Processing Under Pressure

Stress, Memory and Decision-Making in Law Enforcement

Third Edition

MATTHEW J. SHARPS

This publication is not intended to replace nor be a substitute for any official procedural material issued by your agency of employment nor other official source. Looseleaf Law Publications, Inc., the author and any associated advisors have made all possible efforts to ensure the accuracy and thoroughness of the information provided herein but accept no liability whatsoever for injury, legal action or other adverse results following the application or adoption of the information contained in this book.

©2022 Looseleaf Law Publications, Inc. All rights reserved. No part of this book may be reproduced, stored in a retrieval system, or transcribed, in any form or by any means, electronic, mechanical, photocopying, recording, or otherwise, without the prior written permission of the Copyright owner. For such permission, contact Looseleaf Law Publications, Inc., 43-08 162nd Street, Flushing, NY 11358, (800) 647-5547, www.LooseleafLaw.com.

Library of Congress in-publication data
Names: Sharps, Matthew Joseph, author.
Title: Processing under pressure : stress, memory, and decision-making in   law enforcement / Matthew J. Sharps.
Description: Third edition. | Flushing, NY : Looseleaf Law Publications,
    Inc., [2022] | Includes bibliographical references and index. | Summary:
   "The law enforcement expert who understands the human nervous system has   an edge. That information will enhance and support the skills needed to do the job. The law enforcement professional may need that edge to stay alive. Scientific psychologists also stand to gain from a positive relationship with law enforcement and with the world of forensic science"-- Provided by publisher.
Identifiers: LCCN 2021026324 (print) | LCCN 2021026325 (ebook) | ISBN 9781608852406 (paperback) | ISBN 9781608852413 (ebook)
Subjects: LCSH: Law enforcement--Decision making. | Police--Job stress. | Police psychology.
Classification: LCC HV7936.P75 S482 2022 (print) | LCC HV7936.P75 (ebook) | DDC 363.201/9--dc23
LC record available at https://lccn.loc.gov/2021026324
LC ebook record available at https://lccn.loc.gov/2021026325

Cover by: *Sans Serif, Inc.*, Tecumseh, Michigan

Table of Contents

Dedication.. i

About the Author.. iii

Preface and Acknowledgments v

Introduction
    SCIENTIFIC PSYCHOLOGY AND LAW ENFORCEMENT 1

Chapter 1
    THIS IS YOUR BRAIN ON ADRENALINE: THE NERVOUS SYSTEM,
    LONG-TERM STRESS, AND THE WORLD OF LAW ENFORCEMENT 5
        Brains Past and Present 7
            Cortical Powers, Subcortical Limits..7
        The Law Enforcement Officer as Hunter 9
            Suspects, Deer, and Hyperfocus...9
        Brains and Physical Actions... 11
            The Prefrontal Cortex and Its Allies 12
        Subcortical Realities and Processing Under Pressure............. 13
        The HPA Axis—The Core of Fight-or-Flight............................. 15
            Cortisol and Adrenaline.. 16
            The Body's Response to Action 17
        Long-Term Fight-or-Flight... 18
            Real-World Stressors... 19
            Vignette 1: The Officer at Home.. 20
        Long-Term Stress and Law Enforcement..................................... 24

Chapter 2
    ACUTE STRESS: PROCESSING UNDER PRESSURE AND
    COMBAT SITUATIONS 25
            Vignette 2: Damage to the Prefrontal Cortex....................... 26
        Prefrontal Damage, Prefrontal Stress... 28
        Perception and Attention Under Pressure................................. 30
            Sound Anomalies.. 30
            Tunnel Vision.. 31
            Automatic Pilot 33
            Visual Clarity and Sense of Time.. 35
            Memory Loss... 36
            Intrusive Thoughts 36
            Dissociation and Paralysis.. 37
        Tactical Heartbeats 39
        Tactical Stress: A Case History.. 42

- Stress, Cognition, and PTSD 45
  - Combat Fatigue and the Island of Malta 47
  - Other Cognitive Aspects of PTSD 50
  - Vignette 3: PTSD at Home 52
  - Arguments Against PTSD 54
  - PTSD Past and Present 55
  - The Death of Wild Bill Hickok 58
  - Wild Bill Hickok and the Modern Officer 62
- The Importance of Memory 63

Chapter 3
RECONSTRUCTING THE CRIME: THE MIND OF THE EYEWITNESS 65
- A Bit of History 66
- Ancient Memories 70
- Eyewitness Memory in Context 72
- Estimator Variables 73
- Situational Variables 74
  - Light in the Darkness? 76
  - Single-Light Sources 77
  - Occultation 78
- The Interaction of Darkness, Occultation, and Violence 79
  - Passage of Time, Rehearsal, and
     Post-event Information 81
  - The Cognitive Interview—A Possible Remedy? 82
- Target Variables: Cross-Racial Identification,
   Disguise, and Weapon Focus 85
  - Cross-Racial IDs 85
  - Who Was That Masked Man? 86
  - Weapon Focus 87
- Witness Variables 88
  - Children as Witnesses 88
  - Older Adults as Witnesses 89
  - The Chemically Impaired as Witnesses 91
  - Physiological Arousal and the Eyewitness 91
- Important Experiments 92
- An Important Complication 94
- Variables under Law Enforcement Control 95
- The World of the Showup 96
  - Vignette 4: Showups and Lineups 96
  - Conformity 99
  - Really Amazing Conformity 100
  - Conformity and the Eyewitness 101
  - The Showup 102
- Lineups Good and Bad 102
  - Lowered Expectations 103

Chapter 4
CREAM-COLORED VANS AND GRASSY KNOLLS: EYEWITNESS MEMORY IN CONTEXT 109
Gestalt and Feature-Intensive Processing 110
G/FI Theory: A Synthesis for Eyewitness Memory 111
Memory for Guns and Cars 112
    G/FI, Vehicle Recall and the Washington Sniper 115
Eyewitness Memory in Context 121
    When President Kennedy Died 122
    Research Traditions 125
    Police Collaboration and New Experiments 126
    Validating Research for the Real World 127
    Memory for Persons 129
    Lineup Performance 130
    Memory for Weapons and for Peripheral Sources of Hazard 131

Chapter 5
THE INTERPRETATION OF VISUAL INPUT — OR, NEVER AIM YOUR POWER DRILL AT THE SWAT TEAM 133
The Death of Amadou Diallo 135
The Range of Interpretation 137
A Taxonomy of Interpretive Error 139
    Errors in Clothing or Physical Attributes of Perpetrator 141
    Errors in Environmental Detail 142
    Errors in Perpetrator Race or Sex 143
    Weapon Errors 145
    Inferential, Extrapolative, or Imaginative Errors 145
Interpretation in Action 148
    Interpreting the Officer-Involved Shooting 150
    When Citizens Decide to Shoot People 151
Public (and Jury?) Expectations 153

Chapter 6
THINKING TO WIN: DECISION MAKING IN COMMAND AND HIGH-RISK ENVIRONMENTS 157
North Hollywood, 1997 157
European Theater of Operations, 1942 160
    Vignette 5: Inside the Ball 162
Lessons from Past and Present 164
Gestalt and Feature-Intensive Processing Again 166
    Interviewing for Information 168
    Decisions at Tactical Speeds 171

Feature-Intensive Experience as the Basis for Trained Gestalt
Responses: The Strategic Precedes the Tactical 172

Chapter 7
WARRIOR MINDS: THE DYNAMICS OF DECISION 175
Non-Compensatory Realities 176
Factors in Decision Understanding 179
    Front-Loading, or Prior Frameworks
        for Understanding 179
    Explicit Versus Implicit Information 181
    Effective Use of Memory 182
    Horrible Decisions and Why 183
Functional Fixedness and Mental Set 187
    The Push of Pike 188
Cognitive Dissonance 190

Chapter 8
COGNITION IN TACTICAL ENVIRONMENTS I: LITTLE BIGHORN 195
Important Disclaimers 196
What Happened to Custer 197
    The Beginning of the End 199
    Eyewitness Anomalies 199
    George Armstrong Custer, Himself 201
    Psychological Dynamics and Springfield Carbines 203
    Cognition on Reno's Hill 206
    Psychology at Custer's Last Stand 207
Lessons from Custer's Grave 210
    Training 210
    Mission 211
    Command Psychology 211
    Stress 213

Chapter 9
COGNITION IN TACTICAL ENVIRONMENTS II: MOGADISHU, 1993 ... 217
The Seventh Cavalry Revisited 217
The Battle of the Black Sea 218
    Tanks and Tactics 221
    Cognitive Context 223

Chapter 10
COGNITION IN TACTICAL ENVIRONMENTS III: ARDENNES, 1944, AND THE RELIEF OF BASTOGNE 227
The Battle of the Bulge 229
General Patton and the Relief of Bastogne 230
    The Importance of Teams 232

Building Foresight 235
Summing Up—Cognition at the Little Bighorn,
at Mogadishu, and at Bastogne 236

Chapter 11
SPECIAL UNITS – COGNITIVE SCIENCE AT THE EXTREMES 239
Things That Go Boom in the Night: Cognitive
Science and EOD 239
Finding the Bombs in the First Place 240
SMOKE: Effective Cognitive and Field Training for
IED Detection 241
Initial Considerations 242
The Cognitive Basis of SMOKE 243
Errors in IED Search 245
EOD and Education 248
Mental Sets and IEDs 250
The Undercover Officer- Kurtz's River 251
The Social Basis of Undercover Cognition 257
Best Practices for Psychologists and
UC Commanders 259
Cognition on Patrol 260
Science Fiction in the Patrol Context 261
A Personal Note to Sergeants, FTOs and
Senior Officers 262
Summary 263

Chapter 12
**SYNTHESIS: IMPLICATIONS FOR TRAINING AND ENFORCEMENT
IN AN INCREASINGLY RISKY WORLD** 265
Training Facilities, Training Scenarios 266
Increasing Resources for Training 267
Elements of Successful Training 268
Reasonable Trade-Offs 269
Training and Experience in the Context of Stress 273
Administrative Stress 275
Fixing Problems 278

Epilogue
A BRAVE NEW WORLD? 281

Appendix
THE DEVELOPMENTAL CONTEXT OF FORENSIC COGNITIVE SCIENCE .. 287
Teenagers. Tongue-studs, and the
Nature of Development 287
The Young Child as Witness. And as Victim. 291

Cognition in Early Childhood; Or, Why Young Children Are Basically Alien Beings 294
Parenting; Or, God Help Us 297
Adolescents as Witnesses; and as Gang Members. Oh, and as "Child" Soldiers 301
Aging and the Criminal Justice System..306

Bibliography/References 311

Index 323

Dedication

To my wife, Professor Jana L. Price-Sharps, Police Psychologist, and to all the law enforcement officers and commanders who encounter the hazards described in this book on a daily basis.

About the Author

Professor Matthew J. Sharps teaches cognitive psychology, forensic cognitive science and the history of psychology at California State University, Fresno. He has also served on the adjunct faculty of Alliant International University, Fresno, teaching cognitive/affective psychology, neuroscience, and the history of psychology in the forensic clinical and clinical doctoral psychology programs.

At the University of Colorado, Sharps served as a National Institutes of Health research associate. He has taught or guest-lectured at the University of Wyoming, Fresno Pacific University, Stanford University, and Stockholm University, and has delivered invited addresses to the California Reserve Peace Officers Association, NASA-Ames, the Guardia Finanza of the Italian federal police, the South African Police Service, the Unites States Air Force Academy, and to numerous law enforcement agencies, and attorneys' and judges' associations, in California.

Professor Sharps received his B.A., M.A. and Ph.D. from the University of Colorado and also holds an M.A. from UCLA. He is a diplomate of the American Board of Psychological Specialties, American College of Forensic Examiners, a Fellow of the American College of Forensic Examiners Institute, and a Fellow of the Psychonomic Society.

He has published extensively on cognition, and his current research focuses on cognitive psychology in law enforcement contexts, especially eyewitness memory and decision-making under high-risk conditions.

He is the author of over 350 publications, proceedings abstracts, and presentations, as well as the book *Aging, Representation, and Thought: Gestalt and Feature-Intensive Processing*, published by Routledge, an imprint of Taylor and Francis (formerly published by Transaction Publishers).

Professor Sharps has consulted in nearly two hundred criminal cases in California and elsewhere, has served as a research consultant to the Fresno Police Department, and is a graduate of the Incident Response to Terrorist Bombings and the Prevention and Response to Suicide Bombing Incidents schools, New Mexico Institute of Mining and Technology, administered by the U.S. Department of Homeland Security. He is also the author of the blog *The Forensic View* from *Psychology Today*.

Preface and Acknowledgments

The first and second editions of this book, published by Looseleaf Law Publications in 2010 and 2017 respectively, met with very positive responses, especially from law enforcement officers and commanders. I appreciated all the thoughtful comments and feedback very much.

This edition of *Processing Under Pressure* incorporates all of the material presented in the second edition, but includes recent and updated relevant research that was not available in 2017; much has happened in this field in the past five years, and I have tried to select new work of current, critical importance for coverage here. This new edition incorporates new research information in the areas of eyewitness cognition; important updates in crucial areas of law enforcement training; and coverage of important issues in PTSD, that were simply unknown at the time of the second edition. As in the second edition, this new version applies cognitive science to current issues in explosive ordinance disposal and to undercover operations, and demonstrates some special applications of this emphasis to patrol and investigative operations as well, including revised coverage of the infamous Newhall Incident.

Finally, in a new Appendix, the third edition addresses an area that is often ignored or misinterpreted in the criminal justice system: human cognitive development. Children and aged adults are cognitively very different from young adults and the middle-aged, and in view of the relative aging population, and the ever-rising importance of juveniles in the criminal justice system, it is increasingly important for anyone in the criminal justice world to have a solid understanding of developmental differences and similarities, and of how they work. I hope that this new material will be very useful to every reader of this book, and that it may also stimulate important new research.

The main point of this new edition is to provide law enforcement personnel, students, academic researchers, and others involved in the criminal justice system with crucial, current, useful information. I hope and believe that this information will contribute directly to officer effectiveness, safety, and survival in an increasingly demanding world. In that spirit, this new edition of *Processing* is respectfully presented.

In the preparation of this book, I received invaluable advice, information, and assistance from many people in both the law enforcement and academic communities. Responsibility for the content of the book (and, with regret, for the inevitable errors and oversimplifications) is of course my own. The ideas and opinions advanced in the book are also my own, and do not necessarily reflect those of any of these fine people or of their agencies or institutions. However, I would very much like to extend my most sincere thanks to the people who had the greatest influence on its development.

To Chief of Police Jerry Dyer (retired), and to the staff and officers of the Fresno Police Department: I'd particularly like to thank Deputy Chief Patrick Farmer; Deputy Chief Michael Reid; Lieutenant Dennis Montejano; Lieutenant Tim Tietien; Sergeant Dave Gibeault; Sergeant Michael Manfredi; Sergeant Kirk Pool; Sergeant David Selecky; Officer Rod Brisendine (retired); Officer Eric Eide; the late Officer Bruce Fain and Dianna Fain; Officer Gene Johnson; Officer Michael Manzie (retired); Officer Michael Orndoff (retired); Officer Kurt Smith (retired) and my late colleague Officer Michael Scholl, whose knowledge of the arcane and convoluted world of counterterrorism was practically without parallel.

To Chief of Police Robert Nevarez, Delano Police Department, whose expertise, counsel, and friendship have been invaluable over the years.

To Sheriff Tyson Pogue, Sheriff Jay Varney (retired), and Commander Bill Ward of the Madera County Sheriff's Office, who have provided outstanding ongoing expertise, assistance and support of the research conducted for this book.

To Supervisory Special Agent Ray Fragoso, United States Bureau of Alcohol, Tobacco, Firearms, and Explosives; to Chief of Police Darryl McAllister (retired), Union City Police Department, whose extraordinary story, from his days as a young officer, forms an important part of this book, and whose expertise and friendship have been invaluable over the years; to Captain Ed Laverone (retired), Santa Clara Sheriff's Department; to Sergeant Anthony MacWaters (retired), Trinidad, Colorado Police Department; to Brigadier General Gerard Labuschagne (retired), Lieutenant Colonel Stephen McIntosh, Lieutenant Colonel Lindsay Smith, and Lieutenant Colonel Elmarie Myburgh, South African Police Service; to Scott Larsen, former Los Angeles County Sheriff's Department; and to Deputy Les Moore (retired), Alameda Sheriff's Department.

To my outstanding instructors at IRTB and PRSBI, the U.S. Department of Homeland Security schools, New Mexico Institute of Mining and Technology. In view of terrorist threats against individuals in the counterterrorism community, I obviously would not present your names in a public document such as this book; but you know who you are. You do great work. We need more of you.

To my late parents, Joseph A. Sharps, USGS and formerly of the United States Army Counter Intelligence Corps, and Patricia Sharps, and to my late father-in-law, Major Gordon Price, United States Army, who spent the equivalent of several horrible lifetimes under fire in the Pacific Theater during the Second World War.

To Professor, Riccardo Fenici, Catholic University of the Sacred Heart, Rome, Italy, trainer and docent to the academies of the Italian State Police and to the Army of Italy; and to criminologists Dr. Gaetano Pascale and Dr. Pasquale Striano, both of whom spent many years on hazardous duty as officers of the Italian state police forces.

To Dean Christopher Meyer and to former Dean Andrew Lawson, College of Science and Mathematics, California State University, Fresno; to Professor Lorin Lachs, Chair, Department of Psychology; to Professor Constance Jones, former Chair, Department of Psychology; and to my CSUF friends and colleagues, especially Deans *emeritus* Karen Carey, Andrew Rogerson, and K.P Wong; to Professors Mike Botwin, Spee Kosloff and Roy Yockey; to Professors Candice Skrapec and Peter English; and to Dr. Schuyler Wei Liao.

To my friends and colleagues Professor Eric Hickey, Walden University, and Professor Bill Holcomb, formerly of Alliant International University, Fresno; to the late Professor Richard Pasewark, University of Wyoming; and to my friends and colleagues of the Society for Police and Criminal Psychology, including and especially Dr. Gary Aumiller; Professors JoAnne Brewster and Michael Stoloff; Dr. Jim Herndon; Professor. Wayman Mullins; Dr Hank Paine; Dr. Jerry and Ann Serafino; Professor R. Alan Thompson; and Professor Jim Turner.

To Ms. Mary Loughrey, Editorial Vice President, and the outstanding staff at Looseleaf Law Publications. They did a wonderful job and improved the book significantly. Their expertise, experience, and professionalism rendered the whole editorial process pleasurable, seamless, and straightforward, and I can't thank them enough.

To many outstanding students and alumni over the years, including and especially Shari Ahlberg; Dr. Brianna Alcantar; Emanuel Alcala; Amber Allred; Janine Antonelli; Janet Asten; Amy Balmanno; Terri Barber; V. Michael Bence; Amanda Briley; Zack Carter; Hilary Casner; Dr. Sarah Chishholm; Justin Day; Dr. Sandy Schulte; Jordan DeRuiter; Laurel Dunn; Joy Ewart; Dr. Samantha Fasel; M.A. Flemming; Troy Folmer; Brandon Foster; Marcel Garcia; Chelsea Garrett; Dr. Scott Gefeller; Dr. Lisa Giuliani; Dr. Mallory Glasere; Morgan Goodwin; Melissa Griffith; Bill Hayward; Jessica Henslee; Dr. Megan Herrera; Dr. Millie Herrera; Dr. Adam Hess; Crystal Hill; Alexandra Hinojosa; Brandon Hoshiko; David Hulett; Alexis Humphrey; Seth Hurd; Jessica

Janigian; Jenna Jones; Miranda Jones; Ashley Kirby; Nicole Kimura; Dr. Devin Kowalczyk; M.L. Kuhn; Jason Lam; Amanda Lodeesen; Jeremy Lomelli; Mireya Lyons; Dr. Justin Matthews; Hayden McCaw; Dr. Kaichen McRae; Corri Moss; Dr. Sandra Mitchell; Simran Nagra; Kristen Neufer; Dr. Elaine Newborg; Allana Newton; the late Michael Nunes, school psychologist; Dr. Mitch Partovi; Anders Paulsen; Brent Pollitt; Justin Power; Dr. Bethany Ranes; Reyna Renderos; Dr. Brianna Satterthwaite; C.N. Sevillano; S. Sizemore; Marissa Skaggs; Dr. Heather Stahl; Amanda Sunday; Hannah Swinney; Dr. Amy Tillery; Michael Tindall; J.F. Torkelson; Constance Tumlin; Dr. Sarah Van Valkenburgh; Mary Varner; Andrea Vianello; Dr. Amy Villegas; Jason Volkoff; Dr. Kristen Wagner; Angela Welton; Dr. John Williams; Erik Wilson; Carla Wilson-Leff; and Dr. Ellen Woo.

To Jamie and John Colson, Marshal and Molina Colson, and Christopher Dang.

And finally, to my wife, Professor Jana L. Price-Sharps, who, aside from being my personal reason for living, is the best police and clinical psychologist I have ever come across.

To all of these extraordinary people, to the living and the dead: Thank you.

Matthew J. Sharps
Coarsegold, California

Introduction
SCIENTIFIC PSYCHOLOGY AND LAW ENFORCEMENT

P sychologists and police officers frequently don't get along. The relationship can be reminiscent of the one Tom Wolfe *(1979)* described for flight surgeons and pilots. The surgeon may find a reason why the pilot can't fly, just as the psychologist (or, for that matter, the social worker, the counselor, or the psychiatrist) may find a reason why the officer should not remain on duty, a reason that may take a gun and badge.

It is also true that many police officers have their own horror stories of interactions with psychologists. ("So I just came out of a shooting, I mean it was a *good* shoot, the guy shot first and he was cranked out of his *mind*, and all the psych can talk about is whether I love my *mom*!" "I've been on the street eight years, and I've been on SWAT for three, and the guy sits there and wants me to draw a *house* and a *tree* to tell me if I'm *qualified!* And then he won't tell me *why!*" Hell, we don't arrest trees—"what's *wrong* with him?")

It's not a marriage made in heaven.

This is a great pity, because modern psychological science and modern law enforcement have a lot to say to each other. The term "psychology" encompasses a number of fields that have become increasingly differentiable in recent years. Some of these fields are more directly based in logic and evidence than others. Scientific psychologists have amassed a great deal of useful information, again mostly in recent years, which can be important or essential for modern law enforcement professionals. In turn, law enforcement officers are in possession of crucial knowledge and experience that can dramatically enhance psychological science. Both groups, the shrinks and the cops, are in possession of critically useful information, information that can enhance both fields. It is therefore important that both groups try to talk to each other more.

What, specifically, does scientific psychology have to offer the world of law enforcement? The primary subject of psychological science is the human nervous system and what it does. Every law enforcement trainee trying to master the complex environment of the modern police car has a human nervous system. So does every veteran officer entering a dangerous situation, and every police commander supervising that officer. The same type of nervous system exists in every member of the public with whom law enforcement officers interact. There's a nervous system in every eyewitness, and in every suspect or perpetrator. This is true whether or not alcohol or narcotics have influenced the picture, as they frequently do in criminal cases.

This means that the law enforcement expert who understands the human nervous system, and what it does, has an edge. That information, that edge, will enhance and support the skills needed to do the job. At the extremes, the law enforcement professional may need that edge to stay alive.

Scientific psychologists also stand to gain from a positive relationship with law enforcement and with the world of forensic science. The Gestalt psychologist Max Wertheimer held that it was critically important to understand perception, thinking, and memory in real world situations, as well as under the better controlled circumstances of the laboratory *(Wertheimer, 1982)*. A similar perspective was held by Ulric Neisser, often considered the founder of cognitive psychology, and is increasingly held by many others in the field *(Sharps and Wertheimer, 2000)*. The law enforcement realm can provide us with tremendous opportunities to advance our knowledge of mind and brain, for it is in that realm that we truly begin to see *processing under pressure*—the faculties of the human mind at the extreme, under circumstances in which the consequences may literally involve life and death, and in which mentality is stretched to its operational limits.

I am not a police officer. I've never been one. I am an experimental psychologist, and I have studied cognition for over forty years. I have taught a very large number of students, including senior police officials in specialized courses, about the law enforcement aspects of cognitive science. I have served as a consultant or expert witness on cognitive issues in nearly 200 criminal cases, and I have been honored with the opportunity to observe, and on occasion to participate in, law enforcement and special unit training. Most emphatically, though, I am not a law enforcement expert myself. The majority of genuine law enforcement experts are out in the field, in the streets and the cruisers and the stations, enforcing laws. So this book is unlikely to teach police officers anything about police work *per se* that they don't already know.

Rather, the purpose of this book, and of my own research and teaching for some years now, is to show law enforcement experts and psychological scholars how *relevant psychological knowledge can increase the professional effectiveness and survivability of officers in the field*. In the course of most of a lifetime spent studying cognition and the human nervous system, I have been privileged to observe the extreme importance of psychological processes in the high-risk world of criminal justice. I've also had the chance to see how an understanding of the interactions, the places where criminal justice and scientific

Introduction

psychology meet, can prove useful and perhaps essential to the important work of both groups of professionals, cops and shrinks alike. Each group has a lot of information the other group needs, and that information is important. That information gives you an edge.

That information is the subject of this book.

Chapter 1
THIS IS YOUR BRAIN ON ADRENALINE:
THE NERVOUS SYSTEM, LONG-TERM STRESS, AND THE WORLD OF LAW ENFORCEMENT

This first chapter is mainly about the brain and about how it responds to different kinds of stress. The second chapter deals more specifically with cognitive brain functions under tactical and combat stress. This may seem like an awful lot of material about the brain as such, and in fact there are sections of these first two chapters that you can skip over without losing the main ideas in the rest of the book. These optional sections are pointed out as we go. However, it's probably worthwhile to read these chapters all the way through. It's a good idea to know as much about your brain as possible. This is because there are times when your brain is trying to kill you.

The brain doesn't mean to do this, of course. It's just that certain bits of the brain are just not very bright, and they're devoted to doing things that may not work out well, that may in fact get you killed, in the complex environments that characterize modern law enforcement.

About twenty-six centuries ago, the Ionian Greek philosopher Alcmaeon suggested that nerve pathways carry impulses to the brain. He turned out to be right, and since that time we have learned a great deal about the brain and how it acts to make us behave. Yet the brain is still largely a mystery to us. In the average person, it consists of somewhere between three and four pounds of electrochemically active material, vaguely resembling pizza cheese. Not very impressive, on first acquaintance. Yet that mass of electric cheese is fantastically well organized, and it has a history that can't be ignored.

For one thing, the basic layout of the brain is old. Really, really old. On my desk, I have a casting of the brain of a *Tyrannosaurus rex*. This brain came from a dinosaur that lived about seventy million years ago; even so, it's structurally very similar to that of a modern reptile. Reptile brains really haven't changed much at all in the millions of years there have been reptiles, right down to modern alligators and lizards.

If you've read this far, you're probably wondering why we would care about alligators and lizards. Well, in general, most of us don't. However, there are two important things about alligators and lizards that we do need to consider:

1. They're not very bright. They operate more or less "on automatic." With reptiles, a feared stimulus is either attacked or avoided, an edible stimulus eaten, a sexy stimulus courted, and so on, without anything much in the way of rational consideration. Reptiles don't "think" in our sense, but they move around and eat and fight and reproduce perfectly well anyway.

2. Humans, of course, are not reptiles; but amazingly, *we have the same kinds of non-thinking brain centers, many of these in just about the same locations in our heads, as they do, underneath the structures that are uniquely human and that allow us to think.*

Furthermore, many of the structures that we have in common with reptiles generally function "on automatic" in us as well as in alligators. These structures operate together with the rest of our advanced mammalian brain structures (the parts of the brain that think) that reptiles don't really have at all.

When we say *automatic* here, we're *not* saying *instinctive*. That's actually a pretty important distinction. Nobody's suggesting that you're somehow born with "instinctive" tactical skills, for example. But many behaviors, even in humans, have to become relatively automatic, over time and with training and experience, to function well; and to make some of these behaviors work well, we have to use very ancient brain structures that frankly, on their own, just aren't too bright.

The gradual development of the brain was not just a matter of putting complex new structures on top of simple old ones (e.g., *Cesario, Johnson, & Eisthen, 2020*). Some of the things that even reptiles do are pretty complex, although it's also true that we can put alligators in zoos and not the other way around. But the important point here is that we use these ancient, relatively "non-thinking" brain structures— in more or less the same way reptiles do, generally pretty much on automatic. Frequently, we use these automatic structures instead of our smarter, less automatic, uniquely human brain areas. This may become especially, unfortunately, and spectacularly true when we're under stress, such as the stress of a violent encounter with an armed perpetrator.

These brain similarities obviously don't suggest that people "came" from dinosaurs or alligators, but the crucial fact, for modern law enforcement or law enforcement psychology, is that the same kinds of unthinking structures exist in the depths of our modern, human minds, and they do basically the same things that they do in alligators. The problems arise when they do things that might work perfectly well in the relatively simple world inhabited by alligators, but which are wildly off the mark, and potentially deadly, in the very complex, option-filled environment inhabited by the modern police officer.

Brains Past and Present

The next few paragraphs are not essential reading for understanding cognition and law enforcement. However, they do provide a valuable framework for understanding how the brain's structures and activities operate in the law enforcement realm. You can skip to the next section if you like, but if you want a more in-depth understanding of what's going on in your head under stress, this framework will come in handy.

It starts with the fact that, once again, the "automatic" brain structures are very similar to the parts of our brains that are hidden by the *cortex*, the big, gray, wrinkly mass that most people think of when they think "brain." That's why these non-thinking, hidden structures are called *subcortical* structures; in human beings, they are found beneath the cortex. The cortex, Latin for bark (as in the bark of a tree), is on top of, and wraps around, the not-too-bright subcortical structures that keep us awake, control our heartbeat and breathing, and send rudimentary messages to each other and to our bodies. At best, these subcortical messages are pretty simple; we will be primarily concerned here with the ones that deal with high-arousal behaviors such as those involved in fighting or running away. The structures and their actions that are involved in such behaviors are generally grouped together under the term "fight-or-flight" complex.

CORTICAL POWERS, SUBCORTICAL LIMITS

The cortex, on the other hand, is basically what we think with. The cortex, the big gray wrinkly mass, is the main thing you see when you examine a modern human brain at an autopsy, or in a jar in a neuroscience lab. The cortex is the part that looks like wrinkled pizza cheese; but do not underestimate the power of electric cheese.

The cortex is what gives human beings their unique power over the rest of the animate world. Alligators don't have much cortex, by comparison. Neither did *Tyrannosaurus Rex*, for that matter—if you ever see a mounted skeleton of that particular dinosaur, especially one that includes the teeth, you'll immediately see that it was much more of a physical creature than a thinker.

However, our kind of creatures (mammals), and especially we humans, specialize in out-thinking less brainy types of creatures. This is where the cortex comes into its own. When a police officer takes a shortcut across a corner, to intercept a bad guy who runs all the way around that corner, the officer has used his or her cortex to work out the courses and speeds involved. The cortex is where the thinking action is; and the more cortex a creature has, in general, the more and the better that creature can think. Humans, in the terms that matter, have more cortex compared to our body weight than anything else does; but there's an essential point here to be considered. This is the fact that the human cortex *has to work with the simpler parts of the brain*, the ones that aren't too bright, but that let us breathe and eat, fight or run away.

In humans, the cortex has to manage, administer, and command the subcortical structures and, for that matter, the rest of the body, in order to optimize outcomes in law enforcement and in life generally. Our huge advantage is that we can think.

So, we can think. What do we think about? Generally, we think about what we know, or about how our knowledge applies to a given situation. Because what we know is in our memory, a lot of what we think about *is* our memory. It can therefore be argued that more cortex helps a living creature have a better and more developed memory. Memory, as we will see, is hugely important in the world of criminal justice; we will address these issues in Chapters 3 through 5.

Members of our species (*Homo sapiens sapiens*, meaning the wise, wise man—apparently we're so wise that we named ourselves twice) seem to have had fully modern human brains for somewhere between one and two hundred thousand years. We can find skulls of our capacity all the way back to that time and ever since. Our brains have ranged around 1300 – 1500 cubic centimeters in volume for all of that time, and have remained anatomically modern throughout.

At this point, the discerning reader may be wondering why all of this matters, even as a background framework; so let us sum up. These considerations matter because the brains we have, and with which we deal on an everyday basis, *have parts that we can't communicate with very well*: the primitive, not-too-bright, subcortical parts that control our breathing, our eating, and, to a great degree, our running and fighting. We can't talk to these old, reptile-like parts of our brain very well, for the very simple reason that they're stupid. Try talking to an alligator sometime, and you'll see what I mean.

However, we also have our smart, advanced, thinking brain structures, in the cortex, and these have had more than a hundred thousand years of history *during which they were exactly the same as they are now*. In every year of those long, long periods, brains had to be *ecologically valid*—in other words, they had to respond to local conditions *as they were*, whether those conditions included giant sabertooth cats, or mammoths, or shopping malls, or armed humans in the grip of psychoses caused by methamphetamine abuse. In all that time, we had to integrate information from our stupid brain parts and our smart brain parts. We also had to apply that information, correctly, to whatever situation we encountered, whether that situation involved an angry pimp on drugs or an equally angry sabertooth on adrenaline.

The ultimate point: *Much of the brain that developed during the sabertooth age is still with us in the age of methamphetamine, and part of it is not very accessible to conscious awareness.*

This means that the subcortical brain responds simply, to simple stimuli, without much in the way of conscious, cognitive activity. The cortex responds in a more complex, mediated, cognitive way; but sometimes it responds in the wrong *era*.

The Law Enforcement Officer as Hunter

Our ancestors lived, with the same brains that we have, for a vastly longer period as hunters and gatherers than we have as members of modern or even ancient civilizations. Therefore, and especially in view of the considerations discussed in the preceding paragraphs, there are times when we respond to an investigation or a patrol incident as we would have, in the old days, to a mammoth hunt. There are also times when we respond to a gang war in the way we would have responded to a buffalo stampede. Not surprisingly, this type of ancient hunting response, in the modern non-hunting world, can result in a certain degree of error. Sometimes it also results in large numbers of casualties. It's important to emphasize that the brain we have today did not develop, primarily, in the *world* we have today. Gangs have made money from extortion, prostitution, illegal alcohol, or cocaine sales for only a very brief portion of our couple of hundred thousand years. We have had shopping malls, cars, and methamphetamine for even less. Therefore, whenever a police officer answers a call, a very critical question arises: will that officer respond in a manner appropriate to the call, perhaps a gang-related shooting? Or will the officer make use of tendencies in the brain that would be more appropriate to dealing with a giant sabertooth or a woolly mammoth?

SUSPECTS, DEER, AND HYPERFOCUS

Consider an example. Our ancestors hunted deer, often with spears or arrows. Such hunting requires a continual focus on the specific animal a given hunter wants to eat. Now, consider a modern analogy—the point at which an officer enters a room, weapon drawn, and confronts a suspect. As we will see, the officer's perceptual world narrows around that suspect, just as it would around a deer. The officer's focus is entirely on the target—what's the suspect (or deer) going to do? Does he present a verifiable danger (gun, knife, or antlers)? What procedures will best facilitate the capture? All of these considerations make sense, whether you're confronting a deer or a human suspect.

Or do they? I am informed by law enforcement experts that when an officer enters a room containing an armed suspect, that officer is frequently fired upon, by another person, from the side or the rear. The officer may be shot and killed, not by the suspect in his sights, but by an ally of that suspect, another bad guy who took a position in a back corner when he became aware of the officer at the door. The odd thing is that the additional bad guy, perhaps standing in plain sight, is frequently effectively unnoticed by the officer.

The officer in question could have seen the additional assailant, of course, simply by sweeping the room with his or her eyes upon entry, and officers are in fact trained to do this. The unfortunate fact, however, is that the officer whose attention is narrowed, focused directly on the bad guy across the room, may be effectively unaware of the extra assailant in the corner, *even if that assailant is potentially within the officer's field of view.* This is especially true, as we will see, in the grip of the "tunnel vision" that is among the most common effects of the enhanced metabolic rate necessary for success in combat. When there's an additional bad guy in the back corner, a hyperfocus on the suspect out front may betray the officer at exactly the wrong moment.

Deer do not form gangs; humans do. Deer do not have a friend in the corner with a .38; humans frequently form just that sort of association. In the ancient world of hunters, a sharp perceptual focus on the prey, while excluding everything else from your active perceptual field, made sense. However, this is the modern world; you're after a gang member, not a deer. And when you focus on only one of several gang members who plan to ambush you, the chances are that this ancient, deer-hunting focus will get you killed.

In short, an officer may respond to an armed and gang-affiliated suspect the way an ancestor, forty thousand years ago, would have responded to an unarmed, non–gang-affiliated deer. If so, the officer may very well be killed in the line of duty, victim of the brain's tendency to focus on the *center* of a given situation under stress, without adequate attention to the *periphery*. In the past, the deer was in the center, and that was all that mattered. In the present, the bad guy is still in the center, but he has an armed friend in the corner, on the periphery, and that makes all the difference in the world: the officer does not go home that night. In effect, that officer is killed by the distant past, the hunting past, to which his or her brain may still be attuned.

This kind of tragic and all-too-frequent event is often preventable. It is preventable through training. However, that training must be of a specific type; it must incorporate what we know about the nervous system into the prediction of officer performance and survival.

As we will see in subsequent chapters, officers need to receive *front-loaded, explicit, feature-intensive training and practice* in controlling the periphery as well as the center of any given tactical situation, in order both to succeed and to survive. In order to provide that training, those responsible for doing so must be aware of why it's necessary in the first place, and also of the dynamics that make front-loaded, explicit, feature-intensive training generally superior.

In other words, those responsible for training must be aware of what the nervous system generally does in the kinds of situations that officers are most likely to face. They need to understand, at least at a reasonable level, the nature of *processing under pressure*. They must address those aspects of the nervous system's activity that are useful for their trainees, and provide training that enhances those characteristics and abilities; and they must also identify those brain tendencies that are likely to be useless or worse than useless, and provide training that circumvents or eradicates those specific proclivities.

Effective training must work with the way the nervous system is, the way it works in real life. We cannot ignore cognitive characteristics or limitations that derive from the basic nature of the brain itself, and we can't turn the brain into some other, more convenient organ. The brain is what it is. Therefore, a formidable challenge becomes clear: training officers and supervisors must have a solid and powerful knowledge of what the brain is up to in any given situation. Training based in that knowledge will help to provide the edge, the advantage, that contributes to officer survival. This is the edge that lets them go home at the end of the shift.

Therefore, a fairly straightforward, unassuming academic question assumes life or death importance in the law enforcement realm: exactly what is the brain doing in a violent situation, anyway?

Brains and Physical Actions

The following paragraphs discuss basic relevant structures of the brain and what those structures do, especially with relevance to tactical and combat situations. As was the case with some of the material earlier in this chapter, this information is not essential for the reader to understand what happens when an officer encounters a violent situation. However, it will be helpful for those who wish to develop a more complete understanding of how the brain relates to thinking and memory as these cognitive processes operate in the hazardous world of law enforcement. It will probably prove especially helpful to those who wish to develop training systems and scenarios more in line with the actual characteristics of the human nervous system, and with the actual operational parameters of processing under pressure.

The cortex of the brain comes in two relatively symmetrical sides, or hemispheres, left and right. Each of these hemispheres has four lobes: the frontal, which is up front; the parietal, which is right behind the frontal; the occipital lobe, which is behind the parietal and is mainly concerned with vision; and the temporal lobe, in front of the occipital lobe and beneath the frontal lobe.

A full consideration of all that these structures do is well beyond the scope and the space limitations of this book. There are many excellent textbooks that can guide the interested reader further; I recommend Banich and Compton's *(2018)* text for an extensive but efficient treatment of relevant issues. Here, however, we are going to focus solely on those brain structures that are the most important in the law enforcement realm.

THE PREFRONTAL CORTEX AND ITS ALLIES

The first of these is the *prefrontal cortex*, in the very front of the head. It is here that decisions are made. The decision to arrest a suspect or to fire a weapon originates here. So, in more peaceful settings, does the decision to speak in a staff meeting or to hold a press conference. These decisions, too, are functions of the prefrontal cortex. The prefrontal area is involved in other functions, as well: attention, impulse control, good judgment, bad judgment. It is perhaps the most important single area of the law enforcement professional's brain, and it is unfortunately situated way out front, protected only by the forehead, readily available for hard impacts from fists, beer bottles, or dashboards. Do not forget the prefrontal cortex. We'll be seeing it again.

So, the prefrontal cortex essentially makes decisions. Once the prefrontal cortex has decided to act, other parts of the *frontal lobes* are engaged. In basic terms, the *supplementary motor cortex* contributes to the complex sequences of acts involved in the chosen behavior. The *premotor cortex*, also in the frontal lobes, may give the go-code: it contributes to permission to move, to initiate activity. The *motor cortex*, still in the frontal lobes, then allocates the necessary neural commands to the various parts of the body that will be involved in the chosen

Chapter 1

activity; and finally, the body responds to the prefrontal cortex's original assessment.

Other parts of the cortex are involved in any given action as well. The *parietal lobe* tells you where your own body is relative to the action, and helps you to understand what's going on. The *occipital lobe* deals with everything you're seeing, keeping it orderly and comprehensible. The *temporal lobe* deals with your hearing, and helps to distinguish what you are seeing from where it is. Even some of the subcortical structures are helping out nicely: the *cerebellum*, a large, ball-like structure under the back of the cortex, is smoothing your actions for you and "remembering" how to perform essential motor actions, the aiming or driving or unarmed combat skills that you painstakingly learned in training.

So, thanks to the combined efforts of the frontal lobes and their many allies in the rest of the brain and the nervous system, you respond to whatever situation you encounter, whether that situation involves a staff meeting or the arrest of a violent suspect. The cortex and its attendant subcortical structures appear to function as a synchronized but highly flexible computer, delivering what amounts to a ballet of the necessary actions to the nerves controlling your muscles, making it possible to adapt and overcome in virtually any law enforcement situation.

It looks so perfect, at least in the abstract; and yet in reality, the perfection is illusory. Recall the officer mentioned above, so focused on the suspect across the room that he was shot by the unnoticed, but perfectly visible, assailant in the corner. The brain's "ballet" may be synchronized and flexible, but it has limits, especially when applied to the lethal and constantly shifting realities of tactical situations. The way in which a given officer meets those limits may literally mean the difference between death and victory; and unfortunately, some of those limits have their origins in the unreliable, inaccessible, alligator-stupid recesses of the subcortical brain. These subcortically based limits form a major reason why, on occasion, your brain is trying to kill you.

Subcortical Realities and Processing Under Pressure

Most of the time, law enforcement personnel aren't particularly at risk, any more than civilians are. This means that in most of your everyday life, at least by comparison with high-risk situations, you don't need much energy.

You go to the store. You watch a movie. You go to sleep. If you're a patrol officer, you wake up, have breakfast, go to briefing, drive your accustomed patrol routes. You file necessary reports. You go on with your daily routines.

Then comes the call: Need for backup. Shots fired. Officer down. Street address. No further information.

You feel a sharp stab of fury, of *wrong*, compounded with other emotions, when you hear "Officer down." But there's not a lot of time to think about that. Your training and experience take over, and you *act*. Light up the roof. Siren. *Go*.

Suddenly, from the perspective of the nervous system, energy becomes extremely important. The brain concurs. It starts to provide you with what you need.

The problem is that the brain is basically conservative. Over the thousands of years that we were hunters, it kept pretty much to the basics. This means that some of the most important brain structures an officer will use, in the most strenuous and demanding of duties, are the subcortical structures. You remember. The structures that alligators have, too. The ones that aren't too bright.

The *amygdala* is one of these. It sits below the frontal lobes, integrating thoughts with emotions, especially those involved in anxiety and aggression. The amygdala, which provides a kind of bridge between thoughts and intense feelings, is closely wired to the *hypothalamus*, which is a simply amazing subcortical organ of the brain. It is the organ of *homeostasis*, of maintaining a steady state—the right amount of food, the right amount of exercise, the right amount of everything. If you've just had Thanksgiving dinner, the hypothalamus is the organ that tells you that one more piece of pie is too much. If you're thirsty, the hypothalamus tells you to drink a glass of water.

The hypothalamus isn't perfect, of course. If you've just come out of a long, dehydrating hike through a summer desert, temperature 103 in the shade, the hypothalamus may tell you to drink and keep drinking; thanks to the fact that the hypothalamus isn't too bright, you may keep drinking until you're projectile vomiting, or conceivably until you're dead. Just from too much water.

So, these structures aren't perfect, and this imperfection is important. Subcortical structures like the hypothalamus, which make a lot of mistakes, may under extreme conditions drive you to destructive or suboptimal behaviors that go far beyond drinking too much water in the heat. They may help you hyperfocus on the bad guy across the room, and ignore the one behind you in the corner, as we saw earlier. They may use so much energy that your ability to remember what happened, or to reason about your situation, is impaired or effectively nonexistent. They may lead you to do things that in retrospect, or in front of a jury, may seem to have been insane.

However, there is at least some good news. The ineffective or actively dangerous things that subcortical structures may "want" you to do can be overcome, at least to some extent, by means of the *conscious front loading of explicit knowledge.* The right types of training, with the right kinds of cognitive framing, can install an explicit, feature-intensive, prior framework for dealing with the given situation, and such training can be particularly effective.

In short, you can frequently defeat the bad impulses of the brain by means of *training that takes the brain and its activities into account.* The officer who can predict the more hazardous tendencies of his or her own nervous system has an edge in the dangerous world of law enforcement and human conflict. In the fight-or-flight realm, in situations in which an officer must establish a reasoned balance between the use of force and appropriate tactical caution, such knowledge can prove critical.

We'll discuss this in detail in subsequent chapters. For the moment, please keep the following important point in mind: *thanks to the non-thinking structures we all carry in our brains, below the cortex, we may behave in ways that are actively deleterious to officer survival and to operational effectiveness.* This can result from imperfections, going back to the sabertooth ages, in one of the most important systems for the understanding of processing under pressure: The HPA axis.

The HPA Axis—The Core of Fight-or-Flight

The hypothalamus forms the H in HPA axis, which stands for Hypothalamus-Pituitary-Adrenal. Again, this is one of the most important brain systems for the world of law enforcement, and one of the most important to understand.

Basically, here's how the HPA axis works. When you get into a situation in which you perceive the need for fight-or-flight, the hypothalamus receives the information that things are about to get a lot worse, or at least a lot more intense. So, it sends chemical signals to the pituitary gland (the P in HPA). The pituitary then signals the adrenal glands (which form the A).

The adrenal glands aren't brain structures at all. They're situated on top of the kidneys. This places them in a good central location for communicating with the rest of the body at large; and this is exactly what they do.

When the hypothalamus tells the pituitary to inform the adrenal glands (three steps—H to P to A) that things are about to get active and/or dangerous, the adrenal glands go to work. The adrenal cortex of each gland produces *aldosterone,* which reduces secretion of salt by the kidneys (not very exciting, but it helps in the metabolic balancing act that's about to follow), and *cortisol*, which stimulates the liver to elevate your blood sugar and enhances the metabolism of fats and protein.

CORTISOL AND ADRENALINE

Cortisol is what gives you the energy to respond to risky situations, and it's useful, to say the least. Need some extra energy? Some really huge guy on crank coming at you with a knife and a baseball bat? Quick, says the adrenal cortex, have some energy, and it starts shoveling cortisol into your system at flank speed. Basically, when you perceive the need for a lot of extra energy, cortisol slides the equivalent of a rare steak, a cream pie, and a Hershey bar into your bloodstream. This is oversimplified, to say the least, but you get the idea—if you run out of energy while running or fighting, it won't be the fault of your adrenal cortex.

But the activities of the adrenal cortex are almost overshadowed compared to what the adrenal medulla, the other important part of the adrenal gland, is up to. When the HPA axis alerts the body to stress, to the need to fight or flee, the adrenal medulla starts blasting adrenaline into your system as fast as you can take it. It is this adrenal medulla response that truly prepares you for the *fight-or-flight* response, the overriding physiological response that is about to *change your body into another thing entirely*. You are about to become faster, stronger, and more durable than is normally possible. You are literally about to become a superhero.

The adrenaline coursing through the body now prepares you, to the limits imposed by physiological possibility, for combat. It prepares you for a wide range of possible actions. You may have to fight, or run to a better position and then fight, or run from overwhelming force until you can regroup to fight. The adrenal response is therefore flexible. It makes it possible for you to fight, then to run, then to fight some more, run some more, and so on. The adrenal medulla has prepared you for all kinds of high-speed, high-stress maneuvers, without discrimination. It has changed your body into a different kind of thing: a new kind of body that uses a great deal of energy, but that wears out faster than normal in compensation to deal with the peculiar challenges posed by physical danger.

How is this accomplished? How does adrenaline change you into the "superhero" who can do all of these things?

Chapter 1

THE BODY'S RESPONSE TO ACTION

First, in the grip of a fight-or-flight response, your body is not very concerned with the future. So, you effectively stop digesting your food; if you've got to avoid being killed in the next two minutes, the fate of the semi-digested burrito still in your stomach simply fades into insignificance.

You also stop being able to salivate very well; spit is not needed (you're not bothering with digestion at the moment, and that's what spit is mainly for). Fight-or-flight is very much a "lead, follow, or get out of the way" situation. Digestion, together with other physical mechanisms concerned with the basic maintenance of everyday life, essentially gets out of the way. The adrenaline leads and the dedicated fight-or-flight systems follow.

You need more oxygen to fight or to run, which means you need more blood to carry it. So, your heart rate goes up. Most of your blood vessels expand (this is called vasodilation) to accommodate the raging storm of blood that roars through your tissues. Your blood pressure and breathing rate rise, in order to provide more oxygen for your racing, new-and-improved high-volume circulatory system. The combined effect is to strengthen your muscles and to allow you to respond with greater strength and rapidity to any threat that must be overcome (fight) or avoided (flight). You even get an added bonus: your muscles and surrounding tissues become somewhat harder and more armor-like as they are engorged with blood. Many of them are now harder to crush or injure.

So, in the fight-or-flight response, you're superior—you're stronger and faster. Because of other factors having to do with endorphin response under stress, you may not even feel pain as much. With these enhanced abilities, you can run faster, tackle the bad guy with great coordination, hold him down with relative ease. These are good capabilities to have.

However, you pay a lot for these enhanced capabilities, both in terms of physiology and psychology. This is true over both the long and short terms.

We'll begin with the long-term effects of stress, of maintaining at least a low-grade fight-or-flight state, off and on, for weeks, months, or even years. Many law enforcement people wind up doing exactly this; and despite the enhanced performance you experience in tactical situations, the stress of long-term fight-or-flight is not a good idea.

Long-Term Fight-or-Flight

The fight-or-flight state is fearfully expensive physiologically. The body is operating at a higher metabolic rate than it can maintain over time. It's like putting jet fuel in your car—you might get amazing performance, but only until the engine melts.

If you stay in the fight-or-flight condition for more than a brief period, there is excessive wear on the heart and the blood vessels. Because you're not digesting food as well as you would in the absence of this adrenalized state, you're ultimately getting shortchanged on nourishment. As a result, you may start to develop digestive problems, such as ulcers or esophageal reflux. That's the one where stomach acid is puked up into your esophagus, gets sucked into your trachea, and makes you feel as if you're choking to death. These very negative consequences happen as the digestive system fights to do its normal job under the abnormal circumstances offered by the fight-or-flight state.

Your hard, tense muscle tissue starts to degrade as well, because the higher metabolic rate doesn't allow very well for the removal of the toxic by-products of muscle activity that literally build up in the muscle itself. As if these issues weren't bad enough, even the cortisol that helped to give you all that energy has a nasty down side. Cortisol is essentially caustic. Too much cortisol, for too long, starts to degrade body tissues. One area that seems particularly susceptible to cortisol damage is the *hippocampus*. This is a subcortical brain structure that is mainly responsible for the formation of new memories. We'll encounter memory in more detail in Chapters 3 and 4, but for now it is enough to realize that if the fight-or-flight state can mess with your memory or learning powers over time, it's a good idea to limit the amount of time you have to stay in that state and to provide yourself with opportunities to recover from it.

This is not to say that fight-or-flight is inherently bad. You need these responses, for brief periods, if you live in the perilous world of law enforcement. Brief fight-or-flight periods give you the "superhero" powers to take care of tactical business, and you can recover from most of these effects, *provided their influence operates over a relatively short term*. The better shape you're in, in general, the more readily you recover. If you have a brief, intense stress, a few minutes of frenetic activity, the restorative powers of the body are typically sufficient to repair any damage you've sustained, and to get you ready for the next time such a stressor presents itself.

These restorative powers make sense in the terms we discussed above, our responses to our hunting past. Brief intense stresses, followed by relatively extended recovery times, are typical of hunting-

and-gathering lifestyles, the lifestyles enjoyed by our ancestors for the vast majority of all the time we've been on earth. You find the deer or the buffalo, you stalk him, and there's a wild two minutes while you stab him and stick a sharp rock in his head. This is followed by a high-protein feast and a nice long nap. Repeat as necessary or desired.

This pattern of behavior, essentially, is what the HPA axis is for. It works best for short, limited periods of fight-or-flight time.

Not all of the stressors in the ancient world were so brief or limited, of course; but the problem is that, for whatever reasons, our bodies never really developed good methods for dealing with enhanced HPA activity over long periods.

REAL-WORLD STRESSORS

The psychologist, Hans Selye *(e.g., 1976)* has characterized our response to short-term stressors as the *alarm* state. We're pretty good at recovering from that response, especially if we're in good physical and psychological shape. However, if the stress goes on for a long period, Selye holds that we enter the stage of *resistance*, in which the body tries to maintain itself, but the HPA axis goes on pumping extra stress-related chemicals into our systems. If the stresses are not relieved, either through their elimination or through training or psychological interventions to cope with them, *exhaustion* may follow—illness, and possibly even death, may result.

These problems are massively exacerbated for law enforcement personnel. For them, the chronic, long-term stressors that everybody faces on an everyday basis are punctuated by sudden, acutely stressful situations (violent confrontations, chases in cars and on foot, shootings, etc.). These crises provide more cumulative stress than members of most other occupational groups may ever encounter in their entire lives. The cumulative stress helps to account for a wide variety of problems to which officers are frequently prone: digestive illnesses, cardiovascular illnesses, depression, and difficulties in dealing with colleagues, the public, and family.

We're not really good at coping with longer-term stressors, such as those involved in the endless filing of reports. We're not really built for a long life on patrol, sitting in an increasingly cramped and technologically demanding cruiser, surrounded by people who fear us and dislike the fact that we may take them to jail.

Our long past did not really equip us to deal with rude witnesses and victims who keep shouting, "I PAY YOUR SALARY!" We're not good at filing many, many reports, day after day, or at dealing with administrative stresses, over and over again. Our distant past did not prepare us for being told, repeatedly and condescendingly, that we need to learn to "multitask," when all we want to do is get this damned mass of reports off our desk, and we finally got an afternoon to do it, and we suddenly learn that, instead, we have to go to a mandatory six-hour seminar to teach us to be sensitive to whatever the hell it is this week ...

Human beings, including law enforcement officers, need diplomacy in dealing with such situations and in dealing with other people generally. Diplomacy relies on cognition, and, as we will see, many of the most relevant aspects of cognition are significantly impaired under conditions of enhanced HPA activity. This becomes increasingly important when interacting with colleagues or members of the public who are especially irritating, or when dealing with the fact that many family members do not, typically, *really grasp what the officer goes through on a daily basis*. Family problems are fairly crucial for many law enforcement officers. Let's see why.

VIGNETTE 1: THE OFFICER AT HOME

Consider an example. You're a police officer. It's end of shift; you leave the station, drive home, pull into your driveway. You're exhausted. This is because you're on night shift, and you don't get much sleep. Night shifts are inherently hard for everybody, because we are basically diurnal, daylight organisms. If you were a nocturnal creature, such as a raccoon, or a wombat or something, you'd be perfectly happy staying up all night; but since you're a diurnal human, you're already at something of a disadvantage.

In your case, you, like many officers, are at a special disadvantage. Even if you could sleep during the day, you usually don't. This is because your spouse, who is awake during the day instead, expects *you* to stay awake most of the day with him or her as well, and to deal with various family problems during that time.

Today, you have to get up early in the afternoon to go to a parent-teacher conference; your kid threw up on his costume (he was supposed to play a complex carbohydrate in the school play, *Nutrition and Educational Excellence*). The teacher is insisting on an immediate conference because this is *so very serious*. Oh, and the dog ate the income tax return, says your spouse, and then he marked his territory forcefully and damply on the sofa. And the drape swatches came, and they're *all the wrong color*-

Et cetera. You come in at the end of shift, and you sit at

Chapter 1

your kitchen table, and your spouse continues to jabber about this inconsequential crap. You want to go to bed, but instead you listen to this demented circus with only one part of your being. This is because the other parts of your being are still out there on the street, in memory, thinking, ruminating, processing the bad one that happened just last night, a few hours ago—*blood. That was a lot of blood. And* (fill in the name of your partner) *didn't look so good. Didn't shoot, either. Didn't even take cover. Wonder if he'll be okay next time* (next time for what, unspecified, but it doesn't look good). *Family* (of the bloody person) *will probably sue. Probably have an IA* (internal affairs inquiry) *on this one. Wonder what the Chief will say. Sergeant* (fill in a name) *has been on my case—wonder if she'll use this to-*

"Honey?" says the spouse. "Have you heard a word I said? What's wrong with you these days? Aren't you here for me anymore? I'm always there for you-

"—*But I can't even tell you about it. You just don't expose the family to all that—all that—well, all that blood. What was I thinking? Oh, yeah—Partner. Sergeant. Chief. IA. Next week required seminar on Sensitivity in Law Enforcement: Lessons from the Sixties—how am I even gonna* sit *through that—gotta file the report—crap, I'm tired-*

"—I just don't know what's wrong with you," says the spouse. "My friend (here, you should fill in the name of your spouse's most annoying, intrusive and invasive friend)—my friend says (s)he thinks all this police work has changed you—(s)he thinks we should see a counselor. There's this wonderful one (s)he knows who does all kinds of Eastern yoga and philosophy and could help you with your *diet*, because you eat all the wrong things, all that *red meat and coffee—*

You are tired. You dealt with some bad things last night, *very* bad things, *last night*. You *need* your damn coffee—night shift ain't easy at your age, dammit.

So you say some highly negative things in response to your spouse's suggested changes in lifestyle or diet. You say even more negative things about the annoying and invasive friend. You're tired, tired beyond description—your judgment is off, and so you may say these things at high volumes, quite loudly. These things will later be regretted, during your divorce proceedings or fitness-for-duty hearing.

Why did you do this? Why did you yell at your spouse? Hell, you knew what would happen—are you nuts?

No, you're not nuts at all. The problem is that your HPA axis, already stressed, begins to treat the irritating spousal conversation as a *life-threatening event*. The HPA axis, composed of alligator-stupid structures, is not too accessible to your conscious, thinking cortex; and because the cortex itself is not operating at peak efficiency (Chapter 2), your cognitive responses may be substantially impaired. Your cortex has all your advanced cognitive abilities, and it just isn't available to talk right now.

If the cortex were available for a nice conversation, at the critical moment, it would say something like this: *"Calm down. There's nothing to fight or run from here. The threat is illusory. This conversation presents no stimulus that could be overcome by placing the body in metabolic overdrive. Your best bet,"* your cortex would say, *"is to treat this conversation as if it were completely non-threatening, thereby conserving your body's resources."*

Unfortunately, the cortex is essentially off duty, so it doesn't get to say these things to you. However, your HPA axis *is* available for consultation, and, as always, it's not too bright. It has an entirely different message for you: *"This conversation is full of stress. Stress should be met by means of an angry and hugely overblown episode of screaming. Continued stress may require a program of biting, killing, and general mayhem involving blood and possibly exposed internal organs. Time for the rodeo. Light up the roof. Siren. Go."*

So, with the HPA axis shrieking like a banshee in the basement of your brain, you become increasingly unglued and increasingly aggressive. Hopefully, in the ascending levels of verbal hostility that characterize a fight with your spouse, you do not resort to actual physical violence. Some people, of course, do engage in physical assault at this point, which is of course a crime. This frequently forms the basis of domestic disturbance situations, among the most dangerous calls to which officers must respond. However, in most people, most of the time, the cortex is on duty at least to the extent of preventing physical violence against their loved ones.

Nevertheless, you may find yourself speaking loudly and aggressively. You may even scream or shout. At your spouse.

> **And the story continues...**
> Your spouse screams back. This drives your HPA axis into even more alligator-stupid hyperactivity. You scream some more, with greater volume and more graphic language. The spouse escalates in response, and shrieks back at a volume and frequency that may attract bats, or possibly dolphins.
> At that point, the spouse may run out of the room, slam

the door, and call his or her friend—(Remember? The friend with the Eastern philosophy counselor). During their conversation, of course, the friend becomes *deeply concerned* about the safety and welfare of your spouse. The friend, knowing that you are a police officer, decides to call the police to complain about you. If possible, the friend wants to complain to your sergeant. Just to protect your spouse, of course.

Bad, crazy, and embarrassing things ensue over the next several hours. These things may involve your colleagues, other officers with whom you interact on an everyday basis, being called to your house. It is possible that your colleagues, people you know well, may arrest you at that point.

The next day, you are required to see your sergeant to talk about things. Then you see your commanders to talk about the same things even more. Then you may get to discuss the same things with other managers and professionals, people who, of course, are there only to protect the welfare of everyone involved, frequently in triplicate.

You are scheduled for an IA, an internal affairs hearing. God knows what's going to happen there. The IA is scheduled to take place just after the Sensitivity Seminar (oh, crap, you forgot about that thing). You are now carrying quite a bit of cognitive and emotional baggage from this entire nightmare. Your HPA axis kicks in even more. You notice that you don't feel good, that your heart races at odd times, and that you seem to have even more indigestion than usual.

You're embarrassed, you're angry, you're confused. You don't feel well. You don't want to admit it, but you're overwhelmed, and you may feel betrayed by the people to whom you feel closest, the family members and close colleagues who provide what support you actually have.

And that night, in that condition, you go back out there. On patrol.

You're exhausted. You feel sick. You feel like a train wreck. And you're on patrol.

Back out there.

Question: In this physiological and psychological state, do you think you're going to be operating at your peak levels of efficiency, effectiveness, self-control, and civic awareness that same night, on those same bad streets, when a meth addict or a drunken prostitute vomits on your shirt?

Long-Term Stress and Law Enforcement

This scenario was meant as an illustration of what can happen when stresses multiply and are exacerbated on a long-term basis. It was certainly not intended to characterize the average officer; even less was it intended as a caricature.

However, the fact remains that many law enforcement officers are forced to conduct highly complex police operations, under hazardous conditions, while carrying the burden of long-term stressors similar to those presented in this example. Stress is cumulative. Because officers have no choice but to encounter the acute stressors of the streets, it is important for commanders to do what they can to alleviate the chronic stresses presented by administrative requirements and even family obligations. We will discuss this in more detail, together with some ideas concerning how to reduce these types of chronic stress, in Chapter 12.

For the moment, it is important to realize that the officer who encounters the sudden, acute stress of the streets *may already be dealing with the negative effects of long-term stress.* This means that the effects of tactical or combat stress, to which the officer must respond quickly and intelligently, are frequently exacerbated by all of the factors we've discussed this far. The officer must strike a balance, cognitively and effectively, between the need to apply sufficient force and the need to limit that force to the levels demanded by police procedure, and by situation-specific rules of engagement. This is obviously difficult at the best of times; and for these reasons, it is important for everyone working in the criminal justice system to have at least a reasonably good understanding of the dynamics involved. This is true both for the dynamics of long-term, chronic stress such as those we have examined in this chapter, and for the more immediately demanding dynamics of combat, of the short-term stresses which must be successfully navigated under life-or-death circumstances. For the law enforcement officer, both types of stress, the chronic long-term and the acute short-term, may impinge on the nervous system simultaneously.

So, exactly what happens, psychologically, under acute, short-term stress such as that characterized by a chase, a shooting, or a fight, especially a fight involving lethal force? *What is your brain actually doing in combat?*

Chapter 2
ACUTE STRESS: PROCESSING UNDER PRESSURE AND COMBAT SITUATIONS

It's important to recognize that the dynamics involved in long-term stress are very similar to what happens in sudden violent situations. However, in sudden situations, all of these things happen at a vastly accelerated level. This is even true of potentially violent situations. Increased heart rate, vasodilation, enhanced HPA activity; all occur with short-term stressors just as they do in stressful situations that develop over the longer term.

However, in acute situations, these factors typically exhibit a greater intensity; the fight-or-flight response comes on fast and hard. The result is that under acute stress conditions, a fairly consistent set of cognitive tendencies and responses will typically characterize the officer's behavior and, for that matter, the behavior of witnesses, victims, and other civilians impacted by any given violent situation.

Where does this set of responses come from? As we'll see, the basic answer to that question lies in the stress-related activities of the *prefrontal cortex* mentioned above. In order to make sense of that statement, let's briefly review what happens when the body enters the fight-or-flight state.

Blood flow and subsequent oxygenation increase, the body prepares to attack or to be attacked; it is stronger, and faster, than before. However, there is a cognitive downside to this response, operating in tandem with long-term stress problems discussed above. When you enter the fight-or-flight stage, you will recall that your heart rate increases and most of your blood vessels dilate; blood flows in enormous volume to your muscles.

All that blood, and the physiological resources it carries, has to come from somewhere; and, because you don't have to be a genius to fight or run, the body draws a lot of important blood-borne resources from your prefrontal cortex when you're under high stress. The reader will recall that the prefrontal cortex is the part of the brain that is most involved in thinking, concentrating, and deciding among alternatives; and now, under stress, it's effectively starving for oxygen and other essential resources.

This means that in a bad situation, you simply aren't going to be as smart as you are when you're in a calm situation. This, in turn, means that you're going to rely more on your not-too-bright subcortical structures, and, most crucially, on the habits and ingrained patterns of behavior you learned in training. This is a major reason that your training needs to be both realistic and sufficiently flexible to confront the tactical realities of modern law enforcement, under conditions in which your cortex is not operating optimally.

But what exactly do we mean by suboptimal cortical operation, especially with reference to the prefrontal structures that handle such crucial issues as judgment and self-control? In order to consider the cognitive effects of diminished blood flow to the prefrontal cortex, normal under combat or other acute high-stress conditions, let's look at the absolute worst case scenario. Let us first consider what happens when the prefrontal cortex is really out to lunch, when there is actual *damage* to the relevant important prefrontal structures rather than the temporary, less-profound reduction of prefrontal function typical of the fight-or-flight state.

VIGNETTE 2: DAMAGE TO THE PREFRONTAL CORTEX

So there's this young police officer or soldier. He (or, of course, she; but for the sake of verbal economy, we'll stick with "he" in this story), is riding around in a police car in an American city, or is riding in a Humvee in Afghanistan or Iraq. A high-speed chase goes bad, or a mine goes off under the vehicle, and the front of his head bounces very firmly off the windshield or the very hard ceiling. He may or may not lose consciousness; the ER doc or the army surgeon notes symptoms of concussion, but certifies him as fit for duty.

Yet the collision of forehead with unyielding auto part happened, and we can't undo it. The brain was concussed, and in this particular case the associated injuries caused fluid infiltration of the orbital prefrontal cortex (just above and behind the eyebrow) and the medial prefrontal cortex (just behind the center of the forehead). Also, as the guy's head rebounded violently down or back from the impact, the very front of the temporal lobe came crashing down on the sharp bones at the base of the brain case, the sphenoid bones. The sphenoids sliced into the front portions of the temporal tissue like a butter knife going into a loaf of cheese; and now, the injuries lurk there, deep within the brain, like a particularly nasty time bomb.

Over a few days, or weeks, the young guy's colleagues and commanding sergeant begin to notice things about his behavior. He doesn't pay attention as well as previously, and he's prone to attending to the wrong things in the field or in training. He seems to attend to various irrelevant stimuli rather than to the important aspects of a given field situation; attention bounces from thing to thing, stimulus to stimulus, without really processing whatever it is (this is common with orbital prefrontal damage).

Sometimes the reverse effect is observed; the wounded man's attention may seem to focus obsessively on a given object or situation (another common cognitive symptom). His judgment seems impaired, or dulled, or clouded; this is observed in training, and in field performance, and that time when he walked into a Marine bar and explained to a very, very large lance corporal that the corporal's girlfriend looked like she was beaten with an ugly stick. (Such failures of judgment often accompany damage to the medial prefrontal cortex.)

Anyway, the Marine in question planted a well-conditioned fist the size of a brick into the afflicted individual's forehead. After this incident, his attentional and judgment-related problems were exacerbated.

However, the guy did not appear to learn from the experience. Oddly enough, he continued, and continues, to be overly aggressive. He interrupts colleagues and superiors a lot, finishes their sentences, and blurts out remarks that are off-topic or entirely irrelevant to the situation at hand.

Offensive remarks and jokes erupt from this guy in exactly the wrong social contexts. He becomes more verbally confrontational, and he may use physical violence in situations in which a less confrontational or more diplomatic approach is called for. In fact, he has started to use violence in situations in which no such approach is called for at all, literally starting fights on the street. His home life starts to go south; he may verbally or perhaps physically assault his wife, or other family members or friends. Inappropriate and antagonistic comments burst out at briefing or, for that matter, at dinner. Supervisors, colleagues, friends, and family members of the wounded man are confused; he used to be so reasonable, so easy-going, but somehow seems to have *changed* ...

These are common symptoms of prefrontal damage, and probably of damage to the lower forward areas of the temporal lobes. In weapons training, the afflicted individual

> may suddenly swing and fire his weapon at any sound, threatening or not, and fail to remember doing so at the end of the training session. He may show *perseverative* behaviors, responding in the same habitual, repetitive way to stimuli, whether such a response is warranted or not. Perseveration involves the essentially mindless repetition of the same behaviors, over and over. Such perseverative behaviors are often observed with prefrontal damage.
>
> The head-injured veteran has obviously become a serious problem as a soldier, and an absolute nightmare as a police officer. In terms of operational effectiveness, proper restraint in the use of force, and potential for civil liability, this individual may now be vastly worse than useless, despite good performance records and professional promise prior to the injury.

Prefrontal Damage, Prefrontal Stress

Latent prefrontal damage, in some cases associated also with the type of sphenoid-based temporal damage mentioned above, sometimes provides at least a partial answer to that awful question: *"What went wrong?"* It's not a particularly hopeful answer. Medicine and psychology simply do not, at this point in history, provide us with good ways of treating an individual with major prefrontal damage, even if that damage was incurred heroically and in the line of duty.

This type of problem, by the way, may be of special significance to law enforcement commanders of the present and near future. At the time of writing, the ongoing conflicts in Western and Central Asia have placed many young people in harm's way in an environment rich in improvised explosive devices (IEDs). As a result, large numbers of young people wind up smacking their foreheads against armored surfaces with considerable force.

It should be noted that similar effects can be achieved even without this type of direct physical impact. You don't have to have a piece of shrapnel sticking through your skull. A person whose head has been in the vicinity of an explosive blast can exhibit the same symptom picture, if such a blast causes the brain to be smacked around inside the skull itself. Brains are soft, the skull is hard; if you imagine a slab of wet fat rebounding off the inside of a cue ball, you probably have a reasonable working conception of the dynamics involved.

However, whether such damage is the result of direct impact or explosive detonation, these kinds of damage may lead their victims to engage in further impulsive acts reflecting poor judgment (remember the very large Marine in the bar?). These impulsive acts may in turn cause further prefrontal damage, actively exacerbating the existing neurological and behavioral damage. This type of phenomenon is called *positive feedback*, in which an injury contributes to its own consequences in an accelerative manner. As military individuals who have incurred such injuries in the line of duty return to civilian life and aspire to become police officers, commanders may find their administrative and disciplinary work in this regard more cut out for them than anybody bargained for.

However, the severity of the potential problems involved in prefrontal damage affect a relatively limited number of individuals. The potential for such problems in any given case should obviously be noted, provided there is a reasonable basis in a given specific case history; but what do such extreme cases have to do with normal police work, conducted by individuals who have not incurred this type of damage? The answer is very simple: acute stress itself may cause the brain of the normal person, the person without prefrontal trauma, *to mimic these symptoms,* at a more limited, more subtle, but very real level.

Traumatic prefrontal damage illustrates the extreme, the point at which prefrontal ineffectiveness is at its height. As such, it helps to provide a textbook illustration, a clear, high-resolution picture, of the ways that a prefrontal cortex can malfunction with reference to professional behavior in the law enforcement and military realms.

Normal acute stress, such as that which occurs in combat, does not typically result in the very powerful behavioral malfunctions seen in true prefrontal damage. It is important to be clear about this; the extreme *intensity* of the behavioral anomalies observed with prefrontal damage is atypical for the acute stress response. However, the same *kinds* of behaviors, albeit at lower intensities and therefore somewhat more difficult to spot, are observed with acute stress in the normal human nervous system. As we have already seen, the normal adrenal response to acute stress (including such stressors as high-speed driving, being shot at, engaging in a physical or even intense verbal confrontation) is a reduction of the flow of blood-borne resources to the prefrontal cortex. The "symptoms" of this normal human response reflect an attenuated version of the crises seen with prefrontal damage.

Thus, the law enforcement officer, with a normal human nervous system placed under extreme acute stress, can anticipate a behavioral picture that is similar, if massively diminished in severity, to the individual who has suffered prefrontal damage. This behavioral picture will include temporarily reduced attentional capabilities; reduced judgment; reduced consideration of alternatives and of the consequences and probable course of future actions; greater reliance on habitual or ingrained patterns of behavior; and the potential for perseveration, for doing the same thing again and again for no good reason.

In subsequent chapters, we will deal with the specific effects of these factors on memory and on higher cognitive processes, such as strategic and tactical thinking in command contexts. We will find, however, that the abilities to *perceive* and to *attend* properly are at the core of virtually everything cognitive that happens in the acute stress situation. For successful cognitive performance, especially under acute stress, it is critically important to allocate perceptual and attentional resources to incoming stimuli, to one's own actions, and to one's own thoughts, in an ordered and systematic manner that promotes both operational effectiveness and officer survival. These are exactly the behaviors which become impaired under conditions of acute stress.

Let us therefore consider major factors involved in perception and attention. These relate directly to a series of psychological anomalies that, although not well explained at this point in the history of psychology, are nevertheless very common under acute stress.

Perception and Attention Under Pressure

An outstanding and much-cited study of 113 officers, conducted by Dr. David Klinger under the auspices of the National Institute of Justice, is the original source of much of what we know about these anomalies; much of this work is discussed in detail in his excellent book *(Klinger, 2004)* and also in Lt. Col. Dave Grossman's and L.W. Christensen's outstanding book *On Combat (Grossman and Christensen, 2004)*, which, with Grossman's other seminal book *On Killing (1996)*, should be required reading for anyone concerned with these issues. These excellent treatments are recommended to the reader for full consideration of all of the ramifications of these phenomena.

This book will not attempt to repeat the outstanding treatments by Klinger and Grossman. Rather, we will use this important research to address specific questions of processing under pressure, of how the perceptual and attentional anomalies relate directly to the cognitive realm as applied to law enforcement situations. These anomalies are as follows:

SOUND ANOMALIES

Under stress, sounds are subjectively diminished in volume (this is the most common perceptual anomaly reported), or sounds may be perceived as louder than normal (much less common). So, things either don't seem as loud, or they seem louder, than they should. This is of obvious importance in such matters as gauging the distance to gunfire or to an explosion. This phenomenon may prove to be important either in a given tactical situation, or in retrospect, when the officer, victim, or witness must recall that situation in a report or in court (Chapters 3 and 4).

The subjective reduction of sound by stress can be phenomenally powerful. I have encountered several cases in which gunfire, literally within a few feet of the ears of police and civilian witnesses, was clearly confirmed; yet some of these "earwitnesses" reported *a complete and absolute failure to hear the shots fired*. The reader can imagine how this could influence witness testimony regarding much quieter sounds than pistol fire or shotgun blasts.

TUNNEL VISION

"Tunnel vision" is the second most common phenomenon observed (after diminished sound; *(Klinger, 2004))*. The officer who focuses on the bad guy across the room, but fails to notice the assailant in the corner, is the victim of such tunnel vision. So is the officer who, focused on the car he or she is chasing, fails to see the pedestrian who steps into the path of the police car, or fails to hear the clearly articulated command on the radio. As we saw above, such tunnel vision was probably not generally a problem, and indeed may have presented an *advantage* in focus, in much of the ancient world; when hunting a deer or a mammoth, the last thing you needed was to be distracted by a bird or a pretty flower. You needed to focus on the prey animal.

However, when an officer attempts to arrest a felon who happens to have an armed friend in the corner, as we saw above, this same tendency is a potential killer. Operating in the complex context of a modern city street, or in a rapidly evolving altercation involving deadly force, tunnel vision is an enormously serious problem. It means that you are very unlikely to notice peripheral sources of hazard, as opposed to sources of hazard that are perceptually central or that occupy most of your attention. This problem assumes special significance in IED- or ambush-rich environments, in which the failure to notice something out of place, something that simply isn't right for its context, can literally mean that you don't go home that night. The full ramifications of this phenomenon will be addressed in a subsequent chapter.

"Tunnel vision" is frequently seen even in training scenarios with experienced, veteran officers. Consider a training simulation in which shots are fired at one end of a hallway. The shooter is out of sight of officers in training, who enter the simulation at the other end. The trainees, expert veteran officers, rush down the hallway to reach the scene of the shooting, an obviously commendable action.

The problem is that the simulation includes IEDs, distributed liberally on the floor of the hallway. They are in plain sight, but they are *frequently completely ignored even by veteran officer trainees*. Officers may literally kick mock pipe bombs and IEDs out of their way, or run over them as if they weren't there, in their haste to get to the location of the shooting. I have observed this repeatedly in this training scenario, even in the performance of highly-experienced officers.

This is the effect of tunnel vision. Arousal-based tunnel vision, in the scenario described above, effectively creates a focus on what the officers involved perceive to be the most important part of the scenario, the shooting. This focus, or hyperfocus, is so profound that they completely fail to notice mock-lethal hazards, perfectly visible and literally underfoot.

It must be noted that these effects have been observed in training. In the even-more stressful environment of the streets, the officers in question would not have gone home that night.

I recall participating in another training scenario, designed to simulate a probable hostage situation. An individual emerged from a building in which hostages might or might not have been held. This individual could have been a bad guy, or an innocent bystander, or a hostage himself. There was no way to know. Obviously this individual was important. At the very least, he might have had important information about the disposition of forces and hostages inside the building. Yet officers were so intent on entering the building, so hyperfocused, that they ran right past him as if he wasn't there. In such a case in the field, the officers' *tunnel vision* might literally prevent an immediate end to what otherwise might prove to be a prolonged and deadly standoff.

In another training evolution of my experience, a tactical building entry, officers were so focused on their own actions that they completely failed to notice a sniper, standing in plain sight off to one side, but still within fifty feet. In this case, the sniper peppered the wall of the building with paintball rounds. These slammed repeatedly into the wall of the building, within arm's reach of one the trainee officers; the officers literally did not even notice the rounds crashing into the wall near their own heads.

Research, including that of the author, is currently underway to develop training that will help to alleviate these types of problems posed by tunnel vision. An excellent study by Hope and colleagues (*2012*, detailed in Chapter 3), demonstrated experimentally that high arousal contributes very directly to the type of tunnel vision I have observed in training and in the investigation of a number of real-world field situations, reducing the effectiveness of officer eyewitness reportage. We will discuss this further in Chapter 3, and will deal with the ramifications of these effects for law enforcement training in Chapter 12. For the moment, we can say this: it is crucial to recognize that strong tendencies toward tunnel vision exist, and that realistic training must be provided to fight against it. This training should be provided in a variety of realistic environments, reflecting the reasonable spectrum of possibilities that officers may encounter in the field (again, see Chapter 12).

AUTOMATIC PILOT

Under high stress, individuals may operate on "automatic pilot"; in other words, habitual or perseverative behaviors may be observed. A famous and tragic case of this phenomenon was seen in the 1970 Newhall incident in California, in which well-trained officers of the California Highway Patrol (CHP) were killed by heavily armed assailants. Among the many terrible lessons derived from this incident was the fact that the officers tended to respond automatically to the dangers of the firefight *with the exact motions they had learned in training*. This was true whether the motions in question were appropriate to the given situational evolution or not. The most infamous example of this occurred in the case of one officer who had expended all six rounds from his service revolver. With his better-armed assailant still mobile, he attempted to reload his weapon. Revolvers are hard to load under stress, and rather than slamming one or two rounds into the weapon, sufficient to neutralize the threat, *he apparently attempted a full reload of his revolver, as he had been trained, taking the necessary time to do so.* Tactical experts have told me that this was time he could have used against his assailant, if only he had conducted a *partial* reload, one or two rounds to stop the bad guy and save his life. The invaluable time spent in the attempted full reload was, in this case, a lethal artifact of his range training. He was evidently in the grip of "automatic pilot;" and his assailant walked up and killed him.

Prior to attempting the full reload, this officer was also reported to have dumped the spent shell casings into his hand, and then *taken the time to put them in his pocket*, having been trained scrupulously to pick up his brass on the firing range. This would have been another excellent example of "automatic pilot" in action, and for many years it was. Practically everyone in the field, including the present author, was taught about this Newhall Brass-in-the-Pocket Effect, repeatedly, in trainings that ranged from the local to the U.S. federal level; and we carefully repeated this lesson again and again. It is certainly true that after the Newhall incident, the CHP did in fact formulate a rule against picking up expended cartridge cases on the practice range, to keep officers from developing exactly this automatic-pilot habit.

However, in the wake of recent historical research, it appears that the CHP's No-Brass-in-the-Pockets rule was formulated as part of a general training revision in the wake of the Newhall Incident, *rather than as a result of any specific officer's actions.* John Anderson, a retired Sheriff and 33-year veteran of the California Highway Patrol, does not mention the brass-in-the-pocket incident in his authoritative book on Newhall *(1999).* When asked specifically about this omission by Schraer *(2012),* Anderson stated that as a consequence of the Newhall tragedy, the CHP no-brass-in-the-pockets rule was in fact formulated for range training; but, contrary to consensus, and to decades of use-of-force training and academic work in law enforcement, the officer in question had apparently not put the spent casings in his pocket at Newhall. So said Anderson and Schraer, and quite a few others over the past few years.

When the revised no-pocket-brass story of the Newhall Incident first appeared and began to circulate, it met with considerable skepticism. It still does in some quarters. There are still questions about the horrible Incident, and some details are not consistent between sources; but a general consensus seems to have emerged that Anderson and Schraer's viewpoint, now shared with other authorities, is correct.

On the other hand, Grossman & Christensen *(2004, pg. 72)* assert that there have been several occasions on which "dead cops were found with brass in their hands, dying in the middle of an administrative procedure which had been drilled into them," or had been "shocked to discover empty brass in their pockets with no memory of how it got there." More research is needed to clarify these issues with regard to specific cases other than Newhall; but anyway, and for the present, it would seem to be an awfully good idea to get rid of Brass-in-the-Pocket practices in range training, as the CHP did in the wake of the Newhall tragedy. It's always a bad idea to practice the wrong motor programs. *You will fight in the manner in which you were trained;* and that's a statement that will stand the test of time. "Automatic pilot" is a fearsome enemy; the full reload attempted by the officer at Newhall, discussed above, very probably contributed to his death.

Four officers died in the line of duty at Newhall. Their names were Officer George Alleyn, Officer Walt Frago, Officer Roger Gore and Officer

James Pence. A terrible cost; but the CHP ultimately benefitted from the lessons learned by changing its training and field protocols accordingly.

"Automatic pilot," under stress, can be observed in a variety of different situations and applications. In another example, a specific municipal agency had a policy, when necessary, of drawing the service weapon, firing two rounds, and returning the weapon to the holster. As field conditions changed with time, this practice on occasion proved ineffective against some assailants, especially those using such drugs as PCP, and the agency terminated this policy. Prior to the termination of this policy, however, there were instances of officers drawing a weapon, firing two rounds, and returning the weapon to the holster, *even though the assailant continued his attack.*

In one instance, a well-trained, expert officer told me that he fired his two rounds, returned his weapon to his holster even though his assailant continued to attack, and said something like "What the hell am I doing?" He drew the weapon again, and *repeated the behavior.* He fired two more rounds and again *returned the weapon to the holster*, even though the assailant continued the assault. That situation ended with the officer's survival; but the potential consequences are obvious. Here was a case where the officer's cortical "override," his conscious attempt to interrupt and disable his internal automatic pilot, failed to overcome the habits ingrained through training; his prefrontal cortex just wasn't cooperating.

Other instances could be cited, but these serve our purposes: whatever is thoroughly trained into law enforcement personnel, or acquired by them through habit and experience, can be expected to surface under conditions of extremity. This is true even if the behavior in question is a really, really bad idea. Once again, *you will fight in the manner in which you were trained.*

VISUAL CLARITY AND SENSE OF TIME

Heightened visual clarity has been reported under acute stress, and time may seem to slow, giving the perception of more time for necessary actions. (Much more rarely, time may seem subjectively to speed up under the same conditions; again, see *Klinger, 2004*). I have spoken with a Southwestern state police officer who experienced subjectively enhanced clarity, and the subjective slowing of time, under acute stress in a combat situation. He reported having "all the time in the world" for necessary responses to a violent situation in which he successfully apprehended his armed assailants, and to have had an experience of continuously enhanced visual clarity at the same time.

These particular perceptual anomalies sound like great things to have. However, it must be noted that the evidence for these phenomena is anecdotal, and the mechanisms poorly understood at best. It is very unlikely that stress-enhanced visual clarity and personal speed, relative to your apparently slow-moving surroundings, are "real," in the sense that you could actually use them to enhance your performance. It's much more likely that these effects are not real at all; that, instead, these perceptions are unreliable stress-related subjective impressions that may lead to a false sense of confidence. Almost certainly, these phenomena are illusory, creating a false sense of confidence that can get you killed if you believe in them. Therefore, it's not a very good idea to rely on them. You're not supernaturally fast, and the bad guys have not been slowed relative to your responses. You need to move as fast as your training and experience allow.

MEMORY LOSS

Memory loss for your own actions, and for the actions of others, is frequently observed under conditions of acute stress. More rarely in Klinger's work, memory distortions were observed. This will be treated in depth in Chapters 3 and 4. For the moment, however, it is enough to observe that reports of events observed under stress on the part of eyewitnesses, victims, and even trained law enforcement officers (see Hope et al., 2012) tend to be less complete and less reliable than would typically be the case under less stressful conditions.

INTRUSIVE THOUGHTS

Intrusive thoughts are sometimes seen under conditions of high stress. Sometimes officers will blurt these out. Sometimes they will blurt these out in the presence of less-than-friendly witnesses.

This phenomenon may account for many of the darkly humorous remarks that officers, on occasion, make at scenes of human tragedy. Occasionally, officers will tell jokes while dealing with human remains. Sometimes officers will ask each other if they watched the game last night, while collecting evidence at a particularly gruesome accident scene. The reasons for these behaviors are fairly straightforward: You may not want to think about pulling some guy's spleen out of the windshield wipers, and so your mind drifts to something else, like a joke or a football game; and under stress, the mouth will frequently blurt out whatever occurs to the mind.

Straightforward reasons or not, however, such remarks may be misconstrued by members of the public. They may *really* be misconstrued by the media. Those insensitive officers! Those evil officers! How could they be so *callous!*

Whole media and public-relations circuses can result from this type of effect, so it is very important for public relations officers, in particular, to be aware of this particular facet of *processing under pressure:* the fact is that there is very probably nothing wrong with the officers in question. In a normal human nervous system, intrusive thoughts may simply occur to *anybody* in the heat of the moment, and may be blurted out under the worst possible circumstances accordingly. It is very important to communicate these facts to members of the public and the media, most of whom have never had contact with human organs outside human bodies, but who nevertheless may prove amazingly quick to judge. It's obviously important to get this information out into the community before such an incident occurs and requires explanation. Also, it should be pointed out that this type of phenomenon may be characteristic of *any* human nervous system, not just one that happens to belong to a police officer.

However, the information itself is simple and straightforward: under conditions in which the prefrontal cortex is not exercising its normal functions of diplomacy and impulse control very well, any individual is fairly likely to give voice to whatever random thoughts occur at that moment. If that individual is a police officer, those random thoughts then wind up on the front page.

DISSOCIATION AND PARALYSIS

Other important psychologically-based phenomena that occur under high stress include high levels of dissociation, in which an individual may feel utterly disconnected from the situation or from reality itself, and even, on occasion, temporary paralysis. These are rare, but their potential for harm to officer survival and operational effectiveness are obvious.

Dissociation is an extremely important phenomenon that requires a lot more research attention than it has received to date. In research allied to the work discussed in this book, my students and I have dealt repeatedly with dissociative tendencies in our research respondents, as we've examined eyewitness processes in cases of paranormal "sightings" of Bigfoot, ghosts, flying saucers and so on. And before you decide to stop reading right now, these somewhat weird topics are more pertinent to law enforcement than they might initially appear.

First, waves of interest in paranormal "sightings" can be very burdensome to law enforcement agencies. A good example was seen in the "Phoenix Lights" incident of 1997, when a number of people thought they saw lights moving purposefully through the sky in Arizona. God knows what was really going on (the whole thing was probably connected with some U.S. Air Force activity in the area), but a great many people were loudly insistent that Law Enforcement get out there and do something about the Space Aliens. Granted, driving a patrol car in the desert moonlight around the beautiful golf courses of Phoenix and Scottsdale, ostensibly looking for the Klingons or Darth Vader, is probably preferable duty to arresting violent methamphetamine addicts in an alley downtown; but somebody has to pay for everything law enforcement does, and there are only so many officers per shift. If you have to staff the Alien Patrol as well as the real work, something is going to break (see Chapter 12).

Second, as will become apparent in Chapters 3-5, eyewitness evidence is extremely important in criminal investigation. It is also, and quite often, completely wrong. The *extremes* of eyewitness processing are therefore of significant interest to law enforcement researchers, and seeing a Bigfoot, or mistaking the planet Venus for a Klingon starship, are about as extreme as you're likely to get.

Which is why my students and I have conducted research into why people see these things. They are the extremes of the eyewitness errors on which court cases are frequently lost.

And it turns out that there are several specific psychological tendencies that incline people to specific paranormal beliefs. The depressed tend to believe one thing, the hyperactive another *(Sharps, Matthews, & Asten, 2006)*, but there's one psychological tendency that contributes to belief in *everything*—Loch Ness, Bigfoot, Klingon starships—*everything*.

That tendency is *dissociation*.

Not only does dissociation incline you to paranormal *beliefs*; it also inclines you to paranormal *perceptions*. We found that people with higher levels of dissociation were more likely to interpret everyday pictures as paranormal in nature. Most people saw a picture of a kid in a Halloween gorilla costume. The dissociated saw a picture of Bigfoot. Everybody else saw a helicopter at night, from an odd angle. The dissociated saw an alien spaceship *(Sharps et al., 2010)*. And in a recent study, we found that two dust specks that appeared on desert images, the result of an ill-advised camera lens-change in a sandstorm, were frequently interpreted by the dissociated as alien spaceships, once they'd learned that the particular patch of desert in question was regarded as mystical by other people *(Sharps, Nagra, Hurd, & Humphrey, 2020)*.

Dissociative tendencies, in otherwise normal people, can result not only in bizarre beliefs, but also in bizarre perceptions; and if those perceptions are reported as eyewitness memories, imagine the courtroom chaos that could ensue.

To what degree are average law enforcement officers, under high tactical stress, subject to the situational dissociation that may result not from their personalities, but from the exposure of their normal human nervous systems to the stressors which produce, at least temporarily, dissociative tendencies?

Right now, we don't know. We need to find out. But in the meantime, we must acknowledge that dissociation is associated with high stress, and that dissociation not only influences what you *believe*, but also what you *see*.

It's hard to imagine a more important determinant of eyewitness performance, in the civilian witness or the most experienced law enforcement officer.

Tactical Heartbeats

How stressed do you have to be for these perceptual and attentional anomalies to happen to you? Well, that depends to some degree on individual differences, including differences in temperament, physical fitness, experience, and training. However, it is clear that any given human being is more likely to experience these things under high levels of physiological and psychological arousal, the levels of arousal typical of combat.

One of the best ways to measure physiological arousal has to do with heart rate. When we're in the grip of the fight-or-flight response, our heart rates go up for the reasons discussed above. So, we can begin to develop an index of just how aroused you're likely to be when time slows down, the world shrinks to the bad guy across the room, and you don't seem to remember anything of what happened afterward.

For most people in good shape, most of the time, the heart pumps at 60-80 beats per minute, or sometimes a bit higher. This is good for everyday life, but far too low for the metabolic intensity needed for success in combat. Experts in the field *(e.g., Grossman & Christensen, 2004)* believe that the optimal range of heart rate, for operational success and officer survival in combat, lies between 115 and 135; this is the optimal "zone," in athletic terms, for complex motor skills, visual reaction time, and basic cognitive capacities such as those involved in many shoot/don't shoot decisions. Some authorities extend the upper limit of this range to 145.

However, it should be noted that, for most people, fine motor skills begin to deteriorate at a heart rate of about 115 beats per minute. This could be a problem, even at the bottom of "the zone," depending on your duties. Granted, you don't need much in the way of fine motor control in a typical fight; but you might wonder what the loss of fine motor skills does to the accuracy of an officer in the sniper role, in which aim and accuracy are of course crucial, or to the skills of the bomb squad expert attempting to defuse a complex IED.

Beyond 145 beats per minute, for most people, complex integrated motor skills begin to deteriorate. Between 145 and 175, again for most people, all of the phenomena identified by Klinger *(2004)*, and discussed above in cognitive context, become increasingly problematic. Beyond a heart rate of 175, effectively, all hell breaks loose.

Above 175, people begin to lose gross motor skills *(e.g., Grossman & Christensen, 2004)*; they may not even be able to run well. There may be submissive behavior (a *huge* problem for the officer, to say the least), and voiding of the bladder or bowels (also not great for your command presence). The individual may freeze, obviously losing all operational effectiveness while becoming a superb target. Finally, there may be *irrational* fight-or-flight behavior; the individual may fail to fire, or fire at the wrong things repeatedly, or even flee the scene. Operational effectiveness is lost, and the probability of officer survival is dramatically reduced.

In the author's opinion, what happens above 175 beats per minute seems to simulate, rather closely, the symptoms observed when people with actual prefrontal cortical damage are exposed to stressful or complex situations. These symptoms may seem to be at the farthest extremes of human behavior. We might therefore wonder to what degree such massively enhanced heart rates ever occur at all; after all, we have very little hard data on heart rate, or on other measures of human stress such as the electrodermal activity of the skin, from actual combat situations. A firefight is not the optimal situation in which to be wearing time-synchronized heart monitors, electrodermal activity apparatus, or other things with lots of wires wrapped around your arms, and it's a *really* bad time to be reporting your cognitive responses to research psychologists. In fact, if the shrinks were even there, they'd be in the way, or they'd get shot; these are very real problems in the collection of field data for law enforcement research. Researchers in the field are working on nonintrusive ways of getting around these problems right now, but at the moment the whole field is operating at a very preliminary and primitive stage.

Chapter 2

However, some important pioneering work has been conducted in training scenarios, especially by Prof. Riccardo Fenici, working with the Italian police forces *(Fenici & Brisinda, 2004, October;* also *see Fenici, Ruggieri, Brisinda, & Fenici, 1999,* for additional early research). Fenici measured the heart rates of young, almost incredibly healthy Italian male officers in a relatively benign environment, the firing range. These guys were in really great shape; their average heart rate was in the sixties.

Now, remember that these officers were on the firing range. They were aiming at the targets, not the other way around. There was absolutely no physical hazard at all. Nobody was even mad at them. The only possible threat was that another young guy might shoot better than they did.

Police officers are frequently competitive individuals (they have to be), but simple competition is not exactly at the same level as lethal armed combat. These officers, purely and simply, were not in any danger at all.

Their heart rates jumped into the *hundred* and sixties.

Is this the same as 175? No.

Is it awfully damned close? *Yes.*

Do you think that the heart rates might go a little higher if, say, the targets started firing back, were clearly stoned out of their gourds on methamphetamine, and were running toward the officers, screaming and firing on full automatic, in that special semi-bulletproof way that only the truly cranked seem able to achieve?

It's a pretty good bet.

Grossman *(1996; Grossman & Christensen, 2004)* provides a number of excellent examples of police and military behavior that are at least consistent with the disorganized behaviors characteristic of the highest range of heart rates. As we will see in Chapters 8, 9, and 10, well-documented instances of the behavior of soldiers and commanders, in historically well-analyzed military situations, provide similar examples. Many veteran officers can probably recall instances in which their own behavior, or that of colleagues, provided a close fit to the over-175 syndrome; and virtually every veteran officer with whom the author has been privileged to talk can recall instances in which, if behavior did not reach the outlandish levels of over 175 beats per minute, operational efficiency was significantly reduced by physiological response to the stress of specific tactical situations.

Tactical Stress: A Case History

An excellent example of the combined cognitive and perceptual effects of tactical stress was provided to the author by an outstanding senior police officer, Chief of Police Darryl McAllister (retired) of the Union City Police Department in California. Chief McAllister, a highly articulate and analytical commander, encountered this situation early in his career as a young officer on patrol. We have no idea what his heart rate was at the time, of course, but he adapted and overcame the situation; he was forced to kill his assailant, who had already shot another officer and who was in the process of trying to shoot him. McAllister's analysis of the situation yields a textbook picture of the combined effects of tactical stress on even the highest caliber of police professional.

McAllister had responded to a domestic situation. It was his second call to the same house. As he talked with the female victim at her door, he was of course focused on the central aspects of the case and on his discussion with her. She told him that her husband (who had attacked her, and who was therefore the suspect in this case) was gone.

In his central focus on taking her statement, McAllister did not notice what was on the periphery of his environment. The husband was in fact sitting in his vehicle at the time, approximately fifty feet away. Even though Chief McAllister had the car's description and tag number, he reports that he did not see the vehicle or the assailant; the human nervous system's tendency toward tunnel vision, toward a focus on the situation in the center, precluded his search of the periphery.

Another officer arrived. At McAllister's request, he began to search the area. The second officer found the husband, who exited the vehicle and became verbally aggressive. McAllister approached the situation, coordinating his movements with those of the other officer. At this point, the suspect raised a weapon and began to fire. The other officer was shot and badly wounded. Then the suspect turned to shoot McAllister.

McAllister experienced the most common of the sound anomalies. He has no memory of the sounds of the shots, but he did see the muzzle flashes. He also has no memory of drawing his own weapon, but he does remember firing, at a range of ten feet. He also remembers one of his shots striking the assailant's head, at exactly his point of aim. (This illustrates the good side of our ancient, deer-hunting, central-focus tendencies; Chief McAllister's central focus may have prevented him from seeing the suspect and his car initially, but it enabled him to guide his shot perfectly.)

During the altercation, McAllister took cover behind the other officer's patrol car; he leaped behind it without thinking at all. He credits his ability to do this, in the middle of a fire-fight at a range of ten feet, to a training situation two weeks earlier. The training officer had repeatedly required the trainees to fire twice at a target and then to jump behind available cover, a washing machine-sized box placed on the range. McAllister's repeated experience of this training, "over and over," enabled him to repeat the motions involved perfectly; again, under conditions of tactical stress, the officer will tend to revert to his or her most ingrained, least-prefrontally-mediated habits. In some cases, this leads to disaster; but in McAllister's case, his ingrained habits were beneficial ones, acquired during training to which he was, in his words, "particularly attentive." This strongly highlights the need for versatile, realistic training, the motions of which *become* the "automatic pilot"; good habits are better than bad habits, but whichever ones you have, they're the ones you're going to use in any high-stress situation.

What happened next is of significant interest. When other officers arrived at the scene, Chief McAllister was found still taking cover, and still covering the body of his erstwhile assailant with his service weapon. He has no memory of this whatsoever. He remembers absolutely nothing of what he said to other officers at their arrival and nothing of returning to headquarters. He states that he couldn't even remember his locker combination on his return.

This makes perfect sense in the terms discussed above. We have already seen that memory frequently goes pretty much out the window under high-stress conditions (also see Chapters 3 and 4). Consider memory under stress, again with reference to our hunting past. There are only so many cognitive resources to go around, especially in the prefrontally-diminished state of the tactical response. In the ancient hunting world, there was no strong reason to remember, or to be able to describe, the situation you just encountered, at least not in the mind-bending detail required in modern police reports and in court. Cro-Magnon hunter-gatherers, as far as we know, did not have courts, and they certainly didn't file any reports.

So, the witness to a bad situation, whether that witness is an officer, a bystander, or a victim, does not have a brain that has been readily equipped by our ancient past to give a detailed account of the situation per se. Such accounts, of course, are exactly what are required by courts and in police reports, and this discrepancy between the requirements of the modern world and the brain's long history is probably responsible for all sorts of really serious problems in the criminal justice realm.

Officers arriving at Chief McAllister's scene described his state as one of "hyper-focus," and, as stated above, he was covering the body of his assailant with his weapon when they arrived. This is not an illogical thing to do; the author recalls a training scenario, used extensively by Italian law enforcement agencies, in which an apparently dead person leaps up and "fires" at the trainee, frequently to the trainee's total surprise and simulated death. Veterans of the Vietnam war, or those familiar with operations in the Pacific during World War II *(e.g., Tregaskis, 1943)*, will understand the wisdom of holding a weapon on an assailant until you're really, really sure he's dead; but Chief McAllister holds that tactical wisdom had nothing to do with his continued attention to the dead assailant. He was still simply, and absolutely, hyper-focused on the target, on the center of the action without reference to the periphery.

As Chief McAllister's case demonstrates, even the most capable officers experience these effects. These tendencies of the human nervous system cannot be eradicated; the best that can be done is to train realistically, flexibly, and with reference both to tactical and to cognitive realities for the probable range of circumstances under which officers are going to operate.

In view of the importance of these factors for the investigations and court proceedings that inevitably follow tactical situations, it is also critically important for commanders, attorneys, and others involved in the criminal justice system to understand the psychological dynamics involved in such extreme examples of processing under pressure, at least in terms of the basic operation and ramifications of those dynamics. High-risk, high-stress situations happen, and frequently they cannot be avoided. This was the case with Chief McAllister's incident.

Sometimes, of course, tactical situations can be avoided. When they cannot be avoided, they can sometimes be made less lethal. However, in those situations in which lethal force must be used, and in which officers will be subjected to return fire, it may be that specific types of training can be used to match the demands of the tactical situation to a higher level of precision, contributing both to operational effectiveness and officer survival. We will consider such training issues in subsequent chapters.

But how does an officer or commander decide among force alternatives, and among competing tactical possibilities within those alternatives? Keep in mind that this decision must typically be made quickly and under conditions of limited information. How is this all-important decision to be made?

The correct decisions will not be arrived at through perceptual or attentional processes. These, in a way, are handmaidens to cognition; they find the information you need, and they provide a preliminary analysis of which elements of that information are the important ones. However, the right decisions, or the wrong ones, depend on higher cognition: on the processes of thinking and memory that allow us to weigh and assess conditions and resources. These allow us to go with our strengths, rather than our weaknesses. These allow us to use our advanced cortical abilities to devise a *feature-intensive analysis* of the prospects of the given situation. This analysis can be made with reference to a thorough understanding of the cognitive realities that will take over once the HPA axis assumes a controlling influence. The critical thing is to have the careful cognitive analysis in place *before* the tactical situation begins; again, we will see evidence of this in subsequent chapters.

Stress, Cognition, and PTSD

Law enforcement officers frequently encounter horrible things. These encounters may have long-term effects on the human nervous system, reducing both efficiency and survivability on the part of the given officers. When this type of difficulty reaches clinical proportions, it is classified as post-traumatic stress disorder, abbreviated to PTSD.

PTSD is an old problem. In World War II, the same basic syndrome was called "combat fatigue;" in World War I, "shell shock." In the American Civil War, it was "the soldier's disease;" before that, God knows, but you can be sure it was there.

PTSD is a horrendously multifaceted problem in the modern world, in the scientific and clinical realms of course, but also in the legal and civil domains (see the excellent treatment in Miller, 2015). The condition can result from one or more powerful acute stressors, or from the cumulative effect of chronic significant stress. It is a very real problem affecting many law enforcement officers, including some of those who enter law enforcement having undergone traumatizing experiences in the military. The effects of PTSD can, of course, be dramatically accentuated in the presence of the types of trauma-related brain damage discussed above.

PTSD is therefore very complex, deriving from many possible sources and producing a fairly broad spectrum of physical and psychological symptoms (e.g., Rasmussen et al., 2019). Frequently the patient with PTSD will present with many of the stress-related symptoms discussed above, but often on a much more epic scale.

A full discussion of the complexity of the syndrome is far beyond either the space limitations of this book or the professional scope of its author, so I wish here only to focus on some of the *cognitive* consequences and elements of PTSD, in the terms of acute and chronic stress we've already discussed. There is a problem even with this limited consideration, however. At the present moment in history, nobody really understands what PTSD, post-traumatic stress disorder, actually *is*.

The National Institute of Mental Health provides the following description:

> "When in danger, it's natural to feel afraid. This fear triggers many split-second changes in the body to prepare to defend against the danger or to avoid it. This 'fight-or-flight' response is a healthy reaction meant to protect a person from harm. But in post-traumatic stress disorder (PTSD), this reaction is changed or damaged. People who have PTSD may feel stressed or frightened even when they're no longer in danger.
>
> "PTSD develops after a terrifying ordeal that involved physical harm or the threat of physical harm. The person who develops PTSD may have been the one who was harmed, the harm may have happened to a loved one, or the person may have witnessed a harmful event that happened to loved ones or strangers.
>
> "PTSD was first brought to public attention in relation to war veterans, but it can result from a variety of traumatic incidents, such as mugging, rape, torture, being kidnapped or held captive, child abuse, car accidents, train wrecks, plane crashes, bombings, or natural disasters such as floods or earthquakes" *(NIMH, retrieved 2015)*.

Pretty obviously, PTSD can also develop from the experience of being shot, or shot at. Or from shooting at other people, assailants who are trying to kill you. There are many possible sources of PTSD, and law enforcement officers experience most of them. It's important to note, according to NIMH, that the source of PTSD may not be violence or horror directed toward oneself, but also toward others, both loved ones and strangers. This makes PTSD a diagnostic nightmare, producing a bewildering symptom picture (see *Rasmussen et al., 2019*). We don't understand it very well.

But that doesn't mean it isn't real, and fortunately for the law enforcement community, we hear less and less denial of the syndrome's reality. It does mean that we need to understand PTSD much better, from a variety of valid and relevant perspectives. One of these perspectives, one relatively neglected to date, lies in cognitive science.

It is likely that *cognitive mechanisms* may underlie some of the weirder aspects of the syndrome.

For example, young veterans who returned from combat in Western or Central Asia may exhibit a dramatically higher diagnosed frequency of PTSD symptoms than has been the case in previous wars. Many of these people ultimately become law enforcement officers, so PTSD in the case of recent combat veterans is of great importance to police commanders and personnel officers. It's also pretty damned important to the other officers with whom these veterans will work, under hazardous conditions, in the field. But why is this happening? Why are we evidently seeing more PTSD than was apparently the case in previous wars?

COMBAT FATIGUE AND THE ISLAND OF MALTA

The science of PTSD is just beginning, and we certainly can't answer that question on anything resembling a definitive basis. Nor am I suggesting that a cognitive perspective can replace a responsible, comprehensive clinical approach; cognitive considerations may supplement, not supplant, a complete clinical understanding. However, cognitive science suggests at least a hypothetical answer to this question, one which should be subject to future research. The idea is rooted in a rather arcane source: World War II observations by Air Force General Curtis Lemay (LeMay & Cantor, 1965). LeMay, a bomber force commander during World War II, and USAF Chief of Staff during the Cold War, had this to say:

"Take one ordinary mission, or any demanding or dangerous flight. You're frightened beforehand, perhaps... (but) once you're committed... (there's) no chance to be scared."

A quick caveat: I doubt that the late General LeMay would be too crazy about my interpretation of his observations here. For example, the quote above doesn't say anything about the God-awful psychological consequences once you get back on the ground, after the mission. Also, many veterans can attest that fear, tremendous fear, can be present *during* an operation, no matter how busy and committed you may be. LeMay, here, has oversimplified.

However, there's an interesting cognitive implication here, in LeMay's idea that you're so damn busy over the target that it at least *limits* your "chance to be scared." The brain has limited cognitive resources, and if pretty much all of those resources are directed toward your controls or your guns or your bombsight, you may not notice much about your emotional state until later; a number of tactical veterans can also attest to this.

Also, the same limited cognitive resources, *further* limited by all the fight-or-flight factors discussed above, may mean that you're so focused on the core aspects of your mission that *you don't encode sufficient relevant data about the context in which it occurs*. This is important for your eyewitness report of the action, of course (see Chapters 3 and 4 below), but as we will see, it might also be important for later symptoms of PTSD.

One additional point about the quote above, and this is where we get into a possible explanation for the prevalence of PTSD today. There was one thing you were absolutely certain of, in a World War II bomber over Schweinfurt or Peenemunde or Ploesti. This was the fact *that there was no way out*. You weren't getting out of that airplane until it was away from the target, and ultimately down on the ground.

Now, a typical World War II bombing mission took a day at most. But what about longer-periods of chronic stress, longer periods *when there was no way out*? History provides a potentially important example, discussed by LeMay; the horrendous World War II siege of the island of Malta, in the Mediterranean, by the German navy and air force.

Little food or anything else could be brought into Malta; everything had to come in by submarine, not the most capacious type of cargo vessel. LeMay:

> *"You can guess what the food situation was like. Day after day, week after week, the population of Malta was bombed and dropped and shelled. Civilian casualties came to more than 4800."*

The levels of death and destruction were epic; scenes of horror were endemic and ubiquitous, and the God-awful bombardment and carnage went on week after week.

"And nobody ever reported any combat fatigue" (LeMay & Kantor, 1965, pg. 358).

Nobody every reported any combat fatigue. Here, the General was referring to the period of the siege itself, and there are a couple of important cautions to be considered concerning this statement.

First, when you're having the living hell bombed out of you by the Luftwaffe, there's a very good chance that your psychiatric records aren't going to be in apple-pie order, especially the records that are on fire at the time. To say there were no cases of PTSD at all may therefore be a bit of an overstatement.

Second, LeMay has nothing to say about what happened *after* the siege, as military personnel and civilians began to reflect on what had happened to them and their hands started to shake. I don't know, but

Chapter 2

I would be willing to bet that what we call PTSD, the combat fatigue of World War II, was probably *very* prevalent, at least after the shelling stopped.

But *during* the siege of Malta itself, there apparently weren't anywhere near as many cases of combat fatigue, PTSD, as we might expect. LeMay suggests it was non-existent.

Here's the thing about Malta. It's an island, surrounded entirely at the time by angry Germans. There was no possible way off the island, no escape, no stopping the nightmare. Just like the situation in a B-17 over Schweinfurt; except that a bombing mission took a few horrible hours, and the terrifying siege of Malta went on for what must have seemed forever.

What LeMay's observation suggests is that PTSD, basically "combat fatigue," may be strongest *when there is some possibility of ending the danger* (escaping the island, escaping the next mission), *and when this possibility is enmeshed in ongoing uncertainty about prospective outcomes*.

In short, if one cannot escape the danger, PTSD *at the time* may be less likely; if one has some prospect, perhaps uncertain or nebulous of escaping danger, *the probability of PTSD may increase*, as the given individual weighs the uncertain prospects of escaping more combat. It may be the anxiety of *uncertainty*, at least in part, that gets to you over the long term.

Now, in the present long-term conflicts in Central and Western Asia, in which the United States is participating on what appears to be an ongoing basis, military personnel face great uncertainty. Rotations out of combat situations may or may not be final. A given soldier may be home for good, but may also be rotated back into the operational whirlwind, depending on Defense priorities well beyond that soldier's control. There's no way to know.

In cognitive terms, this essentially creates situations in which streams of reasoning divide into multiple different lines of possibility at once. A lot of these lines of possibility may have very negative consequences, *but there's no way to know*. There is a lot of uncertainty: I will do such and such if I don't have to go back into combat, but what the hell will I, and my family, do if I have to go back into the combat environment? It looks like I'll have to go back- oh, good, I just heard that I won't have to go back—oh, damn, it looks like my Reserve or National Guard unit will have to go back after all—oh, okay, if I have to go back into uniform, it will probably be stateside service- what? Joint Tasking? What the hell is Joint Tasking? You mean I may have to go back into the combat zone and work with a *completely different service*? For how long? Nobody knows? *What?*

So, a major implication of LeMay's Malta observation is that PTSD *may be more likely when you have options*, especially after the shooting stops but when more shooting may or may not be in the offing. This may seem counterintuitive—isn't it good to have options? Well, under most circumstances, maybe so; but *if you aren't the one controlling those options*, and if one or more of the options may lead to long-term separation from family and from normal life, or to your own premature, violent death, then the answer is no. Most sane people would prefer to have some of those options *closed* to them if at all possible. Especially the potentially lethal ones.

So, if this interpretation is correct, then a high relative number of uncontrollable options, with the consequent anxiety of *uncertainty*, may prove to be a significant factor in the development of PTSD. It makes sense, although we just don't know, not yet. This idea needs to be thoroughly researched, and real-world research of this type takes a long time and a lot of resources.

But if the basic premise is right, and if the afflicted individual is a police officer who is also a Reservist, or a National Guard member, then he or she may carry this uncertainty, with its cognitive consequences, into the field in law enforcement duties as well.

This would certainly also be the case with those law enforcement officers whose PTSD derived from non-military sources, from their everyday duties. Law enforcement officers, in their unique and very high-hazard environments, face one hell of a lot of uncertainty every day.

An important caveat, which I will emphasize once again: scientifically, this is *hypothetical*. These ideas seem to fit the facts, but we don't know for certain if they operate as suggested, and there's certainly a lot more to PTSD, both in and out of the cognitive realm, than we've discussed here. We need far more research on the subject, solid research, with the collaboration of law enforcement officers and military personnel. But what we know already clearly demonstrates that ex-military personnel frequently carry many of the stress-related symptoms described above into their police duties with them.

OTHER COGNITIVE ASPECTS OF PTSD

People with PTSD often have nightmares. Bad dreams. *Really* bad dreams.

If you're one of these people, don't feel alone. *Everybody* in your world has the dreams. But that doesn't mean the dreams aren't a problem. They rob you of sleep, and of sound sleep, and the resulting

Chapter 2   51

fatigue can seriously mess you up in a demanding law enforcement situation the next day. If the dreams are really bugging you, it's very important to talk to a competent police psychologist, somebody who actually *gets it,* and obtain his or her help. Competent shrinks can usually help quite a bit.

But PTSD can also produce the dreams, essentially, *when you're wide awake.* The underlying processes are different, but the terrifying qualities are just the same. These waking "dreams" are called "daytime intrusions."

Officers are frequently reluctant to disclose these, let alone talk about them. They frequently think these daytime intrusions are evidence of "being crazy," or of descent into madness.

No, they're not. They make a lot of cognitive sense.

Think about those poor guys in the bombers, working for General LeMay in World War II. They were focused, at high levels of arousal, on their controls, or their guns, or their bombsights, as well as on the Messerschmitts which were flashing around like high-speed, heavily armed mosquitos intent on shooting the maximum number of holes through their bodies.

Now, as discussed above, we have a fairly limited level of cognitive resources available at any given time. So, if we're focused like hell on shooting down the Messerschmitts, we will tend to miss a lot of other details in our environment, details that are less immediately lethal.

Therefore, it's a good bet that the brains of the guys in the bombers didn't record a lot of important contextual facts, such as the fact that only here, in this airplane, at this time, is this kind of horrible thing likely to be happening. If you don't record those facts, these crucial where-and-when aspects of *context,* it's very possible that your brain may think that the whole miserable situation could happen again, anywhere, any time.

Like in a department store in Denver, or on a sidewalk in Chicago.

And on that sidewalk, you hear a car backfire, and you duck behind the bombsight (okay, a nearby mailbox, but at the moment your hyper-aroused brain is not particular), and wham—you're back in 1944 in the plexiglass nose of a B-17. It is now very clear that PTSD results directly in *disruptions in memory,* including completely involuntary "flashbacks," the reliving of traumatic experiences (e.g., Bisby, Burgess, & Brewin, 2020) that would be far better left in memory than re-experienced in the veteran's perception of the current real world.

Various environments, and various neurochemical states, can facilitate this entirely negative process. Let's see an example.

VIGNETTE 3: PTSD AT HOME

So there's this veteran of irregular jungle combat in Asia, long, long ago in a country far, far away (with apologies to *Star Wars*).

He was in his easy chair in his living room, years after his combat experiences. He was reading a fairly boring technical article, related to his work, and it wasn't really holding his attention. His wife was out, and his kid was grown and gone. He had long vertical blinds in his living room.

Now, the thing about long vertical blinds is that they sort of look like bamboo. Bamboo, in jungle warfare, is scary. You can hide *anything* behind bamboo—infantry, machine gun nests, even field artillery. Anything.

Now, this guy, like anybody else, knew damn well that the blinds weren't bamboo, but he noticed that they *looked* like bamboo. At first he found this mildly amusing, and then a bit unnerving, and then, even though he knew the bamboo stalks—I mean the blinds—weren't really concealing a threat, he became nervous. Fairly naturally, his mind segued from the boring technical article to thoughts about his wartime experiences.

So, he had a nice glass of Scotch to make himself feel better.

Not his best move.

A few words about alcohol. It's legal. Most cops of my experience won't use illicit drugs, because cops are almost always law-and-order people, and drugs are illegal.

But booze *is* legal, and many law enforcement officers partake, especially when they feel they need a drink.

If you actually feel you *need* a drink, it's an amazingly good idea not to *have* one.

But the fact is that if you're nervous, or depressed, or anxious, alcohol *will in fact make you feel better*.

For about an hour.

Then you'll feel even worse.

Aside from the health consequences of booze, a major problem is that eventually, *it always makes you feel worse than you did before*. You go up, and then you go down, and the down is even lower than it was before the booze.

Unfortunately, many people then decide that the solution

Chapter 2

to their new (even worse) emotional state is: MORE BOOZE!

You need a reason to drink more, of course, and our veteran had one. He knew a lot of people who were dead, who had died badly, very badly, back in those jungles. What more natural than to toast their memory?

Which he did. Quite a lot. With additional glasses of Scotch. And his cognitive and perceptual faculties continued to fragment, as is typically the case when you pour Scotch on them.

Too much alcohol makes you hot and uncomfortable, and so our veteran thought he'd feel better outside. He also felt nervous being inside a house, at this point; after all, the Viet Cong could target one of their ancient French 75mm cannons on any building you're in, so outside feels better. Safer. More places to duck into if the shelling starts.

Granted, there were no angry communists with antique French 75's in his present suburban environment, but when there *had* been, in a much different and earlier setting, his brain hadn't been too particular about recording the *context*, the wheres and the whens; he'd been kind of busy staying alive. His brain had, quite reasonably, placed a priority on his survival, rather than on the context.

But anyway, outside felt better. So he went outside.

But there's a problem with outside. Outside has a lot of trees. You can hide *anything* behind a lot of trees. And outside was also where a lot of bad things had happened to him.

And unfortunately, the outside environment, in the American South, was now an excellent match to the environment in which he had encountered so much horror; and he started to feel even more anxious.

So, to feel better, he drank some nice Outside Scotch in additional toasts to the memory of his dead comrades, and his cognitive systems (which, you'll recall, didn't do a really good job in the first place of recording the *context*, the places and times of his actual traumatic experiences)- his cognitive systems continued to fragment, and he started to feel more anxious, and to notice how much the Spanish moss on his backyard trees resembled the fungal arboreal growths of Southeast Asia, and...

By the time his long-suffering wife came home, she found him in the backyard, carefully examining patterns of sticks on the ground in search of Viet Cong booby traps.

> Now, it's important to realize that this man was not "crazy" in any meaningful sense. He was (and remains) a successful professional man, in a supervisory capacity in a field related to engineering and technology. On any given day, at home, in his office, in a conference room or on a factory floor, he is perfectly normal; but thanks to a weird combination of vertical blinds, Scotch, and backyard sticks, together with the relatively fragmented cognitive nature of his traumatic experiences, on at least one occasion he was right back in the jungle.
>
> His wife, to whom he refers as "a candidate for sainthood," stayed with him. As a result of treatment by a competent psychologist, somebody who *gets it*, he no longer has the daytime intrusions, and he seldom even has the dreams. He continues in his supervisory and technological duties, and has made respected technical advances in his field. He's fine.
>
> So PTSD is not the end of the world; but if this story resonates with you, personally, it's a very good idea to find a psychologist just like his. And for God's sake, put down the Scotch.

So, our veteran has helped us to illustrate the cognitive consequences of PTSD. Eventually he had a happy ending. It happens. It's nice when it happens.

But there are other times when the ending is not so happy, and when it illustrates the potentially terrible consequences of PTSD. There are times when PTSD can kill you, as we will see.

ARGUMENTS AGAINST PTSD

PTSD is often devastating, and devastatingly serious; but despite widespread evidence and an amazingly large number of documented cases, one frequently encounters two objections to the modern characterization of PTSD. Both objections can pose significant obstacles to the successful understanding and treatment of the condition.

The first objection involves skepticism *concerning the condition itself;* various authors and individuals, especially anonymous individuals on the Internet, assert that the condition doesn't exist at all, or that people of the past simply dealt with similar trauma by shrugging it off somehow. It's also suggested that, since the symptoms of PTSD are now well known and readily accessible on the Internet, large numbers of people, including unscrupulous veterans, may be *faking* the symptoms of PTSD, malingering to get money and benefits out of the rest of us. This objection may seem ridiculous to clinicians, researchers, and the very real victims of PTSD; but you encounter this assertion more often than would seem to make sense.

The second objection is more subtle, and may in fact be more difficult to deal with. This is one you usually hear from *veterans and law enforcement officers themselves*, who perhaps should know better, but who nevertheless assert that, sure, PTSD exists, but it certainly can't affect *me*. Other guys, maybe, you know, who don't have the *training* or *experience* that I have… In other words (and this part is usually implied, rather than stated outright), the officer or vet may suggest that if people have the Right Stuff (see Wolfe, 1979), if they're strong enough or tough enough (like him, or occasionally her), this PTSD stuff won't bother them.

How does the responsible commander, officer, clinician, or scholar counter these arguments, which are often believed strongly and defended vociferously?

There are ways.

PTSD Past and Present

Let's deal with the first argument first. *Did people in the past actually have PTSD?*

Well, we have nomenclature for the condition going back at least to the American Civil War, when it was known as the "Soldier's Disease." In later wars, as mentioned above, it was "Shell Shock," or "Combat Fatigue." It would seem that the disorder was at least recognized, even if it wasn't discussed a lot in public, for well over a century or more. There are also many earlier references, harder to document as we move back in history, but still consistent with the modern clinical picture of PTSD.

Many veterans of World War II were very disinclined to discuss their war experiences or the effects those experiences had on them. But some, in some cases, were willing to acknowledge on camera the negative influences of what we now call PTSD on their postwar lives, their families, and their marriages (e.g., Haffner & Gillam, 2003). Their stories are fading with the natural course of mortality; but what has been preserved in text and on film leaves no doubt that *PTSD and combat fatigue were essentially the same thing.*

But what about the idea that the current epidemic of PTSD is a modern fabrication, that victims may, intentionally or perhaps not, be getting their symptom picture from the Internet?

The best way to find out if this could be the case was to examine cases of PTSD before there was an Internet, and before the syndrome became well-known at all, under whatever nomenclature.

So my wife, Professor Jana Price-Sharps of Walden University, and I undertook to find out. First we read a tremendous number of rather dusty old books. Then we embarked on a five-thousand mile field trip in the American West, investigating the scenes of numerous crimes and military disasters of the nineteenth century and earlier, when even the "Soldier's Disease" lay in the future or in obscurity. We walked battle and crime scenes, examined local artifacts, and spoke with local historians throughout, using standardized criteria for PTSD (Sharps & Price-Sharps, 2019).

Among the crimes and battles we examined, from the standpoint of forensic cognitive science (me) and forensic clinical psychology (her) were the murder of Wild Bill Hickok (see this section, below), the gunfight at the OK Corral, the horrible crimes of mountain man John "Liver-Eating" Johnson, the Battle of the Little Bighorn (see Chapter 8, below), the Fetterman Massacre, and other human tragedies going back to the Spanish Entrada.

In every single case, the principle characters in each terrible drama had undergone experiences, in war, law enforcement, or civilian life, *which would clinically predispose a person to PTSD by modern standards.* And *in every single case, we found the diagnostic criteria of PTSD*: failures of impulse control, dissociative processes, impulsive violence, substance abuse, outlandish irritability even by the standards of those violent centuries, failures of concentration, recklessness, and *epic* levels of substance abuse, especially in terms of the ingestion of vast quantities of rotgut whiskey.

In every single case, decades or centuries before anyone had ever heard of PTSD, we found its etiology, its symptoms, and its aftermath. PTSD existed long before the Internet or before the symptoms of the disorder became widely known. *The syndrome, PTSD, is real.*

In the spirit of complete transparency, we actually thought at the time that we'd had one failure to find the syndrome. This was the case of the Fetterman Massacre, a battle of 1866 in which Lakota (Sioux) warriors conducted a complex ambush near Fort Phil Kearny in northern Wyoming. The Lakota lured the infantry command of Captain William Fetterman beyond the bounds dictated by his orders, and he and his command were destroyed. It was long held that Fetterman had impulsively gone beyond his orders in his reckless hatred of his Lakota foes, and, that his failure to concentrate and focus appropriately on the

Chapter 2   57

tactical realities had led his eighty long-suffering subordinates to an unnecessary death (e.g., Brown, 1962).

The problem for us was that Fetterman exhibited none of the normal signs of PTSD. He was not a pleasant person by 21st century standards, true, but there was nothing of PTSD about him at all. He was apparently a highly competent officer of the 19th century, with none of the usual symptoms. So chalk up one failure for our field project.

Until we spoke with local historians, walked the battlefield, and became acquainted with more modern research on the subject (*Fort Phil Kearny/Bozeman Trail Association, 1993; Monnett, 2008*).

It turns out that the initial reckless attack by the U.S. Army on the Lakota, ignoring orders and failing utterly to understand what was really going on, was apparently actually spurred and escalated by a *cavalry* officer, George Washington Grummond, not by Fetterman and his infantry at all.

Horses are faster than foot soldiers, and so it appears that Grummond's horsemen swiftly outstripped Fetterman and his infantry, who may, in fact, have died moving forward in an attempt to rescue Grummond's cavalry command (see *Monnett, 2008*) from the dissociative and impulsive attack ordered by their— how shall we put this—deeply *unusual* commander. Grummond.

Grummond had horrible experiences in the American Civil War, the kind of experiences that might very well have predisposed him to PTSD. Grummond drank like a fish, and while drunk out of his mind he pistol-whipped subordinates, and irritably and impulsively shot at other officers and civilians (including a man to whom he then denied medical treatment). He was also guilty of fairly epic levels of spousal abuse; in general he displayed most of the worst qualities we would associate with PTSD.

Oh, and he seems to have had impulse problems in other areas, as well. When Grummond died, only two of his wives showed up to claim his military benefits.

Lieutenant George Washington Grummond might be considered a 19th-century poster boy for the worst consequences of untreated PTSD, in every important respect. Historians like Monnett (*2008*), and the members of the Fort Phil Kearny/Bozeman Trail Association, have done a great service in clarifying the realities of the battle, and in clearing the record of Captain Fetterman; but they have also given research psychologists a significant bonus as well. We found that every single case of our field investigation, across the American West and back to the Entrada, led to a picture consistent with PTSD in major participants. We found this again and again in the terms of modern symptomatic and etiological characterizations, over a century before anybody had any idea of the concept of PTSD beyond vague allusions to the "soldier's disease."

The symptom picture of PTSD has persisted through history as a natural phenomenon, without cultural or technological overlay to bias our perception of this disorder. PTSD is completely real, and although the factors involved are very complex (e.g. Rasmussen et al., 2019), the symptoms are exactly what current experts currently say they are, and we can prove it.

But what can we say to the second argument against PTSD, that if you have enough of Tom Wolfe's *(1979) Right Stuff,* if you're a real *operator,* hard enough and strong enough, you won't get PTSD. Well, let's look at a specific case and draw our own conclusions. Let's look at a probable PTSD victim whose Right Stuff was virtually impossible for anybody to question. Granted, we can't be absolutely certain that this was PTSD in every respect; but it's suggestive, to say the least…

THE DEATH OF WILD BILL HICKOK

Case histories are always a problem for psychologists. You only have one person in the case; so, you can't use most kinds of scientific analyses on the situation. You can never be sure if your conclusions about the given case generalize to everybody else.

But you can use case histories, at least heuristically, to suggest what's going on. And a really good case history, in the present instance, is what happened to James Butler (Wild Bill) Hickok.

Hickok *(Turner, 2001),* practically the prototype of an Old West hero, was a military veteran, having served as a U.S. Army sniper in the Civil War. He was a highly effective Army scout in the Indian wars of the late 1800s, and a very successful lawman in the tough cattle towns of the American West. He was a hard, pragmatic man, an expert killer when required. And in 1871, he got into a street gunfight.

This might not have bothered him, not much, anyway, under normal circumstances. Hickok, after all, had killed an awful lot of people—estimates vary *(Wilstach, 1926),* but Wild Bill was, to say the least, fairly experienced in the arcana of homicide. He'd been a soldier, a scout, and a lawman—he'd been very successful in a variety of occupations which required killing.

But this gunfight, in October, 1871, was different.

Hickok, for reasons based in a gambling incident, had a shootout with another gambler named Phil Coe. In the course of the fight, in front of the Alamo Saloon in Abilene, Kansas, Coe grazed Hickok's side with a shot from his revolver. This would obviously have produced pain, and

Chapter 2

a fairly powerful "fight or flight" response in any human being, even Wild Bill Hickok. But Hickok, a master of pistol fighting, retaliated by firing both of his revolvers into Coe's abdomen. Coe went down. So far so good, from Hickok's perspective. In view of his history, we would not expect major psychological consequences at this point.

Unfortunately, Hickok's deputy, Mike Williams *(Wilstach 1926* gives Williams' first name as Jim), chose this moment to approach him, apparently from behind. Williams is reported to have had his own revolvers drawn (although published accounts of this incident vary in detail). But, anyway, Hickok, presumably in the grip of "fight or flight," perceived Deputy Williams as a threat. He spun and fired, killing his own deputy.

Bad guys are one thing. Your own deputy is something else.

Now, this was Wild Bill Hickok, for God's sake. A gunfighter, one of the best at that horrific profession that the Wild West ever produced. And yet he'd accidentally killed Williams, his deputy, apparently his friend, his colleague and subordinate. A man who trusted Hickok, his superior, to keep him as safe as duty allowed.

Hickok had blown him away. And Hickok knew it.

Wild Bill had screwed up, and screwed up badly, in the one realm of life where he *never* screwed up.

And—*perhaps*—it changed him; certainly he changed.

It is said that Williams was the last man Hickok ever killed. He'd killed an awful lot of people, but he never killed again. Such a general absence of homicide would seem fairly normal to most people—but this was Wild Bill Hickok. And apparently, he never killed anybody else. Ever.

Hickok, originally, was about as romantic as one of his blue-steel Navy colt revolvers, tucked into his scarlet sash. (As far as romance goes, the whole Calamity Jane thing turns out to be a myth; Hickok apparently had practically nothing to do with her.) Wild Bill, at least Wild Bill Version 1.0, was pretty much immune to the charms of love, and family, and all the rest of it.

At least until 1871, and the death of Williams, when Wild Bill Version 2.0 seems to have emerged.

After the death of Williams, James Butler Hickok fell madly in love with a lady of the "entertainment world," a well-known circus performer. He apparently decided to create a fantasy future for the pair of them, a world of marital joy and peace.

Romantic fantasy; does this sound like the mind of a soldier, scout, and gunfighter? Or does it sound like such a mind *fundamentally changed into another kind of mind entirely*?

Anyway, Hickok left the violent world of frontier law enforcement, and moved to Deadwood, South Dakota, in order to dig up enough gold to finance matrimonial bliss.

God only knows what he was thinking about: love and peace and rocking chairs, and children playing by the hearth? After a violent lifetime on the frontier, after making dozens, perhaps hundreds, of lethally vengeful enemies, was such a prospect even realistic? One can never be sure, of course; people change.

But the Williams incident may very well have been the final straw that drove even Hickok into the throes of PTSD. PTSD frequently places a person at a high chronic level of arousal, and as we have seen, such a level of arousal can lead you to beliefs, perhaps dissociative beliefs, that are not necessarily salutary, or even realistic. Arousal can lead you to beliefs that have their only home in the realm of fantasy. Can you even imagine Wild Bill Hickok happily at peace in that rocking-chair, fireside setting? And can you imagine Wild Bill, cut-away coat, mustaches, and "wide-awake" hat bending in the breeze, twin revolvers hanging by their loading-gates in his scarlet sash, happily driving a pickaxe into a promising yellow rock in some nameless muck-filled ravine in South Dakota?

Apparently, neither could he. His prospecting period lasted about two days. Literally. Two days.

Still immersed in his fantasy world of prosperous marital bliss, Hickok continued to gamble incessantly, looking for the Big Strike that all gamblers seek and almost none ever find. As a former lawman, when he sat at card games, he always insisted on keeping his back to the nearest wall, with a clear view and a "killing field" between himself and any given door; a lot of people wanted him dead, and this simple tactical precaution was practically instinctive.

Hickok, a man of amazingly aggressive tendencies, enforced this back-to-the-wall rule with a grim visage and his hands on his Navy Colts. Fellow card players generally got up, and gave him their chairs; and he maintained his required back-to-the-wall perspective on the doors of any given saloon.

Until August 2, 1876, when another gambler—a young and relatively inexperienced man—refused to give up his back-to-the-wall chair to Hickok.

Was the other gambler suicidal? This was Wild Bill Hickok, for God's sake. What would the famous gunfighter do in this potentially explosive situation? We'd expect an immolation, with the young gambler reduced to a quivering pile of ashes.

Chapter 2

"Okay," said Hickok, who sat down at the gambling table with his back to one of the doors.

Wild Bill Hickok in a passive role, submitting without protest to a young, inexperienced gambler. It's impossible, it makes no sense. But it happened.

Does the reader remember one of the less-common symptoms of high arousal, in which even a hardened law enforcement officer, like Hickok, *may find himself trapped in the grip of submissive behavior?* Hickok's actions on this occasion were at least consistent with the submission of high-level PTSD, perhaps derived from the five-year-old incident in which Wild Bill killed Williams.

At any rate, Hickok passively took a chair with his back to the door. As he became engrossed in the game, a gambling acquaintance named Jack McCall, who had previously lost heavily to Hickok, entered through a door in the front of the saloon in *full view of Hickok*, and circled behind him. Hickock appears to have ignored him completely, with an intense tunnel-vision focused on the cards in his hand. But, after some courage-building contemplation from behind, McCall approached Wild Bill from the back and blew him away. Wild Bill Hickok, lawman and veteran, expired on the wooden floor of the Number 10 saloon in Deadwood. To the end, he is said to have clutched his last poker hand, aces and eights; forever after, the "dead man's hand."

(Incidentally, our study of the layout of the Number 10 saloon in Deadwood strongly suggests that it was Hickok's position toward the middle of the room, rather than his orientation to the doors per se, that was the more important spatial factor in his demise. However, overall, Wild Bill's position at the gaming table certainly indicates a strange, perhaps dissociative disregard of his normal precautions, and a significant failure of his powers of concentration, on the very day of his murder.)

At McCall's trial, the assassin claimed that Hickok had killed his brother. McCall never had a brother. Homicide detectives will not be surprised; there are always weird loose ends. Every time.

But Hickok was dead.

James Butler Hickok, one of the most aggressive and truly *dangerous* warriors of the American West. He was an iron-hard law enforcement officer of epic abilities; but after he shot his own deputy, he appears to have, perhaps dissociatively, entered a fantasy world of peace and connubial bliss. Dissociation is more important than we would generally believe; and as Hickock's fantasy world encountered the hard realities of nineteenth-century Deadwood, he became at least momentarily passive, passive enough to sit in a chair with his back to a door. And, after a lifetime of rock-hard aggression, he died, aces and eights in his hand.

WILD BILL HICKOK AND THE MODERN OFFICER

If the case of James Butler Hickok isn't a fairly likely example of a law enforcement officer in the grip of PTSD-related stress, I don't know what is.

I can't prove it, of course, not with complete certainty. It's a case study. As mentioned above, case studies are largely impervious to our statistical technologies.

But if this sort of thing could happen to Wild Bill Hickok, cold-blooded sniper veteran of the Civil War, Marshal of the American West, Indian Scout and buffalo hunter, tough guy beyond the moral or legal bounds of anything we have in the modern world:

What could happen to you?

PTSD happens to the strongest officers and operators. But PTSD aside, the mental set of the best officers, of course, *is to keep going no matter what.*

And most of them do; and some of them burn out, in the grasp of undiagnosed PTSD. They may have The Right Stuff (*Wolfe, 1979*), but it only lasts so long; the best, the hardest officers, burn out, in ways analogous to the ignoble death of Wild Bill, on that whiskey-soaked floor in the Number 10 saloon, clutching his aces and eights.

James Butler Hickok died in 1876, almost a century and a half ago. We've advanced a bit since then. The modern officer suffering from PTSD has many options that simply weren't there for Hickok, *but the modern officer has to make use of these options, possibly to avoid a similar fate.* If you have these problems, these symptoms, you must understand *that they're not a mark of failure.* They are certainly not a mark of any form of personal or individual weakness.

Hell, as far as I can tell, James Butler Hickok had the same symptoms. Wild Bill Hickok, for God's sake. The very same symptoms.

If Wild Bill's story resonates with you, it would be a very good idea to find a competent shrink, somebody who *gets it*, and acknowledge that you have the same nervous system as Wild Bill Hickok. The same human nervous system. Use modern psychological technology to optimize your performance in the field, to adapt and to overcome the symptoms of PTSD. Hickok didn't have this option; you do, and you can use it for the benefit of your fellow officers and the population you're sworn to protect.

Chapter 2

The Importance of Memory

PTSD is obviously of crucial importance, although, thankfully, it is a relatively small proportion of the general population that suffers from it.

But, as mentioned above, all of us have nervous systems, and all of us use them in similar ways. Our nervous systems process information; our higher reasoning powers, those involved in problem solving and decision making, are directly dependent on the processing of information, the information we have in memory. Information processing, of various types, is therefore key to ultimate operational success, and frequently to officer survival. Information is learned and held in memory; and as we have already seen, memory is not at its best under the tactical conditions frequently encountered in the world of law enforcement.

Here we enter the convoluted world of the eyewitness.

The average person, or the average law enforcement officer, probably thinks in the first instance of an "eyewitness" as a civilian who happens to see a crime as it is committed. This is one kind of eyewitness, of course; but it is also true that there are many other kinds of eyewitnesses as well. Any officer or civilian who observes a crime, or who participates either in the crime or in opposing it, becomes, essentially, an eyewitness to whatever happened, and to whatever he or she did during the action. Anyone who reports on an *officer's* actions is an eyewitness, too. So is anyone who provides a report on events that relate to a crime or a police action, if not on the crime or action itself. All of these different individuals and situations participate in the eyewitness realm, and all are in fact governed by the psychological dynamics that operate in that realm.

For these reasons, it's extremely important to understand the relevant aspects of how eyewitness memory works, as these apply to eyewitnesses who may be officers, bystanders, or victims. Memory provides the raw material for all forms of reports and narratives, ranging from the officers' situation reports to the complex narratives recalled, or created, by eyewitnesses in court. Memory also provides the basis of all reasoning and decision making, including the crucial decisions made by officers and commanders in tactical situations.

Thus, memory is a crucial aspect, if not the core aspect, of *processing under pressure*. The most important aspects of memory for the understanding of cognitive aspects of law enforcement lie in the performance of eyewitnesses, and in the processes eyewitnesses undergo to arrive at that performance. For these reasons, we will consider the minds and memories of eyewitnesses, in depth, in the next two chapters.

Chapter 3
RECONSTRUCTING THE CRIME:
THE MIND OF THE EYEWITNESS

As we've already seen, memory is critically important in virtually all areas of law enforcement psychology, and it tends to get worse under the high-stress conditions that characterize *processing under pressure*, the cognitive processes that operate in combat in many law enforcement (and military) situations. It's a great pity that memory is worse under stress, because the fact is that human memory isn't all that great to begin with.

To some degree, memory for what happened in a given bad situation tends to be better in trained law enforcement experts than in the general public. This is still disputed among academic studies, but the basic fact was demonstrated reasonably conclusively years ago *(Clifford & Richards, 1977)*. However, the superiority of the police over the civilians in this regard is highly *situation-specific*. Clifford and Richards showed that officer recall was better than civilian recall only in situations that lasted for relatively long periods of time—long enough to give directions to a person on the street, for example. For shorter intervals (the time required to tell a person the time, in that study), in which officers did not have time to engage their training, *their memory performance was no better than that of civilians*.

This distinction is critically important. Many tactical situations are over and done with in very short periods of time; a good example came from a homicide on which the author consulted in central California. By chance, the shooter came on a former enemy he'd known in prison. The first chance for a witness to notice that anything was wrong was when the shooter yelled "Hey! I knew you in the Bay!" (Pelican Bay, a California prison where some of the state's more violent convicts are incarcerated.) The shooter drew a short-barreled weapon and fired. His mortally-wounded enemy went down and that was it; in our laboratory simulations of this crime, we were unable to reduce the time from beginning to end to less than half a second, but also unable to extend the time beyond a second and three-quarters.

This is a single example, of course, but it serves to illustrate a fact that law enforcement professionals know well: violent situations encountered by officers, and by civilian witnesses, may run their course before training and experience have much chance to work on memory at all.

And, of course, Clifford and Richards' work did not address the vastly different circumstances of actual, stress-related conflict, in which heart rates can climb to practically unbelievable levels, and in which the reasoning powers with which we monitor our memories simply go out to lunch (Chapters 1 and 2). Although there have been defenses of the reliability of memory in specific contexts (e.g., Brewin, Andrews, & Mickes, 2020), even these defenses acknowledge that memory is at least somewhat malleable; and the malleability of memory can completely derail an investigation or a courtroom proceeding,

A Bit of History

So, eyewitness memory is not great.

Psychologists have been studying it for quite a while. Hugo Munsterberg, often considered the founder of forensic psychology, got the ball rolling in the first decade of the twentieth century *(e.g., 1908)*. However, Munsterberg had a tendency to go beyond his data and to make inflammatory statements, especially in dealing with law enforcement and with real-world cases in court. This did not do his reputation, or the field itself, any favors with regard to credibility. Work on eyewitness memory effectively dried up before it had fairly begun.

However, related work on memory itself continued, and at least one seminal set of studies from the past absolutely requires our attention. This is the work of Bartlett *(1932)*, who worked with both visual memory and memory for stories.

Bartlett would show you an abstract drawing that looked more or less like an Easter egg crossed with a football. This drawing, *"Portrait D'Homme,"* had some spots on it, in a highly distorted schematic representation of a human face. Bartlett would then ask you, over time, to draw this "portrait of a man." Over successive reproductions, over time, the Easter egg qualities, together with the irregularities in the placement of the spots, would vanish.

Instead, people would draw increasingly realistic portraits of a human face. This same type of reconfiguration, based on nothing but personal belief as to what a human face *ought* to look like, was reproduced with different kinds of pictures in situation after situation. People knew that the demented Easter egg of the original drawing was supposed to be a "portrait of a man;" and so, accordingly, they drew pictures that looked more and more like a human face, *and they believed that what they drew was what they had seen.* This effect has not always been replicated (Carbon & Albrecht, 2012), but it's apparently very dependent on other aspects of the given context; just like eyewitness memory in the real world.

You can see this effect even more clearly in a classroom demonstration occasionally used by the author. You show two circles, connected by a long line, to your research subjects. Then, you have a group of them come back later. You ask them to draw "the thing" you showed them before. Two circles and a line: it's a simple figure. Most people get it right; two circles, a connecting line, no problem.

However, now you ask a different group of respondents to draw the *eyeglasses* you showed them earlier. Now, there weren't any glasses to begin with, of course; there were only two circles and a line. However, under these conditions, people start to draw glasses. Many respondents move the circles close together to form lenses, and they turn the long line into a short bridge to connect them. A few *really* interesting people add earpieces. Similar findings emerge with all sorts of visual stimuli, as they did in Bartlett's original work. The simple fact is that people's beliefs, and their expectations, result in radical reconfiguration of their visual memories.

Bartlett also showed that custom and cultural beliefs significantly reconfigured memories of a Native American story. Bartlett's respondents were British, but the motivations and actions of the mythological characters in the story were those familiar to particular American tribal peoples, steeped in the relevant cultural traditions.

American Indian mythological conventions were completely alien to Bartlett's English subjects; and many of them, in their memories, unconsciously *changed* the motivations of characters in the story, to fit British ideas of courage and morality. Unfamiliar Indian names and ideas either vanished or were replaced with something more British, and much of the less familiar cultural material was simply deleted from memory. Modern research in several venues, including work by the author, has confirmed the major points originally described in the verbal realm by Bartlett *(e.g., Ahlberg & Sharps, 2002; Bergman & Roediger, 1999).*

These points, crucially important for any decent understanding of eyewitness memory, or for any aspect of memory under conditions of processing under pressure, can be summarized as follows:

1   Memory is not static, eternal, or unchanging. Rather, memories become reconfigured with time; the more time, on average, the more reconfiguration.

> 2. Memories reconfigure in three directions: brevity, loss of detail, and personal belief. Any given memory becomes "shorter," briefer, as information is lost. Much of this lost information lies in the realm of detail, rather than that of gist or core, of central information. (Because eyewitness identifications are highly dependent on detail, this is a really big problem.) Also, personal belief weighs in. What you think you saw, or even what you think you *should* have seen, may readily become part of the memory itself. What you believe becomes part of your memory, and part of what you will report to the police.

The relevance of these discoveries to eyewitness memory is obvious. Yet even in the wake of Bartlett's landmark work, relatively little specific research on eyewitness memory was conducted until Elizabeth Loftus began intensive modern study of the subject in the 1970s. In a series of justifiably famous studies, Loftus showed a film of a car moving along a country road *(Loftus, 1975; see also Loftus, 1979)*. She then asked respondents to recall whether or not they'd seen a barn in the film. There was no barn, but in view of the rural character of the scene, many people remembered having seen one.

In a later lecture to a professional society, Loftus mentioned the fact that many people in such experiments even supplied the color of the nonexistent barn: Red. Well, most barns are red. This, of course, is the color that our training and experience tends to provide to our mouths when we talk about barns.

Now, again, *there wasn't any barn to begin with*, let alone a red one. People just made one up. They weren't lying, not in any normal sense; but a barn was suggested by Loftus, and the memories of the witnesses obligingly provided one. They even picked a nice color.

In other studies *(e.g., Loftus & Palmer, 1974)*, a car was shown running into another car. When people were asked how fast the car was moving when it hit the other vehicle, they usually provided a pretty good estimate of speed. However, when asked how fast the car was going when it *smashed into* the other car, answers changed dramatically. The car was now recalled as moving at higher speeds, sometimes about double the actual velocity. Also, many respondents also provided a variety of colorful but wholly incorrect details, such as broken glass and other evidence of a high-speed collision.

These experiments clearly demonstrated the effects of *post-event information* on people's memory. When it's implied, post-event, that you must have seen a nonexistent barn, your memory is happy to supply an imaginary barn in a reasonably likely color. When it's implied that a vehicle must have been moving quickly, your memory supplies a kamikaze driver at the wheel of some sort of street-legal Indy car, doing unspeakable damage to everything in his path.

Memories, in short, change. This is important. A witness sees an assailant of one race, and remembers somebody else of a different race, carrying a gun when in fact he was carrying nothing at all. Such testimony can easily send the wrong suspect to prison while leaving the real perpetrator out there in the streets, imbued with fresh confidence.

The same dynamics apply to the memories of a given officer engaged in virtually any critical incident. An officer remembers standing next to a bush during a gunfight and firing two rounds. However, witnesses place that officer next to a mailbox instead of a bush, emptying his or her magazine and *then* firing two rounds from another. The wheels of justice, and of Internal Affairs, take notice. The officer wasn't merely mistaken; he or she *lied* about his or her location, says Internal Affairs, at the time of the shooting.

Charges are filed. There are accusations of an integrity violation, an IA, the end of a career. There are massive civil damages against the disgraced officer.

Yet there was no integrity violation. There was only a human nervous system doing what it's good at: filling in the gaps in memory with plausible possibilities. The officer was actually standing next to a mailbox, but he or she remembers it as a bush, of a similar height and breadth to the mailbox, seen just moments before.

As to the two shots recalled by the officer, versus the entire magazine plus two actually fired, this is an unfortunate aspect of the interaction of psychology with modern police technology. Even in the old revolver days, it was difficult to keep track of shots fired during a gunfight; counting is not a high cognitive priority when people are trying to kill you.

However, in the modern world of the auto-loader, an officer might very well fire an entire magazine, do a "combat reload" in which a new magazine is inserted effectively without thinking, and fire rounds from that new magazine as well. The officer remembers nothing of the first magazine, but counts the rounds fired from the second one to arrive at the number of shots fired, firmly believing this to be the total. There is no necessary integrity violation here; there is merely a failure to recall a smoothly automated action, the *combat reload*, in the heat of battle.

Gaps in memory are also facilitated by the cortex-busting properties of the stress of the moment, as discussed in the previous chapters. Under acute stress, probably more so than under normal conditions, the nervous system congenially fills these gaps in with reasonable suggestions that become part and parcel of the memory. The dynamics of this type of memory error will be addressed below.

All of this makes obvious sense in the wake of Loftus' discoveries. She showed that human memory is not the objective video or digital recorder that many people (including jurors) believe, or want to believe. She also showed that information delivered *after the fact*, post event, can cause memories to metamorphose in reasonably predictable directions. These are extremely useful facts, and very important. Yet the big, shocking question still remains:

How can memory possibly be *that bad*?

Ancient Memories

To recapitulate a theme developed in Chapter 1, the brain has been ecologically valid, adapted to its environment, throughout our long, long past. In the ancient world of the hunter-gatherers, certain kinds of memory were important. You needed to remember the people in your tribe (all twenty of them), where your possessions were (all four or five of them), how to build a fire, and so on. You also needed to be able to remember the things you needed to make a living, the techniques of hunting and gathering. The brain in fact does this sort of thing very well.

But is the brain really more attuned to the limited demands of the ancient world than to the more complex realm of the modern world? My students and I *(Sharps, Villegas, Nunes, and Barber, 2002)* addressed this issue, the question of what sorts of things the brain is good at, in a three-experiment study in which we asked the following question: *What was the most complicated thing hunter-gatherers did?*

Answer: Hunting.

Okay, so what's the most complicated part of hunting?

Answer: Probably tracking and remembering different kinds of animal tracks.

So, we got a bunch of pictures of animal tracks, together with bunches of equally unfamiliar stimuli. We gray-scaled them to the same visual salience and so on, and then showed them to groups of urban California college students. In general (and we asked them), these students had no experience, understanding, knowledge, or interest in hunting, tracking, animals, or even being outside. This was a thoroughly urbanized, modern group of people, living in a modern high-technology society.

Yet these students learned and remembered animal tracks, on average, about *two to three times better than other equally unfamiliar natural stimuli (Sharps et al., 2002).*

Chapter 3

Much complex human behavior probably derives from ancient roots *(Bailey, 1987)*, especially from the hunter/gatherer adaptations of the pre-agricultural world. This makes sense; about 90% of the human beings who ever lived were hunter/gatherers *(e.g., Lee & DeVore, 1968; Bailey, 1987)*. Ten or fifteen thousand years ago, the hunter-gatherer lifestyle was the only way of life that existed. Our animal-track study showed that the ancient world of the deer hunters of Chapter 1, and of the animal trackers of our distant past, are very much with us, buried in the least-accessible recesses of our brains; and our urban college students, much more comfortable with shopping malls than with open plains, with keyboards than with spears, were still really, really good at picking up the bases of the tracking skills of the hunter.

But why are people so bad at picking up everything else? What about our relative inability to recall the faces of perpetrators, or the details of their vehicles or weapons?

Well, in ancient tribes, you very seldom saw a stranger. In our modern world, by contrast, we may see hundreds of strangers every day. Sometimes we may see one of the strangers shoot or rob another one, and then the court expects us to remember exactly which stranger fired the shot, or held up the convenience store.

In ancient tribes, no warrior ever had a Beretta 9mm pistol; yet the court requires the modern police officer to recall exactly how many shots were fired from that specific weapon. As an ancient warrior with a spear, there was never any reason to count the number of rounds your spear held. It was really simple. One.

There were no lawyers or investigators in the ancient world to provide inaccurate post-event information, inadvertently or otherwise (no Cro-Magnon hunter was ever persuaded by a Paleolithic attorney that the mammoth he speared was in fact brown, not grey). Our world has developed faster than the biological basis of our memories. Our generally disastrous eyewitness performance is probably one of the less-fortunate results. Over the millennia, as civilization developed, many peoples (especially and including the Greeks) developed elaborate *mnemonic devices*, systems for remembering almost incredible quantities of text and information. But then the technological miracle of *paper* was developed. After paper became widely available, together with books, literate populations, and the storage of digital information, those mnemonic systems of memory became less important. Ultimately, over the past couple of thousand years of improved information technology, people essentially stopped attending to the training of memory. The use of mnemonics effectively ceased.

So, we now live with our raw, relatively untrained, brain-based memory abilities. These are really, really good at remembering animal tracks; but they are simply wretched at remembering which of the hundreds of total strangers you saw on any given day actually killed the guy in the liquor store, and whether he had a gun or, for that matter, a stone axe. Our memories are fallible, and they change with time and new information.

Fortunately, however, the ways in which memories change can be understood. This understanding can be used by the criminal justice system to work out what's really going on with memory when we are under pressure; when officers' careers are on the line, when the innocent may go to prison, or when the guilty may go free, now filled with extra confidence because they believe they've fooled the police.

Eyewitness issues are not only important for the defense. They are also critically important for law enforcement and for prosecutors. The simple fact is that nobody, defense or prosecution, wants the wrong guy to go to prison. Not just for his sake, for ethical, legal, and humane reasons. These are unspeakably important, of course, but there is another reason as well, one that resonates especially well in the world of law enforcement. This is the fact that every time a wrongful conviction occurs, the *bad guy is still out there*. And now he knows he can get away with it.

Eyewitness Memory in Context

So, we see that memory really *can* be as bad as we thought, and we can at least understand the ancient roots of the problems. Therefore, it would be really nice to know what kinds of situations tend to result in better or worse eyewitness accounts and identifications. What do we know that will help us to evaluate a given case, whether the witness is an officer, a bystander, or a victim?

The study of eyewitness memory has become a major industry in experimental psychology. The explosive growth of research in relatively recent years is astonishing. *Sporer, Malpass, and Koehnken's* excellent general text on the subject, in 1996, had 318 pages. Eleven years later, the 2007 *Handbook of Eyewitness Psychology (Toglia, Read, Ross, & Lindsay; Lindsay, Ross, Read, & Toglia)* had 1,304 pages, and they had to break it into two volumes so the average person could carry it.

So, we know a great deal more now than we did a couple of decades ago. However, paradoxically, this explosion of information may have made important principles of eyewitness memory somewhat *less* available to the people who need it, including attorneys, law enforcement officers, and commanders, who are not themselves specialists in eyewitness memory. If you go to the nearest university library and try to research eyewitness issues for yourself, you're immediately confronted with dozens of specialized books and a near-infinity of highly specialized articles. If you go to the Internet, the term "Eyewitness Memory" turns up, at the moment, over 1,240,000 results; it was about half a million for the same search for the 2017 second edition of this book. The growth in the available reference material is astonishing. What do you look up first, and why? How many years will this take? Have you brought enough food to survive the ordeal, and will they even let you eat it in the library?

For these reasons, we'll summarize the most important elements and principles of eyewitness memory in what follows. Then we'll discuss some special cases, special kinds of eyewitness memory, that have become important in recent years as the character of crime has continued to evolve, and we'll set these in a theoretical context that is useful in understanding how the whole thing works. We'll do this in the rest of this chapter and in the one that follows.

Estimator Variables

Estimator variables, or factors, are the ones you can't control, the ones that are endemic to the situation being witnessed *(e.g., Narby, Cutler, & Penrod, 1996)*. They're usually divided into *witness variables* (is your witness a child, an infant, a person over eighty, or somebody who really, really needs glasses but wasn't wearing them at the crime scene?), *target variables* (what did the suspect look like? Did he have a gun, what race was he or she, was there a disguise?), and *situational variables* (was it dark, or was there a fence between the witness and the suspect?).

The classification isn't perfect, of course; a cross-racial identification in the dark, for example, falls under all three types of estimator variables. However, in general, this scheme works quite well for discussing the factors involved *(Narby, Cutler, & Penrod, 1996)*.

We'll cover some of the most important variables below. For more of the latest information on each, I refer you to all 1,304 pages of the *Handbook* reference above. It's important to stress that the vast majority of the academic information on this huge and expanding subject is valuable, and certainly worthwhile to learn. However, for most non-specialists in the field, the time required to develop a mastery of this torrent of information is simply not available.

Situational Variables

I don't know why anybody needs a professor of psychology to put on a suit, sit in a witness stand, and tell this to a jury, but I personally have spent quite a lot of time in exactly that situation, in erudite exposition of the following fact: *People can't see in the dark.*

I can't imagine why anybody on the planet has a problem with this one, but people do. Witnesses saw the bad guy, in his green and white striped shirt, distinctive haircut, and all, running like hell down a dark street at midnight with no moon and ten-tenths cloud cover.

Objection! They couldn't have seen him, says anybody who's ever seen, well, darkness. This is because it was, well, dark.

Yes, I did, says the witness, I did *too* see him. It wasn't all that dark, or something. So there. (And, by the way, you can see by my manner and bearing that I'm credible, attractive, and very confident.)

A word or two about credibility, attractiveness, and confidence. Credibility can be crucially important in an investigation or in court. People lie all the time, and it's important to establish that a given witness doesn't have a personal axe to grind, or a reputation as an inveterate liar, a "psychopath" (antisocial personality), or a person of numerous other undesirable traits. If aliens or Bigfoot come into the story (and on occasion, they do) it's a good bet that credibility is not high. It's important for investigators and attorneys to consider credibility or its absence dispassionately and in depth, and then to establish the relevant facts. They matter. But credible people tend to be believed at a higher level.

So do people who are attractive. If you're ever accused of a major crime, it's very important to ascertain that you're being accused by ugly people.

However, confidence is more complicated. Most studies have found little or no relationship between witness confidence and the veracity of their stories. A few studies have found such relationships, and a huge academic controversy is currently being waged over who to believe on the subject. Does confidence matter, does it indicate veracity, or not?

There is a lot of solid current research on this issue. Using Enhanced Cognitive Interview techniques, *Paulo, Albuquerque, & Bull (2019)* showed that accounts of those facts about which witnesses were more certain were more accurate than uncertainties or than regular recall. *Pica, Sheahan, Pozzulo, Vallano, & Pettalia (2019)* showed that mock jurors were more likely to believe that a defendant was guilty if the eyewitness had seen "him" 10 times prior to the crime compared to zero times, an obvious bow to familiarity as opposed to the prospect of that familiarity's potential contribution to error. Familiarity with the given suspect would obviously lead to greater confidence on the part of the witness, and jurors would of course be more likely to believe a witness who was familiar with a given suspect—but apparently, people are remarkably bad at *assessing the degree of that familiarity.* Oddly, whether a witness knew the defendant 1, 5, or 10 years ago *doesn't matter to potential jurors*— in a recent study, mock jurors still tended to perceive the witness more positively, the defendant more negatively, and to find the witness guilty more often, no matter how long ago the acquaintance between witness and suspect occurred (Thompson, Sheahan, Pica, & Pozzulo, 2019). Additional factors which bear upon the judgment of witness accuracy and witness confidence lie in the arcane world of signal detection theory (Smith & Leach, 2019). The issue of witness confidence and eyewitness accuracy is by no means straightforward or, at this point, well-understood.

Ultimately, at present, the answer to the question of confidence in eyewitness memory is not satisfying. Basically, it depends on the situation and on the given study. However, what we *can* say is that witness confidence is *frequently not a good predictor testimonial truth*, and that in any given case, where we have a single witness, we really can't tell, to a reasonable degree of doubt and all other things being equal, whether it is or not. Witness confidence in large numbers, or under specific controlled experimental circumstances, may predict witness accuracy; but in the real world of criminal justice, we do not necessarily see a strong relationship, in any given specific case, of evident witness confidence to witness accuracy.

But the fact is that witness confidence, however doubtful as a source of evidence, is astonishingly convincing to any given jury, for good or for ill. Few things are more convincing to the average jury than the confident, credible eyewitness. I have seen juries convinced by such witnesses, even when the crime occurred under conditions of pitch darkness.

At which point we should repeat our mantra: *people can't see in the dark.*

Therefore, a wise investigator or prosecutor will not base a case on witness *confidence*. The witnesses may be right, they may be wrong, but the confidence they display may or may not be related to the truth of their statements. The witnesses in question may just be confident people, or annoyingly overconfident people, or people with low self-esteem who mask it with a display of annoying overconfidence.

This is especially true if they are claiming to have seen what happened in the dark.

Light in the Darkness?

There are, of course, many different versions of "dark." In deep twilight, for example, you can see a little bit. The problem is that as it becomes darker, the *cone cells* in your eyes gradually go off duty. These cells, which are responsible for much of your daylight vision, can see color and are clustered toward the center of your visual areas. They require a lot of light to operate; they're basically daylight mechanisms. As the sun goes down and conditions become darker, the function of the cones is largely replaced by that of the *rod cells*, which don't require as much light energy to operate as the cones. The rods don't have color vision, and they're clustered toward the periphery of the visual areas. They also don't have the same level of acuity, or resolution, as the cone cells; and even so, with this diminished visual acuity, the rods can't see in the dark. They need *some* light, at least a little bit.

For these reasons, in daylight (using your cone cells), you have great resolution and visual acuity. Because the cones are in the middle, so to speak, your best vision is straight out front, not to the sides. Also, unless you're colorblind (an important issue to resolve with many eyewitnesses), you can see color.

Wonderful. You're all set to be a great witness, at least to any crime observed in daylight. However, as everyone in the world of law enforcement knows, lots of crimes, especially violent crimes, happen at night.

As darkness comes, and the rods take over, your best vision is peripheral, because the rods are situated toward the rims of your visual systems. You see in black and white, and your ability to resolve the image you see gets worse and worse. A further problem is that when you see something interesting peripherally, out of the corner of your eye, you may habitually swing your eyes toward it, placing the image toward the centers of your eyes where the cones are, and largely removing your peripherally placed rod cells from the operation. This brings your centrally located cones to bear; this is completely useless, because the cone cells can't see in the dark or even in the low light by which the rod cells can operate. So now, you can't see what you were looking at at all.

This is somewhat complicated, but the upshot is relatively simple: as darkness increases, your visual abilities decrease. There's no getting around it. It gets even worse if you've just come from a lighted environment into a darker one; your eyes, not yet dark-adapted, don't even have the rudimentary abilities of normal rod function.

Therefore, when people tell a police officer about the color of a car, or a shirt, or whatever else they saw in a pitch-dark scene, one of two things is generally the case. One: They're lying. Two, and probably more frequently: They're simply wrong. Their brains are filling in the troublesome gaps in their memories with plausible alternatives, concerning which the witnesses may be both confident and credible. Human brains made up red barns for Loftus; they're certainly capable of making up appropriate gang colors on a bad guy's hat and jacket for the witness on the street.

Of course, the perpetrator might have been illuminated by moonlight, or the light from a streetlight. The problem, however (of *course* there's a problem), is that the moon's silvery glow tends to make you look all silvery, or at least sort of gray and pale. Some types of streetlights may yellow the complexion, or alter the perceived color of clothing. Clearly moonlit or street lit conditions are superior to those of total darkness, but the subtle effects of such light sources must be taken into account.

It's also a big problem if your eyes have to adapt to darkness quickly. Dark adaptation takes quite a while; many minutes may be required, if you start under bright-light conditions, before you can see fairly well under low-light conditions. If you're adapted to brilliant sunlight, and you have to look into a relatively dark environment in a building or in a shaded area, you may have great difficulty in visual resolution.

I once consulted on a case in which this exact problem came up. Officers in a brilliantly sunlit environment, with their eyes adapted to that environment, had to perceive the actions of a perpetrator in a relatively dark environment. They believed that they saw a weapon which simply didn't exist, and they acted accordingly. In this case, the difference between their light-adapted eyes, and the dark environment in which the suspect took refuge, proved tragic for all concerned. The response of the eyes to light and dark is far more important than most people think.

SINGLE-LIGHT SOURCES

Of course, if the perpetrator was seen in the beam of a flashlight, or of a police cruiser's spotlight, there's no question that visibility for that case was vastly better than it would be under conditions of total darkness. However, single-light sources are notorious for changing the relief of a given object, including a face. Go into a dark room with a mirror and a flashlight and shine the light on your face. (Tell your family what you're doing first. Otherwise, it can get really weird.) As you move the light around, you will see your reflection change from normal to unfamiliar to monstrous, as the light hits you from below; this technique was used in early monster movies to make vampires or zombies out of actors, and it'll do the same for you.

The simple fact is that single light sources change what you see. This doesn't mean that the identification made under such circumstances is necessarily wrong, of course, but it does mean that you want to be skeptical about it.

OCCULTATION

Occultation is another big problem; it's one of those things you shouldn't even have to talk about, but the fact is you can't see through a solid object. I recall a case in which a five-foot woman described a burglar who was crawling at the time, making him about two-foot-six in stature at the time of observation. She saw him through a six-foot solid wood fence—not through the cracks; through the *fence*. In fact, there weren't any cracks, not that you could see through, in that particular fence. As an added bonus, it was absolutely pitch dark at the time of the burglary; yet she described the colors and pattern of his shirt.

The time-course of the crime, and the place of arrest of the suspect positively identified by this lady, were such that the suspect would have had to engage in track-star running speeds, for several miles, while carrying a burden of stolen electronics that would normally be an effort for two men to lift. Oh, and by the way, he would have had to jump a high fence, still carrying the electronics, to have been the guy who committed the crime.

However, the lady was confident, attractive, and credible, and the jury bought it. The suspect was convicted, even though it was dark, and she "saw" him through a hunk of wood, and he was neither a track star nor a world-class weight lifter.

If he was innocent, this obviously constituted a personal tragedy of epic proportion, for a man who may literally have had nothing to do with the crime. And if he was innocent, the right guy, the guy who did it, *is still out there*, new and improved with extra confidence and contempt for the police.

It's a psychological principle that we tend to attribute bad things that happen to us to fate or bad luck, but good ones to our own personal abilities. Whoever the real bad guy is, out there, he's unlikely to think he escaped justice due to a statistical fluke. He's more likely to consider himself a criminal genius, and the police officers who didn't catch him to be buffoons. So, the next time, he'll be more confident. More ambitious. Maybe even better armed, in genuflection to his new status as a criminal mastermind.

It is important to bring these simple, self-evident facts to the attention of the courts, the juries, the attorneys: *People can't see in the* dark, and they can't see through stuff that they can't see through. Sometimes the two combine: one of the weirdest cases in my own experience involved my running around a cold crime scene with a field guide to trees. Yes, trees. The crime in question had been committed near a street light, which at least lent some credibility to the witness's ability to see the perpetrator. However, there was a large tree situated between the light pole and the scene itself. This seemed to present no difficulty, at least on first consideration: during the trial, it was shown to the jury that the tree was bare, and the light shone clearly on the crime scene through the branches. There would have been some dappling of the face and body of the perpetrator, as the shadows of the branches moved and cast their irregular shadows, but basically there would have been pretty good, if slightly yellow, lighting at the scene.

Unless, of course, the tree had been in leaf at the time of the *crime*, as opposed to the time of the *trial*.

Which, of course, it was. Fulsome in nature's splendor, the tree in question had been completely covered in amazingly verdant and leafy, well, leaves. The foliage had blocked the streetlight completely and had cast the crime scene into complete and utter darkness.

And, for the last time, *people can't see in the dark*. The witness, with a complete story, confidently presented, had in fact seen nothing.

Lighting and occultation are important, and they are frequently discounted or not considered at all in criminal justice proceedings. In view of the fact that the lion's share of crimes, or at least violent crimes, occur at night, these admittedly simple facts need to be at the forefront of the mind of any investigating officer or prosecutor dealing with a nocturnal crime.

The Interaction of Darkness, Occultation, and Violence

In many violent crimes, convictions are obtained without much in the way of direct physical evidence. Examples include the Peterson and Wesson killings in California. Scott Peterson was convicted of killing his pregnant wife, and the child in her womb, effectively without strong direct physical evidence. Marcus Wesson was convicted of killing his own children, but the physical evidence was contradictory and somewhat confused.

This is the wrong place to go into the evidentiary factors surrounding these two cases, and in fact, having reviewed these cases to the best of my ability, I would not dispute the juries' findings; but it is of interest that these horrific crimes resulted in convictions with a relatively low level of physical evidence.

What causes juries to convict in the relative absence of hard, nonequivocal evidence? What factors are important here? We conducted a study of this phenomenon, specifically pertinent to evidentiary conditions of darkness and occultation *(Sharps, Herrera, and Price Sharps, 2013)*; the idea was to find out what might lead potential jurors to convict under poor viewing conditions, in at least a preliminary attempt to sort out these aspects of the relationship of evidence to juror decision making.

We created scenarios of an armed robbery, in which the level of violence ranged from a simple assault and battery to a sex-crime homicide involving torture. The flight of the suspect from the scene, and his identity, were described by a "witness" in a mock but realistic investigative interview. In the interview, the witness acknowledged pitch darkness at the scene, and further acknowledged observing the suspect's flight from behind a concrete wall too high to see over; without further elaboration, however, the witness said that there must have been enough light, and glossed over the occultation problem posed by the wall. Based solely on this "eyewitness" account, respondents rated, among other factors, the likelihood of the guilt of the suspect.

The results were straightforward and a little frightening. Potential jurors tended to find the suspect guilty more frequently, and to believe in his guilt more strongly, in the more violent conditions. They also tended to notice the problems of darkness and occultation less frequently in these more violent conditions.

In summary, the more violent the crime, the more potential jurors tended to assign guilt and to ignore very basic problems of evidence (darkness and occultation). It seems probable that the negative emotions aroused by the high levels of reported violence reduced potential jurors' tendencies to evaluate evidence critically; in short, more violent crimes resulted in greater juror acceptance of lousy evidence.

It should be noted that this effect, while significant, was statistically relatively weak. This indicates, as one might expect, that the violence of the given crime is only one of many factors influencing the judgment of evidence. Yet we see, in this study, the important fact that the emotion generated by more horrific crimes can be an important factor in the judgment of evidence, and therefore ultimately in the judgment of the entire case. It is therefore incumbent upon investigators and attorneys, dealing with more violent and/or horrifying cases, to pay special attention to the nature of eyewitness evidence in such cases.

Passage of Time, Rehearsal, and Post-event Information

In general, the longer the time that has passed since an event, the harder it is to remember. Also, with more time, we generally see more of Bartlett's reconfiguration, in terms of brevity, loss of detail, and changes in the direction of personal belief.

It's also important to realize that the passage of time does not occur in isolation. It's marked by events, including internal, mental events. Consider a witness, victim, bystander, or officer, who witnesses a crime or an officer-involved shooting. He or she has memories of the event, which are told to patrol officers. Then the story is told again, perhaps to patrol supervisors and then to detectives. Then to friends and family, over and over, and then to district attorney investigators or assistant D.A.'s themselves, and then to defense investigators, and then in discovery, and then...

The point is that stories are told, again and again, before the witness comes to court. Each retelling yields an opportunity for the type of reconfiguration identified by Bartlett, and for that reconfiguration to become part and parcel of *what the witness perceives to be the original memory*, to be recounted in court with credibility and confidence.

Other people can contribute to this reconfiguration, sometimes inadvertently. An officer asks a witness about the suspect's weapon. The suspect knows nothing about guns, is rather proud of knowing nothing about guns, but then spies the officer's 9mm Beretta. Snap. The bad guy was now, in memory, armed with a large, service-type semi-automatic, highly reminiscent of a Beretta 9mm.

The witness, a day later, watches TV with a relative. They see an entertainer, of the same race as the suspect. "Hey, he's just like that guy that robbed you," says the relative. "The guy you described." The witness goes to bed, giving a night's sleep the opportunity to work on the memory (we don't know how sleep works on memory, but it does; you remember less, in controlled studies, if you're not allowed to sleep after learning or encoding the given memory).

And the witness wakes up with a clear memory, new and improved: the bad guy looked just like the entertainer, and he was armed with something like a 9mm Beretta.

Are these just fanciful possibilities? The answer is no. Thanks to the work of Bartlett and of Loftus cited above, we know that time and post-event information can definitely alter memory. We also know that post-event information may come from a variety of sources, internal and external. For what it's worth, I have personally seen all of these effects operating in actual criminal cases.

But is there hard experimental evidence of this type of memory change with regard to eyewitness reportage?

The answer to that one is "yes." In one of my own experiments, *(Sharps, Herrera, Dunn, & Alcala, 2012)*, we showed "witnesses" a crime scene, in which a "suspect" aimed a handgun at a "victim." Then we simply asked them to describe what they had seen, in a "free recall" format similar to the initial stages of most police interviews. This went well; respondents provided us with several times more correct than incorrect details.

However, then we asked them to remember anything else they could about the crime. We asked them three times.

In these repeated queries, respondents provided us with far less information than they had the first time around, and *a much higher proportion of that information was wrong*. On average, witnesses recalled *nearly as much false information as accurate details across the three later queries*. In the third query, in fact, the level of false detail actually exceeded the amount of correct information.

It's important to consider this result with reference to the reconfiguration of memory, described by Bartlett and by Loftus and colleagues and cited above. Eyewitness memory reconfigures, it changes, both from the passage of time and from the influence of post-event information. Our 2012 result shows that *this reconfiguration can begin almost immediately*, with the first rendition of your eyewitness account. And it keeps on changing.

Every time you repeat your story, or are asked more about it, or watch an account of the given crime on TV, a few bits of your memory will be influenced by what you say, or see. You can't help it; and the next time you think about the crime, those false bits may be incorporated into the memory itself, resulting in a few more false bits, which generate even more false bits, and so on.

The more time you have for the inadvertent generation of false memory details, the more your memory will change, and change again. The more you talk about the given event, or see it described on the TV news, the more opportunities you have to decide you were robbed by your local news anchorman. Especially if you don't like him.

THE COGNITIVE INTERVIEW—A POSSIBLE REMEDY?

These problems are widely acknowledged, even though a lot of people who need to know about them don't. But is there any decent remedy for them?

Chapter 3

A number of scholars and law enforcement officers have sought a solution in the Cognitive Interview, essentially an improved system of questioning constructed with reference to the cognitive and affective characteristics of witnesses, and designed to maximize accurate witness information (e.g., *Fisher & Schreiber 2007; Memon & Bull, 1991; Sharman & Powell, 2013*). Although the order of questioning in the Cognitive Interview (CI) is similar to that of traditional police questioning (free-recall response followed by answers to more specific questions), the CI also incorporates an attempt to reinstate the context of the given crime; uses proper spacing of questions to give witnesses time to reflect; frames questions in a manner compatible with the given witness; involves the building of rapport; and encourages witnesses to approach their memory from different perspectives. At the same time, the CI also involves instructions to avoid guessing, and the minimization of constructive recall, a laudable attempt to avoid the problems discussed above (e.g., *Fisher & Schreiber, 2007*).

In general, the CI—an unfortunately confusing acronym for those law enforcement officers who work with Confidential Informants—the CI seems to work well. It's not used as much in the field as scholars would prefer (see Fisher & Schreiber, 2007), possibly because of the complexity of such issues as trying to ascertain what manner of questioning is psychologically compatible with a given witness. Interviews are usually conducted under time pressure, so there may be a tendency, on the part of investigators, to skip the more time-consuming elements of the CI.

But researchers in general have found that, at least with regard to memory for persons and situations, the CI tends to maximize memory performance without increasing the prevalence of false details (e.g., *Memon et al., 2010; Sharman & Powell, 2013*). However, this may not be true across all circumstances, with all variants of the CI. *Ginet et al (2019)* used a modified cognitive interview to study memory conformity. Those interviewed by means of those techniques, by comparison with the results of a more typical structured interview, did in fact report fewer incorrect details, consistent with earlier work; but respondents also reported more confabulated details that were previously introduced by a "confederate" to whose testimony those respondents were exposed. There are a variety of contextual factors involved in CI performance which still require research.

Therefore, it would probably be a good idea for researchers to address the elements of the CI separately and in various combinations in aggregate, to work out exactly what's going on under different circumstances. Let me illustrate.

In several studies, we addressed specific aspects of the CI which it shares in common with the typical police interview; specifically, the order and types of questions involved. As recommended in the CI, we employed general, free recall questioning, followed by specific questions, concerning an important but relatively neglected area: eyewitness memory for firearms.

What we found was more complicated than might have been expected. In one study, we found that the later specific questioning was definitely important, generating significantly more correct details about the given firearm than did the earlier, more general, open-ended free recall questions. So far so good (*McRae, Sharps, & Kimura, 2015*). However, in a follow-up study involving several *types* of firearms, varied on a spectrum of typicality with regard to use in crimes, we found that the more generative specific questions actually resulted in *more* of the types of errors discussed above (*Sharps, McRae, Partovi, Power, & Newton, 2015*). This result was of course in contrast to most assertions about the CI, to the effect that it does not inflate such errors.

These contrasting results do not, however, necessarily provide specific contradictions to any of the work on the CI cited above. For one thing, the earlier work addressed people and situations, not firearms, and that may make a big difference; the brain treats people and inanimate objects very differently, and the processing of situations, entire scenes, must frequently combine aspects of both.

For another thing, we only addressed *one* of the several factors important to the CI in our firearms studies, that being the type of questioning; if we had studied this factor in aggregate with the other recommended techniques (see *Fisher & Schreiber, 2007*, and summary above), the results might have been different. But the point is that we really don't know. This rather unexpected result, with regard to the important area of memory for firearms, indicates that we need to examine all of the factors involved in the CI, in aggregate and separately, for a full understanding of the CI's mechanisms, and for that matter the mechanisms of the traditional police interview. Hopefully, such interactive and systematic research will clarify these issues for investigators in the near future; for the present, it's very important to be circumspect and conservative in the interpretation of the results of any given interview, CI or otherwise.

Target Variables: Cross-Racial Identification, Disguise, and Weapon Focus

I've put these factors together here for a reason: although they seem to be very different kinds of variables, they have important cognitive attributes in common.

CROSS-RACIAL IDS

Let's begin with cross-racial identifications. In general, they're worse than same-race IDs *(Meissner & Brigham 2001)*; witnesses are about 1.4 times more likely to identify a person of their own race correctly, and about 1.56 times less likely to identify such a person incorrectly, than they are with reference to a person of another race. People often assume that this derives from racism, and in some cases they may be correct. However, perfectly normal non-racist human adults frequently make these mistakes. The reasons have to do not with racism, but with familiarity.

Most people are most familiar with people of their own race. They therefore easily discount the features that characterize the race as a whole (darker skin in African-Americans, say, or fair skin and relatively long faces in many Scandinavians). So, people become good at distinguishing the idiosyncratic features that distinguish this particular descendant of Ugandans or Norwegians from others, provided that they themselves are highly familiar with people of Central African or Scandinavian origins.

Suppose I am a native of a Mediterranean island, and am now living in Rochester, Minnesota. I'm used to the olive-skinned, dark-haired, relatively short people most typical of my native island, and the majority of the people I know there are of similar stature and body build to myself. Obviously, there are individual differences between the physical characteristics of the island's people, but through long familiarity I can easily discern and process these differences.

However, in Minnesota, I now find myself surrounded by tall, pale people. These are the descendants of Scandinavians, and most of them have pale skin, relatively great height, fair hair (how many shades of blonde and light brown *are* there?), and light-colored eyes (how many shades of blue and gray and gray-blue and gray-blue with just a hint of green and—?). There are also other differences in such things as the shape of the face, the size of the brows and eyebrows, and so forth.

So how do I, with my previous experience limited to a Mediterranean island, possibly tell the police officer which Neo-Viking took my wallet? "Well, he was tall. And pale. I think he was blonde—blondish. Might have been a Norwegian, or a Swede. Maybe a Dane…"

The problem of cross-racial identification may diminish with increased globalization and increased worldwide distribution of common media. However, for the present, we distinguish each other not by the broadly shared physical attributes common to a given race, but by the defining, idiosyncratic features that characterize the individual *within* the race. We're usually not as familiar with people of other races as we are with our own. Therefore, we're substantially worse at cross-racial identifications.

(Incidentally, race itself is a slippery concept. The reader may have been surprised at my use of "Scandinavian," as a racial type, above; aren't Scandinavians just Caucasians by race? Well, in broad terms, the answer is yes. However, if you can't tell the average Norwegian from the average Sicilian, or from the average resident of Athens, Greece, you probably aren't trying very hard. All are Caucasians, and yet, on average, all possess distinguishable physical characteristics in common with other average people from their own regions (e.g., *Brues, 1977*). Humans have mated with other humans all over the place, and the whole question of race is still one that vexes anthropologists and many other interested parties [see Krause, 2016]. Ultimately, however, the point at which to draw racial lines, from the purely scientific perspective of how to distinguish one person from another in an eyewitness situation, is very much a matter of opinion.)

The upshot: if a person's characteristics differ substantially from the norms we are used to, we're likely to have problems making a decent ID. Such differences in physical appearance and characteristics can occur naturally, as a result of race.

WHO WAS THAT MASKED MAN?

They can also occur deliberately, as a result of disguise.

A decent disguise changes recognizable characteristics. Smart criminals know this. Knit hats or baseball caps are pulled low over the forehead, obscuring hair color, length, hairline, and hairstyle. As a bonus, a cap worn correctly obscures the eyebrows, and it even shades the eyes to reduce certainty as to eye color. Sunglasses may be used to conceal brows and eyes—wraparound styles, and larger sunglasses, can also obscure the shape of cheekbones. Baggy clothes can obscure body type and can hide individual characteristics such as scars or tattoos. I've only seen it used once, but a nylon stocking over the face can compress the facial features and change the overall appearance of the face unrecognizably.

Chapter 3

An effective disguise can render eyewitness identification well-nigh useless. Instead of the modest changes in "what we expect" that drive mistakes in cross-racial ID's, disguise changes *everything* about what we expect, and even what we can see and discern. The one case in my experience in which the criminal made use of a nylon stocking over his head, in the style of the old gangster-movie cliché, stands as a real testament to the art of disguise. The perpetrator, an armed robber, wore a hat and sunglasses as well as the stocking over his head. However, he had also cut or ripped holes in the stocking; this meant that the stocking not only distorted his face, but that *the holes distorted the distortion*. Baggy clothes rendered the characteristics of his body indiscernible. Ultimately, several witnesses, *and a security camera videotape* of the robber, were not enough to make a single solid identification.

However, the thing that really made this guy's outfit was his *gun*.

WEAPON FOCUS

That gun. That thing was amazing. I am not a firearms expert, and perhaps an expert in that area could have identified the weapon positively, but all I can say is that after many viewings, I could not. I'm pretty sure he started with an M-1 carbine, but that was only the beginning of one of the most amazing, viscerally *scary* weapons I have ever seen. He'd sawed pieces off, and he'd put some kind of monster perforated shroud on the thing, and there was some kind of heat-transfer plate, together with some sort of terrifying sighting system, capped off with something that looked like a flash suppressor. An *evil* flash suppressor. Several other menacing and greasy structures protruded from the weapon as well, contributing to the overall murderous gestalt, and the whole gun, frankly, would have induced terror in anybody who saw it. If you were to take that thing into the woods in the fall, the deer would simply surrender. ("Okay! Kill me! Eat me! Stick my head on the wall! I don't care anymore! Just stop pointing that *thing* at me!)

The guy was a criminal mastermind, and one is forced to wonder why he didn't just take all that talent and go get a *job*, for God's sake. However, although the videotape was scientifically useless for identification purposes, it did reveal one important fact. Nobody could tell who the bad guy was; but everybody, all the potential witnesses, were staring at that monstrous gun as if it were the Loch Ness monster and the ghost of Marilyn Monroe combined. The witnesses didn't look at the *guy*. They looked at the *gun*. None of the potential witnesses could take their eyes off it.

This example is perhaps the ultimate illustration of *weapon focus*. This is the tendency to look at a weapon, when it's present, at the expense of observation time on the individual holding it. Weapon focus is obviously a problem; any second spent gazing on a gun or a knife is a second that is not being used to record the facial features, or other relevant characteristics, of the robber, rapist, or murderer holding the gun. Weapon focus, like most other topics in eyewitness memory, is a topic of scholarly dispute (remember those 1,304 pages?), but a landmark study on the subject, that of *Steblay, 1992*, indicated that weapon focus is frequently a significant factor in eyewitness cases.

Identifications are made in terms of feature-intensive analysis, in terms of the witnesses' ability to identify the idiosyncratic features that distinguish one person from another. If we, as witnesses with normal human nervous systems, are unfamiliar with the race of the suspect, it diminishes our ability to make this analysis. If the suspect was in disguise, the feature-intensive analysis becomes impossible—either the relevant features are obscured, or we wind up analyzing the wrong ones. Finally, such analysis requires *exposure time*. We need to see the suspect for sufficient time to make this analysis. Obviously, therefore, the more time we are in contact with the suspect, the better from the standpoint of eyewitness identification (more will be said on this topic below). However, anything that distracts us during this period of opportunity will be deleterious to our ability to make the ID successfully. This is where weapon focus comes in; every moment we spend looking at the suspect's weapon is a moment we didn't spend on his body or face, and if Steblay was correct, it's going to be a problem in a substantial number of real-world cases.

Witness Variables

CHILDREN AS WITNESSES

To this point, we have considered variables that arise from the target (the person being observed) and the situation. What about the witness's personal characteristics and abilities? What if the witness is a kid?

The question of children as witnesses is an important one, and there is a huge body of evidence and debate that has risen around the issues involved. We will address developmental issues in forensic cognitive science, in more detail than you probably want, in our Appendix below.

However, as a rule, the older the child is, the better he or she will prove as a witness on average. Children under the age of five years are highly unreliable, and if the witness is an infant, frankly, forget it. The toddler's nervous system, and certainly that of the infant, is in a state of constant developmental flux, and is simply not the same as that of an adult. Moreover, young children lack the life experience and the cognitive sophistication to be reliable at all. If a four-year-old, for example, is asked to give an account of what happened when he or she was molested at age two, the result, positive or negative, will be effectively useless. The child's nervous system has changed dramatically in the intervening two years, the events themselves typically happened under conditions of great pain and limited ability for observation, and the child has no cognitive reference to frame the events. Preschool witnesses are usually and unfortunately of very little use in criminal proceedings.

Studies have shown *(Pozzulo, 2007)*, for example, that children over the age of five are not necessarily any worse than adults at picking an assailant out of a lineup when a picture of the assailant is present. However, children do tend to pick out more false positives (somebody other than the assailant), and they provide far fewer descriptive details than adults. As children mature through the school years, they get better in all of these respects; but in general, the child will not provide the same level of sophistication in eyewitness situations that adults will, and wise investigators will treat children's eyewitness reports with this in mind. The question is sufficiently convoluted that it's a good idea for any investigator, confronted with a child witness, to seek expert assistance or at least to engage in a bit of study of the issues involved.

OLDER ADULTS AS WITNESSES

Aged witnesses also present difficulties. Individual differences exist, of course, as they do with the testimony of underage witnesses. However, in general, adults in their sixties and beyond tend to be less accurate than younger adults in their recall of environmental details, personal characteristics of assailants and others, and of events themselves *(e.g., Yarmey, 2001)*. In lineup situations, younger and older adults seem to provide very similar levels of correct identifications when a picture of the assailant is present; however, older adults appear to be more prone to false positives. This information is not conclusive; conflicting results do exist in the literature *(Bartlett and Memon, 2007)*, partly because of differences in methodology employed, and perhaps also because of individual differences in the aging process itself. In general, however, eyewitness memory is not likely to be as sharp in older adults, especially in those over seventy, as in younger adults;

differences exist in the cognitive asynchrony with which older adults process visual information *(Sharps, 1998, 2003)*, and these age-related changes frequently make a difference.

It is also important to recognize that older adults may be suffering from perceptual deficits; their hearing and vision are of course frequently poorer than those of young adults. If an older adult witness needs glasses, or a hearing aid, it is important to find out if that adult was wearing glasses at the time, or if the hearing aid was turned on and had functioning batteries. The author dealt with a case in which an older and vastly near-sighted lady, without her glasses, "saw" a suspect, in a cross-racial identification, at a distance that ensured she could not have resolved his features. She later identified him positively as the culprit. She was a very nice lady, very credible, and absolutely confident; and she was wrong. If not for the suspect's absolute and iron-clad alibi, it's very likely that he would be in prison. The bad guy, of course, would still be out there.

Does the older adult have "floaters?" These flaws in the vitreous humor of the eye are more common in the nearsighted, but they increase in size and number in virtually all of us through the aging process. A witness may have 20/20 vision, but if a floater obscured a that witness's view of a murderer at the time of the murder, even momentarily, this would obviously tend to impair the witness's accuracy. The presence of floaters has not, to the knowledge of the author, ever been addressed by the criminal justice system; but it should be. The influence of this frequently age-related factor could be significant in any given eyewitness case.

It's also important, if an adult of *any* age wears glasses, to find out whether the glasses in question have been made to a current prescription. This is especially true for older adults, many of whom are on fixed incomes; glasses are expensive, and visual changes are gradual and, therefore, may escape notice. Your witness may be wearing a pair of glasses ten years old, which are now effectively useless. The same is true of hearing aids; the batteries are expensive, and wearing the hearing aid doesn't necessarily mean it's working well, or even at all. It's a good idea to check these factors, if possible.

So, the eyewitness testimonies of both children and the aged are complicated. In general the most prudent course is to treat them with caution, although without prejudice or unwarranted stereotyping; it's a fine line, and the scientific evidence is not, at this point, entirely conclusive for either group.

THE CHEMICALLY IMPAIRED AS WITNESSES

Although the evidence may be reasonably argued for children or aged adults as witnesses, most psychologists *(Narby, Cutler, and Penrod, 1996)* have been in pretty close agreement, for a very long time, that if the witness is stoned or drunk at the time of the crime, the resultant identifications will suffer. Recreational drugs and alcohol provide a galaxy of toxic effects on the human nervous system, and the abilities to perceive and attend to incoming stimuli, including the complex and fast-moving stimuli that are present in most crime situations, can be substantially impaired in the drunk or drug-impaired. This obviously depends on the type and amount of whatever suicidal hobby equipment is currently coursing through the veins of the user. It's important to note that many crimes occur in the presence of drugs or alcohol, so the testimony of users of various descriptions is often a major issue. A major principle governing this type of testimony lies in the realm of *state-dependent learning*; when a thing is learned in one psychological or physiological state (say, stoned out of your gourd) it becomes harder to recall under the conditions of a different state (sweating in unaccustomed sobriety on the witness stand). For this reason, it's best to treat the identifications of those so impaired with a very high degree of caution, if not outright skepticism, depending, of course, on the degree of impairment at the time of the crime. However, because this is nearly impossible to ascertain after the fact, it's especially important, in the case of the drunken or drug-impaired witness, to try to find corroborating or conflicting evidence as well. Try very hard.

The list of estimator variables we have reviewed is not exhaustive, but everyone involved with the criminal justice system should at least be aware of the important factors discussed above. It's a good idea for law enforcement officers, especially detectives and other investigators, to learn more about this subject as time and resources permit. It's also a good idea for commanders to encourage this learning process, or at least to provide time and resources for investigators to engage in it.

PHYSIOLOGICAL AROUSAL AND THE EYEWITNESS

Another critical witness variable *is the state of arousal of the given witness.* As discussed in detail in Chapters 1 and 2, physiological arousal, especially arousal to the point of "fight or flight," plays havoc with our mental operations, and much of what the fight or flight response does to us is going to have pretty massive effects on our memory. Tunnel vision, for example—if you don't see elements on the periphery of a given scene at a point of high arousal, you're certainly not going to remember them.

So, the symptoms of "fight or flight" can operate on memory. But what about processes within the memory system itself? How does arousal influence those processes, and their outcomes?

These are not easy things to study. Memory is best addressed in laboratory settings, for one thing, and producing any kind of arousal, let alone extreme arousal, is legally and ethically risky in human laboratory subjects. Human research is actually governed by very high standards of safety for research participants. Under most circumstances, in most laboratories, it wouldn't be ethically possible to produce the levels of arousal in which we're interested here.

Even so, there have been some excellent studies, especially with police officers and military personnel as respondents, and the results have been pretty revealing.

A possible difficulty with these populations comes up immediately. Cops and soldiers are trained people, and they've self-selected into dangerous occupations. To what degree do their results generalize to the witness population at large? It's a reasonable question, but recall the work of *Clifford and Richards (1977)* cited above. In that study, police officers were in fact better eyewitnesses than non-officers, but *only if their training had time to operate*. When the event to be witnessed was of very short duration, officers performed at a level no higher than that achieved by civilian control respondents. This demonstrates at least a reasonable continuum of abilities between law enforcement and other witnesses.

It can't be denied that with enough observation time, police officers were shown to be superior witnesses; but what that really means is that whatever results we get with cops, and probably soldiers, the results we get with civilians are likely to be even *worse*.

And as we will see, eyewitness memory under conditions of stress, of physiological arousal, is bad enough already.

Important Experiments

We don't have the space for a comprehensive review of all the relevant research here, but let's focus on a few especially important studies.

One excellent example was conducted by *Morgan and colleagues (2004)*. Their research participants were military personnel, including Naval and Marine Corps aviators, participating in a survival school interrogation resistance course. Such courses are amazingly intense; the instructor/interrogators put trainees through some truly horrible experiences, similar to what they might encounter if captured overseas. The instructors stop short at the point of genuine injury; but pain and massive discomfort are involved.

The military respondents in the Morgan, et al. research were subjected both to relatively low-stress and to relatively high-stress interrogations. The low-stress situations did not involve direct "physical confrontation." The high stress situations did.

The analyses and assessments of the trainees' performance were complex, but for our purposes things basically come down to the following points. First, memory in the high-stress conditions was generally worse than in the low-stress conditions, although there were exceptions. Second, only a day after their interrogations, many of these military personnel (and most of them [59%] from the high-stress condition) *could not recognize their interrogators*.

Now, when somebody has his face a few inches from yours, as he roars like a tiger and physically confronts the living hell out of you for half an hour or so, he's going to capture your attention. You'll probably, well, observe him. A lot.

Yet many of these young, well-trained men, in excellent physical condition, couldn't even *identify* him a day later.

There's a lot more to the Morgan et al. (2004) study than this, and interested readers are directed to the journal article itself. But the takeaway conclusion is clear: stress can play holy hell with your memory. The physiological arousal of a high-stress interrogation (or a mugging, or a rape, or an armed robbery) can pretty well rob an eyewitness of any prospect of accurate memory. Physiological stress, in this context, is a really big deal.

Another outstanding relevant study was conducted by *Hope, Lewinski (Force Research Institute), Dixon, Blocksidge and Gabbert (2012)*. Hope, Lewinski and Gabbert are University researchers. Dixon and Blocksidge are officers of the London Metropolitan Police. I mention this to underscore the importance of collaboration between academic researchers and police officers in this type of research; the result of such collaboration is frequently excellent research.

And this was an excellent study. The procedural details were, as usual, complex, and the study addressed a number of variables (interested readers are referred to the journal article); but basically, the authors compared two groups of police officers, one of which engaged in a grueling heavy-bag workout, and one of which merely watched the workout. The officers then moved separately from the training gym to a realistic field setting, a trailer containing an unpleasant (and very loud) resident.

A number of memory indices were addressed, but ultimately, the results boil down to the following: the officers who worked out on the heavy bag fared far worse than the control officers in virtually every area of memory. Memory for the trailer, for its loud inhabitant, for a bystander who could be seen by the officers on their way from the gym to the trailer, even for the briefing the officers had attended earlier—all were recalled more poorly by the workout group than by their control counterparts. The exertions of the workout group had contributed to physiological arousal, which in turn had contributed to deeply lousy memory.

We could cite additional studies, but these serve to illustrate the point; memory is generally worse under conditions of high physiological arousal than it is when the subject is calmer, even in trained law enforcement officers.

An Important Complication

A point of confusion, frequently encountered in court proceedings and in classrooms, lies in the distinction between *arousal* and *emotion*. Obviously we tend to associate the one with the other; but in fact, their effects on memory can be very different. In general, and with relatively few exceptions, higher physiological arousal is associated with poorer memory, as demonstrated in the work of Morgan et al. and of Hope et al. cited above. Emotion, on the other hand, can actually be associated with memory *improvement*. These effects may be relatively specific; *Burke, Heuer, and Reisberg (1992)*, in an early attempt to untangle this mess, found that emotion tended to improve memory for *gist* and for basic information associated with the core of a given event, but to reduce memory for more *peripheral details*. This may only be true for more emotionally arousing events, however; another study *(Laney, Campbell, Heuer, & Reisberg, 2004)* found that thematically arousing events, in which the key factor was empathy, tended to be better for more peripheral factors as well.

An important study of cognition in the presence of trauma, of *processing under pressure,* may shed some light on these issues. *McKinnon et al. (2015)* examined the memory of passengers for a frightening event in which they were personally involved, the emergency landing of Air Transit Flight 236 in 2001. The passengers' memory for the details of their experience was compared with their and others' memory of the 9/11 terrorist attacks in the same year, and for a contemporaneous, emotionally neutral event. More details tended to be recalled concerning the Flight 236 near-disaster than for either 9/11 or the neutral events.

How is this possible? Well, there are several intriguing hypotheses concerning the underlying neuroscience *(McGaugh, 2003)*, but ultimately, if you think about it, you have a lot of personal involvement if you're about to plunge into the Atlantic in a defunct airliner. This means that you're going to direct an awful lot of attention to what's going on around you, and much of that activity will fall well within your expectations; for example, passengers correctly reported memories of donning life jackets, receiving instructions to help children, etc. Everybody knows the basics of crash preparation, so many of these details may have arisen from expectation as well as from true memory.

Now, the 9/11 tragedy was horrible, but most people weren't personally involved in it, and their specific expectations about what was going on around them at the time wouldn't have been particularly memorable; indeed, in the McKinnon et al., study, very little difference was observed between memory for 9/11 and for neutral events.

In short, it may be that *personal involvement* may have a lot to do with concentrating your mind on a given emotional event, and with subsequent memory improvement, although there are clearly a lot of other factors operating *(McKinnon et al., 2015)*. At this point, we're not very clear on what all of them are.

To sum up, however, it appears that we have the following situation: Strong physiological arousal tends to impair memory quite profoundly, especially in the eyewitness realm. This appears to be true for everybody, law enforcement officer or not. For a variety of reasons, not all of which are understood, however, emotional involvement can actually *promote* memory, although in the eyewitness realm, that mnemonic effect may be confined to specific types of details (Burke et al., 1992; but see Laney et al. 2004). The emotional state of a given witness, as well as the arousal state, should therefore be considered in any given case. Arousal and emotional involvement may very well operate in opposition to each other; however, arousal generally seems to "win," resulting in poorer memory in high-arousal situations, especially in the directions of reduced detail (brevity), gist, and personal belief.

Variables under Law Enforcement Control

All of the variables we've discussed to this point are estimator variables, those that are not under police control. An understanding of these variables is important, in that it can help the investigator gauge the probable veracity of a given statement or identification. However, the annoying fact is that there's not much you can do about estimator variables, not after the fact.

However, law enforcement *can* control the way in which eyewitness information is elicited; and this can mean the difference between a good conviction of a serious bad guy, and the punishment of the innocent while the guilty go free, still out there and filled with renewed evil confidence. But what is the best way to ensure against the errors inherent in eyewitness memory?

The World of the Showup

VIGNETTE 4: SHOWUPS AND LINEUPS

An officer is patrolling the streets of a small rural town. It's late at night, but it's still hot, with the peculiar smells of modern chemical agriculture drifting in the hot motionless air. A call comes in: home invasion, robbery, violent crime.

Light up the roof. Siren. *Go.*

En route, the call is modified. The officer is diverted to pick up the victim and the witnesses. The bad guy, I mean the suspect, has been picked up by another unit. He's being held at a particular street address. He seems like the right guy, the bad guy. Everybody's pretty *sure* he's the bad guy. After all, he's the right race, right hair, right clothes: jeans, dark t-shirt, sneakers, baseball cap.

So, the officer picks up the witnesses, and the victim. The two witnesses, in support of their friend the victim, crowd into the back of the cruiser with her. The victim is still crying and talking alternately; loudly, quickly, irrationally. After-effects of stress; normal. As the witnesses are packed into the car, the officer remembers to admonish all three not to talk to each other. In most such situations, of course, the witnesses are separated, and they absolutely *should* be separated; their tendency to talk to each other, to modify each others' stories with *post-event information*, is well-known. However, this is a small department. So few cruisers, so many bars, and it's the weekend. Necessity prevails; the officer admonishes the witnesses, *don't talk to each other*, and heads for the location of the suspect's arrest.

Chapter 3

Maybe the officer uses the siren; go quickly, get this over fast, get back to work. Probably the officer does not; but even so, there's still engine noise, ambient noise, the constant blare of the radio traffic. The officer also has to concentrate on driving, at a good speed, through Saturday-night traffic, so it takes a while for him or her to hear the whispering from the back seat—"you think he had a mustache? No, he didn't—I didn't see a mustache." The officer turns in the driver's seat, admonishes the witnesses again, briefly and with a bit of asperity. Unfortunately, just then, the officer has to turn his attention back to the gravel truck that just pulled in front of the Crown Vic at two miles per hour. Hit the brakes, hit the lights, swerve around it. The officer hears the whispering again, and delivers yet another impromptu admonishment— "Ladies (or gentlemen), please *knock it off*! *Quiet*!" but the damage is done, and two blocks later, the annoyingly assured self-appointed leader of the witness/victim group starts whispering again.

Only a block to go. The hell with it.

The officer, with his talkative cargo, arrives at the scene. A sergeant comes over to admonish the witnesses yet one more time—*we don't know for sure if this is the guy*—...; but let's face it, the tableau is compelling. Overwhelmingly compelling. There's another big, official, black-and-white cruiser parked by the curb, the red and blue roof lights spinning. The rotating roof lights change the color of everything, in the scene surrounded by darkness, every second or so. The spotlight of this police car is trained on the bad guy (oops—I mean, the suspect), sitting there on the curb in a pathetic, guilty-looking posture, in handcuffs (is it possible to look *innocent* in handcuffs?), providing a textbook example of a single-light exposure effect, distorting the features of the suspect to the level of unrecognizability. Three police officers, tall, strong, in perfect uniforms, their duty belts hung with weapons and their glinting badges clearly visible, surround this sorry specimen of obviously criminal humanity. Actually, the cops are just standing there, waiting to get this over with and get back to work, but they look so *official*. And (they look like) they're *guarding* him. Wow, he must be *dangerous*.

So, the witnesses, who just spent the last twenty minutes in the cruiser changing each other's stories, are confronted with a person who looks very like the perpetrator. After all, he's the right color, or race; he's probably close to the right body build, since the police picked him up based on a description; and he's wearing the right clothes.

Granted, in many places in America any male you're likely to see on the streets after dark is dressed in very similar clothes, but at least this guy is plausible as the perpetrator. This is especially true in the distorting glare of the single-source spotlight, and in the fact that he's surrounded by all the trappings of the official world of criminal justice. He's exactly what you'd expect.

The witnesses, laden and armed with all this post-event information, pile out of the cruiser. On seeing the bad guy (or at least somebody who looks a lot like the bad guy), the victim bursts into tears. The dominant member of the group begins to hug her, while screaming angrily "THAT'S HIM! THAT'S HIM!" in the general direction of the suspect. The dominant witness is convinced; if that wasn't the bad guy, then why would the victim be crying? The third, more diffident member of the group, takes it all in. He or she realizes that everybody else thinks that this must be the bad guy, further realizes that the suspect at least looks pretty much like the bad guy, and quietly makes a positive ID to the nearest officer. The victim hears this, becomes even more certain it's the bad guy, sitting there in handcuffs on the curb. She begins to sputter out yet another positive ID. All three witnesses have come to the same conclusion. They're confident, and they're credible.

But are they right?

The fact is they could be. The suspect matched the description. Of course, lots of people match the description. Also, the single-light source that distorted the suspect's features, the defining details that identified him within his race, further contributed to the conditions that allowed the suspect to match the description even more. The physical details that might have distinguished the suspect from the actual perpetrator were now distorted or invisible.

Nevertheless, the witnesses could be right; but there are two additional important factors here, both of which were under the control of law enforcement, and both of which resulted in the fact that this identification is highly suspect. This is important: *these factors were under the control of law enforcement,* and so their negative influence could have been excised entirely.

These factors, and their documentation, are important for prosecutorial as well as investigative reasons. If brought out in court, these uncontrolled factors, *conformity* and the use of the field identification procedure, or *showup*, would very likely result in an acquittal whether the suspect in question was actually the bad guy or not.

Conformity

The first of these factors lies in the fact that the witnesses had the opportunity to talk to each other. It's of paramount importance to keep the witnesses separated so that they can't. It's so very important that it's worth the extra time and expense to get extra cars out there to transport witnesses if necessary, and to assign officers to keep the witnesses apart and out of earshot of each other. The reason for this is essentially simple: *people conform*.

At first glance, this doesn't exactly seem like news. Obviously, people tend to conform. Most people wear the same fashions as other members of their group. This tendency may hit its high point in junior high school, but it's also vastly present in adult settings as well. If you don't believe this, and you're a senior officer or commander who typically goes to work in a suit, try going in tomorrow wearing brown or gray casual suede shoes, or a shirt in an unusual color. You'll be the talk of your whole department for about a week.

Human beings live in groups, and we are very, very sensitive to the feelings and ideas of those groups. Therefore, most of us find it very important to conform with reference to group norms.

In groups, people start "bonding" over the things they have in common. In a given group, for example, we all start talking about how we love the same sports team or the same politician. Some people in the group, of course, may love a different team or politician. No problem; they leave our group, join some other people with the same ideas, form their own group, and bond conformingly over their shared hatred of our group.

Everybody understands these dynamics, at least at a visceral level, and so the reader may be wondering why I'm even bringing it up. The answer is that so far we've talked about only higher-level, social phenomena involving complex opinions and preferences. However, conformity reaches down much farther than that, to very basic levels. We don't just conform to social things such as fashion and opinion. We do so all the way down to *perceptual conformity*, to the point where we will reconfigure what we see, or at least think we see, into accordance with other people's opinions. In other words, it's easy for other people to convince you that you've seen something that wasn't there at all, or vice versa.

Really Amazing Conformity

The most dramatic illustration of this fact was made by the psychologist Solomon Asch *(e.g., 1956)*. The basic experimental format was very simple. Asch showed his experimental subjects lines of different lengths, and essentially asked them which lines were the same; the subjects were to match lines of the correct lengths. The differences in length between the lines were visually obvious: one line was longer, and one line was shorter, and nobody had any problem telling the difference.

Until, of course, Asch put his subjects in a social setting, with other people who were actually and clandestinely working with him. The individual subjects didn't know that the others they encountered were really working for Asch, and that they were in on the thing; they thought the others were just random participants in the experiments, like themselves.

Anyway, these other people seemed to have something wrong with them. They all seemed to think the shorter line was the longer, or vice versa and, through their responses, they let the real experimental subjects know this in no uncertain terms, by means of their responses to the questions. In early trials, they all chose the correct answer; but in later trials, they all chose the wrong answer, and they all chose the same one. This sent a fairly powerful message: You think A (the short line) is shorter than B (the long one)? Oh, no, we all think that B is shorter. Don't you think that B is shorter? We all think that B is shorter. Why do you think A is shorter?

Now, if you are the poor hapless real subject, the obvious conclusion is that something is wrong here. If you're the real subject, it seems most likely that you'll come to one of three conclusions. Either all the others have some weird visual problem you don't know about; or they're all crazy in some way; or (most likely) there's some trick going on. It's obvious that B is longer, not shorter. These people are wrong.

This is neurologically pretty simple, as neurological things go. The long line takes up more of your relevant eyeball tissue than the short one. The eyeball tissue sends this message to your occipital cortex (the visual part of the cortical brain), and you come up with the inescapable conclusion: Short lines are shorter than long ones. This is not hard.

Yet the results of this study were simply amazing. Under this mild social pressure, Asch's respondents went along with the group, on average, a bit over one third of the time. And even more respondents did so at least once, if not repeatedly; they changed their minds and reported, essentially, that the long line was shorter than the short one.

This ought to be impossible; but it happened, again and again. These results are effectively incontrovertible: Under even mild social pressure, human beings, on average, are willing to deny the evidence of their own eyes, even in simple visual situations. This lets them feel like *part of the group*; they will be, so to speak, in with the in crowd.

Conformity and the Eyewitness

The ramifications for eyewitness phenomena are obvious. Eyewitness situations in the field are vastly more complex than those that occur when you look at a simple line in good lighting. There are facial features to be processed, locations and spatial relations to deal with, weapons or their absence, occluding street clutter—real eyewitness situations are enormously more complicated than Asch's simple laboratory situation. Real situations give the witness much more room to wobble, much more room for post-event information to work its evil ways, and much more leeway for social pressure to change the memory of the witness into another thing entirely.

This is why you have to keep the witnesses separate until their reports are generated and recorded. This is not just important; it is absolutely essential, worth whatever resources need to be deployed to keep this separation airtight. Law enforcement officers want to make good arrests, arrests that will lead to valid and appropriate convictions. If witnesses have not been kept separate, their evidence is *extremely* questionable; this questionability will come out in court. When this information does come to light, if you've got the wrong guy, he goes free. Hooray. However, if you've got the right guy, this massive error in procedure may very well mean that a criminal goes free. And he's still out there.

If social pressure can have this much significance under conditions of visual simplicity and good lighting, imagine how much worse life can get when the identification is made under conditions of darkness (except, of course, for the single-light source of a cruiser spotlight), while the suspect is surrounded by officers and sitting in a handcuffed position. Identification techniques like this, single-suspect viewing techniques, are used all the time, of course; but the fact is that they shouldn't be.

THE SHOWUP

As many readers will be aware, this procedure, in which witnesses are brought to view a single suspect, is called a field identification procedure, or *showup*. The showup clearly has its uses; for example, if officers are chasing an armed killer who may or may not massacre somebody else in the next few hours, it's a very good idea to make sure whether or not they've got the right person in custody, right away. Under such circumstances, the properly documented showup would probably be viewed as justified by reasonable people.

However, under circumstances in which time for a more leisurely identification is available, the showup is much harder to justify. Some years ago, the late Attorney General Janet Reno convened a working group under the aegis of the National Institute of Justice to review and make recommendations for eyewitness procedures *(Department of Justice, 1999)*. Now, anyone familiar with General Reno or her record is unlikely to consider her to have been a bleeding heart liberal. Yet even her group's NIJ guide holds that showups are prone to an "inherent suggestiveness," and that their proper venue occurs "when circumstances *require the prompt display* [italics mine] of a single suspect to a witness." Even then it is suggested that, when there are multiple witnesses, the other witnesses (kept scrupulously apart) should probably be subjected to other identification procedures as well *(DOJ, 1999, pg. 27)*. The showup is really not your best bet for an accurate ID.

Even so, and pretty obviously, the roving armed killer of the previous paragraph might very well warrant a showup—the circumstances might require *prompt display*. However, when a suspect is picked up and there's no reason to expect that anybody else is running around out there with a gun or a chainsaw, there's usually enough time to conduct a procedure less fraught with methodological evil and the potential for losing a good case: The lineup.

Lineups Good and Bad

In a lineup, of course, a picture of a suspect is displayed to the witness, together with a number of "foils," pictures of similar individuals. The witness is supposed to choose the suspect, if present. (Note that lineups can also use actual people, rather than pictures, but this is fairly rare for obvious reasons of practicality). Lineups can also be administered without the actual suspect present, in order to control for the prospect of "false positives"; however, this is probably not a very common procedure in real-world police work, again owing to practical considerations. Even so, the witness is supposed to be admonished that the suspect may or may not be among the alternatives. Lineups at least force the witness to make a choice among plausible alternatives, rather than simply to decide whether a given plausible suspect is plausible enough.

In a properly conducted police lineup, the suggestiveness of surrounding officers and handcuffs is removed. Lighting is good, and not derived from a streetlight or a single light source in the dark. So, in general, whenever possible and consistent with public and officer safety, the lineup should be used instead of the showup. It's less convenient, but it's more reliable and it will probably win more cases, especially in situations in which multiple witnesses, who have been kept scrupulously apart, make the same strong lineup identification.

Lowered Expectations

The reasons for this may be considered under the heading of a cognitive concept, the *satisficing search*. As we will see in subsequent chapters, this concept is typically applied to the realm of decision making, elements of which are crucial here. Granted, an eyewitness identification depends on the witness's *memory*—but the witness is also engaged in *decision making* as he or she selects the suspect believed to be guilty.

In satisficing, a person who must choose among alternatives *tends to pick the first one that satisfies his or her minimum requirements*. Satisficing characterizes much of everyday cognition.

As a real-world example of satisficing, consider the author's search, thirty years ago in Laramie, Wyoming, for a pickup truck to buy. I wanted a four-wheel drive longbed for less than $5,000; these were my minimum requirements at the beginning of the search. I developed other requirements as the search continued, of course; the first truck I examined was a $4,000 4-WD longbed, but the wheels were missing. The seller assured me that he could get me some wheels cheap from some relative, but I did not buy the truck; I discovered that my minimum requirements involved wheels.

Second truck: had wheels but no engine ("… but that's no problem, we'll go git my brother and he'll git a good shortblock in there no problem, jest cost about…"). I didn't buy this one either; minimum requirements now included an engine.

You might wonder why it took me so long to add these minimum requirements to my initial set. That's simple: in my naïve and untutored innocence, I never thought that anybody would be such an idiot as to try to sell a truck without them. Wheels and engines were already among my minimum requirements, of course, but implicitly—not explicitly—I simply assumed that any truck for sale would have them.

Of course, I was wrong. The third truck had been used as a semi-mobile facility for keeping chickens, especially in the cab and under the camper; the vehicle was liberally festooned with unwholesome chicken byproducts and a smell that would have killed any chicken-fancying fox suicidal enough to go in there. New minimum requirement: No damn chickens. I didn't buy it.

Finally, I found a used truck. Four wheel drive; longbed, $5,000 exactly; wheels, an engine, and mercifully devoid of any evidence of chickens. The truck fit all of my minimum requirements. I bought it.

The following day, the miserable thing broke down in my driveway.

Did I get the best available truck? Probably not; I didn't explore the whole universe of possible trucks, available for purchase, in southern Wyoming at that time; I just bought the first one that *fit my minimum requirements* ($5,000, longbed, no chickens, etc.). I *satisficed*.

In other settings, people do this all the time; you want a green sweater, but all they have is an olive-green one. Okay, it's green enough; you buy it. The store's out of fat-free milk; oh, well, 2% is low enough fat for you; you throw it in the cart. People often pick the first one, of whatever it is, that fits their minimum requirements. This may be true when they seek a career, or, God help them, a spouse—these facts probably contribute quite a bit to the incomes of career and marriage counselors.

What does the satisficing phenomenon, the situation in which you pick the first of a number of alternatives that satisfies your minimum requirements, have to do with eyewitness identification? Simple: in a showup, you as a witness have only one alternative. If that alternative, the suspect, *fits your minimum requirements*, you may very well satisfice and pick that suspect as the perpetrator.

You may, of course, be right. However, if your minimum requirements are that the bad guy has to be a medium-sized male, with a medium complexion, medium hair length, and wearing a t-shirt, jeans, and sneakers, it must be confessed that an appreciable portion of the male population of any given city is in danger of being chosen as your bad guy. This is especially the case in the bad light or single light of a nocturnal showup, when the suspect is handcuffed and surrounded by the police. Effectively, you satisfice; and effectively, the suspect goes to jail, guilty or not.

The lineup reduces the tendency to satisfice. This is a major advantage of the lineup over the showup. In a lineup, you have to pick one of a group, and comparison of the features of the group members may demonstrate to you that many, if not all of them, satisfy your minimum requirements. Minimum requirements, therefore, can no longer serve as your gold standard; you need more. Therefore, you're less likely to satisfice. You're more likely to pick a suspect, or a foil, who matches your memory more precisely.

Even so, the lineup is not perfect. One of the persons depicted may look so much more like your assailant than the others that you pick that person, just from the coincidence of the match between his or her features and those of your memory. Also, there is great contention in the field right now between advocates of sequential double-blind procedures and believers in more traditional simultaneous "six-pack" photo arrays (see *Mecklenburg, Bailey, & Larson, 2013*). The double-blind sequential method requires that the lineup administrator be unaware of the identity of the suspect photo, if indeed the suspect is present in the lineup at all. It also requires that the pictures be shown only one at a time rather than side-by-side, which is suggested to reduce the tendencies of witnesses to pick the "best" photo, the one closest to memory, from a simultaneous "six-pack" *(e.g., Mecklenburg, Larson, & Bailey, 2008)*. Advocates of the more traditional simultaneous method often question the value of the double-blind sequential method relative to the six-pack, especially in terms of the logistics, the additional time and expense involved for the double-blind sequential system. New concerns have also recently been raised about the methods used to demonstrate the power of the sequential method, but the questions remain unresolved at the present time (e.g., *Mecklenburg et al., 2013*).

There are theoretical questions, as well. For example, it has always seemed to the author that the sequential method might be more liable to the type of satisficing errors discussed above, as only one person is compared at a time to what might be the witness' minimum requirements for positive ID. Perhaps witnesses would be more likely to pick the first person who fits their minimum requirements, even erroneously, when alternatives are presented one at a time; the cognitive process would be similar to that involved in my personal truck selection debacle.

However, I must confess that this is speculation; at the moment, no data exist at all on the satisficing question as it relates to lineup method, and an important study, among others, has made a strong case for the superiority of the double-blind sequential method. In a large-scale field study *(Mecklenburg et al., 2008)*, the Illinois State Police showed that the sequential double-blind method resulted in about 30% fewer false identifications than did the traditional method. However, it also reduced suspect identifications by about 15%.

Most lineups conducted in the U.S. today are still conducted as six-packs, and the jury is still out in the criminal justice world as to what the best method actually is. Psychologists often differ with police officers on this question, and the relative merits of the techniques "remain unsettled" *(Mecklenberg et al., 2008)*. Ultimately, however, there is general agreement that the lineup is better than the showup, and should be used instead whenever circumstances permit.

> *The construction of the lineup matters, of course. Consider several instances, from the author's case files and from other sources, of things you don't want to do or see:*
>
> - Don't have a suspect of one race in among five "foils" of a different race.
>
> - Don't have your suspect clean-shaven while everybody else has a beard, or vice versa.
>
> - Don't dress your suspect in a button-down shirt while everybody else is in a jail uniform, and *especially* don't match that shirt to the witness's description. Your suspect, if present in your lineup, should be visually very similar to your foils.
>
> - Don't have your suspect's face filling the entire photo menacingly, while everybody else is seen as a tiny head somewhere in the middle of the photo.
>
> - Don't photograph your subject against a different color background than everybody else.
>
> - And for Heaven's sake, don't pin a large post-it above the head of your suspect, a glowing goldenrod indicator of guilt, when nobody else has one.
>
> Your suspect, if present in your lineup, should be visually very similar to your foils.

In all of these cases, of course, the lineup was biased by the way in which it was constructed. In the majority, the obvious biases posed a significant credibility problem for judge and jury, gleefully pointed out by the defense and met with rage and gnashing of teeth by the prosecutor. In fact, these modifications had rendered the lineups effectively useless.

However, the fact remains that a *properly conducted* police lineup, involving positive identifications by several witnesses who did not have the chance to influence each other's stories, and also supported by strong physical evidence, provides very powerful evidence in court. Even with a perfectly conducted lineup, of course, a given identification can be wrong; the paramount importance of good physical evidence cannot be overemphasized. However, the fact remains that a solid, well-conducted police lineup frequently provides very compelling evidence in court.

At this point, we have considered many of the most important factors in eyewitness memory. We have considered crucial estimator variables, which are not under the control of law enforcement officials. We have also considered witness separation, showups, and lineup procedures, which are subject to police control. We have mainly focused on person identification, in part because this has been the major focus of the field of eyewitness identification generally.

However, there are a variety of important factors we have not discussed. What about weapon identification, and the identification of vehicles? What about memory for important inanimate details of the crime scene?

Also, frankly, is this all? Is all we get from a scientific consideration of eyewitness memory a series of disconnected facts, to be applied when possible but without any central organizing principles?

In the next chapter, I wish to address these questions, using data from my own research as well as that of others. We'll also set this discussion within an overall theoretical framework that has proven to be of use in understanding eyewitness memory, as well as for the understanding of aspects of higher reasoning that are directly important in field and command decisions.

Chapter 4
CREAM-COLORED VANS AND GRASSY KNOLLS: EYEWITNESS MEMORY IN CONTEXT

In the previous chapter, we dealt with a number of the facts, in isolation, that govern the eyewitness realm. In this chapter, we will go a bit farther into the next logical step. We will try to put the pieces together into a coherent account that will help to make the whole business more comprehensible, and that may also help the law enforcement professional make some decent predictions concerning witness accuracy in specific cases.

Let's first approach this synthesis by discussing the questions it's meant to address. Consider a case on which the author worked some years ago. A shooting in the door of an apartment, while the witness's kids were apparently crawling around her legs in a frenzy of terror, constituted the main issue to be tried. As the trial commenced, the type of weapon used assumed central significance, as is often the case. The witness provided a clear, confident, credible memory of the weapon: a large, police-type semi-automatic pistol, something like a Glock or a Smith & Wesson M&P.

The problem was that the evidence was uncertain to begin with. So, as post-event information was provided to the witness by various attorneys and their cronies, the weapon became reconfigured, altered, in her memory. The weapon she remembered changed from a clear representation of a semi-auto to that of a revolver.

It's hard to imagine how anybody could confuse those shapes. Semi-autos are blocky; revolvers are rounded, with pronounced bulges at the cylinder and grip. However, it got worse. At some point during the trial, the weapon morphed from a revolver into an ice pick.

Yes, I said an ice pick.

This was maintained with confidence for a while, until, with the shifting demands of the trial, the ice pick turned back into some unspecified type of gun. During the course of this amazingly malleable testimony, each new weapon type was confidently asserted to be accurate, despite that fact that the witness clearly didn't really have a clue concerning the weapon in question.

At first inspection, this entire situation seems impossible. How could a person turn the blocky shape of a large autoloading pistol into the unmistakable bulging lines of a revolver, then into the stark simplicity of an ice pick, followed by an indeterminate "some kind of gun?"

Well, if the mind were some kind of recording device, as often seems to be assumed in investigations and in court (and especially by juries), this would be a serious question. If you record a football game on a DVD, it doesn't magically turn into a soap opera or a game show when you play it back. So, if the mind were a recording device, we'd have to devote quite a lot of time to really lousy answers to this apparently profound question.

However, the mind is not a recording device, and in light of the research of Bartlett and of Loftus discussed above, the answer to this question becomes simpler. Memory is not a veridical record of what has been seen. It is, instead, the reconfigured product of initial encoding, post-event information, and general reduction in the directions of gist, brevity, and personal belief. The witness in the gun-gun-ice pick-gun case did not encode the features of the actual weapon at all. She had no *feature-intensive* depiction of a given type of weapon in memory. Rather, she encoded something along the lines of "some kind of weapon," a general, *gestalt* framework for something vaguely weapon-like, which was therefore massively susceptible to the negative influences of post-event information discussed above.

Gestalt and Feature-Intensive Processing

The major point of this discussion actually lies in that distinction between *feature-intensive processing*, in which a person processes veridical details of a scene (or a gun or a car or a face) and *gestalt* processing, in which there is little attention to the details that might assist in making an accurate identification *(Sharps & Nunes, 2002; Sharps, 2003)*. Our witness in this case had a gestalt representation of general weapon-ness in her mind, without any understanding or knowledge of the features of a given weapon that might have resulted in a correct identification.

Gestalt processing, such as that exhibited by this witness, does not mean that the details, or the internal structure and meaning of a given situation, are absent from the situation to be understood or processed. However, the important point is that these feature-intensive elements of the situation don't generally make it into memory. Most people don't encode, for example, a short-slide blue steel .45 ACP; they encode "some kind of gun." Most people don't encode a specific 6'3" individual of probable Swedish descent, with a slightly sallow complexion and a sort of dark-gold hair color, fading into brown; they encode a "real big guy," or if the investigator is lucky, a "real big blond guy."

In a series of papers, the author and students have developed a practical synthetic formulation, the Gestalt/Feature-Intensive (G/FI) Processing Theory, that deals with these facts *(Sharps & Nunes, 2002; Sharps, 2003)*. This theory has been successfully tested in the realms of reasoning *(Sharps & Martin, 2002; Sharps, Hess, & Ranes, 2007)*, education *(Sharps, Hess, Price-Sharps, & The, 2008)*, addictive behaviors *(Sharps, Price-Sharps, Day, Nunes, Villegas, & Mitchell, 2005; Sharps, Price-Sharps, Day, Villegas, & Nunes, 2005; Sharps, Villegas, & Matthews, 2005)*, adult memory, cognition and aging *(Sharps, 1998, 2003 for reviews)*, and other areas as well. Thus far, the theory has been shown to be both useful and reliable; and, as we will see, this has proven to be the case in a number of studies applying these ideas directly to eyewitness memory and identification.

G/FI Theory: A Synthesis for Eyewitness Memory

The gist of G/FI is that the two types of processing, gestalt and feature-intensive, are not separate entities; rather, they lie on a continuum. People in eyewitness situations frequently encode the original memory in a "gestalt" manner, with little actual attention to details that might assist in making a correct identification. However, later analysis of the situation, especially under circumstances in which others (e.g., attorneys and law enforcement officers) are directing and framing the analysis, the processing of the initial, relatively sparse gestalt memory moves in a more "feature-intensive" direction, in which a relatively slow and meticulous analysis of elements of the initial situational configuration is undertaken. The problem here, of course, is that the initial gestalt configuration was relatively devoid of the details needed for feature-intensive analysis in the first place; and as Bartlett demonstrated, such details may be readily fabricated, wholly unconsciously on the part of the witness, from vague impressions, later information, or other sources. Feature-intensive analysis is only going to be helpful if the features to be analyzed were there in memory to begin with; and an understanding of this fact, and of the dynamics involved in G/FI analysis of eyewitness memory, gives you an edge.

Consider the weapon identification situation discussed above, in which the extreme metamorphosis from gun to ice pick was observed. The witness in question had little or no knowledge of firearms. Under such circumstances, a relatively gestalt encoding of "some kind of gun," which with a little pressure would become "some kind of weapon," was practically inevitable. However, suppose instead that the witness had been a police officer, or a recently discharged veteran, and that the weapon had in fact been a Beretta M9A1. This more expert witness would have recognized its characteristic shape, very different from that of a Glock or a Smith & Wesson, easily distinguishable from a 1911 .45 ACP, but clearly an autoloader. Moreover, this obviously more expert witness might have registered the standard black grips, positive thumb safety, and proprietary Bruniton™ non-glare finish; more specific features particular to that type of weapon. All of these features, resulting in an obvious capacity for feature-intensive analysis, would have encoded at the initial crime scene. This would have constituted a truly feature-intensive memory.

In this hypothetical case, would it have been possible for the relatively expert witness to mistake the M9A1 for another member of the Beretta 92/96 series, or even a Beretta Vertec, especially in view of the fact that part of the weapon was of course obscured by the grip of the assailant? I would suggest that such an error might very well occur; those autoloaders, similar in design and finish, could probably be mutually mistaken under rapidly evolving tactical circumstances, even by a witness of relative expertise.

However, is there any possibility, however remote, that the relatively expert witness would be likely to mistake a Beretta for the blocky shape of a Glock? Unlikely. How about a wheel gun, a revolver? Pretty much impossible; an autoloader is an autoloader. An ice pick? Ice picks ain't autoloaders; see above.

So, a relative expert on something is less likely to misidentify it than somebody without that expertise. Hardly world-shattering information; but what is important here is the underlying dynamic. The reason expertise makes this difference is that it promotes, or permits, feature-intensive analysis; therefore, if we can identify other factors that promote FI analysis as well, we stand a better chance of predicting the veracity of a given eyewitness.

Memory for Guns and Cars

It's amazing how often weapon identification (and, as we'll see shortly, vehicle identification) comes up as an important factor in investigation and in court. It's perhaps equally amazing how little scientific attention has been directed to these issues. So, my students and I conducted a study to address the issues involved *(Sharps, Barber, Stahl, & Villegas, 2003)*. We examined firearms identification under ideal laboratory conditions—excellent lighting, no occultation, no excessive arousal—in the clear understanding that whatever happened in the field, under stressful, cognitively demanding conditions, would generally be worse.

And frankly, what we found in the lab was bad enough. In that study, correct response rates for semi-automatic pistol identification were slightly less than half correct. A nondescript short-barreled revolver of a type frequently used in crimes was identified at a rate of only 43%, even though it had been seen in perfect lighting only minutes before.

(It should be noted here that horrendous firearms recognition performance is not confined to handguns, but occurs with long guns as well. In a recent study [Herrera, Sharps, Swinney, & Lam, 2015], we found, essentially, that the average person couldn't tell a rifle from a decidedly sub-lethal spring-fired Daisy BB gun; people kept mistaking the BB gun for an actual rifle, or perhaps a shotgun. This is obviously a matter of potential importance as long guns, of various types, are becoming more frequently used in crimes).

There are some mitigating factors. For example, more familiar handgun types were better recognized than less familiar types; the .45 automatic Colt pistol (ACP), familiar to practically everybody from a thousand war movies, was better identified than a relatively unfamiliar nine-millimeter weapon of European manufacture (Sharps et al., 2003).

At first glance, these results may seem useful but rather obvious—of course, the more familiar gun is remembered better than the less familiar. But why? Well, pistols, like other objects in the world, have characteristic shapes and features; if people have seen numerous .45 ACPs in the movies, they've been "trained" in a way, albeit inadvertently, to recognize the features of that weapon. This is important; none of the respondents in our series of studies were firearms experts, and on average they reported little to no experience with firearms. Yet their repeated exposure to commonly depicted weapons rendered them better witnesses, with regard to these weapons, than otherwise, even without demonstrated expertise. In other words, *conditions that are conducive to feature-intensive processing are conducive to better eyewitness memory; conditions that are less likely to foster FI processing, on average, predispose witnesses to poorer performance.* These principles appear to hold true even in the absence of demonstrable expertise.

An additional result from this weapons identification study really highlighted this effect, the influence of feature-intensive processing. Our civilian research participants were not very familiar with guns, but they were substantially more familiar with revolvers and semi-automatic pistols than they were with true assault weapons, such as Uzis. This means that, all other things being equal, the familiarity effect discussed above should have taken hold, and the witnesses should have remembered pistols better than assault weapons. Yet they did not; the average rate of recognition for pistols overall was 49%, and the average rate for assault weapons, Uzis and so on, was 71%. Why?

The answer is not simple, but it is straightforward. The effect of familiarity seen in pistol recognition was not some magic inherent in familiarity itself. Rather, it derived from the predisposition for FI processing that familiarity made possible. FI processing, not familiarity per se, was the key; and the simple fact is that assault weapons are larger and more complex than typical handguns, providing more features for even relatively unsophisticated witnesses to work on.

For example, Uzis have folding stocks; .45 ACPs do not. The individual witness may not know a folding stock from a goat, but he or she will notice the folding stock, and perhaps describe it internally as the big coat-hanger-looking-triangle-thing at the back of the weapon. The witness may even take a moment to ponder something on the order of "What the hell is that?" as he or she looks at the folding stock, increasing the depth of processing *(Craik & Lockhart, 1972)*, the amount of attentional and cognitive resources that a witness directs to the given situation. This directly contributes to the opportunity for FI processing *(Sharps, 2003)*. Assault weapons have all sorts of features that a witness could compare, in an FI manner, to familiar things—coat-hanger-shaped folding stocks, candy-bar-shaped magazines, sights with definable geometric shapes, and so on. All of these are definable features, and all are candidates for the enhanced FI processing that leads to more effective eyewitness ID.

This interpretation is also supported by our study of long-gun recognition, cited above (Herrera, Sharps, Swinney, & Lam, 2015); in that research, we found that a rifle which presented more features, a bolt-action weapon with a sling and telescopic sights, was correctly identified more frequently than was a lever-action iron-sight rifle, which presented fewer features for identification.

So, at this point, we are on our way to a practical predictive theory of eyewitness identification. Good theories simplify things, and G/FI seems to be leading in precisely that direction. You can't see features well in the dark, or from behind things, or when you have only brief exposure times. All of these, as well as other "estimator" variables discussed in the previous chapter, therefore swing the pendulum more toward gestalt than toward feature-intensive processing in the case of an average witness to an average crime, with consequent diminution of accuracy. You can't deal with features as well if you aren't very familiar with them, or if you're looking at something else. Cross-racial identifications and weapon focus fall into line, respectively; we can explain these phenomena in G/FI terms. In a cross-racial situation, the witness may rely more upon the gestalt impression of the face than on the idiosyncratic features that identity the specific individual in that race. Weapon focus results in less visual time on the face and body of the perpetrator; this robs the witness of the opportunity to engage in the relevant FI processing.

So, in G/FI theory, the investigator, DA, or juror has a potentially powerful predictive tool at his or her disposal. Taking the eyewitness picture as a whole, in any given case, those identifications that are more conducive to FI processing, overall, should generally prove more accurate. Those that are less conducive to FI processing should tend to produce more gestalt representations in memory, with consequent loss of accuracy on average. These gestalt representations are not only less likely to be accurate, they are also more readily reconfigured in the presence of post-event information (remember that ice pick?), simply because they possess fewer definable features to anchor the given representation, to keep that representation from veering off track. In other words, if you remember the trigger guard and magazine of a specific handgun, there is no way for your memory to turn that handgun into an icepick. In the absence of feature-intensive recall of trigger guards and magazines, however, a general gestalt concept of "weapon" can become, in the mind, anything from an icepick to a handgun to a bazooka.

However, there is another aspect of G/FI theory that goes in an entirely different direction. Sometimes, under special definable circumstances, FI processing can *hinder* the formation of a proper representation. This occurs under circumstances wherein *a very limited set of features informs the witness's representation*, to the degree that this very limited set of features masks the inadequacies of the generally gestalt nature of the bulk of the representation itself.

G/FI, VEHICLE RECALL AND THE WASHINGTON SNIPER

This requires some clarification, to say the least; so let me illustrate this point with another of our studies *(Villegas, Sharps, Satterthwaite, and Chisholm, 2005)*, in which we addressed vehicle identification. Vehicles, like guns, are frequently important in investigations and in court cases, and I can give no better example of this than the Washington Sniper case of 2002. Many readers will recall that in that year, two young men went on a "shooting spree" *(Blades, 2005; Horwitz and Ruane, 2003)*, in which twenty-three victims were killed or wounded, the majority in the Washington, DC area. This reign of violence "terrorized" the entire population of the area for three weeks (Blades, 2005).

It is obvious that the most terrible cost of such a spree is to the victims and their families. However, there are other costs as well. Every state trooper, municipal police officer, or deputy sheriff who responded to a sniper-related call, real or imagined on the part of the caller, was unavailable for other law enforcement duties. How many violent crimes, robberies, or burglaries occurred because patrol resources were busy at the time with sniper-related calls? How many crimes went unsolved because detectives were following up on credible and confident leads to the sniper that had no basis in reality? Every sniper call took scarce enforcement resources away from other police work; and every such call had to be paid for.

This is one of the most important aspects of eyewitness memory in the modern world: The proclivity of the confident and credible eyewitness, who is nevertheless completely wrong, for sending law enforcement resources on wild goose chases. When this happens, it of course reduces the force available for agencies to direct against real crimes, and it may have a real and deleterious effect on police department budgets already strained by reduced funds and enhanced crime rates. Should rates of domestic terrorism increase as well, as many analysts currently believe to be likely in the future, this problem will assume even greater significance.

And frankly, this problem had already assumed enough significance with the Washington sniper. Several witnesses reported strong sightings of the sniper's vehicle: In their minds, it was definitely a white or cream-colored box truck, which was often referred to as a "van" in communications and by the media. As we'll see below, the precision of language cannot really be overestimated as a factor in criminal investigations. Some people refer to a box truck as a "van," as in "moving van," where others refer to a moving van as a "truck" and confine the word "van" to minivans and the like. This meant that a lot of people, including a lot of law enforcement officers, were distracted by a hell of a lot of pale boxy vehicles- imprecise language dramatically inflated the number of different kinds of vehicles that people might be frightened of, looking for, or inclined to report to the police.

But anyway, law enforcement finally had something useful to go on. Pale vans and similar vehicles were stopped and searched all over the place, with no results whatsoever, for a very simple reason: The actual vehicle driven by the sniper was a blue Chevrolet Caprice.

White van to blue Chevy Caprice. You can't get any wronger than that, and wronger isn't even a word.

Chapter 4 117

What happened? Well, it's not hard to figure out. White or cream-colored vans are very popular with a whole variety of tradesmen, locksmiths, plumbers, electricians, delivery people, etc. Vans are great because you can securely lock up your tools and supplies in them in a way that would be impossible with a pickup truck, and pale colors such as white and cream don't show dirt very well; you don't have to wash your vehicle all the time. Therefore, in virtually every city in America, including Washington and its surroundings, white or cream-colored vans and little pale box trucks are scurrying past you all day, delivering flowers, bearing locksmiths to stranded motorists, carrying plumbers to plugged toilets, bringing the electrician to fix the fuse box after little Jimmy electrocutes the dog, and so on.

So, consider the following scenario. The Washington sniper takes a shot at you. You, a civilian, panic. All of the dynamics discussed in Chapters 1 and 2 seize your body and your brain in no uncertain terms. You dive behind a Volvo, hitting your head on the pavement as you go down. You look, confusedly, at the street before you. You are frightened and confused, perhaps in shock. In this state, you search wildly for your assailant.

Now, the Washington sniper and his friendly helper are long gone, of course, borne off to safety and freedom in their Chevy Caprice. So, in your frantic search, you don't see the sniper, the helper, or the blue Caprice. You see none of this, but you do see the white van belonging to Bert's Lock and Key crossing the intersection before your temporarily crazy eyes. Remember, you are looking for the fleeing vehicle of your assailants. Bert and his van fill the bill quite nicely; remember the process of satisficing? So, you confidently report Bert to the police; and within minutes, every officer from Silver Spring to central Virginia is pulling over every locksmith and delivery van in sight. Which means, of course, that those officers are not available for the other duties that keep piling up. The sniper goes on his merry blood-soaked way while police officers spend hours pulling over plumbers and bakery guys.

Cases like that of the Washington Sniper are poison for police departments, including state police agencies. Such cases create a horrific imbalance of resources. Public and media opinion demand that something be done about the most salient threat, the sniper, leaving all the other prosaic, everyday, bread-and-butter threats unaddressed. And much of this, at least in the case of the Washington Sniper, came about as a result of the perceptual juxtaposition of a blue Chevy Caprice with a cream-colored minivan.

How could people be so fantastically lousy at vehicle identification? Well, of course, they could simply decide that the next vehicle they saw

(Bert's) was that of the sniper—but could they make other pertinent mistakes as well?

The answer is a resounding *Yes*. In our experiments *(Villegas, Sharps, Satterthwaite, & Chisholm, 2005)*, we effectively repeated the gun-ID work discussed in this chapter, but with vehicles rather than weapons. What we found was, quite frankly, astonishing: Despite people's protestations of being highly vehicle-savvy, their accuracy on average was 23.81%. In other words*: Three-quarters of the time, under ideal, well-lighted, no-stress conditions, the average person was likely to be wrong about what vehicle he or she saw just ten minutes before.* Highway patrol and motor officers, take note.

With reference to G/FI theory, a fascinating pattern emerged from this already rather interesting pattern of total failure on the part of our witnesses. It had to do with color and vehicle type.

The stimulus items, the actual vehicles we used in our experiments, were small die-cast cars. We used these little models, instead of the real thing, for the simple reason that the photography of real cars, outdoors under daylight conditions, makes it virtually impossible to standardize conditions of light and shading to a reasonable degree of experimental precision. The use of these little cars conferred an additional advantage as well: It meant that we had perfectly controlled conditions. We had vehicles that were absolutely identical as to color, but different as to model; and vehicles that were absolutely identical as to model, but different as to color. Moreover, the colors and the models of any given type were also completely identical.

The results were interesting and quite a bit worse than we expected. The reader will recall that, on average, people's recognition rates for common handguns ran slightly under fifty percent. However, in this experiment with cars, as opposed to guns, fewer than *one-quarter* of our sample got the vehicle right, under conditions that were vastly superior to those typically encountered in the field. Incredibly, 8% of our respondents identified more than one vehicle as correct, despite the fact that they had *only seen one vehicle*. If anyone is still inclined to treat eyewitness memory as unfailingly accurate, I would just like to refer that individual to this fantastically stupid result.

However, the most interesting results with reference to G/FI theory had to do with the *color* and *type* of the vehicle, especially with reference to *inaccurate* identifications. Of our respondents, 17.46% inaccurately selected a vehicle of the same color as the "target" vehicle, the one they had seen initially, even if it was a completely different kind of vehicle. However, only 9.52%, a little more than half as many, inaccurately selected a vehicle of the same model as the target vehicle, but of a different color. In other words, in this study, vehicle color was approximately twice as important as vehicle model in the generation of errors. People were about twice as likely to mistake a red pickup truck for a red car as they were a red sedan for a green sedan, or a black pickup truck for a red pickup truck.

Why would this be? The answer lies in G/FI theory. We've already seen that FI processing is more powerful for memory than G processing. Here's the critical point: Color is more feature-intensive in nature than is the information you use to perceive vehicle model.

This is a complex point, so let's pursue it a little further. If you see a red car, including "red" as part of the overall thing you see, this is feature-intensive, FI, in the purest sense of the word. The main feature of the vehicle you've seen is the color red, period. Because you can articulate this in language ("red" is a linguistically definable color), "red" becomes an irreducible and incontrovertible part of the eyewitness representation: You saw a feature-intensive red thing, a thing with a clear, definable feature of redness, and that's it.

However, let us consider the problem of vehicle model. Unless we know the name of the specific model, how do we define it? Answer: By the shape.

Okay, so how do we define shape? What, for example, is the name of the structure at the back of the roof that curves down to meet the curve of the rear fender where it meets the back door frame?

Trick question. There isn't any name for that particular piece of the car, at least not one that I could find out about. In fact, there isn't any commonly accessible name for many of the curves and contours that make up the body of a car (or of a gun, or a human body, for that matter). We encode such complex features not in terms of their existence as features, but in overall, gestalt organizations—in terms of the G (gestalt) in G/FI.

Now it becomes clear why a red pickup truck was mistaken for a small red car, but a small black car typically was not. The nervous system of a witness is challenged by an investigator, who asks, "What did you see?" The nervous system responds: "I saw a red thing," because the feature-intensive comprehension of "redness" far outweighs any of the vague, amorphous details that come from the processing of the gestalt curves and contours by which we recognize a particular vehicle model. So, when that nervous system is again confronted with the prospect of a vehicle of the correct color, the rest of the representation frequently goes out the window. Never mind the rest of the details, most of which have receded into a gestalt blur; I can remember that the car was red, that's what I saw and that's the one thing, the one feature, about the vehicle that I can name. My nervous system doesn't care about the differences in shape between initial representation and final testified outcome, at least not as much as it does about similarities and differences in color. The shapes of different parts of a given vehicle are processed as relatively non-definable gestalts. They are therefore cognitively subordinate to the features that my nervous system can truly grasp in an articulate form, the feature-intensive elements, such as the verbally comprehensible and feature-intensive concept of "red."

> **Let us summarize and add a caveat to the G/FI principles outlined above:**
>
> - Conditions that are conducive to feature-intensive processing are conducive to better eyewitness memory; conditions that are less likely to foster FI processing, on average, predispose witnesses to poorer performance. These principles appear to hold true even in the absence of demonstrable expertise with reference to the object type (e.g., gun or vehicle) in question.
>
> - (Caveat.) However, in a generally gestalt and therefore malleable representation, a given FI detail such as color may become so important, in the mind of the eyewitness, that it subsumes all other aspects of the representation. This may actually lead to *in*accuracy; color, for example, as a verbally articulable concept, may become more important in the mind of the eyewitness than more gestalt details of shape and relief. This can lead to over-dependency on FI processing at the expense of veridical G (gestalt) aspects of the given representation.
>   As a result, any reasonable alternative of the same color as the initial representation may be identified positively but incorrectly (the redness of the vehicle may overwhelm the less-articulable details that distinguish the shape of a car from a truck).

So, from a practical standpoint, how can this information provide an edge for the investigator? These findings suggest a fairly straightforward answer. The investigator must first ascertain whether a given witness's account of a crime is predominantly gestalt in nature, relatively free of the details that promote accurate memory and identification, or, more rarely, a relatively feature-intensive, detail-rich account. (Obviously, it should be ascertained that these details, these features, *actually conform to the reality of the crime* as determined by evaluation of physical evidence and other verifiable eyewitness reports.)

If the more gestalt situation is the case, emphasis on given features, such as the redness of the car (or, perhaps, on the color/race of the suspect, may be misleading. An isolated element of FI processing may overwhelm less feature-intensive elements of the representation in the witness's memory, to the extent that the memory cannot be trusted at all.

Another caveat is in order here. A rich variety of verifiable FI details may support the veracity of given eyewitness's memory, *but only with reference to the elements of the situation to which those details pertain*. I may remember all the details of the gun correctly, but not even have been looking at the car. I remember exactly where the mailbox was, from behind which the shots were fired, but I may have missed completely the details or even the existence of the bush beside it. There are such things as individual differences, and many different factors can determine where a witness directed his or her gaze; many different factors can also influence the interpretation of whatever the witness believes was there.

In short, strong FI memory of a given aspect of a situation really says nothing pertinent about memory for the rest of the situation.

However, if a *specific* memory is relatively rich in relatively verifiable details, and the circumstances surrounding the memory were such as to promote a high level of accurate, well-understood feature-intensive processing, then the overall account from that witness concerning the elements so described is more likely to prove reliable. The investigator therefore has a greater likelihood of success in basing further evolutions of the given investigation on the reports of the relatively FI witness.

Eyewitness Memory in Context

These findings within the context of G/FI theory, while not absolute, can at least give an investigator an additional edge in coping with the inconsistent and malleable world of eyewitness memory. However, thus far we have discussed only isolated elements that might be present within a crime scene—guns and vehicles. What about the rest of the scene, including the suspects themselves?

Real crime scenes are remarkably complex. Frequently, the witnesses to actual crimes are under fantastic levels of stress during their encoding periods, when they are actually observing the events of interest. As we've already seen in Chapters 1, 2, and 3, this means that their mental processes, on average, are pretty much out to lunch while they're encoding the crucial memories. Therefore, to say it nicely, certain oversimplifications and outright errors tend to emerge.

WHEN PRESIDENT KENNEDY DIED

One of the best-documented cases of eyewitness variability in recorded history is to be found in the infamous assassination of President John F. Kennedy in 1963. The conclusion of many thinking people, including the thinking people on the Warren Commission *(1964)*, was that the assassin, Lee Harvey Oswald, acted alone from the Texas Book Depository with a Mannlicher-Carcano carbine. Certainly the mechanics of the situation would justify this conclusion.

However, many eyewitnesses, together with those who wished to be taken for eyewitnesses, told a different story. Depending on the witness, Oswald either did or did not fire on the President; let's face it, nobody actually saw him take the shots. "Witnesses" also claim to have seen assassins, or their weapons or furtive movements, on the infamous grassy knoll, behind the slightly less infamous wooden fence, or in a number of other locations. A motorcycle officer with an open microphone was here, there, or everywhere at the time of the crime, and the general chaos of screaming and running produced a galaxy of conflicting reports. These reports, of course, have formed the nucleus of what might be termed a conspiracy industry. In my attempt to conduct at least some basic research on the whole miserable mess for this book, I was confronted with the *clear and indisputable facts,* if you've got the right kind of mind, that the President was definitely assassinated by Oswald, acting alone, and also that he wasn't. Both stories are maintained with equal confidence, and as to credibility, it's very much in the eye of the beholder.

The same confusion pervades the entire case. *If* Oswald committed the crime at all, in the elastic minds of the witnesses, the reader can find authorities who are incontrovertibly certain that Oswald acted alone, or with the help of agents of the Soviet clandestine services. Or with the aid of Cuban terrorists of various affiliations. Or with the help of most of the agencies of the federal government (at least so far nobody's accused the Park Service), or the Mafia, or other elements of organized crime, or organized crime operatives friendly to certain famous actor/singers who apparently didn't like Kennedy, or possibly somebody who was really ticked off over the whole alleged Marilyn Monroe thing.

Everybody has a theory, and everybody is sure that his or her theory is right.

Chapter 4

Some of the confusion surrounding Kennedy's death may derive from the *precision of language* factor that we saw complicating matters in the Washington Sniper case above. For example, many people became obsessed with the course of the "magic bullet" which struck both President Kennedy and Governor Connally of Texas, who was riding in the same limousine. Since Connally was riding in front of Kennedy, it appeared to many people, and to the producers of a Hollywood movie on the subject, that the bullet had to move laterally between Kennedy and Connally to inflict the wounds on the two men, a physical impossibility.

But the problem was in the *language,* not the physics. If Connally were *directly* in front of Kennedy, as is implied on a Gestalt basis by saying something like "the Governor was seated in the car in front of the President," then the course of the bullet implies that it was both sentient and capable of gymnastics. However, although it's technically correct that Connally was seated "in front" of Kennedy, the Governor's seat was actually a jump seat, set lower than the President's seat "behind" him, and was also offset toward the center of the car. When you diagram or model the actual positions of the Governor and President, you find that no ballistic magic is needed; the bullet flew straight and true with no significant deviation.

Experienced investigators will sympathize with the problem. In non-specific Gestalt (G) terms, "in front" seems to imply one man sitting directly in front of the other. One must get into the feature-intensive (FI) specific details of "in front, but lower and offset to one side" to see what was really going on, and to avoid the development of yet more deeply unusual conspiracy theories, some perhaps involving space aliens. A crucial lesson that devolves from this example: use very specific, feature-intensive language in interviewing witnesses, and without biasing their accounts, guide witnesses to higher levels of specific FI details. Linguistic specificity is your friend in any given case.

But the simple fact, in the Kennedy case, is that the conflicting eyewitness accounts muddied the proverbial waters to an incredible degree, far beyond the circumstances surrounding the Incredible White Van Effect seen in the Washington Sniper case. This in turn has resulted in a galaxy of theories, ranging from the plausible to the completely ludicrous. The case serves as an outstanding example of what happens when witnesses really get going with the dynamics we've already seen, and of the fantastic difficulties that these effects may create for the investigator.

Incidentally, in view of this discussion, a few readers may wonder what the author's personal take on the whole Kennedy business is. I think that Oswald was the assassin, and that he probably acted alone, although he may have *attempted*, probably with little or no success, to recruit assistance or co-conspirators from a variety of sources. My reasoning is that this is the simplest explanation that seems to fit the facts as we have them today. Vincent Bugliosi [2007], in his well-documented and truly massive volume on the subject [1,612 pages, and that doesn't count the computer disc that comes with the book and that contains additional notes], certainly comes to the conclusion of Oswald-as-lone-gunman, as he compellingly sledgehammers every possible conspiracy theory into crumbling oblivion. However, although Oswald-as-the-lone-gunman is my best guess, I must confess that I don't *know*, not with scientific certainty. I don't know for certain, and I don't think anybody ever really will. The witness accounts of the shooting and of related events are simply too variable, too conflicting, and too messy. About all that can be said is that this tragic and historically important crime serves as yet one more impetus for a better understanding of what happens to witnesses in real-world contexts. The most important lessons from the aftermath of the Kennedy assassination, from a psychological perspective, lie in the horrendous unreliability of physiologically aroused witnesses to a violent crime. This is especially true after the witnesses have had a while to let their imaginations, their conversations with other people, and the possible presence of TV cameras work on their memories.

Also incidentally, this horrific assassination provides additional evidence of the fabulously bizarre effects of stress on the human nervous system [see Chapters 1 and 2 above]. The historian William Manchester *[1967]* recounts that in the wake of the assassination, the President's entourage and personal staff drank a rather fantastic quantity of hard liquor [remember, this was the '60s]. The result of this orgy of alcoholic excess was that *none of them got drunk*. The stuff was like water to these people under these circumstances. According to Manchester, the effect of imbibing enough booze to fill the Reflecting Pool was zero to zip under the fantastically stressful circumstances following the President's death. If this doesn't convince you that psychological stress can alter your neurophysiology profoundly, nothing else will.

The upshot of all of this: it is clear that we need a better understanding of eyewitness memory, not solely in isolation but also *in context*. As we've already seen, there has been an enormous amount of research attention directed toward eyewitness memory, especially the identification of suspects *(e.g., Sporer, Malpass, & Koehnken, 1996)*. Sufficient research has been conducted that a relatively general consensus has emerged among experts in the field in all of the areas discussed above *(Kassin, Tubb, Hosch, & Memon, 2001)*. So far, we've also seen the utility of the Gestalt/Feature-Intensive Processing theoretical formulation *(G/FI; Sharps & Nunes, 2002; Sharps, 2003)* in the area of eyewitness memory. To review briefly, this formulation shows how memory works along a single continuum, from relatively "gestalt" processing, which is quick but not amenable to detail analysis, to "feature-intensive" processing, which is slower but more detail oriented. Witnesses usually encode the original memory in a "gestalt" manner, with little actual attention to the details important for a correct identification. However, especially under circumstances in which others (e.g., attorneys and law enforcement officers) are directing and framing witnesses' analyses of their own memories, the processing becomes more "feature-intensive," and a relatively slow and meticulous analysis of elements of the original representation is made by any given witness.

The problem is that the original gestalt representation formed by that witness was likely to incorporate few of the details needed for FI analysis. As Bartlett originally demonstrated, and as our experiments have affirmed, such details may be readily and unconsciously fabricated from vague, gestalt impressions or from later information.

Research Traditions

Most of the research on eyewitness memory has been conducted within two broad traditions. In the first, simple eyewitness phenomena, such as face identification, have been examined under beautifully controlled laboratory conditions. The advantages of this approach lie in the control and precision that are possible under these conditions. The disadvantage is that you really don't know what would happen if you put the same phenomena in real-world context.

In the second type of approach to eyewitness identification, the experimenter generally places a group of people in some social or educational setting. Somebody then carrying a gun, or possibly wearing a bear suit, comes running into the crowded environment and does something evil. The experimenter then asks everybody what they saw.

This type of experiment tells you a lot about context, and it frequently has a greater degree of "ecological validity," direct application to the real world, than does the more typically arid laboratory experimental framework. The disadvantage of this more "naturalistic" approach, though, is that experimental precision and control go out the window. This kind of research, making use of live (or video) simulations of crime events, or even of field studies to the degree possible, may be a massive improvement in terms of ecological validity;

but this type of study is of necessity less controlled *(Morgan et al., 2004)*, and is therefore substantially harder to interpret.

POLICE COLLABORATION AND NEW EXPERIMENTS

My students and I wished to get around the disadvantages of these disparate approaches by borrowing from the best characteristics of both. We conducted a systematic series of studies, using realistically created, ecologically valid scenes, in which you could evaluate one thing at a time in context with strong experimental control over a series of related studies. We used crime contexts derived from modern police training. These contexts, or scenarios, were developed with the advice and assistance of senior police SWAT and field training officers, people who know what goes on in the street and who can advise a civilian investigator, like the author, when he tries to put in something stupid.

This is important, and I wish to emphasize this point. We absolutely need research collaboration between research psychologists and law enforcement experts. Police officers know the world of law enforcement, and experimental psychologists know how to design experiments. Neither group knows how to do the other group's job. This is one of the reasons why I, the author, try to do all of this research in collaboration with police experts. Experimental psychologists, including the author, are not cops; we don't know what cops know. Cops, on the other hand, have not spent years studying experimental design, statistics, and the other arcane skills involved in setting up research that will actually and unambiguously *tell us what we need to know*. There is only one way, in the author's opinion, for the study of eyewitness phenomena and other aspects of police and forensic cognitive psychology to proceed constructively. This is to seek active, mutual collaboration in these research projects between law enforcement experts and experts in experimental psychology. Psychological research in forensic and law enforcement contexts, again in the opinion of the author, *absolutely requires collaboration with police experts*. We're weakest alone; we're strongest together.

Anyway, my students and I began this series of studies to help bridge the gap between the two major research traditions in the field, the hyper-controlled approaches and the less-controlled naturalistic approaches. Also, because most previous research has been mainly concerned with memory for persons, we wanted to address memory for important inanimate elements of crime scenes as well, also in context, but with the greatest degree of experimental precision possible *(Sharps, Hess, Casner, Ranes, & Jones, 2007)*.

We used high-quality digital photographs of ecologically valid crime scenes. These, again, were developed in consultation with expert police officers highly experienced in tactical realities and in the kinds of situations encountered by witnesses in the real world. The scenes employed depicted a potentially violent crime scene, in which a male or female perpetrator appeared, armed with a Beretta handgun. The scene was either a "simple" one, with few distracting objects, or "complex," including a "victim" threatened by the armed suspect as well as typical street clutter.

We also included peripheral sources of hazard in the complex scenes. An "explicit" explosive device (a disarmed surplus hand grenade) and a potential "implicit" explosive device (an army ammunition box that might or might not have contained explosives, but that was clearly out of place in the street scene and that was placed next to the hand grenade) were included and placed on the ground near the perpetrator. The reason for this inclusion was straightforward: such weapons and ambush tactics have become increasingly important in real-world criminal and terrorist operations and may very well be deployed by perpetrators in any given scene to which police have to respond *(Gelles, 2006)*. (We'll address issues of bomb detection in Chapter 11 below.)

For the sake of control in the case of weapon identification, in one set of conditions, the Beretta was replaced by a power screwdriver, which the "perpetrator" might have been pointing or waving around in an argument with the "victim." The major importance of this manipulation will be addressed in the chapter that follows, in which we consider the *interpretation* of what is perceived and remembered.

The conditions for all scenes involved excellent lighting (strong sunlight), extended exposure time, and relative comfort; the witnesses were seated and facing a movie screen on which the scenes were projected. There was no occultation of important elements of the scene and, of course, unlike much of the real world, there was no danger.

VALIDATING RESEARCH FOR THE REAL WORLD

So how are these movie-theater, you-could-be-eating-popcorn conditions "ecologically valid"? The validity lies in the use of the complex, real-world scenarios; but as for these idealized conditions, their selection was simple. In an actual crime situation, evolving rapidly in uncertain lighting and with the potential occultation of important elements of the scene, performance will typically be worse than what we obtained given the known dynamics of human visual cognition *(e.g., Narby, Cutler, & Penrod, 1996; Spoehr & Lehmkule, 1982)*. In other words, whatever we found, it would not be as bad as what happens in the field; and once again, what we found was bad enough.

Nearly two hundred college students participated in this work. People often question whether college students form a good sample for research, but in this case we were not concerned. These were first-year students at a university in which freshman attrition rates are relatively high; intellectually, this group was pretty similar to the local urban population. These students also formed a pretty good sample, in terms of demographics, personal histories, and diversity, of the general population. The exception was that these college-aged individuals were of course generally young and in good health, and a vision test showed that they had good eyesight.

As with the experimental conditions, the use of this healthy, eagle-eyed population meant that, in general, real-world results would be even worse. In keeping with this philosophy, we allowed all participants to see the scene for a full five seconds. Law enforcement experts are generally in agreement that a firearm assault situation, such as that depicted in our scenarios, may be violently concluded in less than a second *(e.g., Montejano, 2004; Moore, 2006; Tietjen, 2005)*. Therefore, our witnesses had substantially more viewing and processing time than would typically be the case in the field.

Again with the aid of senior, experienced police field-training officers, we constructed a realistic police interview, questioning the witnesses on a variety of physical and interpretive characteristics of the scenes and of the individuals shown in them. The results of this were subjected to standardized scoring *(Sharps et al., 2007a for details)*, in order to get an idea of what people actually remember about perpetrator and scene when information is requested in the format of a typical police interview.

In addition to this experiment, a second study of nearly fifty "witnesses" addressed the six-pack line-up identification of the perpetrator under these standardized conditions. Witnesses saw the given scene for five seconds. This was followed ten to fifteen minutes later by a six-pack photographic lineup recognition test, administered according to Department of Justice (DOJ) guidelines *(1999)*. A simultaneous lineup procedure was chosen, as this remains the technique most typically used by real-world law-enforcement agencies *(Wogalter, Malpass, & Burger, 1993; see also Mecklenburg, 2008, 2013)*, despite research that generally favors sequential lineups, as discussed above (e.g., MacLin, Zimmerman, & Malpass, 2005; Wells, 1993; Wogalther, Malpass, & McQuiston, 2004; see also Mecklenburg, 2008, 2013).

So what happened? What did we find?

Memory for Persons

Well, some of what we learned was not too bad. The average accuracy for witness recall of perpetrator clothing was 80.3%. Scene complexity made only a modest difference here: more complex scenes resulted in only 3.3% less accuracy than did simple (visually sparse) scenes. People were 12.6% better at describing a female perpetrator's clothing than that of a male; the atypicality of a female perpetrator of a gun assault probably resulted in more witness attention to her as an individual, resulting in the better description of her clothes. On average, women were 7.46% better than men at describing perpetrator clothing, although this must be interpreted with extreme caution as we had far more women than men in the study *(Sharps et al., 2007a)*.

On average, memory for the physical appearance of the perpetrator (and remember, this was under ideal conditions) was not so good: the level of accuracy was only 70.6%, obviously leaving a bit of room for reasonable doubt. Something really peculiar was also observed here. In addition to the questions on weight, height, and age, which required a verbal description of each, we also elicited *numerical* estimates of each of these variables. The result was almost incredible: *there was no identifiable correlation between numerical and verbal estimates.* In other words, a descriptive term like "fat" or "thin" or "short," on average, had no identifiable relationship with the same witness's numerical estimates of the same quantities.

Neither numerical nor descriptive reports, at least within the research framework that we used, were identifiably superior to the other. However, it is clear that whether an officer at the scene requests qualitative or quantitative estimates of a suspect's height and build matters a great deal. The wrong type of estimate, for a given witness, may elicit completely inaccurate results, results that might prove to be completely at odds with that witness's memories if those memories were to be elicited in another way. This finding obviously requires more research attention, but for the moment it highlights the fact that eyewitness memory, far from being a veridical record of what happened, is constructed in terms of whatever information the witness has at the point of elicitation, including the types of questions. The investigator is not only dealing with memory, but also with interpretation; again, this will be addressed more fully in the next chapter.

LINEUP PERFORMANCE

Fifty witnesses were also exposed to a typical police lineup, only ten or fifteen minutes after viewing the crime scene. Forty-seven of them provided usable data. Once again, the crime scene showed the male perpetrator, armed with the Beretta, under ideal conditions. This meant that the only "visual transformation" the witnesses needed to deal with was that the perpetrator was seen in profile in the crime scene, and the perpetrator and foils were of course depicted full-face in the lineup. There doesn't seem to be any current data on this subject, but in a typical real-world crime situation, witnesses do not have the opportunity to gaze on a suspect, full face. Actual perpetrators are typically in motion, and their faces are frequently hidden by a partial disguise such as a hood, cap, or even a stocking mask; conditions are seldom optimal *(e.g., Narby, Cutler, & Penrod, 1996)*. Thus the simple transformation from profile to full-face in static images, under ideal conditions, as was the case in our study, would seem to pose little challenge compared to the use of lineups in real-world forensic practice *(e.g., DOJ, 1999)*.

However, the results led to little cause for optimism. Out of 47 respondents, only 5 were able to identify the perpetrator correctly. Photo position in the lineup made a slight difference, regardless of correct or incorrect identification: position 5 (center, bottom row) was slightly more likely to yield a correct identification than position 3 (more visually peripheral). The context also made a difference. Four of the correct IDs came from the simple condition; only one individual in the complex (and therefore somewhat more realistic) condition made the identification correctly. However, although context and lineup photo positions did make a difference to overall accuracy, the end result was that only about 10% of witnesses were correct in their identifications. Again, accuracy is probably likely to be lower in more complex, and hence more realistic, visual situations.

This may at first seem contrary to other findings in the broad field of recognition memory. For example, recognition memory has sometimes been shown to be quite good for detailed pictures *(e.g., Nelson, Metzler, & Reed, 1974)*, although performance declines with shorter exposure times *(e.g., Loftus & Bell, 1975)*. However, we should note that these studies did not necessarily map well onto lineup identification of an individual. For example, the Nelson et al. experiments addressed memory for an entire picture, presented in entirety at encoding and retrieval, rather than the more minimalist items typical of lineup usage. It is also true that the dynamic conditions of a real-world crime scene may result in *more* opportunities to see a suspect's face from different angles than was the case here, possibly improving performance sometimes under some conditions. Different levels of foil similarity in a given lineup, and other conditions of, for example, a simulated crime scene might also be expected to play a role in raising or even lowering this average. However, at least within our research framework, these results stand: with regard to a single visual change in the aspect of the individual to be identified, and under ideal conditions, lineup performance was frankly lousy; only one person in ten was likely to make the identification correctly. At the very least, this finding shows that lineup results, even when obtained from properly conducted police lineups *(DOJ, 1999)* must be viewed with extreme caution.

MEMORY FOR WEAPONS AND FOR PERIPHERAL SOURCES OF HAZARD

A full report of these findings is available in Sharps et al. *(2007a)*. But, to summarize here, average performance across conditions was again unimpressive; the average accuracy was 68.9% for weapon memory. Contextual factors were important for witness abilities to identify the gun in the hands of the perpetrator, as opposed to the power screwdriver used as a control. The simple scene yielded better performance than the complex scene by 4.12%, the male perpetrator resulted in better performance than the female by 22.28%, and the gun condition was massively superior to the screwdriver condition by 211%.

This result warranted further scrutiny. It turned out that in the screwdriver condition, out of 103 respondents, 92 were in error, suggesting that the screwdriver was in fact a firearm. Only 5 were uncertain as to what they saw, and a mere 6 correctly identified the power tool. Once again, this result was obtained under ideal conditions of lighting and exposure, and with an exposure period several times longer than what typically occurs in real-world criminal activity. Even so, most witnesses identified the power screwdriver, with its little red end-cap, bit holder, and all, as a gun. This finding may prove useful in explaining the cases in which civilians and police mistake an innocuous object for a gun; rather than having anything to do with the integrity of the officer or witness, this kind of error may very well derive from the characteristics of the human nervous system itself *(Sharps et al., 2003)*. This is an error of *interpretation*, and the processes involved will be discussed in the following chapter.

The reader will not be surprised to learn that identification of peripheral sources of hazard, the mock-up explosive devices planted in the scene, was also poor. As mentioned above, we placed a deactivated pineapple hand grenade in plain sight on the ground between the perpetrator and the victim. This was planted next to a metal war-surplus ammunition box that, whether it contained enough explosives to send the entire scene to Mars or not, definitely did not belong in the context.

Only a single respondent, out of 94 in the relevant conditions, saw and reported the hand grenade, even though it was in plain sight and viewed under the superior observation conditions described above. Not a single individual identified the ammunition box as a potential source of hazard, even though it was placed within a foot of the hand grenade and was clearly an anomalous object in this "normal" street crime scene.

What does this tell us? Taken together, our results with reference to Berettas, screwdrivers, grenades, and ammo cans strongly suggest that the most important results here stemmed from *violation of expectations (Sharps et al., 2007a)*. In an argumentative or potentially violent confrontation, we expect to see a gun, not a power screwdriver; and so our minds manufacture a gun when all our eyes see is a power tool. We don't expect to see a grenade on the street at all, and although our eyes must register it (and ongoing eye-tracking research in our lab has proven that the eyes of a given witness generally do track over and encounter this weapon; *Hess & Sharps, 2006*), our brain somehow filters it out. This is also the case for the ammo can; the mind would have to infer the presence of explosives in such an object, requiring a depth of processing that at the moment is simply not available to us; and so these objects, placed in plain sight in good lighting, are passed over as if they did not exist at all. This is obviously a problem of epic proportion in IED-rich environments such as those currently encountered by military forces overseas, and is likely to become increasingly important in domestic law enforcement *(see Gelles, 2006, and Chapter 11 below)*.

Thus, ultimately, a full understanding of the dynamics underlying the relative poverty of eyewitness performance necessitates an understanding of *interpretation*, as well as of perception and of raw memory. As we will explore in subsequent chapters, interpretation is also a crucial element, perhaps *the* crucial element, in the success or failure of law enforcement command decisions. For these reasons, we will consider the nature of interpretation in the next chapter.

Chapter 5
THE INTERPRETATION OF VISUAL INPUT — OR, NEVER AIM YOUR POWER DRILL AT THE SWAT TEAM

A friend of the author's, an experienced patrol and training officer, once responded to a call in which a potentially armed suspect in a violent crime had taken refuge in a back bedroom of an apartment. It was one of those scary ones; the apartment was dark, the layout unfamiliar, and the officer, weapon in hand, had to "clear" room after room. He was without backup, but the circumstances dictated the need for an immediate apprehension, so he courageously went in on his own. At the darkened door of the bedroom, he heard the muffled movements of the suspect across the room, behind the bed; good cover. Seasoned officers can imagine my friend's psychological state in a direct way that the author cannot; heart pounding, sweat-and-cold at the same time, all the personal hell of Chapter 2 coursing through his body as he entered the room, weapon ready, to confront an armed bad guy in the dark. Would he go home that night? *Who knew?*

And who knew what was going through the suspect's mind? The subjects of arrests are often abusive to the arresting officers, making a great show of bravado. However (although many police officers I have met are unaware of this), bad guys are frequently afraid of the cops; and in a weird way, they may even respect them as well. Gang affiliation and similar experience can make an enormous difference here; of course; but the fact remains that the average non-affiliated felon is typically going to be quite uncomfortable when the police come for him.

Here's the bad guy, hiding in a dark apartment. He knows he did something wrong. Really, really wrong—wrong enough to place him outside society, and for the cops to come after him. He knows he has no training for combat; if he's had any, it was probably naïve at best and wholly nonsensical at worst. He may have a gun, he may not, but he probably has not spent the necessary hours honing the perishable skills to use it effectively in combat. And now he's up against the blue storm. The officer coming after him is a serious professional, with training the bad guy doesn't understand and may not be able to imagine. The bad guy has at least a vague, gestalt awareness that the officer is probably practiced and expert, wearing body armor and carrying all kinds of serious bad-ass artillery. If the officer is a K-9 specialist, the bad guy may be confronted by what he perceives as a highly crazy, violent wolf-dog who may *eat* him, for God's sake. And the ultimate back-up is the SWAT team, good Lord, with submachine guns and flash-bangs and *helicopters* and *snipers* who can shoot your eye out at *five hundred yards* and...

The bad guy sweats. He freaks. He can't think. He is Chapter 2 incarnate. A weird mosaic of fear, aggression, hate, more fear, and a heart rate that would kill a rat wash over him; and finally, in the grip of a lunatic state that defies description, he acts.

Frequently, he acts crazy.

In my friend's case, the bad guy reared up over the bed and aimed his shoe right between the patrol officer's eyes.

That's right, I said his shoe.

God knows what was going through this guy's fear-ravaged cortex, but he aimed a size-10 leather shoe at the officer. The officer saw the metallic glint of the shoe polish in the minimal light from a street-lit window; saw what must have been the slide and barrel of a blue-black automatic aiming at his head and—

He didn't fire.

The officer was squeezing the trigger and grip of his weapon at the moment the shoe made its dramatic and menacing appearance, but "something told him" that he shouldn't shoot, and so he didn't fire. He proceeded to arrest the armed suspect, having deprived him, legally, of the shoe in question. He personally attributes his restraint, literally, to divine intervention. Who knows, he may be right.

But he didn't fire.

Can you imagine what would have ensued if he had? The media headlines would have been epic: *Rogue Officer Kills Unarmed Man. Gun-Happy Cop Murders Unarmed Citizen. Bereaved Relatives Extol Massacred Victim's Virtues, Demand Vengeance. And Also Money.* Yet the fact remains that the suspect was there, in the dark, aiming a long black shiny object at the officer. If the officer had fired, he would clearly have committed a tragic error. But would that officer really have been *morally* at fault, under these circumstances, for failing to recognize the insanely unlikely fact that the guy was threatening him with a size 10 wing-tip?

Exactly why someone would aim a shoe at an armed officer must remain a subject for conjecture; but the fact remains that people aim all kinds of crazy things at the police. To the author's knowledge, these things, to date, have included a shoe; a cordless power drill (in Tacoma, Washington; *Associated Press, 2007)*; a toy rocket; a sprinkler nozzle; and realistically-designed pellet guns almost impossible to tell from the real thing.

But all this is practically nothing compared to the Diallo case.

Chapter 5

The Death of Amadou Diallo

Amadou Diallo was shot and killed in 1999 by New York City police officers *(e.g., Gladwell, 2005)*. Diallo's behavior was not exactly that of an innocent man. When he was challenged by plainclothes police, he ran. He did not respond to police commands, although this may have been due to his tendency to stutter, which could have prevented a proper verbal response, and perhaps to language issues. As Diallo ran, he came to a door and was apparently in the act of trying to open it and flee through it when the police caught up with him. He became increasingly agitated. At that point, he began to rummage in his pockets while turning his body away from the officers. Ultimately he drew a dark, squarish object from a pocket, which he raised in the direction of the officers. His grip on the object and the angle of view apparently presented only the dark, rectangular top of the object to the officers. At least one plainclothesman perceived the top of this object as the slide of a semi-automatic pistol. The officers fired, killing him. The object, as has been extensively publicized ever since *(e.g., Lee, 2005)*, turned out to be a wallet.

Ultimately, this incident was a tragedy on all sides. Probably because of fear and emotional arousal, and perhaps exacerbated by communication problems, Diallo ran from police and made motions similar to those that a real suspect would make in grasping and drawing a weapon. The whole incident evolved very quickly and under horrendous viewing conditions from the visual perspectives of the officers. However, public perception of this tragedy was not exactly surprising. The officers were Caucasian. Amadou Diallo was not. Rather than considering the contextual and psychological influences involved, the shooting was widely attributed to racism *(see Gladwell, 2005*, for extended discussion).

One wonders what the officers could have done differently. How does one ascertain, in the few brief moments of a foot chase, that a non-communicative person has limited English abilities, or that he tends to stutter? How do you pinpoint the source of his agitation? When you see the top of what appears to be a .45 in his hand, and he swings it toward you, how do you crank up your vision to the point that you see blue-black leather instead of blue steel? Assuming that personally you have the eyes of Superman and can see an X-ray outline of the wallet in his hand, how would you communicate this quickly enough to fellow officers, under tactical circumstances, in time to prevent what in their minds was proper defensive fire? Gladwell *(2005)* subtitles his account of the shooting *"The Delicate Art of Mind Reading,"* and I concur; mind reading is in fact what the officers would have had to do to prevent the tragic outcome. Because real, reliable mind reading is, as far as we know, simply impossible, this outcome seems to have been practically foreordained.

Yet none of these considerations really seemed to matter to much of the public or the media. A similar, less-publicized situation was seen in the pellet-gun robbery mentioned above; there were a number of *ad hominem* attacks, in local media and "on the street," on the officers involved. It seemed incomprehensible, to many people, how officers could possibly mistake a pellet gun, built specifically to resemble a real firearm, for the same type of real firearm in the dark.

Such incidents are not uncommon and attributions of racism, malice, and various integrity violations generally result. Various media and web-based sources publish what amount to databases on police shootings, including those made under circumstances such as those cited above *(e.g., Lee, 2005)*. The Diallo case even inspired a famous singer to write and perform a popular song *(Gladwell, 2005)*. Yet these allegations frequently cannot be substantiated at any level; while, as Gladwell points out, the Diallo case was not "exactly exemplary police work" *(pg. 197)*, "there was no evidence that the four officers in the Diallo case were bad people, or racists, or out to get Diallo" *(pg. 197)*.

This type of effect, in which officers mistake a nonlethal object for a firearm, is not common in terms of occurrence per police contact, but the effect does exist and has been extensively reported. As noted above, an individual in Tacoma, Washington, was shot and killed by police officers when he pointed a "small black cordless drill" directly at the officers after threatening to shoot them *(Associated Press, 2007)*. In Central California alone, we have had the aforementioned toy rocket, some pellet guns, and the Incredible Shoe Effect. More recently, a Northern California teenager, wielding a very realistic AK-47 which turned out to be a replica, was shot by officers who saw it, very simply, as a real AK. Many other examples exist; there are, quite simply, a lot of cases in which various relatively innocuous objects have been mistaken for firearms.

We must be absolutely clear here, and I wish to quote directly from a previous article in the service of this clarity: *"These considerations certainly do not excuse or justify unwarranted use of force; although it is certainly true that inappropriate or excessive use of force, including deadly force, does occur (e.g., Grossman, 1996), no sane person would condone or excuse the shooting of innocent persons under any circumstances.* However, especially in view of the enormous professional, personal, and legal costs that frequently face officers in situations of genuine or alleged wrongful death, it seems unlikely that the most parsimonious explanation of the majority of these errors is lack of integrity on the part of the police. It seems likely that these errors more typically result from fundamental characteristics of the human nervous system, placed under heightened stress" *(Sharps & Hess, 2008, pg. 57).*

The Range of Interpretation

So, in general, it appears that these tragic types of mistakes are errors typical of the human nervous system, and that they are errors of *interpretation*; they occur when perceptual input is changed erroneously in the mind itself. The shoe or the wallet is interpreted as a gun. The replica AK becomes the real thing. All eyewitness errors, including those discussed in the previous chapters, involve interpretation in its broadest sense: I see a tall man, and reckon his height as over six feet, using my knowledge of size and measurement. I *interpret* his height. My eyes perceive yellow in the hair of my assailant; I register this intellectually and, by comparison with other possible hair colors, as blonde. I *interpret* the hair color. I see an AK-47. I fire.

It is obvious that the same sorts of intellectual processes are involved in the types of innocuous object/gun mistakes seen here. The square top of the wallet is compared, very quickly and under horrible viewing conditions, with other reasonably likely prospects in the mind of the officer, and what pops up in the officer's brain is the slide of an autoloading pistol. A toy rocket is brandished and the tubular structure of its lower stage calls up an interpretation as a gun barrel. A realistic replica AK-47 is seen as, well, an AK-47.

Yet there is more going on. The interpretation of light-brown-hair-to-blonde is a very direct one, with very little mental mediation involved. The interpretation of a wallet-top as a gun slide requires more *cognitive mediation*—you have to know what a slide looks like, and have some experience of how weapons are typically held for this interpretation to work. Clearly even more intellectual mediation, of some sort, was involved in the patrol officer's decision not to fire when confronted by the Incredible Shoe-Wielding Bandit described above.

Mediation is key. One of the most important, and annoying, things that I incessantly repeat to my students is that *there is continuity in the nervous system*. The brain has modular qualities, of course, as we saw briefly in Chapter 1. Different parts of the brain do different things. The back of the brain does your basic seeing, the temporal lobes do your hearing for you, and so on. Yet when it comes to interpreting what you see and hear, these boundaries are by no means as well established as many people think. In an early paper on experiments in my lab *(Sharps & Price, 1992)*, for example, we were able to demonstrate a substantial sharing of processing resources between vision and hearing. This means that, at a representational level, the most parsimonious explanation is that these types of perception combine in an emergent manner. Vision and hearing must to a degree coalesce rather than remaining completely segregated, and that coalescence depends in large part on local demand characteristics, on what the brain is using that coalescent representation *for (Sharps, 2003)*. The brain contains billions of nerve cells, tens of billions in the cortex alone; and each of these cells makes, on average, thousands of connections. The brain is an astoundingly interconnected system, and the same circuits are frequently involved in a whole variety of different activities. The upshot is that there is quite a lot of *processual continuity*, things held in common, among the various activities subsumed under the general heading of "interpretation."

In other words, there is continuity in the processes involved in memory and cognition. These processes are stitched together and integrated in all sorts of ways. The errors that people make therefore derive from a spectrum of inputs and from their interpretations of those inputs. This, in turn, means that those errors derive from a *range* of interpretations rather than from different, discrete processes. There are simple interpretations, such as "yellow hair equals blonde." There are more complex, mediated interpretations, such as "specific features of a wallet in the dark, in an officer's expert opinion and tempered by his/her experience, equal the slide of a 1911 .45 ACP." Finally, there are insanely complicated interpretations, such as "this guy's overall pattern of shouting, hyperactive, and aggressive behavior, in this context and on this street, together with his gang tattoos and the fact that he's wearing a heavy coat in the summer, and the fact that he is currently reaching into that coat and pulling out a large tubular object—well, all of this input, taken together, equals a serious bad guy on crank who is about to open up on my cruiser with some genuinely ugly artillery."

There is a *range* of interpretation for any given stimulus input, simple or complex; and it should be reasonably obvious that the more complex the situation to be processed, the more complex will be the cognitive mediation involved. Therefore, the more complex the situation, the greater will be the potential for errors and for *compound errors*, based on the use of earlier errors as cognitive input. As we will see in subsequent chapters, the same processes, and the same proclivities for error, also extend to the much more cognitively mediated domains of command decision and tactical planning.

So, from the standpoint of learning what we can about the cognitive processes involved in the at-risk world of law enforcement, we want to learn everything we can about interpretation in that context. We need to learn the ways in which the external stimuli we perceive are interpreted and converted into the internal information on which we take action, action that may have the most serious of consequences.

What is the best way to do this? Well, in experimental psychology, one of the most useful ways to address a cognitive phenomenon is essentially to test it to destruction. In other words, to find out what happens when the processes involved *fail*. What kinds of errors do we make, and under what circumstances?

We will return in this chapter to experiments that directly address innocuous-object-to-gun mistakes, the kinds of things that happen when a wallet or a shoe are interpreted as guns. Before we do this, however, it is necessary to understand more about the nature of integration, and the ways in which faulty integration can produce mistakes, some of them fatal. We can see this most clearly, once again, in the systematic world of eyewitness research. We will therefore consider work, deriving from the standard contexts discussed in Chapter 4, on the specific question of *what happens when eyewitnesses fail:* The question, in effect, of failures of interpretation.

A Taxonomy of Interpretive Error

At first glance, the reader may fairly question the relevancy of eyewitness issues here. What does the civilian eyewitness to a crime have to do with the police officer who mistakes a wallet for a firearm?

The answer lies in my repeated mantra to my students: *There is continuity in the nervous system.* Eyewitnesses are people who see a criminal act, but who typically do not act to prevent it or to engage the criminals involved. Police officers are people who see a criminal act, but typically do act to prevent it or to engage the perpetrators. Police action and engagement, of course, are based on officers' interpretations of their perceptual input, just as witness accounts are based upon theirs. So, in examining witness errors, we are doing something more than simply providing a court-friendly account of how eyewitnesses screw up. We are examining the degree to which the human nervous system, in general, is subject to errors of interpretation.

The participants in this study *(Sharps, Janigian, Hess, & Hayward, 2009)* were 215 college-aged adults. The scenes used in this study were the same as those used in our previous work and described above *(e.g., Sharps et al., 2007a; Sharps & Hess, 2008)*, the intent of which has been to provide a "bridge" between highly controlled experimental studies and more ecologically valid, but less controlled, efforts in simulated crime scenes. Again, these photographs depicted a potentially violent crime scene, in which a male or female suspect was shown armed with a Beretta handgun, or was shown unarmed and holding a power screwdriver. The male and female suspects were both Caucasian, although there was agreement that it was harder to determine the race of the male, a dark-haired man with relatively dark skin, than that of the female, a blonde with a relatively light complexion. This fact, as will be seen below, is important for the question of interpretation.

As in the previous research discussed in Chapter 4, each witness viewed only one scene (with a male or female perpetrator, either armed or holding the screwdriver), and we used the long 5-second observation interval from our previous studies. However, in this experiment we also used a 2-second and a "tactical speed" 0.5 second interval, as well. As noted above, law enforcement experts are generally in agreement that a firearm assault situation, such as that depicted in our scenarios, may be violently concluded in less than a second *(e.g., Montejano, 2004; Moore, 2006; Tietjen, 2005)*. So, we wanted to understand how shorter encoding times, more realistic in terms of the conditions typically surrounding real-world crimes, influenced reconfiguration, interpretation, and interpretive errors.

A bit more detail on the scenes themselves might be helpful. The suspect or perpetrator stood in a gravel driveway, with a shed, a house wall, and some shrubbery in the background, and some garbage cans, a ladder, and other "street clutter" in the foreground and surrounding the action. In the gun condition (as opposed to the screwdriver condition), the weapon (unloaded, with all studies conducted under police supervision) was "aimed" at a female "victim" in her early twenties. The viewing conditions for all scenes involved uniformly excellent lighting (strong sunlight).

To elicit witness accounts, we made use of the same police interview procedure used in our previous work *(Sharps et al., 2007a)* and discussed in Chapter 4. The scoring system for the errors and error types was relatively straightforward and is presented in full in the authors' article on this research *(Sharps, Janigian, Hess, & Hayward, 2009)*.

The ultimate result of this work will not surprise readers who've come this far: People made a lot of mistakes. Interestingly, whether witnesses saw the gun or the screwdriver made no significant difference; this may seem surprising at first glance, but would not be surprising at all *if most people mistook the screwdriver for a gun*. We'll deal with this issue later in this chapter.

For the present, the mistakes in question all fell within five overall types, which were as follows:

1. Errors in clothing or physical attributes of perpetrator — 188%
2. Errors in environmental detail — 91%
3. Errors in perpetrator race or sex — 23%
4. Weapon errors — 57%
5. Inferential, extrapolative, or imaginative errors — 124.5%

Percentages over 100% indicate that, on average, each witness made more than one mistake in the given category of error. We'll deal with these error types one at a time.

Errors in Clothing or Physical Attributes of Perpetrator

Witnesses focused heavily on the perpetrator, and not surprisingly made a lot of errors in what they saw. People wear several items of clothing, but they only have one body, and so witnesses tended to make two to three times more mistakes in clothing than in physique. It was also seen that people tended to make more erroneous *changes* in clothing and physique than they did errors in the *addition* of details, which would have required more depth of processing and therefore would have been more mentally effortful. This is consistent with previous work *(e.g., Meissner, Sporer, & Schooler, 2007; Sharps et al., 2007a)* demonstrating that these are highly typical and prevalent errors.

Errors in clothing and physical characteristics, though common, involve very limited interpretation. They are more of the "yellow hair equals blonde" variety of error, and are of greater interest in what they say about the inaccuracy of eyewitness memory in general than in what they can tell us about interpretation. However, even here we see some influence of context on interpretation. We found that witnesses made more errors with reference to *changes* in the physical characteristics of the female assailant (for example, changes in hair color or erroneous estimates of age), but *added* more erroneous features (e.g., beard, hairstyle, or lack thereof) to the male. (Direct quotes: "Male had a mustach" *(sic)*; "Has shaved head and facial hair.") Men's faces are more amenable to change than women's, simply because of the difference in proclivity to grow facial hair. As a result, even at these basic perceptual levels, witness expectations about what does or does not characterize a bad guy, in terms of facial and cranial hair, had the opportunity to work on their memory and to develop interpretive errors.

Errors in Environmental Detail

Similar effects were seen in descriptions of environmental detail. There was one major reversal; here, people tended to *add* details more than they *changed* details. This is a case in which the type of stimulus item perceived by a given witness trumps the power of depth of processing. With environmental features, it is simply easier to add than to change details. Let's face it, how do you change the details on a bush? From leafy to extra leafy? So, it was the additions that tended to be seen more. Also, and not surprisingly, people tended to add small things rather than large things to their memories; most people did not add an extra building or two, but many added a small bush or something similar.

At some level this doesn't seem too bad: okay, the witness added a bush, but it was just a little one. However, at another level, this ought to astonish us. Witnesses *added whole structures and objects to their memories*, structures and objects that in fact didn't exist at all. This is even more bizarre if you think about it from the following standpoint. If you see something that isn't there, it's typically classified as a visual hallucination. This is a symptom typical of the most severe types of psychological disorders, the psychoses, or of certain types of brain pathology. However, as far as we know, none of our witnesses were suffering from any of these extreme types of pathology. Therefore, it appears that when something that isn't there at all shows up in your *memory*, as opposed to your *perception*, it isn't evidence of a severe illness at all; it's standard operating procedure. Nonexistent bush? No problem. Shove it in there. No shaved head or gang tattoos? Oh, why not—let's stick 'em right in there with the memory, with the things that actually were observed, and at the same level of belief on the part of the witness. This is the fantastic level of erroneous interpretation of which memory is capable, even with reference to relatively concrete things like bushes and structures.

These findings have important practical applications. Consider a hypothetical case, in which an officer recalls standing in the front yard of a house, next to a tree, just prior to a violent arrest. The officer's report is contradicted by credible witnesses: *No, Officer X was standing in the driveway, nowhere near the tree. Maybe he was near the mailbox*, say the witnesses.

If the locations of officers and suspects, at any given point in the developing arrest situation, should later become an issue in the investigation or trial of the incident, this type of discrepancy may literally result in a charge of integrity violation against the officer. In fact, he or she may have done nothing wrong at all; the officer may

Chapter 5   143

simply be a victim of the human predilection for misremembering environmental features *(e.g., Cutler, Penrod, & Martens, 1987; Loftus & Bell, 1975; Wells, Memon, & Penrod, 2006)*. This type of error, so simple in its inception, may prove devastating to officers involved in the complex and shifting physical world of actual police work.

But it gets worse.

ERRORS IN PERPETRATOR RACE OR SEX

About 9% of respondents erred in the race of the perpetrator, and, as you would expect, this was more likely (3.5 times more likely) to happen with our dark-skinned dark-haired male than our light-skinned blonde female. This clearly shows the effect of interpretation; you work with what you've got, and a pale blonde limits your choices in a way that a dark brunette does not. No major surprises here.

Okay, there was one surprise. Counterintuitively, errors in race were more likely to be made with longer (5 seconds) rather than with shorter (2 or 0.5 second) exposure times.

How is this possible? Shouldn't errors be more typical when witnesses have less time to encode the relevant information?

Only if you discount interpretation. We have already seen that our male perpetrator was relatively racially ambiguous. Witnesses who viewed him for a short period had less time to encode the ambiguous features that resulted in misinterpretation. Witnesses with longer exposures had more time to consider his features in context and to allow their interpretations to carry them away into erroneous speculative realms.

This result seems to make no sense in terms of raw perception. However, when you consider *interpretation* as well as *perception*, the pattern of results falls into a recognizable and unsurprising order. Interpretation in this case had a chance to work on erroneous attributions; and the longer that opportunity went on, the worse the misinterpretation became. So, we can readily explain these results with regard to racial misidentification.

However, what happened with the sex of the perpetrator, and for that matter with the sex of the victim, frankly blew us away. These results were completely unexpected: 6%, over one in twenty, of our witnesses decided that our female victim was a male, and 8% got the gender of the perpetrator wrong as well.

Across human races, there are a lot of physical similarities and overlaps between the two sexes which might be confused. However, without getting into details, our perpetrators and victims were decidedly, in physical terms, members of their own sexes. Yet somewhere between one in twenty and one in ten of our witnesses apparently couldn't tell whether they were male or female.

Exposure time made a difference, of course. The gender of the perpetrators was more likely to be confused at 0.5 seconds' exposure time than at 2 or at 5 seconds' exposure time. Here interpretation was not so critical; if a witness had enough time to encode the secondary sex characteristics of the perpetrator or victim, the relative lack of ambiguity tended to reduce the need for much interpretation at all, with consequent diminution of errors.

However, as we've already seen, very few violent situations are resolved over the leisurely five seconds of our longest conditions. Most resolve themselves at much shorter intervals, similar to the 2-second and 0.5-second conditions of our study, and at these speeds, with regard to gender, all hell broke loose. Half a second provides very little time for the accurate feature-intensive processing that would result in correct gender identification. Over 90% of witnesses, of course, got the genders right; but nearly 10%, a forensically important proportion of the population, got them wrong.

What happened?

There was no significant difference in erroneous gender assignment between the male and female perpetrator. So why would people decide they had a female perpetrator when they in fact saw a male? Well, the reader will recall that we had a female *victim* in all conditions. Although this may seem incredible, there appears to be no other reasonable, parsimonious explanation: I suggest that witnesses *actually confused the perpetrator with the victim,* especially when processing time was extremely limited. If so, this highlights the crucial role played by interpretation in questions of eyewitness identification. The witnesses who made this error must have been mistaken on the question of whom, male or female, they saw holding the gun. The demonstration of this type of confusion is of obvious importance in arrest, investigation, and court.

When errors in gender went the other way, in cases in which witnesses substituted an imaginary male perpetrator for our female assailant, it seems most likely that the confusion of gender resulted from social expectation.

Statistically, men commit more violent crimes than women, especially with guns, and it seems likely that the expectation that a male, rather than a female, would be more likely to be involved in a violent assault is responsible for the ultimate gestalt representations in which witnesses mistake a female perpetrator for a male. The term "gestalt" is particularly important here: the relatively short encoding times under which these errors occurred would have reduced the feature-intensive analysis of secondary sex characteristics, which in turn would have prevented these errors. (Obviously, in the case of gender, the necessary level of FI processing that would have prevented errors would be substantially less than that required for the prevention of racial errors—the *degree* of FI processing is clearly of importance in resolving the differences in errors of race and sex.)

We cannot be certain that these explanations are correct, although they seem to be the most reasonable and parsimonious ideas at the present time. The end result of all of this, however, is that about a tenth of our witnesses, under ideal viewing conditions, thought they had seen a bad guy instead of a bad gal, and vice versa. Human beings are very conscious, and at a very elemental level, of sex differences and characteristics. Yet these results clearly show that errors of interpretation can disrupt even these very basic, primal perceptions; and if the mind can do this with sex, what could it do with guns? Or power screwdrivers? Or, for that matter, wallets or shoes?

WEAPON ERRORS

Similar effects of exposure time were seen with reference to the tendency to mistake the power screwdriver for a gun. Two-second and half-second exposure times were worse for this type of error than five seconds for obvious reasons: the shorter encoding periods provided less opportunity for accurate FI processing. This was also true for the production of failures to see the gun at all in the appropriate conditions.

Clearly, at the tactical speeds typical of many if not most violent confrontations, witnesses tend to make errors about weapons, or about whether weapons were present at all. In this research framework, those errors were made more than half the time *(57%)*. We will deal with the ramifications of this error type below, in this chapter; but clearly, in cases similar to those of Diallo and other gun/innocuous object mistakes, there is a great deal going on cognitively that, on most occasions, probably has nothing to do with racism or prejudice.

INFERENTIAL, EXTRAPOLATIVE, OR IMAGINATIVE ERRORS

This is the category in which we saw the greatest effect of interpretation. Recall the work of Bartlett, in which experimental subjects reconfigured both visual and verbal memories in the direction of their personal beliefs, in the direction of their knowledge of the world, and in the direction of what they expected to happen. Loftus' results in the realm of eyewitness identification, discussed above, fall into the same category; you may not have seen a barn, but if the nice psychologist tells you there was a barn in the film, your reconfigurative proclivities are happy to manufacture one in your memory, to the satisfaction of all concerned; and, of course, your imaginary barn is a nice shade of imaginary red.

So, when we began this study, we knew that people imagine things in the crime scenes they've observed. However, we had no idea the situation was as bad as it in fact proved to be. The overall incidence of inferential, extrapolative, or imaginative errors *(124.5%)* was high, with each individual, on average, making more than one of this type of error, adding their own special imaginative/hallucinatory twist to the already insanely complex world of criminal investigation. The results seemed incredible, and yet they happened.

We provided no backstory, no information about the crime or the circumstances leading up to it at all. However, when asked *what they remembered* in the scene itself, an amazing 62% of witnesses, on average, dreamed up at least one wholly fictitious idea of how this situation developed or how the perpetrator or victim came to be in these circumstances. These fabrications were typically reasonable, but were still not inherent in what had been seen (typical examples: a holdup, a threat, or an argument. A less typical example: "female with gun appeared to be angry about a housing/rent dispute... the female who had the gun pointed at her maybe evicted the gunholder." There was also a reference to the perpetrator as "the terrorist.") Again, these fabrications and fantasies were reported as factual memories.

About half of the witnesses also provided an account of the emotional state of perpetrator or victim, or of their intent (again, from a brief observation of a photograph, with no other information provided). These stories too were generally reasonable (typically involving anger or fear); but reasonable or not, there was no basis at all for these ideas, reported as remembered facts.

Over 10% offered some account or speculation as to what happened next, *after the scene they had observed had been completed*. In other words, these witnesses made up stories about what the perpetrator or victim did *later,* after the action depicted in the photograph. These stories were reported as veridical memories. These amazing memories of a nonexistent future generally featured the actions of the perpetrator. Granted, many of these were reasonable and at least recognizably speculative (direct quotes: "Hiding, possibly. Long gone, perhaps." "Probably gone from the scene."). However, others featured explicit material apparently based on nothing at all ("she turned and faced him in a threatening manner within 21 feet."). Based on these accounts, it is reasonable to suppose that the majority of respondents who "remembered" a future action had at least an implicit awareness that they were treading into the realm of the speculative. However, it is absolutely clear that some witnesses, thankfully in the minority, did not. They really believed, credibly and confidently, that they were reporting events based in reality.

I saved the best for last. The reader will remember that our witnesses observed a scene in which two total strangers were engaged in some form of hostile interaction. There was no conceivable personal connection to the witnesses at all. Yet two of our witnesses *actually placed themselves in the scene* in some way, reporting these practically hallucinatory personal participations as memories. This result, bizarre as it was, was, in fact, conservatively interpreted; in fact, *thirteen* witnesses, not two, made some passive reference to personal involvement in the scene ("There is a lady standing in front of me... holding a gun." "police officer... maybe wouldn't believe me..."). These references were not included, of course, because they weren't necessarily "errors"—rather, these responses probably reflected consideration of the situation observed from a personal standpoint, an *as if* standpoint, perhaps rooted in thoughts about how the given witness would respond in a similar situation. The scientifically conservative view is that these responses reflected personal consideration rather than false memory. However, it is not unreasonable to see this type of personal reflection as a pathway to the kind of wholly artificial, not to say crazy, tendency to place the self in a situation in which one had no actual personal participation at all. In two cases, as discussed previously, the witnesses somehow *entered the situation personally* in their imaginations, and constructed their memories accordingly. ("There is a lady out in my yard with a gun... pointing toward my house... waiting for someone to come out of my house to shoot... I am really scared... and I don't know what to do.")

I need to emphasize that we really don't have a clue about the processes, or the personal factors, that may have resulted in these specific accounts. However, the fact that we were able to document this weird effect, which is thankfully very rare, may help to explain all sorts of situations in which people claim personal involvement in fantastic episodes, ranging from forensically relevant situations to alleged supernatural encounters *(e.g., Sharps, Matthews, & Asten, 2006)*. People may very well hold wholly artificial memories as if they were veridical; and given this type of confidence, it is very difficult to see how an investigator would develop evidence, with or without a polygraph, that the incidents in question are wholly fictitious.

From the standpoint of G/FI processing theory *(Sharps & Nunes, 2002; Sharps, 2003)*, we would expect these types of results to derive from situations that were encoded in a more gestalt manner, as opposed to a feature-intensive manner that might tend to point out the inherent contradictions in the fabricated story when compared to the FI reality. However, we have already seen that elements of crime scenes tend to be encoded in a more gestalt manner, providing fertile ground for reconfiguration or wholesale fabrication. Furthermore, we would expect these processes to be exacerbated under stress, because of the intellectually limiting processes of stress described in Chapters 1 and 2. Witnesses who provide erroneous backstories, elaborate tales of the future actions taken by a perpetrator, or even legends of personal involvement in the given crime are not necessarily lying, at least in the conventional sense of the word. Rather, they only need to have beliefs or personal characteristics that may "bleed" into the relatively gestalt initial representation of whatever it was that actually happened. In the eyewitness realm, *interpretation may become memory*.

Interpretation in Action

These results show the importance of interpretation in the memory aspects of *processing under pressure*. Memories can be influenced, altered, or just plain fabricated from active interpretation as from initial encoding and representation. Once again, *there is continuity in the nervous system*. Interpretation plays an active role in memory; it also plays an active role in thinking, in decision, and in action, especially under the circumstances that typically characterize processing under pressure.

With this as a background, let us return to the gun/innocuous object effects with which we began this chapter. To mistake a black square object in the dark, such as the top of a wallet, for the slide of a semi-automatic pistol, or to mistake a near-perfect, full-size pellet-firing facsimile of a firearm for the real thing, does not necessarily impugn the character of a given officer in question. It does show that the officer has a human nervous system, and that he or she is capable of interpreting a given object in light of personal and professional knowledge and experience.

In such cases, in which emotions tend to run very high, the human proclivity for interpretation forms a fairly nasty two-edged sword. Anyone with access to a TV must be aware that there is a tremendous number of fictional characterizations of corrupt police officers available for public consumption. For what it's worth, informal canvasses of the author's students and colleagues indicate a much greater familiarity

Chapter 5   149

with highly negative police portrayals, such as those presented in the movie *Training Day*, than with older, more positive portrayals such as those of the *Dragnet* or *Adam-12* TV series. For one thing, the positive portrayals tend to be in black-and-white; the good cop on TV is generally an artifact of an earlier age. Today, media bad cops seem to draw a much bigger audience share than media good cops. The bad cops are in color and high-def.

The end result is as follows. People see a movie. In this movie, corrupt cops shoot another corrupt cop in order to get corrupt money, which they will undoubtedly use for more corruption. This movie forms the most recent exposure to police matters, and for some the *only* exposure to police matters, for the people who just watched it.

Now, these same movie-watchers are exposed to, for example, the facts of the Diallo case, perhaps with a journalistic slant or bias that presupposes evil or ill-will on the part of the police. Choose which of the following options best reflects these people's probable interpretation:

A. Gosh, this was a tragic consequence of inadvertent actions on the suspect's part. These actions were inaccurately interpreted by the police, even though based on their knowledge and experience, as a lethal response to their lawful challenge. Gee, perhaps a better awareness of human psychological characteristics, both in the law enforcement community and in the population at large, would help to prevent such tragedies in future.

B. THOSE CORRUPT EVIL COPS KILLED A POOR INNOCENT VICTIM BECAUSE THEY'RE LOUSY, #%@#$!%! VICIOUS (rac-, sex-, or fasc-)ISTS! SUE THEM! JAIL THEM! OFF WITH THEIR HEADS!

Which response, A or B, do you anticipate? As you read the news, which response, A or B, is typically more characteristic of real-world situations?

Interpretation again. Popular perception of these mistaken-object effects, even in tragic cases with huge consequences, may have more to do with highly unrealistic public and mass-media expectations, and with popular ideas about deadly force, than with putative racism or integrity issues on the part of police. People decide, they interpret, what they want to be the truth; and the general levels of irritability and hostility keep rising.

When a police officer confronts an armed suspect, decisions with lethal consequences must frequently be made in under a second *(e.g., Gelles, 2006; Montejano, 2004; Moore, 2006; Tietjen, 2005)*. Consider all of the things that must come into those rapid decisions: suspect's movements; suspect's armament if any; suspect's point of aim; the presence of others who may be in the officer's probable field of fire; et cetera; and a lot of the time, all of this high-speed low-drag cognitive processing is happening at night, with poor lighting or no lighting at all. Don't forget that a suspect's weapon may be occluded or partially occluded by clothing, posture, or architectural structures *(e.g., Narby, Cutler, & Penrod, 1996; Sharps, Barber, Stahl, & Villegas, 2003)*. Under these conditions, it's not hard to see how a wallet could become a .45, or a shoe could become practically anything at all.

INTERPRETING THE OFFICER-INVOLVED SHOOTING

If a police officer is unfortunate enough to actually shoot somebody, a variety of bad things begin to happen to that officer almost immediately. The procedures depend on the individual agency, of course, but typically the officer is placed on administrative leave or on "inside" duties. The officer's weapon is almost always confiscated. (The gun is gone; can the badge be far behind? Officers will attest that having their gun taken by their Department is, if not the worst thing that can happen to them, at least a very, very bad thing from an emotional standpoint.)

The officer is interrogated, and interrogated again. Depending on the agency and local law, the shooting, if it resulted in death, is usually treated formally as a homicide, and the officer is grilled as any other suspect would be by homicide detectives. Realize what this means: *That officer is seriously suspected of the most serious crime possible—a homicide.*

(I have mentioned this fact in my classes on some occasions. Students frequently roll their eyes and sanctimoniously explain to me that the homicide detectives, under these conditions, would undoubtedly treat their fellow officers far better, and with far more kindly human feeling, than they would a civilian suspect. At this point, I would expect that many of my law enforcement readers will begin to roll *their* eyes. Yeah, right. Homicide detectives just *love* patrol guys. We go on dates together. We scamper through the meadows and pick flowers together every May. It's all just one, big, happy family. By the way, I'd like to sell these idiots the Brooklyn Bridge.)

For non-police readers, let me qualify. There may be exceptions, of course, but in general detectives are unlikely to give patrol officers any sort of break under these conditions. They may, in fact, pursue a case involving a fellow officer with as much vigor as humanly possible, especially if they think he's guilty and that his guilt may tarnish the badge. The simple fact is that an officer who shoots somebody is in extremely serious trouble unless he or she is cleared by what is usually a demanding and detailed investigation.

If nothing else, this disparity between reality and common civilian belief serves as an example of the almost incredible naivete that many, if not most, civilians bring with them to the consideration of police issues.

The upshot of this entire diatribe is as follows. The officer who shoots somebody is in serious, serious trouble. A bad shoot can end a career. A really bad shoot can end a career and place the officer in prison. In prison, an ex-officer probably has no future at all, especially if the truth about his former career comes out. At that point, he is likely to make many new friends he doesn't really want.

Given all of this, is it really the most parsimonious explanation that officers go around casually shooting people for racial or political reasons? Or do cognitive and perceptual principles form a more reasonable explanation for many, if not most, of the genuinely terrible *cognitive interpretations* that may lead to the type of tragedy seen in the Diallo case, and in many other cases as well?

We decided to try to find out *(Sharps & Hess, 2008; also see Force Science News, 2009)*.

WHEN CITIZENS DECIDE TO SHOOT PEOPLE

We used the same crime scenes we'd used in our previous studies, the ones with a perpetrator holding a Beretta or a power screwdriver. You'll recall that most people, in the Sharps et al. *(2007a)* study, tended to confuse the screwdriver with the gun.

Now, here's the big question: Does this tendency—to interpret the tool as a pistol—also influence their actions? What would the average citizen do in an officer's place, if faced with a similar situation? In other words, does the average person, faced with the question of whether he or she must fire upon an armed perpetrator, integrate the necessary information about weapon versus non-weapon? Can the average person recognize a gun, as opposed to an innocuous object, to arrive at an accurate decision and a subsequent correct action?

We also decided to use the same study to address an additional question, one with real and alarming consequences for public and jury response to any given OIS (Officer Involved Shooting): Regardless of what action the average person would take when faced with an armed assailant, what would he or she typically expect the *police* to do in the same life-or-death situation?

We used our usual college population again, 125 of them this time. We showed them our scenes, over a realistic spectrum of tactical response times; the alert reader will recall that these scenes depicted an assailant, either pointing a 9mm Beretta handgun at a "victim," or waving a power screwdriver at her in what might be construed as an argument between her and the cable guy, or a dispute with a contractor or construction worker. (We also used "victimless" scenes for the sake of experimental completeness; *see Sharps & Hess, 2008*, for details.) Again, excellent lighting and a complete lack of occultation characterized the scenes; this means that the situation was a whole lot better, from a perceptual standpoint, than the average situation confronted by a police officer.

Before we showed the scenes, we told our witnesses, using a standard protocol, that they would encounter a situation that might or might not involve a crime or a source of danger. Then we told them that they could "intervene to protect yourself or others if you see an individual holding a weapon."

In other words, they could shoot him.

Some of our subjects were asked to demonstrate their decision to shoot, or not, by pushing a button on an electronic timer, so we could gauge reaction speed. Others were literally told to shoot, if they decided to do so; we gave them a toy dart gun, one of those suction-cup things, and let them actually try to blow the bad guy away with a model gun. (Granted, a real gun or a Simunitions weapon would have been better, but it is amazingly difficult to get permission to use something like that on a modern University campus. Obviously this dart-gun condition was not intended to mimic the complex dynamics involved in firing a real weapon, but we wanted to provide preliminary information on whether the act of raising and aiming a "weapon" might influence the ability to ascertain the need for a shooting response. The answer is that it didn't very strongly, although there was a low-grade effect that bears further investigation.)

So, what did we find? Well, patriotic readers will be happy to learn that the Spirit of '76 is alive and well; about 88% of our civilian respondents fired at the armed perpetrator when he was aiming a handgun at the victim. Almost nine out of ten shot the bad guy, or at least shot at him.

Unfortunately, about 85% also shot the cable guy. The guy with the screwdriver.

There is a lesson here. Never point a power tool at anybody, or the average person apparently will kill you.

Just as in our earlier research *(Sharps et al., 2007a)*, when witnesses could not, in general, distinguish the gun from the power tool, in this research *(Sharps & Hess, 2008)*, the average person interpreted *and acted upon* the same information; there was no significant difference between the numbers of people who killed the armed assailant and the numbers who killed, to all intents and purposes, the cable guy. The average citizen proved incapable of telling a screwdriver from a Beretta and acted accordingly.

The same people might very well have responded in the same way to a wallet in New York, or a power drill in Tacoma, or even a toy rocket in central California.

This point should be reiterated. In this study, under ideal viewing conditions, the average person decided to kill an unarmed individual, based on a mistaken *interpretation* of a screwdriver for a gun. Yet, as reactions to tragic cases such as that of Amadou Diallo indicate, the same people expect the police to be able to make this type of distinction under conditions of darkness, occultation, high levels of arousal, and—

Just what do people expect of the police, anyway?

Public (and Jury?) Expectations

This was the other question we addressed in this work *(Sharps & Hess, 2008)*. The intent of this experiment was to address the second question posed above: to determine how untrained people *felt that a police officer* should respond to a given situation involving gun violence.

Forty-four people participated in this one. We used our same standardized scenes again; but this time, we only used the ones with the gun, with the armed assailant.

Before we ran this study, we submitted these scenes to three senior field-training officers and a senior police commander, who were asked to evaluate proper police reaction to these scenes. You'll recall that each of these scenes depicted an armed assailant, aiming a service Beretta at a young woman. Beretta 92s are not small guns; and our assailants, both male and female, were rather imposing people. Thus, on a gestalt level, what you really had in these scenes was the Devil pointing a siege howitzer at Polly Pureheart. The only thing to do in this situation, tragic as it was, was to shoot the perpetrator.

This was not solely a subjective reaction. In the opinion of *all* of our senior and tactically experienced officers, this situation, as depicted, absolutely required a shooting response. According to our experts, any police officer encountering this situation *must fire on the perpetrator*, who in their opinion was depicted as posing a lethal armed threat to an unarmed person.

Our civilian respondents did not agree. Overall, only 11.36% of respondents felt that a shooting response was called for, *in a stimulus situation that was deliberately crafted to create an absolute necessity for a shooting response.* Responses varied somewhat with both gender of observer and gender of perpetrator, but ultimately this experiment showed that about nine out of ten people were of the opinion that an officer should never fire in this situation, despite the fact that 100% of our senior police officer referees saw that the situation absolutely required a shooting response.

If these results extend to the real world, and there is no reason at this point to think they shouldn't, they have serious implications for any officer involved in a jury trial of an officer-involved shooting. Apparently, given a randomly selected twelve-person jury, only one or at most two jurors are likely to see a shooting as justified under any circumstances whatsoever. Hopefully this incredibly negative conclusion would be mediated by other factors in court; but at this point, we have no evidence that this would be the case. This study indicates that the cop who shoots a perpetrator, for absolutely valid reasons, is likely to be in *serious* trouble when he or she goes before a jury.

The reasons given by respondents for their views on this subject were varied. Some felt, for some reason, that the daylight and the public conditions of the situation depicted would keep the perpetrator from firing. Others concocted elaborate sets of rules of engagement, or conditions, under which the officer might fire. Several respondents wanted the suspect to fire first, before the officer would be allowed to fire. Of course, in that case the victim would probably already have been shot to death, but this fact seems to have eluded the respondents in question.

Others wanted the suspect already to have committed murder (no word on how the officer was to determine this). Some required the officer to attempt to "convince" the suspect to drop his or her weapon; how such counseling was to be inserted, on a practical basis, into the middle of a gunfight was of course unaddressed. My personal favorites literally invoked the need for clairvoyance on the part of the police, saying that an officer should not fire in this situation because the suspect "did not look like she wanted to kill."

The sources of these fabulously unrealistic expectations must remain obscure; but the source of one whole class of responses was fairly easy to pinpoint. A number of respondents held that if the police had to fire, they should shoot the perpetrator's leg or arm, because, for

Chapter 5

example, "a shot to the leg is relatively harmless, if he is trying to escape, which means he is most likely guilty."

It is difficult to tell, here, whether the grasp of wound dynamics or of constitutional law is the more appalling; however, we have a pretty good idea of the putative source of this "shoot-'em-in-the-leg, shoot-the-gun-out-of-their-hands" perspective. Movies and television shows frequently depict exactly these amazingly unrealistic events. Therefore, many of these unbelievably naïve responses may have derived from just this source: a confusion, on the part of the public, of media depictions of police work with the real thing.

Shootings take place quickly, typically under circumstances that limit cognitive mediation to an extraordinary degree. Yet the results of our studies reveal that interpretation is key, even under these reduced circumstances. The interpretation of what is and is not a weapon is obviously crucial; but equally crucial is the later interpretation, under the cognitively-limiting circumstances of physical arousal, of whether or not the actions taken were appropriate. Even under the relatively primal, relatively high-speed conditions of a gunfight, cognitive interpretation moves swiftly to the fore as a major factor to be considered in understanding, or in judging, what happened in a given situation.

Given these findings, it is clear that interpretation must assume a central role under any circumstances more conducive to cognitive mediation. Such circumstances, of course, are not limited to those engaged in moment-to-moment, life-or-death tactical operations or to those who witness them. Interpretation also plays a crucial role in situations under which command decisions are made. This includes not only tactical decisions, but also strategic and administrative decisions. It is therefore very important to understand the factors that influence interpretation in command context; and, as we are about to see, those factors frequently make the difference between acclaimed success and catastrophic failure. We'll address these factors in the next two chapters.

Chapter 6
THINKING TO WIN: DECISION MAKING IN COMMAND AND HIGH-RISK ENVIRONMENTS

North Hollywood, 1997

On February 28, 1997, the infamous North Hollywood "Shootout" took place.

The facts were straightforward. Two gunmen robbed a Bank of America branch in North Hollywood. They wore home-made body armor. They were armed with several illegally modified fully automatic rifles, together with other firearms.

The robbers were serendipitously observed leaving the bank by Los Angeles patrol officers. Patrol and detective reinforcements were brought up. When challenged, the robbers opened fire with both semi-automatic and fully automatic fire on the officers, in an effort to breach the patrol containment. Civilians on the street were also targeted by the gunmen, intentionally or inadvertently.

The patrol officers were heavily outgunned. Their 9mm handguns and slide-action shotguns were unable to pierce the body armor of the gunmen. At one point, officers commandeered heavier weapons and ammunition from a local sporting goods store, in order to augment the inadequate weaponry standard for LAPD patrol units at that time.

SWAT officers assembled at the scene, and at that point the LAPD forces had sufficient firepower to defeat the bandits. One of the robbers, heavily wounded, shot himself; the other died of his wounds. Ten officers and seven civilians were wounded after over forty minutes of combat.

The tactical response of the LAPD was extremely commendable. Officers were initially outgunned; yet, through sheer courage, they held a containment perimeter until SWAT units could assemble and defeat the threat with their superior weaponry. Law enforcement experts are in general agreement that the overall conduct of the LAPD operation on this day was tactically exemplary.

Yet some of my students, perhaps less expert, disagree. They ask questions. Why were so many wounded? Why did it take over forty minutes to defeat the bandits? Okay, so they were wearing body armor—why didn't the cops just shoot 'em in the head?

As we've already seen, the average person out there is not exactly an expert on weaponry. They've seen the actor Tommy Lee Jones shoot a gun out of a guy's hand with a pistol; why can't the real cops do the same thing?

Any law enforcement officer has the answer: *Because it's impossible, idiot. Er—I mean, that is to say, sir or ma'am, the actual dynamics of weapon handling, ballistics, and ammunition considerations preclude that level of precision at range with a handgun or with a shotgun.*

There. That's better. But the fact remains that sniping somebody in the head with your Beretta or Glock, under tactical conditions and at any kind of range, is generally a non-starter. Also, it should be fairly obvious that a shotgun generally fires shot. Shot is not particularly effective for shooting somebody, with great precision, in the head at long range. Remember also that the bandits were wearing body armor—the only way to defeat such armor at range, in the absence of a precision shot to some unprotected area of the head, is to use a rifle with the right kind of ammunition.

So why didn't the patrol officers simply pull out their patrol and tactical rifles, their M-16s, AR-15s, Ruger Minis or whatever, and shoot the bad guys in the head or through weaknesses in their armor?

Well, that might be a reasonable question today, when many LAPD officers are armed with rifles in their cars, to some extent as a result of that bad day in 1997. However, at that time, patrol officers typically *didn't carry rifles in their cars.*

Everybody knew they might need them; everybody knew that modern levels of urban violence might require them. A little additional thought would have revealed that the situations that might require rifles would be most likely to arise unexpectedly. Yet front-line LAPD officers, the people most likely to be in initial contact with exactly those situations, had no access to rifles as standard equipment at all.

The Evil Spirits of Hindsight rise sanctimoniously to taunt us with the obvious questions: *Why not? What the hell were you people thinking?*

The SWAT people did have rifles, ready to hand in their cars, which is one reason LAPD SWAT was able to deploy so quickly and so effectively on that day. However, as is typically the case, it was patrol people, with their service pistols and shotguns, who bore the brunt of the assault for the first bad minutes. If any of the responding patrol officers had a rifle to start with, of course, the whole thing might have been over and done within a few minutes, or even a few seconds, with a couple of decent shots and no casualties except the robbers. Yet in this rifle-free environment, such a relatively safe outcome was clearly impossible.

The Evil Hindsight Spirits again: *So why weren't the patrol people adequately armed for the modern crime environment?* Well, the LAPD as an agency was aware of the problem, and some LAPD officials had

Chapter 6

apparently lobbied for patrol rifles for some time. Yet no action was taken to provide them.

Why? In hindsight, you would think that anybody, with or without police expertise, would have seen the obvious need for enhanced weapon capabilities. Los Angeles even in 1997 was huge, the urban area of the LA Basin was even huger, and violent crime was not exactly unknown there. Certainly by the 1990s, high-capacity autoloading handguns had replaced law enforcement's old stand-by six-shooter pretty much everywhere. Anybody who saw a single cops-and-robbers movie during that time would have been aware of this. Even cursory research would have revealed that the .38 Special cartridge, regarded in my father's time as a fairly awe-inspiring, life-taking thing to be shot with, had been largely replaced by generally superior 9mm or .40 caliber ammunition as police standards. The few exceptions to this, such as the highway patrolman's .357 Magnum (capable of cracking an engine block, and popular with old timers, in some places, who preferred the perceived reliability of the wheel gun) were typically even more powerful. The accelerated operational tempo of police work that required these superior weapons was not exactly a state secret.

These changes were well known by the 1990s, and they clearly attested to the need, on the part of 1997 law enforcement officers, for some seriously high-powered, accurate tactical ordinance. So, the LAPD experts lobbied the authorities for rifles, and those who held the purse strings apparently said No Soap. LAPD patrol units would have no rifles, and LAPD officials did not press the issue to the point at which the civil authorities would cave. It was a big issue, of course, but not *that* big. Life went on.

The Hindsight Spirits again (they will be with us for much of the next two chapters): *"Why? Why do such things happen? What is going on in people's heads, psychologically, when they do really bonehead things that seem so obvious, in retrospect, that they seem almost incredible? Doesn't there have to be a solution to these kinds of errors in judgment and decision making?"*

Well, there was a solution, and it came out of that very bad day in 1997 when everybody changed their minds. Blood-soaked crises, with their terrible human and economic costs, frequently result in policy changes. And the policy changed. In order to carry a rifle, a given LAPD officer today must pass a rigorous course and examination, and must continue with periodic rifle training as well; nobody just started passing out patrol rifles to everybody who wanted them. However, today, LAPD Metro division patrol units are typically armed with rifles, and many other qualified officers throughout the city have them as well. So, today, when a patrol officer encounters a situation that requires a rifle response, he or she is either adequately equipped or moments away from somebody who is. So, the policy has changed; but it required a highly destructive catastrophe to point out the need for this change.

The Hindsight Spirits (remember them?): *"You guys really need to come up with a better way to foresee the obvious. Before the human and economic costs come up and bite you in the policy."*

By the way, in 2009, the Mayor of Boston said he would not approve the request of the Boston Police Department for M-16 patrol rifles, although he would approve them for special units. This, of course, would have duplicated the conditions obtaining on the day of the North Hollywood Shootout. The decision was apparently influenced by questions from "community leaders" (Fresno Bee, 2009, May 31). The lessons of the Shootout were nowhere in evidence.

European Theater of Operations, 1942

The lack of rifles that fueled the North Hollywood shooting may at first seem to have been an isolated incident, a bureaucratic foul-up of an unusual type. It wasn't; and the more things change, the more they stay the same.

In 1942, the United States was thoroughly embroiled in the World War II air campaign against the German Luftwaffe. Since 1940, the United States Army Air Corps [USAAC, which became the Army Air Forces, USAAF] had been committed to what Gen. H.H. Arnold referred to as "a strategy of high-altitude precision bombing of military objectives" *(Correll, 2008)*.

This sounded good—and it required good bombers. By the time the United States entered the Second World War against Japan, Germany, and Italy, after the Japanese bombing of Pearl Harbor in 1941, the United States had an outstandingly durable long-range bomber, the B-17, and a somewhat less durable but even longer-range bomber, the B-24. Other bombardment aircraft such as the medium B-25 and 26 were available, but the heavy 24s and 17s would carry the brunt of the assault, initially in North Africa and then against Fortress Europe.

These were big, generally reliable planes, bristling with .50 caliber machine guns. They were impressive machines of war, they inspired confidence, and they were shot down like ducks, in fantastic numbers, by German fighter planes as soon as they made their major combat debut in 1942. The reason for this was simple. There were no effective, long-range fighter aircraft to escort them. Effective fighter aircraft had not been developed for the American services. The best the Americans could come up with, at a combat-ready production level, was the Curtis P-40, a durable flying tank that had the maneuverability of, well, a tank. P-40s didn't even have the range to escort the American Eight Air Force

Chapter 6   161

bombers, deployed in England in 1942, to their targets inside Germany. At least not so that the fighters would have enough gas to get back.

Why hadn't anybody addressed the fighter problem? Simple. Nobody thought there was one.

To quote Air Force journalist John Correll *(2008)*, "The Air Corps regarded the bomber as its principle weapon. Furthermore—on the basis of very thin evidence—the Air Corps concluded that new bombers such as the B-17 and the B-24 flew too high and too fast for pursuit [fighter] aircraft to catch them and that bombers could operate over enemy territory *without fighter escort.*" (*Pg. 61*; italics mine.)

Does anybody see a parallel yet?

Financial and public-opinion overseers of LAPD: "No rifles. For some reason, we do not notice the accelerated operational tempo of modern law enforcement. Therefore, no rifles."

U.S. Army Air Corps: "No escort fighters. For some reason, we do not notice the accelerated operational tempo of modern aerial warfare. Therefore, no escort fighters."

The dynamics are the same, and that's good, at least from the standpoint of our understanding of *processing under pressure.* Similar dynamics imply the prospect of similar solutions, to be rooted in a fusion of police and cognitive science, and in empirically proven training. Let's move on.

The British, who'd been at it against the Germans since 1939, had long since learned the folly of sending their Lancaster and Wellington bombers up against the bad guys in daylight, when Nazi ME-109 and Focke-Wulf fighters ruled the world. In effect, the British had had the aerial equivalent of the North Hollywood Shootout to teach them that they needed modern long-range escort fighters; but because the British didn't have enough decent fighters of any description, they quit trying, at least on the daylight front. They sent their bombers in at night, instead. In general, it worked. In a time when effective night fighter planes had not yet been developed by the Germans either, the British strategy of night bombardment set city after city of the Thousand-Year Reich ablaze.

The British Royal Air Force (RAF) Bomber Command tried to explain this logic to the USAAF.

Result: Zip. The British experts (like the LAPD) tried to convince the American guys who were not yet experts (like the LA purse-string authorities) of the validity of the hard lessons learned.

With no effect whatsoever. The Americans, *committed* (remember that word) to daylight precision bombing, kept sending their guys in. Without fighter escort.

What was the result?

Vignette 5: Inside the Ball

So you're the late uncle of the present author, and you're an enlisted guy bent triple inside the "ball," the ball turret on the underside of your B-24 Liberator, flying from Egypt to Yugoslavia. Usually you're the tail gunner, but organizational charts don't always work out perfectly at war, and today you're squashed into this Godawful little ball. Several hours ago, you ascended, in your heavy flight suit and jacket, from the North African sands. You were sweating like hell.

However, now you are shivering, ice forming on your eyebrows and in your nose, your electrically-heated flight suit working about as well as it usually does. You are hanging in your ball under the belly of your B-24, flying through the freezing gray-blue cloud-frost world of this cramped horrible turret over southern Europe; can't see through the ports, everything in the turret freezing up, can barely move, twin .50s taking up half the room in this ----ing ping-pong ball slung under the belly of this lumbering four-engine monster, and then there's a scratchy, barely audible voice coming over the 'phones, "Bogey—Bogey—No, three bogeys" and then, the caller forgetting the carefully drilled-in intercom formulas, "MEs! There's a bunch of 'em on our four! About four! Four o'clock low! Get 'em! JeezSSSTSSTT!" The caller, today's tail-gunner, abandons his throat-mike for his guns.

And in they come, the fighters, the Luftwaffe, as you crank the turret around (slowly—so slowly—why can't they build this thing to *move*?) and the *lichtblau* belly of an ME-109 flashes past like something from a science-fiction movie that won't be made for another thirty years. And a brief thought goes across your mind, one of those intrusive ones that happen under the stress of combat, and you wonder why the hell they call that color *lichtblau*, light blue, it looks like the damn cold dirty white-gray underbelly of a shark, and the shark plane flashes past, and you fire thirty or forty big .50 rounds into the Yugoslavian cloud-bank that has become your world, but the German Shark is long gone. You might as well be firing a BB gun at the wall of a bank because you can't see and you can't hit and the traverse rate on the turret is the speed of a club-footed cow, and the fighter jock in the 109 streaks past, unhurt, immortal. The damn Nazi shark lines up your number 7 bomber, your 24, your guys, and his cannon start to spit, and 7 *comes apart*, my God, the port wing came off, spew of oil and

Chapter 6

> metal, and burning fuel, and the whole ship drops into an inverted spin, and the 109 shark roars past in some Teutonic victory role, off to seek other fat lumbering American bombers, and you pray for the guys in 7 to get the hell out of that burning fuselage, and you see one 'chute, but the chute itself is on fire, and the poor bastard falls toward Yugoslavia with that charcoal mummy of a useless chute at, you remember for no good reason—there's that combat intrusion again—32 feet per second squared, and he falls out of sight to his death, and nobody else—*nobody else, for God's sake*—gets out of 7, and she's on fire, the blue flame etching the fuselage around the wing joints, and the gravity must be unreal in there, everybody screaming, cursing, pinned to the structure of the plane herself as she spins down toward the unforgiving Balkan granite below. And you lose her in the pearly clouds; ten good men dead. And you notice your breathing, the fast hiss-hiss into your oh-two mask, you become aware of your own thundering heartbeat as the bombardier's voice comes in over your 'phones, deliberately calm but still urgent and dripping with semi-controlled terror, "hssssss—Bogey, bogey, twelve o-clock low," and you crank the turret around as fast as mechanically possible, cramped bent triple in this horrible cold-metal ping-pong ball of a turret, sweat in your eyes, and you try to wipe it away savagely, your helmet in the way, cursing, praying, praying, cursing ...

But all of this, of course, was the feature-intensive reality of a bomber crewman, trying to fend off fast, maneuverable, cannon-armed fighters with the relatively light and ineffectual armament of his slowly turning turret. For the Brass, the higher commanders, no such feature-intensive concepts were readily in evidence. They were living inside comforting gestalts, such as the idea that "... the B-24 flew too high and too fast for pursuit aircraft to catch them... bombers could operate over enemy territory without fighter escort" *(Correll, 2008,* pg. 61). So said the Brass.

No, it didn't—and, no, they couldn't—said the guys who lived through those horrible missions in the Balkans, and to Ploesti, and in the B-24s and B-17s over Schweinfurt and Regensburg. The bombers needed fighter escorts. Desperately.

The idea of the self-escorting bomber gradually died in the face of horrible losses and bitter experience. Eventually, long-ranged fighter aircraft, especially the P-51 Mustang, became available to escort the heavy bombers all the way to and from their targets. Eventually, after staggering losses, it became evident to the powers that be that bombers could not typically really defend themselves against the sleek and deadly Nazi Messerschmitts and Focke-Wulf's. Specialized escort aircraft were needed to combat them.

However, for several years there, people like the author's uncle were sitting ducks. For many of them, the intrusion of feature-intensive reality into the comforting gestalts held by their commanders came one, or two, or a dozen missions too late.

Lessons from Past and Present

Why didn't the aviation experts of the American air forces figure things out earlier, before they had to suffer through their own psychological and aerial equivalent of the North Hollywood shootout? Keep in mind that the British had already had their equivalent of North Hollywood, as Lancasters and Wellingtons and good men in sheepskin jackets fell out of the sky like gut-shot geese; and they had learned enough hard lessons about daylight precision bombing that they only engaged in it at night. They tried to explain this to the new American airmen, but *the explanation didn't take.* No sweat, said the Americans. We have better technology—and, besides, we're committed to the strategy of daylight precision bombing. *Committed.*

Other information was available. There was strong information, aside from that derived from the British experience, supporting the idea that daylight bombing without good fighter escorts would lead ultimately to defeat. The terrible lessons of the Spanish Civil War, which the Germans had learned so well in the development of their relatively high-tech fighter arms, were also freely available to the USAAF; and yet the importance of fighters was ignored. Bomber development was advanced to the level of the B-17 and B-24, fabulous weapon systems for their time. Yet American fighter development, which could have kept pace, remained at its best at the level of the P-40; a durable and heavily armed low-speed aircraft, with the maneuverability of a really good modern minivan.

So the Americans sent their guys up, without fighter escort, in daylight; and they died. One medium bomber group, attempting to bomb the Netherlands, suffered 100% losses *(LeMay & Kantor, 1965).*

The Hindsight Spirits again: *Why?* Why couldn't American commanders heed the lessons of the Spanish Civil War, and the British experience, to recognize the importance of a crash program of escort fighter development to match American superiority in bomber development? *What was wrong with them?*

Answer: The same things, psychologically, that were wrong with the LA authorities who did not authorize patrol rifles in time to deal with the nightmare of the North Hollywood Shootout.

So, perhaps we can blame these things on individuals, on unthinking authority figures who keep screwing up. There's something wrong with them. This type of explanation, this attachment of blame to the stereotyped incompetent authority figure, is typical in human crises. In a way, it's comforting: A bunch of idiots screwed up, but that was only because they were stupid. If only I had been in charge, everything would have been alright.

The problem is that this conclusion, so typical in human affairs, is usually completely wrong. It carries with it implicit accusations that are entirely unjustified.

First of all, hindsight is inherently sanctimonious. The Monday-morning quarterback can always feel good as he contemplates the errors that he wouldn't have made on Sunday if only he'd been calling the plays.

Second, what was "wrong" with the decision makers in these cases was the same thing that is wrong with all of us: We have human nervous systems, and such systems operate under specific laws that tend to reduce our abilities to extrapolate what we know into what probably will be.

Let's face it: We'd probably all make the same damn mistakes in the same situations. The author, and the readers of this book, would in all probability have screwed up the fighter escort situation in 1941, and the LAPD rifle policy in 1997, every bit as badly as the people who were actually there, making the decisions *under pressure*. One might even suggest that few of us would have shown the courage and adaptability shown by the LAPD and by the guys in the bombers in dealing with the crises once they had arrived.

As we see, the faults in bad decision making are often attributed to the idiosyncratic attributes of the people making the decisions, period, and although it's unjustified it's easy to do. *Why did this happen*, ask the Hindsight Spirits. *Because the people involved were idiots*, we usually answer, and we all go home with a sanctimonious sense of Monday-morning satisfaction.

It must be admitted that every so often, this is true; this sanctimony is occasionally justified. Hitler's decision to invade Russia was a boneheaded move that probably only he could have made, and so on. Stupidity and lunacy do exist, of course, and they exist in individuals. However, even though exceptions do exist (e.g., Hitler), idiots and lunatics are not generally the individuals making important decisions. The people involved in the Incredible Anti-Rifle effect in Los Angeles were generally regarded as sober, reliable, capable people. The officers behind daylight precision bombing were generally distinguished soldiers and expert aviators in their own right *(LeMay & Kantor, 1965)*.

Whenever a catastrophe or crisis arises in human affairs, our tendency is to try to find somebody to blame. Yet what if the fault is not typically in the individual? As we have already seen in eyewitness identification and in perceptual interpretation, what if the fault is typically in the processes of interpretation used to understand the context to which the decision must be applied? What if the problem isn't idiosyncratic, stereotyped stupidity, but that decision makers are human, with human nervous systems?

At first glance, this may appear intolerably pessimistic. Decision failures are inherent in the processing characteristics of the human nervous system? What sort of chance does that give us? We're all doomed!

No, we're not, because *many of those processing characteristics can be modified through appropriate training*. It is true that certain specific aspects of the processing characteristics of the human nervous system do tend to lead to elements of decision failures. However, these may be identified across situations that otherwise may seem to have little in common, such as the 1997 police emergency in North Hollywood, and the entire Western world at war in the skies over the Mediterranean and Europe. The fact that we can identify these characteristics means that they can be experimentally isolated and analyzed. This, in turn, means that you can train people not to make these kinds of mistakes.

This, in turn, means that more officers will go home at end of the shift.

Gestalt and Feature-Intensive Processing Again

In our discussions of eyewitness memory, and of eyewitness interpretation, we saw the importance of feature-intensive (FI) processing. The person who has an FI knowledge of weapon parts and characteristics will usually turn in a better eyewitness account of a specific firearm than the person who registered the same weapon, in a gestalt (G) manner, as "some kind of gun or something." The conditions that lead to better FI processing lead to better eyewitness memory, as they do to better interpretation of what is seen.

We have also learned *that there is continuity in the nervous system*. This means that the characteristics that foster FI processing are likely to lead to better interpretation of complex information in decision situations, as well as relatively simple information in eyewitness situations. You'll get a better decision outcome, on average, with a strong FI analysis of the input on which that decision is to be based.

To illustrate this principle, I included the gunner's-eye account of aerial combat given above in Vignette 5. If you can conceive, on a feature-intensive basis, of a sleek fighter plane flashing past a slowly turning turret; if you can visualize the cannon-fire of a Messerschmitt in direct battle with the machine-gun fire returned from a low-visibility metal ball on the bottom of a vastly less agile aircraft; if you can understand that level of sweat and lethality on a point-by-point, feature-intensive basis, you're in a much better position to understand the realities of that combat situation than is someone who does not. An individual who does not understand these factors, instead, may have a simple, gestalt idea such as "commitment" to daylight precision bombing; but that person will probably not understand the deadly feature-intensive world to which that gestalt must be applied.

In the case of the air war with Germany, if you'd conducted a proper level of FI processing, it is still possible that you might not have decided for certain to allocate major resources for fighter development. However, it's almost certain that you would have taken the time to look into the issue thoroughly. On the other hand, if you'd had a single gestalt idea of the conflict, such as "As an American general, I am committed to the principle of daylight precision bombing," you'd have been in serious trouble. In fact, you would have been in the trouble that actually materialized in combat. Your gestalt statement, the statement of your belief in daylight precision bombing, really needed to be broken up into individual, discrete, feature-intensive terms.

This concept is not exactly original with the present author—for example, the philosopher Socrates suggested the importance of the same sort of define-your-terms analysis, although in different language that did not lend itself readily to the kind of cognitive consideration we're doing here. But in modern G/FI terms, it becomes easier to understand how to implement such crucial analyses. Let us think about the difference between feature-intensive analysis and gestalt acceptance of individual truisms, using the air war as our example.

Gestalt—"As an American general." Does that mean that my policy is based more on my status and affiliation that on rational empirically based evidence?

Gestalt—"I'm committed." Isn't commitment an emotional state? Should I base the scientific and engineering decisions involved in running an air force on my emotions?

Gestalt—"Daylight precision bombing." What, all the time? Many situations (breakfast, mowing the lawn, Christmas morning) don't require any kind of bombing at all. That may sound fatuous, or even ridiculous; but given that there are many situations in the world that don't require bombing, daylight precision or otherwise, couldn't there be *military* situations, as well, in which tactics other than daylight precision bombing would be appropriate, or even superior? Unless there's no choice, is it wise to commit inflexibly to *any* course of action, or should we remain flexible, whenever possible, to alter our decisions in the face of new logic and evidence?

Also, how precise is our precision? Data acquired at the time demonstrated that the anticipated precision of the bombing campaign was nowhere near what it was expected to be; in feature-intensive view of that fact, shouldn't we review what we're up to?

It is also important to consider, on an FI basis, what is implicit in a given term such as "daylight precision bombing." Although unstated, the initial concept involved self-escorted bombers operating without fighter escort. This was the real problem; yet explicit consideration of this issue may have been constrained by the fact that this concept was implicit, rather than readily available in the overarching idea of daylight precision bombing.

Thus, based on our joint consideration of the North Hollywood shootout and of the World War II daylight precision bombing campaign, we can already start to make recommendations for better decision making.

- *Learn to recognize gestalt statements, concepts, and policies.* Break these down into their components for careful, feature-intensive analysis. What do we really mean by a given term? Does that term carry with it implicit baggage (e.g., no rifles, no escort fighters) that we accept on an implicit basis? This type of FI processing is going to be helpful all by itself.

- *As a commander or administrator, you need to interview the people who actually have to work with the given equipment, or who have to work within the given policies.* Try to get a ground-eye, feature-intensive view of how that equipment and those tactics are actually used, and of their advantages and deficits across a realistic range of possible situations.

INTERVIEWING FOR INFORMATION

This next recommendation is not as easy as it sounds. I use the term "interview" above because it is not enough to "talk" with subordinates about equipment or policies.

Chapter 6   169

Suppose a chief or deputy chief simply asks an officer, informally, how he or she feels about the new police cars, or about the new policies. The officer is likely to notice the brass on the chief's collar, and possibly on the chief's hat, and is therefore likely to come up with the obvious response, the one he or she thinks the chief wants to hear: "The new cars are great! Just Grr-REAT!"

Dammit. You don't want tiger impersonations, you want information. So, your best bet is not to ask such an open-ended, ill-defined question in the first place. If you, as a chief or other commander, really want to know about the new cars, you need to ask *feature-intensive* questions, either orally or, probably better, on short written questionnaires that can be filled out anonymously. You don't want a general gestalt impression (The cars are GREAT! The cars SUCK!). Rather, you want specifics. Ask about ease of quick exit from the vehicle. Ask about placement of computer controls and shotgun mounts. Ask about visibility and ease of visibility through rear windows. Ask for specific evidence, instances of times when the specific features of the vehicle either failed or worked well in a given field situation. You want feature-intensive information here; general gestalt impressions are not going to help you formulate policy, and they're not going to help you identify problems or advantages among the various models under consideration ("Lieutenant! Buy more cars that are great! Stop buying cars that suck!" "SIR-YES-SIR!").

Not all that helpful.

Important questions may even warrant a formal anonymous survey, in which, for example, officers of different levels of experience might be asked to give 1 to 7 ratings on different features of a patrol car, or on different advantages or disadvantages of a new training program. The problem is that the conducting of such surveys is actually a science, and all kinds of things get in the way of accurate responses; the reliability and validity of your questions, the order and phrasing of the questions, all sorts of things. So, if you want to conduct a serious survey of something, your best bet is to make inquiries at a local university and consult an expert on surveys to help you set it up. Most University professors have institutional commitments to regional and community service, and will therefore frequently be glad to help. When you need expert assistance on a given task, such as the construction of a valid survey, it's a very good idea to ask for it.

However, on a more informal basis, let us say that you hear informally that everybody in your agency thinks that Car X is GREAT and Car Y SUCKS. This, once again, is merely a set of gestalt impressions, but it does indicate that there's some kind of problem with car Y. So, the wise commander or administrator will make every effort to acquire feature-intensive information on specific aspects of the vehicle known to be important for the success of a police car. You do not want to base crucial decisions on gestalt impressions. Instead, you want the best, most accurate FI information, from the people who are in the best positions to have acquired it, to inform decisions that may have life-or-death consequences. A successful preemptive response to the North Hollywood Shootout, for example, would have involved the serious consideration of feature-intensive information, obtained from patrol people, on whether or not their duties in the LA of those days warranted the carrying of rifles in their cars. In another example, 1940s air commanders might have canvassed their pilots and aircrews for explicit feature-intensive information, such as that given in Vignette 5, to inform their decisions. FI information is the key to effective understanding; effective understanding is the key to effective decision making.

Incidentally, it's important for a law enforcement commander or administrator to consider the sources of the information that he or she uses to inform any given decision. A full consideration of the concepts involved in this very complex issue is well beyond the scope of this book. However, it's pretty obvious that the person to ask about the day-to-day operation of a patrol car, to continue the example above, is *the officer who drives it*, not the engineer who designed it, or the sales rep who sells it. The engineer and rep have vested interests.

The commander or administrator also wants to get measurements of opinion from a number of officers *of different characteristics*. Senior officers have more experience, but they may also have preferences that have arisen from habit, rather than from objective considerations. Junior officers have less experience with alternatives. Personal idiosyncrasies can damage the validity of data, so you want to spread such idiosyncrasies out as much as you can. In the patrol car example, it would even be a good idea to ask officers of different physical *sizes* about issues such as visibility, ease of movement, and ease of egress. The vehicle may be great for a person who is five-foot-four, but an officer a foot taller can barely get in and out of the thing. It's important to ask about all operationally significant aspects of the car (or the gun, or the helicopter, or the policy) that might reasonably enter into its operation.

So it's best to verify the expertise, understanding, and even the motives of in-house personnel and of outside experts. It is also important to elicit the relevant information in intelligent and well-thought-out ways. Once these criteria have been met, the administrator or commander is in a better position to build the feature-intensive picture of the given decision situation that will maximize the positive outcomes while avoiding the potential for catastrophic error.

Decisions at Tactical Speeds

An important point must be addressed here. Many command decisions must be made swiftly, without the opportunity for long-winded FI analysis. People are shooting; you have to act, and you have to act now. What is to be done in those situations?

The answer has to do with *preparation*; specifically, the front-loaded, explicit, feature-intensive preparation within which training and experience are used to form the effective gestalt responses that provide for swift, effective performance in combat.

FI processing is effective because it is relatively complete, but it has a downside: it is slow. Gestalt processing does not involve the intricate evaluation of FI processing. This is also a downside, of course. As we've seen in detail above, G, Gestalt, processing is inherently less comprehensive than its FI counterpart. However, G processing is *fast*, which is probably why we have the ability to do it at all. In fact, many situations that require speed really do not require FI processing at all, or would be actively hindered by it.

Hunting is probably the quintessential example of such a process. You see the deer, and you fling a spear at him. If you get it right, the result of this Gestalt process is deer meat. But suppose, instead, that you approach the hunt on an FI basis. You spend a lot of time, again on a feature-intensive basis, forming a committee to consider the feasibility of prospects for some tribal spear-based anti-deer action during the coming fiscal year. Then you settle in for a long conference entitled "Excellence in Paleolithic Deer Hunting: Myths and Realities," the purpose of which is to draw up a deer-based position paper, with input from all deer constituents and stakeholders, on potential future deer prospects...

You'd starve to death.

This is obviously a ridiculous example, but it serves its purpose: the outcome of such an FI approach to the high-speed, low-drag world of an actual hunt would be massively unfortunate. In other words, if you tried to apply FI processing to the act of killing a deer, you'd starve.

So here, in a nutshell, is the summary of G/FI tradeoffs. Where FI processing is not necessary, G processing provides for fast, accurate cognitive outcomes (as in killing a deer). Where FI processing *is* necessary, FI processing, although slow, is the only way to achieve an accurate cognitive outcome (as in deciding to provide tactical rifles or escort fighters).

Errors are made when people try to apply G processing, which is intellectually easier as well as faster than FI processing, under conditions in which FI processing is essential. Under these conditions, where G is inaccurately substituted for FI, you miss things *(see Sharps, 2003, for extended discussion)*. Some of these things are important, and failures to consider them have already been seen, in the North Hollywood fight and in the early bomber losses of the Second World War.

So, when you have to move fast, you want a well-trained, highly appropriate G process governing your response. When you have time to think things through, when you're preparing for the sorts of situations that may require a fast G response at a later date, you want to be processing in FI terms, considering all reasonable aspects and ramifications of reasonably likely courses of action.

Therefore, it's beginning to look as if we might refer to G processing as the *tactical* mindset, while FI processing might be called the *strategic* mindset. When an officer confronts an armed perpetrator, and the perpetrator swings his weapon to aim at the officer's chest, FI processing is the last thing the officer wants to be doing. What is necessary is a smooth gestalt completion of the necessary motions to draw, aim, and fire the service weapon—extraneous thoughts need not apply. The same is true of tactical driving—while trying to negotiate narrow, crowded city streets during a pursuit, sweating out the tenuous balance that yields the maximum speed consistent with public safety, an officer, or commander, cannot be thinking detailed FI thoughts about the scenery. The well-trained gestalt response is absolutely the way to go here, just as it was absolutely *not* the way to go when strategic, FI processing was needed.

When the commander, administrator, or officer is thinking about how things are or how they should be done, FI processing is the obvious cognitive process of choice. In tactical extremity, however, well-trained G processing is usually the way to go. It should be reiterated at this point that gestalt and feature-intensive processing are ends of a continuum, rather than discrete types of process; and, as ends of a continuum, situations that partake both of strategic and tactical characteristics may result in a mix of the types of cognitive process employed.

Feature-Intensive Experience as the Basis for Trained Gestalt Responses: The Strategic Precedes the Tactical

Now, here is the crucial point. We've discussed the well-trained Gestalt response. How does it become well-trained? *The answer to this is that G responses typically begin as series of FI concepts.* Feature-intensive processing is the precursor to gestalt processing. The better and more complete that the precursor FI processing is to begin with, the more effective, on average, will be the resultant G processing in the tactical situation *(Sharps & Nunes, 2002; Sharps, 2003)*.

Think about learning to drive. When you first get behind the wheel, everything is feature-intensive: which pedal is the clutch and which is the brake (crucial distinction)? What is the order of signaling, braking slightly, down-shifting-involving-the-pedal-which-is-the-clutch,-not-the-brake, turning the steering wheel, and not hitting the baby carriage on the sidewalk, when you engage in the mind-boggling complexity of your first left turn? *Everything* is feature-intensive and not very effective.

However, and gradually, the discrete barriers between the feature-intensive operations begin to break down, and smooth, coordinated gestalts, involving sequences of integrated control movements, begin to form. The behavioral elements of the driving process, which began as relatively discrete features, ultimately coalesce in the mature driver into a series of coordinated, domain-specific gestalts by which you drive smoothly and effectively. In fact (AUTHOR'S DISCLAIMER: *DON'T EVER* DO THIS IN TRAFFIC, OR EVEN IN A REAL CAR), you will find that if you start thinking, in a feature-intensive manner, about the various actions you use to drive a car, your driving performance is likely to suffer catastrophically until you knock it off and start driving in terms of matured gestalts again. The FI elements of your earlier driver's training were essential in forming the smooth, expert G responses; but you don't want to go back to the slow, step-by-step world of FI processing when you're trying to get out of the way of a speeding ambulance, any more than you want to start thinking about the mechanics of your Beretta in a firefight. Under tactical circumstances, to quote the shoe ad, you just do it. You make the coordinated, trained, matured gestalt response.

This same process of learning and training, in which FI steps coalesce into fast, effective G operations, is ubiquitous. It's seen again and again, in all sorts of training. Handling a firearm, using a nightstick, fighting in unarmed combat, driving, swimming, flying a helicopter, riding a horse; all begin as a relatively unrelated cluster of FI movements that, through guidance and practice, become the smooth G motions of the expert. That expert is now capable of responding to any relevant situation with fast, gestalt behaviors which do not require FI analysis to achieve their goals effectively.

So, to reiterate, why can't we use gestalt processes all the time?

Answer: because if you do, you wind up with the North Hollywood Shootout, or with burning airplanes and crews falling out of the sky at the hands of the Luftwaffe. Strategic planning and thought must be feature-intensive. *Feature-intensive analysis and training, conducted before you get into the combat situation, are what make for effective gestalt responses once you're actually in that situation. These gestalt responses are usually at the core of tactical cognitive processing. On the other hand, strategic thinking is virtually always characterized by feature-intensive processing.*

To fire a service weapon effectively is a gestalt process, but the training leading up to that effective gestalt system is largely feature-intensive, at least in its initial stages. The mature tactical firing response: that is what has become gestalt, through practice and experience. On the other hand, decisions as to what types of training are optimal, or the formulation of department deadly force policy, should be *extremely* feature-intensive. Firearms policies should absolutely not be formulated at the crime scene, at the time when effective deadly force must be used with gestalt speed and efficiency.

Tactical driving of a patrol car is a gestalt process. However, again, the training that leads to effective tactical driving involves many feature-intensive processes; and the relevant command decisions concerning what cars to buy, how they will best be used, and the maximum speed policies in any given urban or rural setting, must be calmly formulated under even more feature-intensive conditions.

In a nutshell, everybody involved in a given tactical situation will have to make effective gestalt responses to that situation; but the training and strategic thought that lead up to those responses must be feature-intensive if the end-product gestalt responses are to be effective. As we will see in the following chapters, one of the most dangerous things for a commander is to be in the grip of a tactical mindset *prior to the onset of the need for that mindset*, during the preparatory period when the best information available must be assessed in a feature-intensive manner. Effective decision making is complex; it requires analysis which may not be possible once things really start jumping.

So, the effective commander wants to use FI processing to make the decisions which will lead to the best training, equipment, and deployment once a situation requiring G processing begins. The successful commander will therefore want his or her FI processing to be of the most comprehensive, least-impeded quality possible. Therefore, it is worthwhile to consider the nature of decision making, and the factors that may enhance or sabotage the successful command decision. This is what we will do in the next chapter.

Chapter 7
WARRIOR MINDS: THE DYNAMICS OF DECISION

Decision making is one of the most enigmatic of human activities. Human beings are literally by definition intelligent (again, *Homo sapiens sapiens* means the wise, wise man). And yet, as we've already seen, human thought is often overshadowed by "mindlessness" *(e.g., Sharps & Martin, 2002)* when it comes to actual decision making. As humans, we can create space flight, but in actual operations we can make simple math errors like the one a few years back that resulted in the destruction of the very expensive Mars orbiter *(Cowen, 1999)*. We can understand the arcane chemistry of pesticides, following which we make the decision to spread them indiscriminately all over the landscape, with amazingly nasty consequences for our air, our water, and our own health. We can decide not to give our patrol people rifles, or not to supply our bombers with fighter escorts. There are many other examples *(e.g., Dorner, 1996)*.

How is it that human beings can possess high intelligence and yet make such bad decisions? There has been a tremendous number of books, nice long ones, on this subject. Much of this research has derived from a tradition called behavioral decision research *(BDR; e.g., Bazerman, 1998; Camerer, 1995; Cialdini, 1988; Freedman & Fraser, 1966; Gilovich, 1992; Kahneman & Tversky, 1972, 1979; Medin & Bazerman, 1999; Tversky & Kahneman, 1972, 1973, 1974)*. The approach has been generally successful in approximating and modeling real-world contexts, but has generally focused on game theory, leading to questions of generality to other areas of decision making *(Garnham & Oakhill, 1994; Payne, 1973, 1982)*, especially to more contextually based questions *(e.g., Gauvain, 1993; Blanchard-Fields, 1986; Park, 1992; Sharps & Wertheimer, 2000)*, such as those that law enforcement people encounter all the time.

If you want to know more about the classic BDR approach to decision theory, the references given above ought to point you in' the right directions. However, one of the things about game theory is that the people being studied generally have a limited set of options for their decisions, and they generally know the rules.

Limited options with rules: This is generally the case for what we call *compensatory* reasoning. In compensatory reasoning, you decide among a limited set of options. This is what we often use in formal reasoning, in business and similar contexts: okay, we now have a list of all possible mutual funds and their histories; which ones do we want to buy? We have only three specific brands of canned beans in the only grocery store in town; which one will give us the best value?

Compensatory reasoning, for what it's worth, is how the Mongol emperor Kublai Khan used to pick his wives. There was a particular Tatar tribe called the Ungrat, who were known to produce the most beautiful girls. Because the Khan wanted only the best, these ladies were apparently the only ones he'd consider. He therefore had a limited set of options. Every year he'd have a hundred of these comely lasses shipped to him. Then he'd have them inspected overnight by older women, who would weed out all the snorers, all the ones who had bad breath, and so on. These would be sent home, with or without some lovely consolation prizes (history is silent), and Kublai would take the lucky winners, six at a time in rotation, to "obey any orders he might give" *(Marco Polo, quoted in Lamb, 1940, pg. 282; Bergreen, 2007)*. Those lucky girls.

There are a few minor discrepancies in the details of this story *(eg., Marsden, 1948)*, but overall it's a textbook example of compensatory reasoning. It's also easy to remember, for obvious reasons. Kublai got to choose among a strictly limited set of alternatives (attractive Ungrat girls), according to specific rules (no snorers or hyena-breathed individuals moved on to the finals). These rules were intended to provide him with the best of the best.

Non-Compensatory Realities

The problem is that most of real life simply doesn't work this way. Most of the time we don't have all of the options for any given decision set before us, nor do we know whether or not we *do* have all the options. In short, we usually don't have enough resources to engage in compensatory reasoning. Instead, most of the time we reason in a *non-compensatory* manner. Generally, then, we pick one option at a time, and we *satisfice*: we pick the first option that fits our minimum requirements. The reader may recall that this is what happened to me, the author, during the pickup truck search briefly detailed in Chapter 3; I satisficed. I bought the truck that seemed to fit my minimum requirements, but the resultant rolling wreck was the worst vehicle I ever owned. In fact, when it broke down and refused to run, literally the day after I bought it, it ceased to fit one of my most basic, fairly obvious minimum requirements (that the engine would start). I didn't have enough accurate information about that truck, at that time, to succeed in my goal of being able to drive around.

Accurate information, processed in a feature-intensive manner, is paramount for success in our generally non-compensatory world; but it is important to realize that minimum requirements, and the ability of a given choice to fulfill those requirements, may change through time.

Classic examples of this fact lie in the unfortunate areas of marital and career dissatisfaction. Spouse and career choices are almost always non-compensatory, for everybody except Kublai Khan, anyway, and these choices are generally made at relatively young ages, in the absence of more mature experience. In the case of spouse selection, young adults generally go somewhere they can find other young people. Then they pick the first potential mate who *satisfices* for them, who satisfies their minimum requirements, whatever those requirements are at the moment. Then they date, or otherwise associate, with the lucky chosen winner for a while. If both partners are still in there satisficing over a mutually agreeable period of time, still satisfying their partners' minimum requirements, it's typically time for the altar.

It's the same basic process for careers. Young people go to school, and they pick the first career that satisfies whatever interest, income level, and/or aspirational criteria the given young person sets as acceptable minima. Thus, they satisfice.

The problem with this approach is that *conditions and minimum requirements change*. This is especially true if you do your important satisficing when you're young and relatively inexperienced, as is frequently the case with reference to spouses and careers. Conditions change; this is true whether a non-compensatory, satisficing approach is used to decide among trucks, spouses, careers, or tactical alternatives. Trucks break down. Formerly ambitious spouses stop going to work or start drinking. Travel-related jobs that were exciting when you are young become exhausting and tedious when you get older; and, of course, tactical situations are notoriously fluid in virtually every respect.

This is one of the major problems that training, experience, and understanding must confront. Non-compensatory, satisficing reasoning is among the worst possible ways of dealing with a changeable world. However, the simple fact is that *non-compensatory, satisficing reasoning is generally forced upon us, as humans, by the nature of that world*; we almost never have all possible alternatives before us, and we seldom have all the facts. So, in general, we're stuck with non-compensatory, satisficing reasoning. It's what we have to do.

Compensatory, non-satisficing decision making is of course occasionally possible in the real world; but sometimes, there are changes in the conditions that supported compensatory reasoning in the first place. You must frequently alter your original compensatory decision strategies to new, modified, non-compensatory realms.

This is complex, so let's give an example. Suppose that the day after Kublai Khan had acquired his year's ration of Ungrat beauties, he had chanced to meet a truly wonderful non-Ungrat lady (perhaps pageant-winner Miss Outer Mongolia 1283 A.D., riding on a donkey or a yak or something). She may have been far more to the Khan's liking than this year's batch of Ungrats, but technically she was off limits: non-Ungrat, and the nice old ladies of the Snore Patrol hadn't had a crack at her. In such a case, Kublai would not actually have gotten the best possible bride, Miss Outer Mongolia, because although he and his advisors *thought* they had had complete information in the first place (non-snoring Ungrat brides are always the best), in fact they had not. In such a case, compensatory reasoning would have in fact been in error in the first place, because complete information was not actually available when the decision process began. Kublai would have been out of luck.

The point of this rather demented example: Sometimes we may think we *are* operating in a compensatory cognitive universe, in which we have all possible alternatives before us and all facts are at our fingertips. We've thought of everything, we've considered all possible alternatives. However, even if that's true, something unexpected (such as Miss Outer Mongolia) *can always rear into the picture and change all the rules.* Such an apparition may change even the framework, the context, within which those rules were supposed to operate. This may prove to be especially true in the constantly shifting real world of law enforcement, in which cognitive processing, processing under pressure, must prove similarly fluid in order to be successful. We will see concrete examples of this in the subsequent chapters.

Still, it's crucially important to make valid decisions in a constantly changing world, and one of the best ways to do this is to prepare for it. Such preparation can be enhanced enormously through a knowledge of how decision making works, of the dynamics that produce successful command decisions.

Decisions have two critical components. The first is accurate information relevant to the situation. The second lies in our *understanding* of that information, our ability to interpret it. Frequently, and especially in the world of law enforcement, there may be no way at any given time to enhance available accurate information; you may, so to speak, have to go to war with what you've got. However, the responsible commander or administrator can dramatically improve his or her decision success through the enhancement of understanding. *How is this to be brought about?*

Factors in Decision Understanding

Again, there is a huge literature on this subject. What I wish to do here is to present some of the most important principles in a directly applicable way that can enhance or diminish the quality and influence of understanding in law enforcement situations.

FRONT-LOADING, OR PRIOR FRAMEWORKS FOR UNDERSTANDING

In a well-known study, Bransford and Johnson *(1972; also see 1973)* showed that virtually incomprehensible passages of text could be rendered entirely comprehensible, and memorable, by means of a guiding or organizing picture or relevant simple phrase made available just prior to passage presentation. They presented participants in these experiments with paragraphs that seemed to make no sense. Some of the wording from one example*: "If the balloons popped, the sound wouldn't be able to carry because everything would be too far away from the correct floor. A closed window would also prevent the sound from carrying... a break in the middle of the wire would also cause problems. Of course, the fellow could shout... the string could break on the instrument... the best situation would involve less distance..."*

Total gibberish—and the participants responded to this total gibberish in predictable ways. They couldn't remember what had been said, and their understanding of the material was effectively nil.

However, when Bransford and Johnson presented an organizing picture to their experimental participants, *before* these subjects encountered the "gibberish" paragraph, their understanding and memory of the paragraph improved dramatically. The picture showed a man playing an electric guitar, the amplifier of which was suspended by balloons outside the open upper-story window of a young woman, who was leaning out the window listening to the music; the amplifier was connected to the guitar by a long wire. In the picture, and quite obviously, the young man was using this demented apparatus to serenade the woman in the window.

Suddenly the disconnected nonsense of the paragraph made sense. *Balloons—wire—problems with closed window—less distance*—gotcha. Makes sense now. Participants now had a *prior framework for understanding*, and they were able to remember and to *interpret* the formerly nonsensical paragraph in reasonable ways.

Bransford and Johnson demonstrated this effect with several situations involving pictures, or simple organizing statements, that rendered otherwise nonsensical materials comprehensible. This worked well when the organizing information was *front-loaded*, provided prior to the paragraph; the same effects generally don't work, or work very poorly, when the information is provided later. They were also able to demonstrate similar effects with organizing *phrases*, so this effect has been demonstrated in the verbal as well as the pictorial realm of prior information.

Some readers may be scoffing at this point; never mind the paragraph, the picture didn't make any damn sense either. Nobody would do that with a guitar, the balloons couldn't hold up the amp, et cetera. However, in a very real way, that's the whole point of the experiment. Even though the situation was novel, and apparently nonsensical, the installation of *a prior framework for understanding* prepared the respondents to understand the situation, to remember its elements, and therefore to act accordingly. The effect of front loading, of the installation of a prior framework for understanding, gives you an edge *even when you confront the unexpected, or the apparently nonsensical.*

Many things encountered by law enforcement and in military settings may not make sense, and many of them appear entirely novel at first encounter. The need for rifles in the North Hollywood Shootout apparently didn't make sense to the authorities holding the purse strings. The need for effective long-range fighter escorts didn't make sense to the bomber enthusiasts among early World War II air commanders. The idea that some nutcase with a mail-order carbine could take out the president of the United States from a book depository window apparently didn't make much sense for those responsible for President Kennedy's security. The unexpected and apparently nonsensical rears its ugly head all the time in the world of law enforcement; the commander, or administrator, or officer in the street is frequently confronted with nightmares from Hell that only seem to make sense after the fact. The point of the Bransford and Johnson experiment, with regard to our concerns here, is that front-loaded training can even prepare you to deal more effectively with the completely unexpected and the hitherto unimagined.

This is why training that *front-loads reasonable responses to the range of reasonably likely possibilities* is so important. It gives you the edge. It gives you the understanding to make reasonable, effective decisions while everybody else is running around wondering how such-and-such a terrible thing could happen to them on their watch.

Front-loaded understanding, the prior framework for processing under pressure, is a commander's best friend. But what elements of training should be front loaded?

The answer follows in the next section; the answer is that you should frontload *absolutely explicit and noninferential information* whenever possible.

Explicit Versus Implicit Information

In a nutshell: the human nervous system responds more effectively to explicit information, in which connections among important elements are made explicit, than it does to implicit or inferential connections.

A wonderful example of this principle was provided by the work of Haviland and Clark *(1974)*. They presented research participants with connected sentences that either required inference, such as *"John took the picnic out of the trunk. The beer was warm,"* or that did not require inference at all, as in *"John took the beer out of the trunk. The beer was warm."* The latter type of item, in which you didn't have to infer that there was beer at the picnic, was more readily assimilated.

Let's look at this effect, the effect of implicit or explicit information, in another classic conjoined-sentence item *(Reed, 1992, pg. 275)*. Here it is: *"Ed was given lots of things for his birthday. The alligator was his favorite present."*

Huh? How did an alligator get in there? Did somebody give it to him? *Who would give somebody an alligator?* Was it a present, or a threat? Did it eat party guests that Ed didn't like? What the hell?

The conjunction of these two alligator sentences, which requires inference, doesn't make very much sense to those who read the item, at least not quickly. However, when the linked sentences are changed to *"Ed was given an alligator for his birthday. The alligator was his favorite present,"* comprehension becomes substantially better.

Now, this utterance is almost as demented as the first one. Who the hell gives alligators…

But that's not the point. Just how crazy the material is, *how novel or unexpected,* doesn't matter. Even though the situation in the second alligator utterance was as novel and unusual as in the first, the fact is that the connection in the second utterance was *explicit*. You were told, up front and in no uncertain terms, that this poor guy was given an alligator, presumably by some lunatic, and that somehow, perhaps through the miracle of interlinking pathologies, he really liked the evil carnivorous reptile in question. The *explicit connection* between the sentences made all the difference. In short, the novelty wasn't so important; the clear and explicit connection of one thing to the other was. One can see a similar effect operating in Bransford and Johnson's work; even though the balloon-serenade was bizarre, the prior framework for understanding provided by the picture made the text comprehensible.

So, if we combine Haviland and Clark's explicit-versus-implicit connections with Bransford and Johnson's prior frameworks for understanding, we have an important recommendation. It applies to anyone; commander, administrator, or officer, or anybody else who is forced by circumstance to sail the dark seas of *processing under pressure.* That recommendation is to train your people and yourself, in front-loaded, explicit terms, and with reference to prior frameworks for understanding, to deal with the *reasonable spectrum of possibilities* that you, and they, may encounter.

> **Examples:** *We have replaced patrol car model X with patrol car model Y. The commander should arrange for the officers to learn exactly why this was done, explicitly. Train them before they start using car Y, very explicitly and in feature-intensive terms, about its operational features. Train them in the features of car Y especially as those features contrast explicitly with those of car X. Another example: in writing field orders for a complex arrest or a SWAT evolution, make each step stand out in explicit connection to the step before and the step to follow. Make certain that all officers involved have an explicit prior framework for understanding their own role, and the interaction of that role with the actions of others immediately involved. To misquote Admiral Nelson, a police commander cannot do much wrong if his or her orders, and training of self and subordinates, are front-loaded and explicit.*

Such orders and training, of course, must be held in memory. As we have already seen, memory is notoriously unreliable. So, what aspects of the cognitive systems involved in memory can be used to enhance memory performance, as opposed to making it worse?

Effective Use of Memory

As we have seen, the human memory system is insanely complex, and oceans of ink have been spilled by people like the author in an attempt to understand it. However, one of the more important things that emerges from all of these studies is that memory, fairly productively, can be separated on most dimensions into *long-term memory* and *short-term, or working, memory*.

There is overlap between these systems. In many areas of modern experimental psychology, it works better to treat working memory and long-term memory as integrated systems. However, for present purposes, this venerable distinction will be seen to be useful.

Long-term memory is, effectively, your archive or library of everything you've learned, at least the things that you can remember, going back through your entire life. Working memory, on the other hand, holds the elements of memory with which you are working right now, and it has a more limited duration and capacity than does the long-term system. The ways in which these systems are interlinked are fantastically complex *(Baddeley, 1990*; also *Sharps & Price, 1992; Sharps, 1998, 2003)*, but on a practical, applied level, we can say the following: if a given item or element of a situation is currently in your working memory system, it's likely to have an influence on your decision process. If it isn't, if it's tucked away or filed in the myriad information stacks of long term memory (LTM), its influence is likely to be somewhere between minimal and nonexistent *(Lesgold, Roth, & Curtis, 1979)*.

Over the years, my students and I have conducted some studies of this factor *(e.g., Sharps & Martin, 2002; Sharps, Hess, & Ranes, 2007b)*. The basic question we wanted to answer was a very fundamental one: *Why do people do stupid things?* Why do we make stupid decisions, when we have access, in memory, to all of the information we would need to keep from doing so?

HORRIBLE DECISIONS AND WHY

We examined this question in terms of people's approval of decisions that had led to horrible consequences; we drew these decisions from a variety of real-world sources. We changed a few details to avoid potential embarrassment (and lawsuits) from the people involved, but the basic gist of each decision was the same as it had been in reality.

These decisions came from executive, business, educational, environmental, and public health venues, and we wrote the items up so that in each one, the basic problem to be addressed was presented to our research subjects, followed by the decision that had been made to deal with that particular problem. However, we left out the negative consequences. Then we asked our respondents to rate the decisions.

To give one example, we had a situation in which an impoverished school had no money for anything; the ancient textbooks were rotting, teacher pay was horrible, the classrooms looked like something from a medieval hut, and so on. It turned out that a computer company was willing to provide this school with matching funds to buy (their brand of) computers. The decision was made to acquire the computers. Hooray. Classroom Technology. Computers for The Children. Education improved, problem solved. Hooray.

Amazingly, most of our respondents thought this decision was just great. They thought this about all the other bad decisions, too.

The reader will probably already have figured out the fly in this particular ointment. The offer was for *matching* funds, meaning the school would have to cough up the rest of the money. Which, of course, the school did not have. What were they supposed to do, pawn the rotting textbooks? Replace the school lunch program by letting the kids catch and eat the rats nesting in the roof? The school had committed to paying half the cost of these expensive computers out of non-existent funds.

Yet everybody in this part of the study thought this was just great. Somehow they failed to perceive, or to predict, the negative consequences of the decision.

However, in other groups, those exposed to our *contextual information condition*, we also provided the respondents with a bit of pertinent information: the fact that *if you use money for something now, it won't be available later for anything else.* We provided this information in the immediate context of the decision consideration, during the period in which people were actively working on their analysis of the given decision in their working memory.

When we provided such simple information to our respondents, *in immediate context,* approval of the bad decisions dropped like a rock. The effects, statistically, were large: those provided with contextual information exhibited far greater understanding of the decisions and their potential consequences. However, this effect only occurred *when that simple information was presented in the immediate context of the decision consideration.*

Now, nobody has to be taught a simple fact like the one about the matching funds, or any of the other simple facts we provided in the contextual information conditions. We proved that by submitting these facts to other groups of respondents, and by rating their knowledge of this information. Virtually everybody knew all of it (*if you pay money now, you won't have it later; if you catch all the big fish, what you'll have left is little fish*; and so on). People already *knew* this stuff.

But if everybody already knew the relevant facts, then why did we have to present them in the immediate decision contexts? Why didn't the people who were cheering for the bad decisions "import" this information from their long-term memories to aid in their consideration? What went wrong for the people who did not have the contextual information, and therefore were overjoyed at stupid decisions?

The reason this happened, and the reason why critical information is often left out of decision-making contexts, is that such information, *even if present and available in long term memory, is not immediately present in the context of the decision.* However, if information is immediately present in that context, in working memory, it strongly influences outcomes. A number of other studies by the author and colleagues have shown that contextual information of different types can be used by adult respondents, across the adult lifespan, to improve cognitive performance in a whole variety of areas, including spatial memory *(Sharps & Gollin, 1987a, 1988; Sharps, 1991; Sharps & Martin, 1998; Sharps, Foster, Martin, & Nunes, 1999)*, mental rotation *(Sharps, 1990; Sharps & Gollin, 1987b; Sharps & Nunes, 2002)*, and regular, nonspatial memory *(Gollin & Sharps, 1988; Sharps, 1997; Sharps & Antonelli, 1997; Sharps, Martin, Nunes, Neff, & Woo, 2004; Sharps, Martin, Nunes, & Merrill, 1999; Sharps & Price-Sharps, 1996; Sharps & Tindall, 1992; Sharps, Wilson-Leff, & Price, 1995)* in both the visual and auditory realms *(e.g., Sharps, 1998; Sharps, Price, & Bence, 1996; Sharps & Pollitt, 1998)*.

The provision of simple information, even if already known to the respondent, has a positive effect on decision making *if that information is in working memory at the time*, if it's made available to the respondent in the proximate context of the decision. This is the same type of effect suggested by the work of *Bransford and Johnson (1973)* discussed above, as well as by other work *(also Kintsch, 1979, 1994)*. In the absence of such information, as seen in this research and in other work *(e.g., Dorner, 1996; Wertheimer, 1982; see also Kintsch, 1979, 1994; Sharps & Wertheimer, 2000)*, decisions tend to have a "mindless" or extremely narrow quality that, especially in the case of law enforcement decisions, can result in catastrophic consequences.

> **Summing Up**
> *In order to facilitate the best decisions, the commander, administrator, or officer needs to make certain of the following facts:*
>
> - The information at hand, relevant to the decision to be made, is as accurate and complete as possible.
>
> - This information should be front-loaded, available as a *prior* framework for understanding, to the greatest degree possible *(e.g., Bransford & Johnson, 1972, 1973)*. Training and experience are obviously great sources here.
>
> - The information should be made explicitly and visibly related to all relevant phases of the decision. Ideas must have direct, noninferential linkage to the concept to be understood *(Haviland & Clark, 1974)*. It's especially important that explicit relationships between present information and previous ideas about the situation be identified and considered *(e.g., Kieras, 1978)*. This point will be considered in detail in the next section of this chapter.

- The necessary information must be immediately present in the context of the decision, available to working memory *(e.g., Lesgold, Roth, & Curtis, 1979; Sharps & Martin, 2002; Sharps, Hess, & Ranes, 2007).*

- With the exception of tactical situations in which trained, gestalt responses may be the optimal or only possible courses of action, analysis of explicit elements of a given decision, immediately available to working memory, should be made in explicitly feature-intensive terms. There should be a deliberate, conscious effort to identify gestalt concepts and to break them down into relevant, step-by-step features.

The use of white boards in "war room" settings can be of great help here.

Obviously there's nothing new about white boards, but the factors discussed here provide some developments in *how* they can be used. We may still place an endless list of talking points, drawn up as they occur to people, on a given board; but it's imperative to have another board up there as well, or two or three of them, on which to establish, explicitly, the relationships between critical elements to be considered. These points should be visible at all times, immediately available to working memory, during decision consideration. Working memory has limitations; a person can, in general, handle about seven organized units of information at a time in working memory *(Miller, 1956)*, but the fact is we're better at dealing with only three or four at a time *(Mandler, 1967)*, or maybe five in a pinch *(Mandler, 2011)*. This is one of the reasons you should only have three or four white boards up there, and, actually, only one or two would be better.

Any complex decision in the real world requires consideration of considerably more information than is held in three or four organized units of information, or even in seven of them. Therefore, visual aids to working memory, especially those that are organized in direct, logical, explicit ways that make use of prior frameworks for understanding, can prove to be crucial in maximizing decision effectiveness and in reducing potentially catastrophic consequences.

The cognitive psychology underlying these recommendations is admittedly complex. However, the recommendations themselves are fairly straightforward and can readily be adapted by law enforcement experts to a variety of decision situations. One point that has not been fully explored, however, is why it is so important that explicit relationships between present information, and previous ideas about the situation, be singled out for consideration in depth. Part of this is obvious, of course; the relationships between the prior frameworks for understanding and the current given situation can provide a strong cognitive edge for decision makers. This is good if those prior frameworks were "installed" through meritorious training and experience; *but what if the wrong frameworks are installed by accident?*

Functional Fixedness and Mental Set

Conversations with homicide detectives, tactical specialists, and other law enforcement experts on the arcana of violence have revealed an interesting fact to the author: Most people don't seem to know a weapon when they see one.

Guns, sure. Knives, pretty much. But the simple fact is that large numbers of people are assaulted and battered, sometimes to death, in rooms that provide a plethora of options for armed self-defense.

Very few household implements provide much in the way of useful defense against a firearm assault. However, in the absence of guns, options for personal defense are virtually endless. Paperweights can be thrown or used to multiply the force of a blow. Kitchen drawers full of silverware provide a variety of options, including throwing the whole drawer at an attacker's head and fleeing while the contents provide the equivalent of a cut-rate fragmentation bomb. Heavy ashtrays may have discus-like properties. All sorts of tools provide lethal potential, and various items of light furniture make dandy war clubs. Wine bottles, the edges of tennis rackets, pointy-cornered-toasters, entire rock collections—the list of things which victims could use to whack their assailants to death, or at least to delay their assailants' progress and facilitate escape, is essentially endless.

Now, in the absence of hard data, all I can say is that I would bet that all of these things have been used, somewhere and by somebody, as weapons. However, the fact remains that most people, surrounded by all sorts of potential weapons, fail to use any of them to deter or defeat any given attacker.

Why?

The most likely candidate for this phenomenon is a nasty process known as *functional fixedness.* This occurs when you do not recognize that a given object could be used for other than its intended purpose. If you need to drive a screw at the office, and you don't have a screwdriver, you may be a victim of functional fixedness; there's no way, you think, to complete the task. However, if you recognize that a nickel or dime would fit the slot, and you could use the coin to drive the screw, you have overcome functional fixedness: you have realized that the coin, normally used to pay for things, can also function as a sort of awkward screwdriver. Screw driven, problem solved.

A large bottle may make a dandy war club, but functional fixedness may rear its head. Bottles are used to contain liquids, not to break skulls; so you stand there holding your bottle as your assailant kills you. You are a victim of functional fixedness.

Innovative uses of objects, such as coins or bottles, usually involve some element of the overcoming of functional fixedness, just as the *absence* of innovation often involves a failure to overcome it. One might be able to find some level of functional fixedness in the events leading to the North Hollywood shootout, for example; rifles are used by the military, shotguns and pistols by the police. Therefore, our police do not need rifles.

As the reader will recall: Yes, they did.

The North Hollywood example, however, bleeds out of the world of functional fixedness and into the closely related world of *mental set*. In broad general terms, functional fixedness deals with objects, and mental set with concepts. Mental set, again in general terms, might be thought of as a functional fixedness of *ideas*.

This is why the lead-up to the North Hollywood situation might be thought of as midway between functional fixedness and mental set—it concerned objects, rifles, but also the question of their use, an idea. The same may be said of the daylight precision bombing controversy of the 1940s—the objects were airplanes, but the idea of their use was the more important aspect of the situation.

THE PUSH OF PIKE

Mental set has been an important impediment to tactical thinking for centuries. Ancient wars were typically decided, at least in large part, by what came to be called the "push of pike"—massed infantry formations assaulting each other with pikes, effectively poking each other with pointy sticks. This went on from Ancient Egypt, or even earlier, into the European Middle Ages.

Effective muskets were finally developed during the late Middle Ages *(e.g., Dyer, 1985)*. You would have thought that this development would have changed the nature of warfare for all time. Initially, however, it did not. Pikemen, with their long pointy sticks, still predominated on the world's battlefields, and as for the musketeers, they would typically fire off a huge volley and then insert bayonets *directly into the muzzles of their muskets*, turning these high-tech weapons into, well, pointy sticks. Then they'd charge and poke the enemy with them, just like everybody else. Mental set prevented most commanders from seeing the potential of the musket; muskets were basically used as pikes with a one-shot difference, and that was that.

It was a Swedish king, Gustavus Adolphus, who overcame this particular mental set and made the musket work. It should be noted that this was in the 1600s, two or three centuries after fairly decent muskets first became reasonably available. The lesson here is that established, institutionalized mental sets may take a long time to break down.

Anyway, instead of having a bunch of pikemen together with a few musketeers, who would fire all at once, plug bayonets into their muskets, and poke the bad guys in unison, Gustavus Adolphus increased the ratio of musketeers to pikemen. He had muskets modified for easier use, and had relatively shallow serried ranks of musketeers fire volleys into the packed masses of opposing musketeers and pikemen they encountered. The effect was perhaps similar to the creation of a multi-man machine gun. The Swedish king even modified artillery for easier battlefield use; the flexibility and intensity of Gustavus Adolphus' firepower resulted in slaughter after slaughter.

Gradually, Gustavus' ideas took hold, and other armies began doing exactly the same thing. However, a hundred and fifty-odd years after Gustavus' time, they were *still* doing the same thing, in the grip of military mental set. British musketeers massed in formations, their smooth-bore muskets at the ready, wearing high-visibility red coats with white belts often crossed approximately at heart level. This would have been fine against forces armed with smooth-bore muskets, which were the best weapons available a century earlier and which have a limited range; but rifling had been invented, and the American colonists, with their long rifles, frequently sniped the beautifully visible British regulars off the field from hundreds of yards away. Just as Gustavus Adolphus' tactics broke age-old military mental sets and changed everything, the existence of the rifle eventually forced a change in the mental set that had initially led to formations of brightly clothed musketeers; but it took decades, and many lives, for this lethal mental set to die entirely.

Rifle formations, operating not out in the open but from behind cover, proved well-nigh impossible to dislodge through the nineteenth century, as the American Civil War was to demonstrate. Facing such a formation with another such formation frequently produced nothing but stalemate, as the trenches of the First World War were to prove so vividly. One way to attack such a formation was at speed. Charging horse cavalry could sometimes break entrenched rifle or even artillery formations, although typically at horrifying cost, as the infamous Charge of the Light Brigade was to prove during the Crimean war. Cavalry was of course more normally used for reconnaissance and skirmishing duties, and when it was used against massed rifles, the result was frequently catastrophic. Nevertheless, it was occasionally successful.

But then the machine gun was invented. A massed cavalry charge could be easily annihilated by a few traversing machine guns, as the First World War was to prove beyond a shadow of a doubt. Cavalry could not survive on a battlefield dominated by the interlocking cones of fire emanating from machine guns. Yet horse cavalry, even in the presence of the machine gun, persisted in the U.S. Army into the first years of the Second World War.

Then the tank came along...

The point is straightforward and clear: in general, military forces fight any given war, initially, with the techniques of the previous war. Pikes continued to be used long after muskets should have replaced them. Muskets, and musket tactics, continued to be used long after rifles should have replaced them. The horse cavalry that could sometimes defeat massed rifle formations lingered long after its nemesis, the machine gun, appeared on the field. Additional (and perhaps controversial) examples of mental set in tactical matters could be drawn from more recent history, but the point is made: historically, every time a new military tactic is devised, armies and commanders have tended to hold onto it long after it becomes lethally worse than useless. This is the practical result of *mental set*: soldiers frequently fight a new war, with its new technologies, using the technologies and tactics of the previous one. The results are frequently catastrophic. The power of mental sets has been sufficient to change history and to create astronomical numbers of casualties, and mental sets take a very long time to die.

Therefore, it is a wise commander, in military or in law enforcement service, who will take the time to apply front-loaded, explicit, feature-intensive cognitive analysis to the mental sets which he or she may retain in any given tactical situation. Mental sets are essentially habits of mind. Some, if based in a rational analysis of current tactical exigencies, may be useful; others prove catastrophic. In general, however, negative or damaging mental sets have gestalt characteristics that may be countered by means of careful feature-intensive analysis. This analysis, of course, is conducted with reference to prior frameworks for understanding, explicit connections between important logical elements, and with all relevant information immediately available in the context of working memory.

But what if we don't *want* to do all of that?

Cognitive Dissonance

This question is by no means as ridiculous as it might at first appear. Mental sets, habits of mind, die hard; but they die especially hard if we have emotional investments in them. The technical term for this is cognitive dissonance *(Festinger, 1957)*. It's typically hard to demonstrate in the laboratory, but it basically boils down to the following point: if you have a firmly held idea which is contradicted by another belief, or by the realities you encounter (which may include the realities of your own behavior), this produces a *dissonance*, in the grip of which you may have to go through some fairly fantastic mental gyrations to avoid admitting the reality. You have an investment in your firmly held idea which is hard to let go, evidence notwithstanding.

The practical upshot of this principle is that the more you pay for a given thing, the more you tend to value it. If you buy two original paintings by great artists and they both turn out to be fakes, you'll probably accept expert opinion that the one for which you paid $49.95 is not, in fact, an original Rembrandt. However, the one you paid $45 million for is another matter. The expensive painting, for you, is likely to stay an original Rembrandt no matter what the experts say, and you'll come up with demented excuses for the fact that Rembrandt appears to have placed delineated numbered regions underneath the paint. It may be a paint-by-numbers picture, possibly of a clown holding a balloon, but by Heaven, for you, it's a Rembrandt paint-by-numbers clown picture and that's what it's going to stay.

Cognitive dissonance occurs in many other realms, as well. Psychologists and other scientists frequently cling to outmoded, outdated ideas, even ideas that have been proven wrong or grossly oversimplified. They've spent so many years, and so much work promoting and believing in them, that intellectual change, the rejection of the old and disproved in favor of the new and proven, becomes psychologically impossible. Another example: historically, it's much harder to arrive at peaceful solutions once battles have been fought, and once the nations involved have invested in any given war in terms of money, materiel, suffering, and human life. Cognitive dissonance rears its head; we've sacrificed thousands of lives, and billions of dollars, and now you expect us to negotiate? It's unconditional surrender or nothing; and the given war goes on.

Every police officer of experience has seen cognitive dissonance operating. The undercover operative who will not abandon the long-term objective that he has pursued for months, even if his cover has probably been blown. The detective who will not abandon an incorrect theory of a given case, and the pursuit of a given suspect, even though new evidence proves that the guy didn't do it. The tragic case of the patrol officer who, for medical reasons, is no longer able to work effectively, but who conceals those reasons to his or her own ultimate detriment and to that of the Department. The assistant district attorney who continues to prosecute the original suspect, even though the person who actually committed the crime is now in custody (this last example is thankfully very rare, but it does happen).

Cognitive dissonance also applies to the commander whose tactics have not met with success, but that have cost lives and time, and who therefore continues to pursue the same tactics with continued lack of success. And continued casualties.

All of these are examples of the pernicious influence of cognitive dissonance; and all should prove preventable through the proper level of feature-intensive analysis on the part of commanders, administrators, and officers.

This is the important point: *Functional fixedness, mental set, and cognitive dissonance are pernicious.* However, all can be prevented to a great degree if the law enforcement professionals involved understand their own cognitive processes, and if they are willing to take the necessary steps.

Let us repeat and expand the important steps to be taken, from a cognitive standpoint, to enhance the effectiveness of decisions.

1. The information at hand, relevant to the decision to be made, should be as accurate and complete as possible.

2. This information should be front-loaded, available as a *prior* framework for understanding, to the greatest degree possible. Training and experience are obviously great sources here.

3. The information should be made explicitly and visibly related to all relevant phases of the decision. Ideas must have direct, noninferential linkage to the concept to be understood. It's especially important that explicit relationships between present information and previous ideas about the situation be identified and considered.

4. The necessary information must be immediately present in the context of the decision, available to working memory.

5. With the exception of tactical situations in which trained, gestalt responses may be the optimal courses of action, analysis of explicit elements of a given decision, immediately available to working memory, should be made in explicitly feature-intensive terms. There should be a deliberate, conscious effort to identify gestalt concepts and to break them down into relevant, step-by-step features.

> 6. Past performance and ideas should be carefully reviewed on a feature-intensive basis. This is true of the individual officer, commander, or administrator, but it is also true on an institutional basis. What have we done in the past, in similar situations? Did it work? If it did, have conditions changed, or is the present situation sufficiently dissimilar that older ideas, even if they are enshrined in policy, no longer prevail? How much investment do we have in a given idea, and how habitual has our implementation of that idea become? This analysis should be made explicitly. The results of this analysis should be forced, perhaps through the use of visual aids involving white boards, into working memory during the consideration of new decisions. Finally, the results of this analysis should be front-loaded, before the situation to which the analysis applies confronts the officers and commanders involved.

It is important to emphasize that these are important aspects of the *cognitive* bases of decisions. They do not supplant the knowledge and experience of tactical experts in any way. Yet an understanding of these principles, and their application in the harsh real world of law enforcement, can supply an additional edge, an additional tool to contribute to operational success and to officer survival. Cognition is not solely concerned with actions and reactions in the outside world; it is also concerned with itself, with understanding the nature of the interior mental processes of the brain. If we can apply intelligence and understanding to our own mental processes, as we do to the exigencies of the real world, we are in a better position to make rational decisions that, plainly and simply, are more likely to succeed. Such rational decisions are more likely to allow everybody to go home at the end of the shift.

Examples of this perspective abound, and they are eminently worthy of study. In the next three chapters, we will consider the importance of cognitive factors in several well-documented historical incidents of processing under pressure, with an eye to a better understanding of the complex interaction of cognitive processes and the very real, dangerous world in which they are applied.

Chapter 8
COGNITION IN TACTICAL ENVIRONMENTS I: LITTLE BIGHORN

In previous chapters, we have seen the effects of stress and arousal on cognition. We have seen the basic operation of perceptual, attentional, and memory systems as they relate to the world of law enforcement, and finally we have discussed important facets of reasoning and decision making, also as applied to law enforcement and command contexts.

The cognitive contexts of law enforcement, the contexts in which these processes operate, vary considerably in terms of the types and levels of risks involved. Some such contexts resemble ordinary business meetings, although the consequences of the decisions that result may be substantially greater, in terms of eventual life-or-death consequences, in the law enforcement realm.

Other law enforcement contexts, of course, are not at all like business meetings. Many law enforcement contexts have a much greater urgency. The cognitive dynamics involved are those of military situations, and the tactical evolutions that result may be virtually indistinguishable from those of military operations.

Even so, tactical situations in law enforcement usually differ in important respects from military contexts. Military operations are frequently concerned solely with the achievement of tactical objectives. In contrast, law enforcement operations, while concerned with tactical success, almost always incorporate a paramount concern for civilian safety, including the safety of suspects and perpetrators to the degree possible.

This is not typically the case in military operations. There are exceptions, of course, and such exceptions have occurred with increasing frequency over the past half century; but it should be noted that military operations are notoriously less successful than otherwise when questions of civilian safety and related concerns must be factored in.

In law enforcement, this question of "collateral damage" is virtually always present if not paramount. Police officers seldom face a platoon of bad guys in an open field. Police officers are much more likely to face bad guys concealed in a house in a densely populated area, armed and hiding among family members and other innocent parties who must not be harmed. This frequently renders tactical situations even more difficult, again from a cognitive perspective, for law enforcement specialists than for military personnel.

Nevertheless, the cognitive dynamics discussed in the previous chapters operate in both military and law enforcement situations of *processing under pressure.* What happens under stress to the military mind is processually no different than what happens under stress to the law enforcement mind, as has been demonstrated so well by Grossman *(1996; Grossman & Christensen, 2004).* It is, therefore, helpful for law enforcement experts to consider these cognitive dynamics in well-documented military contexts, of which history provides a number of excellent examples. This is in part the case because the extreme stresses characteristic of military environments often throw cognitive dynamics into very sharp relief.

This type of historical analysis is becoming increasingly important in the development of better understanding of real-world psychology. For example, this is one of the approaches taken by NASA for the consideration of the psychology of long-range space flight *(e.g., Suefeld, 2008, August).* Because nobody has ever actually taken a long-range space flight (between the planets, for example), the psychological dynamics involved have been studied through the analysis of similar situations, specifically historical examples of long-range maritime exploration. The stresses created by close shipboard quarters, limited resources, long periods of enforced close contact with other crew members, and the prospects of the unknown are held to be similar in space and at sea.

Similarly, we can gain a better appreciation of the dynamics of processing under pressure through the examination of specific tactical situations. In this chapter, and in the two that follow, we'll examine three of these situations: the Battle of the Little Bighorn, which was a tactical failure on the part of the U.S. Army; the "Battle of the Black Sea," the infamous "Black Hawk Down" incident in Mogadishu, Somalia, which was technically a success but which nevertheless produced a high relative casualty rate; and finally, the successful if casualty-ridden counterattack of the U.S. Third Army against the German forces encircling Bastogne during the Second World War. These actions, in the *psychological* judgment of the author, can provide us with excellent examples of the dangerous aspects of cognitive processing under high risk circumstances, as well as examples of the enhancement of the relevant cognitive processes through training, experience, and cognitive preparedness for tactical success in both the military and law enforcement realms.

Important Disclaimers

The author is a cognitive scientist, not a military man or police officer. Consequently, I would not presume to judge the military or tactical aspects of these operations, many of which are still subjects of dispute among genuine military experts. Where I touch on military

Chapter 8 197

issues, or on accounts of actual battlefield tactics, I am merely repeating the work of military historians. I have no intention of presuming to say anything new, critical, or laudatory about the tactical situations, or about the abilities of military personnel, involved in these well-documented battles. All of these fall well outside my areas of professional knowledge.

Rather, what I hope to do in these chapters is to show how the actions of the officers, soldiers, and operators involved in these three important actions are *consistent* with the cognitive dynamics we have discussed in depth above. This is not to say that Generals Custer, Garrison, or Patton were actually experiencing such-and-such a thought at 2 P.M. on a given day in 1876, 1993, or 1944; such assertions, though they are occasionally made in military histories, would require an author to possess both a time machine and some form of telepathy to verify. So, I will not assert, for example, that General Custer was in the grip of cognitive dissonance as he approached the Medicine Tail Coulee. Neither I nor anyone else could know that, not for certain. What we *can* evaluate is what we know of his actions in terms of their consistency with given known cognitive dynamics. This will help us to see how those dynamics might be operating, and how the same dynamics would be expected to operate in an officer or commander, in either the law enforcement or the military realm, approaching a similar situation today. A consideration of processual consistency between given cognitive dynamics and well-documented battlefield behaviors may give the modern police officer or commander an additional edge in the field; an additional tool which may contribute to operational effectiveness and officer survival. It is for those who *are* police or military experts, not for the author who is neither, to judge the utility of this approach.

What Happened to Custer

A fantastic amount of ink has been spilled in attempts to understand the Battle of the Little Bighorn. There are hundreds of books about Custer, numerous films about Custer, and even books about the books about Custer *(e.g., Elliot, 2007)*. With all of this scholarly and popular attention, the facts of the situation become difficult to disentangle from the opinions.

The opinions, of course, have changed. When the author was a boy, Custer was a great hero. By the time the author was a teenager, Custer was generally depicted as deranged at best, or as a sadistic emissary of institutional violence and racism at worst. Today—well, today, people convene near the battlefield every year to re-enact the battle. They ride horses, wear uniforms. Some are there for reasons of genuine scholarly or avocational interest in the historical reenactment. Others are there, of course, purely for the show. Bang, ka-pow, very exciting.

Still other individuals have ridden up to the Cavalry monument, with the blessing of the Park Service, believe it or not, and counted coup on it, whacking the monument to the dead, the mighty mass gravestone, with sticks *(Elliot, 2007)*. Others write poetry devolving from the battle, somehow conflating that very harsh, hot day in 1876 Montana with the Civil Rights Movement.

In short, today, the Battle of the Little Bighorn serves as an historical Rorschach, co-opted or shanghaied by the political or psychological needs of its various partisans. So today, it all depends on whom you talk to. It is, therefore, potentially helpful to start over, to ignore most of the conflicting networks of opinion in favor of the basic facts; and the facts are these.

In late 1875, a U.S. government decision was made to force Great Plains Indian tribes, especially those traditionally if inaccurately known as the Sioux, on to reservations. This action was taken in the wake of Sioux objections and attacks consequent on American incursions into the Black Hills, and on American railroad building. The Black Hills were claimed by the Sioux who had, of course, wrested those territories from other tribes earlier, and who therefore regarded the Black Hills as their territory by right of conquest. Sioux rights to this territory had been affirmed by the United States by treaty, but especially after the discovery of gold in the Hills, increasing numbers of White miners and others entered the area. Attacks and counterattacks commenced; the 1876 Sioux Campaign began.

After a series of U.S. military maneuvers and skirmishes on the plains during that winter and spring, activities that were hampered by the generally horrible weather, three military columns were assigned to converge on Sioux concentrations in what is now southeast Montana. One column was under General George Crook, one under Colonel John Gibbon, and the third was under General Alfred Terry and, of course, included Lt. Colonel George Armstrong Custer, operational commander of the Seventh Cavalry *(Utley, 1973)*.

So it was that in June 1876, Custer found himself in the vicinity of the Little Bighorn River, near what may have been the greatest concentration of Plains tribal peoples ever seen. (The size of this village is now disputed, but practically every aspect of the Little Bighorn battle presents the same problem. What we can be certain of, however, is that it was a really, really big village.)

Predominant among the inhabitants of this village were the "Sioux" tribes, mainly Unkpapa, Blackfeet, Brule, Oglala, Two Kettle, Sans Arc, and Miniconjoux. Together, they might best be called Lakota (related to

Chapter 8   199

Dakota, or Nakota), meaning "Allies," which is what they called themselves.

Northern Cheyenne were also present in the vast extended village, as were representatives of the more southerly Arapaho. There were somewhere in the neighborhood of six to eight thousand people in that village, an estimated 1,500 – 2,000 of whom were warriors *(e.g., Donovan, 2008)*.

After dividing his forces, perhaps not the best move in view of the circumstances, Custer was going to take this huge force on, in mortal combat, with just over two hundred men under his personal command.

THE BEGINNING OF THE END

The orders Custer was given were a bit odd and somewhat amorphous. The intent was for his command to converge on the Lakota camp together with the other two columns, which would have made sense. However, he was also apparently allowed leeway to attack before linking up with the other units if he saw fit. At one level, this makes a kind of sense. In 1876, before the advent of efficient battlefield communications, it was logical to give a subordinate commander some freedom, to refrain from binding him to inflexible field orders. At the same time, it might have made more sense to have given Custer somewhat less flexible directives, to have given him guidelines for cases of reasonable eventuality. However, this did not happen, and Custer was essentially free to get with the program and be a team player or to charge on his own. It should surprise no one that he decided to charge.

In the pre-dawn darkness of June 25, Custer's scouts, under the command of Lt. Charles Varnum, ascended a hill in the Wolf Mountains, some miles from the village. Their purpose was to scope out the territory; the geographic eminence that they climbed would become known as the Crow's Nest. From these heights, the gigantic village was visible. A considerable distance was involved, of course, but the scouts could discern not only the village but even the villagers' ponies. Varnum himself was unable to make out the ponies, or the village itself for that matter; on the other hand, his eyes were inflamed, probably from trail dust. Acknowledging his temporary visual impairment, Varnum took the scouts' words for what they saw, and it was reported back to Custer that there was, very simply, a huge and hostile village out there. So, Custer climbed up to the Crow's Nest to see it, too.

EYEWITNESS ANOMALIES

Unlike Varnum, Custer does not seem to have had anything wrong with his eyes; but he couldn't see the village either. The scouts tried everything they could think of to get Custer to see what they saw, but somehow he simply couldn't make it out. It's traditionally been said that this was because of "morning haze," but that would mean that somehow the morning haze worked on Custer but not on anybody else.

The village was huge. Custer's Ree scouts began their death songs—nobody was getting out of there, nobody was going to survive the battle, if they went up against the forces such a mighty village would surely mobilize. Yet Custer couldn't see the ponies, the village, or even the colossal clouds of smoke that rose from the fires of the thousands of hostile people below.

There is a mystery here, because in 1908 a photographer named Curtis went to the Crow's Nest to check things out. He was able to distinguish cabins, individual cabins, on the site of the village from his perspective at the Crow's Nest, which seems to suggest that Custer should have been able to see exactly what Varnum's scouts saw. On the other hand, perhaps Curtis was in the wrong place *(e.g., Connell, 1985)*; nobody seems to be certain of the precise spot, and the author has found various published estimates of the distance from the Crow's Nest to the battlefield. On yet another hand, however, if Curtis was anywhere near the right place, his perspective on the faraway battlefield would not have been much altered by an error of, perhaps, a few degrees of arc. In short, it's hard to explain Custer's failure to see the enormous village spread out before him. I have driven and hiked around the area surrounding the battlefield, armed with a decent pair of binoculars. For what it's worth, I was able to make out the faces of children, playing in the Little Bighorn River, from substantial distances, and at least to see people and activity at the river from ranges of several miles wherever the topography afforded an unobstructed view. Seeing an entire village would have been child's play. The Little Bighorn lies in a valley, but the valley is in the middle of the Plains. It is a clear, open place, where vistas stretch for many miles—yet Custer could not make out the largest Plains Indian village in history from the Crow's Nest *(Connell, 1985)*, when apparently everybody else could. "Otoe Sioux"—Plenty Sioux—Too many Sioux—muttered the Rees; and yet Custer couldn't see them.

So maybe Curtis had the wrong hill, or perhaps I was there on especially clear days, or possibly Custer had the same trail-dust problem as Varnum even though nobody mentioned it at the time; but perhaps, instead, what we are seeing here is the effect of *processing under pressure*—specifically, the influence of stress on visual perception, and most especially on *interpretation*. Custer, in effect, was an eyewitness to that village, as were his scouts; and as we have already seen, extreme stress can alter eyewitness performance substantially.

And Custer was under extreme stress.

Chapter 8

GEORGE ARMSTRONG CUSTER, HIMSELF

Custer was, by any standards, an unusual man. In the American Civil War, he won his generalship at a very young age, based on his very aggressive command of the cavalry placed in his charge. There were heavy casualties, but for some reason he was never among them. He wore a distinctive uniform with a red bandana at his throat for additional distinction, and he led from in front—his men began to wear the same bandana in imitation of their leader, and they literally followed him into hell. Many of them died. Custer, though he took the same risks, did not.

After the Civil War, things did not go as well for Custer. Like most officers in the Union Army, he suffered a massive loss of rank. His Volunteer Army generalship was converted into his Regular Army rank of captain, although by the time of the Little Bighorn he was a lieutenant colonel again. As was the custom, however, he was still politely referred to as General; perhaps a consolation, or perhaps a continual painful reminder of what he had lost.

Custer was always impulsive. As Connell *(1985)* put it, when he was challenged, his instinct was to charge. At one point on the Plains, he went hunting, and he tried to kill a buffalo with his pistol (think about that for a minute—Buffalo? Those huge things with the big horns, the giant muscles, and the serious attitude problems? *He was shooting at those things with a black-powder pistol?*). But anyway, that's what he did, and he got so excited that he blew the brains out of his own horse, rather than those of the buffalo, completely by accident. His men found him wandering around the prairie afterward, and in his own book *(Custer, reprinted 1995)*, he treats the whole thing in a jocular fashion—*killed my own horse, fell off, buffalo ran off, ha-ha, my gallant lads turned up and everything turned out jolly. Cheers. Ha-ha.*

An unusual man.

Psychologists, like the present author, could have endless fun wondering if that spill from the horse caused the sort of prefrontal trauma we saw in Vignette 2, and what effect that might have had later at the Little Bighorn, but that's all it would be, fun and endless unfounded speculation. Let us move on.

Custer's impulsivity wasn't confined to the slaughter of bison and horses. In 1867, he really, really missed his devoted wife Libby, so he deserted his command and rode several hundred miles to be with her. The Army was not amused; he was court-martialed.

In 1876, Custer had the temerity to testify against Secretary of War William Belknap, concerning Bureau of Indian Affairs corruption. He also testified against Orvil Grant, brother of U.S. Grant, president of the United States. This did not go over well with the president, a man not noted for leniency. This was especially the case because Custer had also, at one point, arrested Grant's son, Captain Fred, for being drunk.

Between the AWOL incident and his direct attacks on the president's friends and family, Custer's career was, not to put too fine a point on it, in the toilet. President Grant actually forbade Custer's presence on the mission that led to the Little Bighorn. Custer himself suffered dramatic humiliation at Grant's hands, and a tearful session of begging, literally crying and pleading on his knees before his superiors, before Grant would allow him to go.

George Armstrong Custer, the great cavalryman, the young general, the fearless soldier, crying on his knees to save his career—how much more stress could a man experience?

His command of the Seventh Cavalry had not been entirely stress-free, either. Custer was a harsh disciplinarian, sadistically so by modern standards, and excessive even by the standards of the nineteenth century. As a result, he was frankly and generally hated by many of his men, who expressed their displeasure through amazing desertion rates. (Desertion was common in the Army of the West, but Custer seems to have hit the jackpot in this respect.) The men who didn't desert were effectively untrained. Most were urban people, with limited understanding and tolerance of such things as winds and plains and horses. Many had little or no training in the handling of their accident-prone trap-door carbines. Some of the few men who actually were trained veterans had been under Custer's command before in Texas, and his astonishingly excessive discipline during those days had produced the obvious effect: a generalized and unhealthy hatred of all things Custer. To compound his staffing problems, most of Custer's most important officers, including Captain Frederick Benteen and Major Marcus Reno, also appear to have hated his guts. In the general wave of demotions that followed the Civil War, pathological professional jealousy was endemic in the officer corps, and Custer, a self-appointed prima donna and martinet, perhaps came in for even more than his fair share. At any event, there was a definite anti-Custer faction in his own regiment, bitterly opposed by a pro-Custer faction involving some of his own relatives; at the end of the day, the Seventh was very far from being an integrated unit, and Custer had to face these disturbing facts (e.g., *Connell, 1985; Donovan, 2007*).

In summary, Custer's career was on the ropes. The President—the All-Powerful President of the United States, the Army of the Potomac's Thunder-Wielding God of War, President General Ulysses S. Grant himself—bore a powerful personal grudge against him. The reader will recall the effects of cognitive dissonance, the fact that the more you pay, the better you like; Custer had paid an enormous amount to be out there, dusty and overheated, in the wilds of Montana. He had begged on his knees, tears in his eyes, and called in a lot of favors from his commanders and colleagues to achieve this command. Somehow, those favors would have to be repaid. He had a mixed reputation. The AWOL trip to see his wife; a number of incidents like the Incredible Buffalo Gunfight with his own horse; these things followed him like rude court jesters in the otherwise carefully orchestrated military parade that was his life. He was in trouble. He was many, many miles from his home in Michigan, or from his more familiar haunts east of the Mississippi. He was traveling over a dusty, wind-blasted, sun-slammed grassy desert without a tree in sight, a place in which his many Indian enemies seemed able to melt into the textures of the Plains themselves. His men hated him for what we might perceive as his nearly insane levels of discipline. His officers hated him because of personal differences, professional rivalries—whatever. Custer was effectively alone and widely hated, and operating in an alien environment he barely understood. His career was in very, very serious trouble; and he was in command.

Thus, certain levels of stress were involved, both of the chronic type we discussed in Chapter 1, and of the more immediate acute type discussed in Chapter 2.

So there he was, on the Crow's Nest, looking down into the largest concentration of hostile Plains Indians in the history of the world. His professional scouts, Mitch Bouyer and Lonesome Charley Reynolds, could see the village. His Ree recruit scouts could see the village, too; they were singing death songs. Expert opinion; and Custer ignored it completely. Big village? Who cares? I can't see it anyway. Don't know why, don't care. There are Indians down there, and I'm going to attack them, and that's that.

Light up the roof. Siren. Go.

PSYCHOLOGICAL DYNAMICS AND SPRINGFIELD CARBINES

As we will see, other members of the Seventh Cavalry demonstrated similarly horrible eyewitness performance, together with truly wretched judgment. However, even if Custer had seen the massive village below, even if he'd considered the full magnitude of the forces deployed against him, it might not have mattered, to him or to anybody else. Incredible as it may sound today, neither Custer nor the other officers involved in the 1876 Sioux Campaign were concerned with the prospect of defeat. Their fear was that *the hostiles might get away.*

There seems to have been a profound *mental set* concerning this issue. Recent Indian battles, including the Wagon Box Fight and the Fetterman Massacre *(see Chapter 2; Monnett, 2008; Utley, 1973)*, had provided solid evidence that the Plains tribes posed a powerful military challenge. They used complex and effective tactics, and although many warriors were armed with traditional weapons, many were frequently better armed for short-range combat, with their civilian repeating rifles, than was the Cavalry with its single-shot carbines. The Plains Indians, in short, constituted a powerful military force not to be trifled with. Yet in the minds of the Army officers, including Custer, there seemed to be no question that the U.S. Army would defeat the Indians under any circumstances. From the officers' cognitive, mental-set-driven standpoint, the Army was superior, the Indians militarily inferior. So, there was simply no concern about the prospect of military reversal or defeat. Such prospects were inconceivable. Instead, the inflexible, adamantine mental set was simple and specific: *Don't let them get away.*

This mental set manifested itself in other destructive ways. Custer had refused to take Gatling guns (primitive rotary machine guns) or infantry support for his cavalry, on the premise that these units would be too slow to keep up—he had to move quickly to keep the Sioux and Cheyenne from scurrying away before he could get to them. (The Hindsight Spirits, of course, are still with us: hindsight renders this picture vastly more ridiculous than it could possibly have been in foresight.) The upshot, however, was that he was facing the Indian forces with horses and carbines. The carbines, as mentioned above, were single-shot trap-door Springfields, slow to reload and with an alarming tendency to jam, as their copper cartridges became deformed in their breaches and became difficult or impossible to extract under field conditions.

Now, it is true that many, probably the majority, of the Lakota and Cheyenne did not have modern repeating rifles. Some had war clubs, or bows and arrows. Some had old-fashioned muzzle-loading rifles, devastating on a shot-by-shot basis but taking forever to reload. A few warriors probably had Spencer or Springfield carbines like those of Custer's cavalry. However, alarming numbers of the Indian warriors were armed with Henry or Winchester repeating rifles; not as accurate as the cavalry Springfields at range, true, but they could fire over and over again as the poor bluecoat soldiers tried desperately to yank jammed copper cartridge casings out of their single-shot carbines. If the Indians could get close enough, in great numbers with these superior weapons, the Cavalry would stand at an appreciable military disadvantage.

So, the Cavalry was massively outnumbered. The Cavalry was, in many cases, outgunned. The Cavalry's reconnaissance of the battlefield was hampered by the scout commander's dust-blindness, and by the inexplicable inability of the commanding officer to see the enemy at all.

Chapter 8

In hindsight, to attack under these circumstances appears effectively insane; Custer would have been far better off waiting for reinforcing columns to catch up and aid in the attack, as he had in fact been ordered to do in the first place. In hindsight.

But was there any way to use *foresight* to avoid what happened?

Well, in order to do so, a very high order of feature-intensive processing would have been required, within several categories of thought. Custer would have had to consider comparative weapon range, weapon type, and probable prevalence of weapon type of opposing and friendly forces. He would have had to consider size and disposition of opposing and friendly forces, together with probable conditions, state of nutrition and rest, use and disposition of transport (horses and ponies); state of training, readiness, and terrain familiarity on the part of his own men (this was a problem—again, many were recent recruits from urban backgrounds). All of this feature-intensive processing, this strategic, feature-intensive thinking, would have had to be calmly conducted by Custer, or at least by his officers, there in the terrible summer heat *before* the battle; and because his most important officers (Reno and Benteen) would barely speak to him, and their level of alcohol use at the time was apparently epic in scope *(Connell, 1985)*, the only person Custer could really depend on for this monumental piece of integrative FI thinking, if it had ever happened in the first place, was Custer himself.

And remember: Custer was under stress.

Under stress, the simplicity of Gestalt reactions is far more appealing than the mental effort of feature-intensive analysis; and the gestalt reaction was very simple, and well-rooted in mental set, especially for Custer. Despite his personal declaration that everything he did in any battle was the result of painstaking study of imaginary military situations, there is no real evidence that Custer made any substantial, strategic, FI consideration of what he was about to do, or of how it would all turn out. Custer appears to have been in the grip of the tactical, gestalt mindset well before the battle began, rather than in the feature-intensive, strategic mindset more conducive to planning a battle. The evidence is consistent with a relatively pure set of mental-set-driven, Gestalt responses: *Don't let them get away. Charge.*

As it turned out, the Sioux and Cheyenne had no intention of getting away. Custer split his forces on that hot day of June 25, 1876, and ordered Major Marcus Reno to employ three companies in an attack on the southern end of the village. Reno did so; the attack failed, and Reno and his men retreated under fire to a nearby hilltop. They dug in and held out for nearly two heat-blasted, thirst-crazed, terror-inducing days. Reno's conduct on this occasion is still a subject of ferocious dispute among Little Bighorn authorities and aficionados.

COGNITION ON RENO'S HILL

The siege on the hilltop provides a valuable interlude, at least from the standpoint of cognitive science. Here we see the direct interaction of the forces of stress and of interpretation on the accuracy of eyewitness memory in combatants, as opposed to civilian bystanders.

Many combat incidents afford insight into this topic. For example, military pilots and aircrew are notorious for inflated estimates of the numbers of enemy aircraft shot down *(e.g., Ford, 2007)*. However, there are mathematical as well as psychological reasons for this phenomenon in aerial combat. If you shoot at a plane, and I shoot at a plane, and it explodes, we're both likely to claim a victory, doubling our real scores. This is especially true if the tunnel vision of actual combat, discussed above in Chapter 2, prevents our seeing each other's aircraft as we focus on the enemy at hand. So, with reference to aircraft totals, the role of psychology as such is certainly not the only damaging influence; but there on Reno Hill, overlooking the Little Bighorn, no such confounds existed. The eyewitnesses had no possible sources for erroneous interpretation of what they saw, for their mistakes, outside of stress and psychology.

And what mistakes they were. "Renegade whites" were seen riding with the Indians—these imaginary renegades even carried imaginary company guidons, the little swallowtail flags that distinguished individual cavalry units. Exact repetitions of cavalry bugle calls were heard, or imagined, and it was inferred that the non-existent renegades had white renegade buglers with them. Some men, there on that hot, thirsty hilltop, saw columns, relief columns, of army troops racing to their rescue. They heard the bawled commands of the imaginary officers in command of these nonexistent regiments. These "columns" seemed so real that Reno's troops fired guns and blew a bugle call to guide them in, and the imaginary approach of these much-desired reinforcements elicited cheer after cheer.

As is often the case, these stress-induced hallucinations, these eyewitness errors, had at least some basis in fact. Some Indian warriors took cavalry clothing or accoutrements from defeated soldiers, and put them on or brandished them. It was therefore perfectly possible for a stranded trooper on Reno's hill to see figures wearing blue riding by, or to see those bluecoats carrying swallowtail guidons. This fact may seem to "explain" the eyewitness errors nicely; but let the reader think, in feature-intensive terms, of what the given cavalryman was actually seeing. The apparition before him might have been wearing a blue coat, but the coat in question was probably torn and almost certainly left open. Its wearer would be shirtless beneath the blue cavalry battle-dress, or perhaps wearing buckskin; he would have moccasins, not boots; he would be carrying a traditional Indian weapon or an excellent civilian repeater, not an Army trap-door Springfield. His style of riding would differ in almost every detail from the typical style of a soldier. He would generally be darker-skinned than the average soldier, with longer hair and with tribal decorations such as face paint and warrior's feathers; and his horse would usually be a pinto pony, not a cavalry mount, marked very differently and generally astronomically smaller than any horse used by the Army.

The reader can probably think of additional visual anomalies, but these suffice to prove the point. Under stress, what a person sees can be readily re-interpreted and reconfigured, by means of the cognitive dynamics discussed above, into an unrecognizable facsimile of whatever was actually seen.

At some points during the Little Bighorn battle, troopers attempted to take cover behind prairie dog mounds, the little hills of earth that the rodents heap up around their burrows. These are tiny mounds of loose dirt, and anyone who has ever seen a prairie dog town will realize immediately that they afford no protection at all. The troopers' actions here seem crazy, insane, unless you realize that this is a classic example of tunnel-vision-related gestalt reasoning. That little hill is made of dirt. Dirt can be used as a barricade. So, I'm hiding behind it. Excuse me if, in the arousal state typical of deadly combat, I fail to engage in a feature-intensive analysis of the size of the given prairie-dog mound, and the average density of its earth deposition, as the terrifying blast from a Spencer rifle or a Sharps buffalo gun rips my head off.

Reno, his officers, and his troops were eventually rescued from their hilltop. No such luck befell Custer. He took about two hundred men—the generally agreed figure is 211—to attack the Sioux and Cheyenne at the northern end of the village. As is well known, there were no survivors.

Historians have debated this maneuver endlessly. Why did Custer split his forces? Why did he attack such an enormous group of warriors with such a tiny band? Again, certain answers to these questions are unlikely ever to be forthcoming. However, we can suggest psychological processes that are at least highly consistent with what happened.

Psychology at Custer's Last Stand

Custer's career on the plains was by no means as active, in terms of pitched battles, as his career in the Civil War. However, at a previous engagement in 1867 on the Washita River, he had employed similar tactics. There were several physical similarities to the Little Bighorn situation. The attack was made on a large village, inhabited both by warriors and by noncombatants. The village was situated on the banks of a river; and on that day, Custer's division of forces prevailed, although one of his units was isolated and exterminated by the Cheyenne warriors. Indeed, at one point, the Indian forces appeared to be massing for a counterattack that might have yielded results similar to those of the Little Bighorn. Custer employed a subterfuge, in which he feinted along the river in force; the Indians altered their positions and the disposition of their warriors accordingly, and Custer was therefore able to withdraw successfully, having inflicted a significant, controversial, and much-debated defeat on the village.

We have already seen the influence of mental set on behavior. When we have an idea of how a thing should go, we often behave accordingly, in a gestalt manner. Such behaviors are more likely under stress, and we have already seen that Custer was under psychological stress, both acutely and chronically. The Little Bighorn situation was a lot like the Washita—big village, river, mix of combatants and noncombatants. In the tunnel vision that often characterizes stress responses in tactical situations, one might very well respond to these gestalt characteristics without considering, on a feature-intensive basis, the major differences between the military situations. These include the facts that the Little Bighorn was a *really* big village, and that unlike the Washita, there was probably no element of surprise operating in Custer's favor.

Custer, under stress, may have reverted to the mental set he had learned at the Washita. Certainly the evidence is consistent with this perspective, although, again, we will never be absolutely certain. He divided his forces and attacked downstream. Of course, some of these actions may have derived from Custer's estimates of practical military necessity at the time, rather than from a cognitive tie to the Washita. But in any event, he charged, lunging along the river with a portion of his divided forces as he had at the Washita; and he met the mighty charge of the Sioux and Cheyenne, near what would later be known as Last Stand Hill.

Last Stand. A heroic name, and one that doesn't sit well with modern sensibilities. Recent scholars have gone to great lengths to de-emphasize the heroic aspects of this battle, at least with regard to heroism on the American side. They point out evidence of disorganization among the troopers, poor battlefield dispositions, evidence of jammed Springfields and desperate attempts to pry the deformed copper cartridges out of the nonfunctional weapons. Why all of this seems unheroic seems difficult to say; the troopers were surprised, they were outnumbered, and they were in many cases outgunned. And

Chapter 8

they died. Most of them died fighting, under hopeless circumstances, in an entirely alien place. If that isn't a Last Stand, I don't know what is.

Questions swarm like Plains mosquitoes in summer. If Custer was aware of the size of the village, of the magnitude of the forces that confronted him, couldn't he have backed off at the last moment? Couldn't he have held his forces in readiness, in a reconnaissance pose, and waited for reinforcements, as he was in fact supposed to do?

For what it's worth, I doubt it, and the reason has to do with the phenomenon of cognitive dissonance, the process discussed above in which the more you pay, the better you like. Custer had staked his career and reputation on this campaign. He had literally cried and begged on his knees for this command. He had ridden that long, hot, boring, backside-busting distance across the plains from Fort Abraham Lincoln in what is now North Dakota to this looming battlefield on a Montana river. He'd paid an enormous price to get here. He knew it, and he felt it. He had bought this chance for an epic victory at great price, and he was not about to release his grip, bought at so dear a cost on so many dimensions, on that victory.

The cognitive dissonance involved must have been insuperable, and Custer did what he was best at. He charged.

Let us consider a final piece of evidence for the tactical tunnel-vision consistent with Custer's behavior. It is probable that the last surviving cavalryman to see him alive was Giovanni Martini, who had anglicized his name to John Martin. He carried a message from Custer to the rest of his divided forces just before things got really nasty on Last Stand Hill. Martini reported Custer's last words, at least his last words heard by any American survivor of the Little Bighorn. Martini was a recent immigrant who apparently did not speak English very well. His testimony has therefore been subjected to a significant level of sanctimonious scholarly doubt. In fact, his report of Custer's words varies curiously among published sources, although the gist is always the same; I've chosen Connell's *(1985)* version for the present work. Be all that as it may, what Martini reported was this. As Custer saw the overwhelming forces arrayed against him and his troopers; as pretty much all of the fighting Sioux and Cheyenne in the world came roaring toward the Medicine Tail Coulee and up the Greasy Grass Ridge into his face; as most of the fighting Sioux and Cheyenne in the world who weren't in his face were surrounding him from behind; as he faced total obliteration of himself and his command from a gigantic, superbly-led, well-equipped military force astronomically larger than his own detachment; Custer shouted a gleeful rallying cry to his men:

"Hurrah, boys, we've got them!"

Lessons from Custer's Grave

Again, it is not the author's place to comment on the military aspects of the Little Bighorn battle. Besides, practically everybody else has already done so. However, there are certain things we *can* say, psychologically, about this battle, things that are directly relevant to modern law enforcement and military operations. These are things that could have been corrected, either through training or through a feature-intensive analysis of what was about to happen. This, once again, is of course hindsight. Neither Custer nor anybody else can be blamed for having failed to see the future. However, now that we're *in* the future, we can use that hindsight productively to keep similar things from happening again. *So what have we learned?*

TRAINING

Most of Custer's men arrived at the battlefield with very little training in the handling of their mounts or their weapons. Obviously, they would have benefitted from a realization, in Washington, that a longer period of standard military training was essential in producing desirable tactical outcomes. This, of course, would be recognized by any modern police or military commander. However, what might be less obvious is the importance of front-loaded, terrain-specific training, delivered in an explicit, feature-intensive manner, on which the individual trooper could build future successful tactical gestalts. Bransford and Johnson, discussed above, have shown us the importance of front-loading, of providing a prior framework for understanding. How many men, other than those with Custer's doomed personal command, might have survived at different points if provided with something like the following front-loaded, explicit instruction: "The Great Plains provide few points of natural cover. You may have a tendency to hide behind something like a prairie dog mound, or a rotten log or something, but it won't work. If you have to retreat, keep riding erratically until you reach an arroyo, or a big rock, or something really substantial behind which to take cover." Then, the men could have practiced this on a relatively featureless piece of ground. The need for realistic training, for the provision of simulated hazards similar to those that will actually be encountered in the field, is already known to every competent training officer; recall Chief McAllister's training officer, discussed in Chapter 2, who insisted on realistic field drills in the taking of cover behind large, substantial objects. Verbal instruction may be denigrated in favor of real-world, motor-skills training; but the point here is that *the two should be used together*. Front-loaded, explicit, feature-intensive instruction should be provided, in order to yield the best prior framework for understanding the exigencies of field training. This will

Chapter 8

contribute to performance in the field, when the real thing happens. This will help officers survive; simply and starkly, more of them will go home at the end of the shift.

MISSION

Custer was provided with nebulous orders. Either wait for us, said Terry and Gibbon, or don't wait for us. A failure of the *precision of language* rears its head again (see Chapter 4). Rather than providing Custer with a feature-intensive table of contingencies (for example, if there are more than X hostiles, wait for the other columns and establish a perimeter; if there are fewer, you may attack without divided forces, etc., etc.,), Custer's superiors provided him with a vague set of gestalt semi-directives. Custer's orders were something along the lines of, "Wait for us, or at least we'd like you to wait for us, to close the jaws of this mighty military trap we've set up, unless you decide not to wait for us and you'd rather attack. But we'd really rather you wait for us." It sounds more like the maunderings of an indecisive lover than a military directive. Custer was given a situation in which appropriate command initiative blended, in a gestalt manner, into an amorphous set of general preferences. There was nothing explicit in his orders; all was implicit, and as Haviland and Clark showed us above, implicit concepts are difficult to grasp and therefore highly subject to interpretation. Without a clear sense of exactly what the mission was, it is not surprising that Custer put his own personal stamp on it. It is also not surprising that Custer's personal stamp involved a tunnel-vision-based, effectively suicidal charge.

COMMAND PSYCHOLOGY

Again, with reference to the Custer battle, this is an anachronism. Nobody could, or would, have thought of this in 1876. However, in a perfect world, Custer should have met, probably a number of times, with somebody who understood cognitive science. (Cognitive science, of course, did not exist at the time—we're talking about a *really* perfect world here.)

Custer should have had some front-loaded, explicit, prior frameworks for understanding himself and his tactical proclivities:

> Previous military successes are no guarantee that the same tactics will work twice. Realize that when things go bad, you're going to rely on previously loaded gestalts. Make certain that before a battle, you consider in depth, on a feature-by-feature basis, whether a previous tactic is being employed because it is the best, or because it's what you always do. Also realize that

when you are under the acute stress of tactical command, and every commander who has a human nervous system will do this, you are likely to experience cognitive tunnel vision. You are likely not to see hazards on the periphery, or to consider them in sufficient depth if you do see them. Rely on the proven competence of scouts to tell you of these hazards, and make sure you incorporate these hazards into your tactical planning. You may not even be able to see things in front of you (such as gigantic villages?), but if several competent people tell you that they can see them, either take their word for it or order additional reconnaissance to confirm or deny their reports.

And for God's sake, *be flexible*. If you always charge, ask yourself if charging is the right course of action, tactically, in a given situation, or if you're just operating out of mental set. Be willing to create contingency analyses, and take your own mental tendencies into account when you formulate them. Be aware of your own proclivities toward cognitive dissonance.

Concerning Custer's shout of "Hurrah, boys, we've got them!" when faced with overwhelming odds: actually, there was nothing wrong with the sentiment, at least at that point. Any competent police officer will tell you that when you enter a tactical situation, defeat is not an option, must never be an option. Cognitively, effectively, *you are going to win*. It doesn't matter if they bring dogs, chains, a Tiger tank, and a bazooka, and all you have is a jackknife and four feet of dental floss, *you are going to defeat the enemy*. Period. No question. Victory is the only option. You will win. That is the only possible tactical mindset, both for victory and for officer survival, and the gestalts that form it must be inflexible and adamantine.

However, that's the *tactical* mindset. The *strategic* mindset is a whole different ball game. Strategic thinking is essential, but it has to be completed well before the onset of any action that will require a tactical mindset. The feature-intensive analysis and psychological considerations characteristic of strategic thought are absolutely essential, but you have to do them before the rodeo starts; *you have to do them before things get bad*. You, as a commander or officer, must do all of that feature-intensive cognitive work *before* all hell breaks loose.

This means that you, as a commander or officer, must do something that is personally very difficult. You must consciously transform yourself, at the point of battle, from a cognitive, feature-intensive, psychologically knowledgeable analyst into a non-stop, victory-assured, gestalt-functioning warrior. The one is dependent upon the other. The strategist must conduct a feature-intensive analysis of the prospects of defeat, and of what to do about them, well in advance. The tactician, who is of course the same person a few minutes or even seconds later, *must not allow these considerations to enter the head.* Under optimal circumstances, the necessary actions have already been explicitly front-loaded into smooth, tactically effective gestalts. Light up the roof. Siren. Go. And because of all that prior, strategic, psychologically minded FI analysis you conducted *before* you went into battle, you will usually win once you are *in* the battle. You are professionally effective. You maximize officer survival.

And you go home.

Stress

As we have seen, Custer was under an amazing amount of stress. He also must have been under the influence of cognitive dissonance and of a number of potentially damaging mental sets. The highly impulsive Custer, whose very impulsivity was one of the characteristics that made him an outstanding cavalry officer, was not likely to be able to pull back and wait for reinforcements, or even to make the feature-intensive analysis needed to realize that such a move might be necessary. What was needed here was a highly flexible commander who could charge or pull back as changing battlefield conditions dictated. Custer, at the Little Bighorn, was not that man. Even as a superior cavalry officer, at that moment in his psychological life, he should not have been placed in a situation in which tunnel vision and mental set could work their nefarious magic and get his command blown away.

I recently had the opportunity to talk to two outstanding Explosive Ordinance Disposal (EOD bomb-squad) officers. These are men who routinely and voluntarily enter the worst environments in the world. Their job is to dissect and destroy complex, murderous devices that make spitting cobras look like children's toys. These guys have absolutely nothing to prove.

They know this, but not from a sense of machismo. They know it in a highly constructive and feature-intensive way. They understand that they have human nervous systems, and that after many minutes, or hours, or minutes that seem like hours, of doing insanely technical and intellectually demanding things to demented satanic devices, they get tired. Sometimes they get too tired to continue.

So guess what they do.

They stop.

These are people who really understand the dynamics of *processing under pressure.* They realize that their fine motor skills have been tired to the point where they are no longer operating at peak efficiency. They recognize the point at which their cognitive skills, the product of the malleable human nervous system, have been reduced to suboptimal levels. So, they stop. They leave the given device, and they tell another bomb technician what they've done and where they were going with it. Then the new technician suits up and does the same dangerous, precise, highly technical work until his or her brain is about to fry. Not until it's fried, for God's sake; at that point, they'd make mistakes and the damn thing would go off. They work only until they recognize that their efficiency is about to become impaired. Then they have another expert continue with the disposal. It's a calm, well-thought-out, psychologically balanced procedure; and when they're done, the bomb is disabled, or it is in a condition to destroy. No civilians die, no buildings are blown into rubble, and everybody gets to go home. We will discuss these dynamics in a subsequent chapter.

Can you imagine George Armstrong Custer as a bomb tech? *"Hurrah, boys, I've got it!"*

Boom.

This does not mean that Custer was necessarily a bad officer. It does not mean that President Grant, so to speak, should have taken Custer's gun and badge. However, it should be noted that "good" and "bad," as global terms, are frequently fairly useless for characterizing a police or military officer. The fact remains that there are officers, like Custer, who are good at one thing, and others who are good at something else. There are wonderful patrol people who make abysmal detectives, and vice versa. There are outstandingly innovative and independent patrol officers whose independence becomes an absolute nightmare in the necessarily coordinated, team-player world required by effective SWAT operations. Custer was a man who charged. Under stress, from a modern perspective, we would expect him to be a man who charged even more than usual. What was required at the Little Bighorn was a man who was capable of charging, but who was also stealthy and thoughtful, and able to consider strategic ramifications in feature-intensive depth before committing the Seventh Cavalry to the all-in gestalts of a cavalry charge. What was needed was a strategist who, at the right moment, would turn himself into a warrior, a warrior who lived, for the duration of the battle, in a purely tactical mindset.

The problem is that Custer seems to have been in a tactical mindset *all the time*. Might it not have been better to assign him to a new command, one in which his genuine skills would have been precisely tailored to the situations he would encounter? At the same time, might it not have been better to use the extraordinary power of Presidents and military commanders to take some of the stress off of him, so that when he charged, the charge would be the best?

Chapter 8

If Grant, or Custer's superior Sheridan, or somebody else in authority had reassigned him, would Custer have been upset?

Probably.

On the other hand, would the Seventh Cavalry have been slaughtered?

Maybe not.

Mental set. Cognitive response to stress. Inadequate training. Vague, non-explicit gestalt reasoning concerning the mission itself. Failure to distinguish the strategic, feature-intensive mindset *before* the battle from the trained, gestalt, tactical responses required for victory *in* the battle. All of these contribute to military and to police tactical failures, and all can be prevented or reduced. However, this prevention and reduction require that commanders and officers understand relevant psychological issues, that they have a strong grasp of the principles of *processing under pressure*. That understanding provides an extra edge, contributes to professional effectiveness, contributes to officer survival.

Custer's superiors did not have that edge. Neither did Custer.

He died; and he took a lot of the Seventh Cavalry with him.

Chapter 9
Cognition in Tactical Environments II: Mogadishu, 1993

The military disaster of the "Battle of the Black Sea" in Mogadishu, Somalia, is sufficiently well known that there is even a Hollywood movie about it (*Black Hawk Down*, the title taken from the excellent book by Mark Bowden *[2000]*).

It must be said at the outset that technically, this incident was a military success; the military objectives were achieved. However, they were achieved at the cost of two very expensive Black Hawk helicopters destroyed by enemy action, two additional Black Hawks badly damaged but successfully landed in friendly territory, the deaths of eighteen American soldiers, and the wounding of seventy-three others. These are not huge numbers, but they are significant in proportion to the forces deployed; and in any event, they are too many. Also, these American casualty figures do not include the thousand Somalis, including three to five hundred dead, who were also casualties of this battle. The Battle of Mogadishu was by any standards a human tragedy.

Also at the outset, I wish to disavow any criticism of the commander of these forces, General William Garrison. For one thing, it is not my place to make such criticisms; and for another, Major General Garrison was in an unusual situation. He was a Special Forces expert, in command of very independent forces, Army Rangers and Delta Force operators. His acknowledged role was less that of a traditional battle commander than that of the man who provided what his operators needed in the field *(Bowden, 2000)*.

This battle took place in relatively modern times, and is, therefore, perhaps a more sensitive and controversial subject than the Battle of the Little Bighorn. Yet, as we will see, the similarities between these battles, in terms of consistency with identified cognitive processes, are substantial.

The Seventh Cavalry Revisited

During the operations of the Ranger and Delta forces in Somalia, several intelligence and tactical failures had already occurred; media and political pressure were now considerable. Commanders and soldiers were under significant stress as a result, and under considerable pressure to perform. They were under pressure to do something right, something spectacular, something *right now*.

We need not dwell on the ways in which pressure from superiors and the public can degrade performance, as they did at Mogadishu, because we have already considered these factors under the very similar circumstances obtaining at the Little Bighorn. The psychological similarities of this pressure-cooker situation to the pressures on Custer and his command are obvious.

As with the Seventh Cavalry, there was also professional division within the ranks of the forces involved *(Bowden, 2000)*. Although the Rangers tended to idolize the Delta operators to some degree, this was not reciprocated; some of the Delta people considered the Rangers relatively unprepared for the mission and had limited confidence in them. Neither of these elite groups held their nearby colleagues of the Quick Reaction Force (QRF), or its soldiers and officers of the famed 10th Mountain Division, in high esteem. Again we see the similarities, psychologically, to that hot, bad day in Montana.

The reader will recall that Custer and his commanders did not consider potential Indian resistance to be a significant factor. Their mental set was that the Indians would be defeated, and that the main problem was that the Lakota and Cheyenne would get away. In the same way, the American forces in Somalia did not consider potential Somali resistance to be a major factor. The Somalis weren't expected to put up much of a fight, even though there were vast numbers of armed, hostile Somali warriors in Mogadishu, just as there were vast numbers of armed, hostile Plains warriors in the village at the Little Bighorn.

The hot dusty plains of Montana draw closer and closer, in terms of cognitive psychology, to the hot dusty plains of Somalia.

The Battle of the Black Sea

The basic facts of the battle are fairly straightforward. The operation itself, in fact, bore resemblance in intent to a normal police operation. It was to be a coordinated apprehension and arrest.

In this, the Black Hawk incident differed from the Custer battle significantly. At the Little Bighorn, the military objective was to defeat an opposing force. In Mogadishu, the intent was to arrest two bad guys, specifically two senior lieutenants of the warlord Mohamed Aidid. The Rangers and Delta operators were simply going out to arrest a couple of guys. The same thing police officers do every day.

One might see the ghost of Custer's vague orders here. Was he supposed to wait for reinforcements, or charge on his own? Exactly what criteria were to be used to make this decision? In the case of Mogadishu, we have a similar situation, at least tacitly. Was this a police situation, in which the military, in a police role, was supposed to arrest two men? Or was it a military situation, in which a battle was to be fought?

Clearly the equipment, personnel, and planning needs differ, to a potentially catastrophic degree, between military and law enforcement situations; but in the absence of a direct, explicit awareness that the

Chapter 9

question of whether a given situation is to be a police arrest or a military battle exists at all, commanders might very well act as their own idiosyncratic proclivities and experiences would drive them on an implicit level. They might, for example, supply their ground forces with equipment more suitable to a police role than to an environment of military, warfare-level conflict.

There is some evidence that this was the case at Mogadishu. The evidence is not conclusive; but it is there.

Aidid's lieutenants were known to be in a particular building in Mogadishu. The building was perilously close to the Aidid stronghold of Bakara Market, but this does not seem to have been a major factor in the tactical planning of the operation. Again, nobody expected the Somalis to put up much of a fight.

The intent was to airlift Ranger and Delta operators into the operational zone by means of Black Hawk helicopters, supported by smaller attack helicopters. A ground convoy was to rendezvous with the airborne force after the Delta operators, supported by the Rangers, had captured Aidid's lieutenants. Then the airborne troops, with the Aidid lieutenants in tow, were to return to their base with the ground convoy.

Speed and surprise were crucial. The convoy consisted of three five-ton trucks and nine Humvees, and these vehicles were crewed by Rangers, Delta operators, and U.S. Navy SEALS. There were no armored vehicles, no tanks or armored personnel carriers (APCs); just Humvees and trucks.

The troops involved were elite soldiers, among the most talented and best-trained soldiers in the history of the world. The fantastic firepower of the Black Hawks, and of the supporting AH-6 "Little Bird" attack ships, was like something out of science fiction. All of this led to a certain sense of confidence, to say the least, among the troops and their commanders. They entered the combat zone with a powerful *mental set*: their fantastic firepower could overwhelm anything the Somalis threw against them, and as stated above, the Somalis were not expected to be able provide anything in the way of effective countermeasures.

The ghost of Custer is clearly felt. The mental set: *Don't let them get away*. No fear of effective retaliation. Only a fear that the targets might escape, might scurry off before we can get them.

And like the Sioux and Cheyenne, the Somalis had no intention of scurrying off.

As the mighty aircraft flew in, that afternoon of October 3, 1993, their crews noticed piles of burning tires in the city below, creating beacons of smoke which were visible for miles. These tires had been burning since morning, and the American forces knew it. They also knew that this was how the Somalis signaled each other of the imminence of an American attack. This was how the Somalis conveyed the need to gather, in great numbers, to repel the American forces. It was clear that surprise, on which so much depended, had been lost completely; yet this fact had no effect whatsoever on the American operation. It went forward entirely as scheduled.

Certain cognitive factors reared their ugly heads, just as they had with Custer.

Mental set: They can't put up an effective resistance, anyway. We are invincible. There was a belief that the Black Hawks, over "a Third World dump like Mog" were "damn near indestructible" *(Bowden, 2000, pg. 88).*

Cognitive dissonance: the attack is planned, we've already got everybody in the trucks and in the air, and we've already invested in and committed to this attack. Besides, we've already paid a lot, in terms of our own responses to negative media and political attention to previous tactical failures, and we sure aren't backing away from high-value targets now. Light up the roof. Siren. Go.

Arousal-based tunnel vision: the burning tires are irrelevant. The targets, the Aidid lieutenants, are of great value. We see their capture in our minds, we perceive the prospect of success. Large numbers of Somali fighters with automatic weapons—well, those we don't see. We also don't consider the fact that the warren of tightly packed, irregularly placed buildings, piles of uncollected garbage, and narrow, twisting passageways provide many points of concealment. We don't think about all that cover for anti-aircraft snipers, who, with cheap rocket-propelled grenades, can in fact knock a high-tech, super-armed Black Hawk out of the sky if the helo crew doesn't see the bad guy first, which they're frankly unlikely to do with all that chaos and cover. Those prospects are on the periphery, and, as the reader saw in Chapters 1 and 2, the periphery is seldom seen or considered when we have a given deer, or a bad guy, or a group of Aidid lieutenants in our sights.

No time for all this. *Light up the roof. Siren. Go.*

Things began to go awry. There were problems with the Somali confidential informant who was supposed to point out the lieutenants' house. One of the Rangers fell while rappelling into the zone from a Black Hawk. He was grievously wounded and required evacuation. In fact, this particular rappel required a far longer descent than any that had been practiced in training, although this factor was probably unimportant in the Ranger's devastating fall.

Yet concerning the fantastically dangerous long rappel: does the reader recall Custer's men, whose training, such as it was, was entirely inconsistent with the prairie-dog-infested West? The Rangers' *valuable* mental sets, the good ones intended to lead to better gestalt responses in combat, and so painstakingly engendered in repeated practice, were geared to shorter ropes; the long rappel could have been even worse.

Regardless, these elite troops were able to adapt and to overcome the situation. The Delta operators captured the Aidid lieutenants, together with a number of lesser Aidid adherents who were not initially targets of the operation, but whose capture provided a substantial bonus.

Then they put their prisoners on the ground convoy.

TANKS AND TACTICS

Here we must consider a question concerning which I can claim no professional knowledge. However, the issue has been raised by military experts, and by experts on the battle *(e.g., Bowden, 2000)*, the most prominent of whom is Col. David Hackworth *(1997)*, who was frankly not too crazy about the whole operation or about General Garrison either. In any event, here's the question:

Wouldn't it have been better if the ground convoy had been composed of armored vehicles?

If the convoy had had M-1 Abrams tanks at point and rear guard; and if the vehicles between had been mighty Bradley fighting vehicles bristling with weapons; and if additional Abrams and Bradleys had guarded the flanks on the nearest parallel side streets, the Bradleys carrying heavily armed infantry troops who could be swiftly deployed and recovered in the event of flank threat; and if that whole co-ordinated show of America's roaring armed might had come barreling through the ragged streets of Mogadishu like an avenging god, an unstoppable juggernaut of bad-ass armor-clad doom—well, wouldn't that have been better?

This point has been debated endlessly by actual military experts. It has been pointed out that armored vehicles were vulnerable in the narrow streets of Mogadishu; yet the eventual recovery column was composed of armored vehicles, M-48 tanks and Condor armored personnel carriers (APCs) belonging to allied forces, and they got in and out just fine.

(It should also be pointed out that when the armored column finally broke through to the besieged Ranger and Delta survivors, there wasn't enough room on the Condors for everybody. A number of Rangers and Delta operators actually had to run through the streets to escape, in a display of heroism, that unpopular term, that may have never been surpassed in military history.)

Whether or not armor would have been "vulnerable" on ingress when it was just fine on egress is an interesting question; however, prior to the operation's inception, the whole vulnerability thing was raised by Allied forces who frankly did not want to commit their valuable tanks and APCs. So why didn't the American forces have American armor? Well, in fact, tanks and Bradleys had been requisitioned for the QRF, but these armored forces had been withheld by those holding the American purse-strings; questions of economy, questions of opinion.

The ghosts of the North Hollywood Shootout, and the voices of the valiant LAPD officers who had no rifles, join those of the Seventh Cavalry in Montana, together with the banshee shriek of the Hindsight Spirits: *There should have been American armor. You guys should have deployed some serious lethal monster American tanks to the party. You would have been effective. You would have contributed to soldier survival.*

You would have gotten home.

On the other hand, the armor had been requested for the QRF, (Quick Reaction Force), not for the Rangers and Delta operators. They saw themselves (mental set again?) as members of fast-moving strike forces, not men to be encumbered by slow, bulky, regular-army tanks. Whether they were right or not, the author would not presume to know or to comment. However, the fact remains that they didn't have any tanks or APCs.

What they did have was Humvees, together with a few trucks whose only armor consisted of piles of sandbags.

Most of the military experts with whom I have talked hold the Humvee in high regard as a military vehicle. However, the Humvee has always reminded the author (again, not a military expert) of a four-wheel-drive police car on steroids. In 1993, the top turret of a Humvee didn't usually even have protective exterior armor, and the whole vehicle had, and still has, *windows*. Windows help you see out, of course, but they also help the bad guys see in, and they are a positive boon to anyone who would like to kill you by shooting you, well, through the windows. The Humvee's windows are putatively bullet-proof, but of course that depends on what kind of bullet you're shooting them with. Also, the bullet-proof quality of the windows is entirely lacking when they're rolled down, and a lot of them were, that hot day in Mogadishu in 1993. It's *very* hot in Somalia, just as it is in southern Montana in the summer, and large numbers of good men were shot through those windows, in those souped-up, tricked-out, four-wheel-drive police cars, as they desperately strove to complete their military mission.

The Rangers and Delta operators were expected to arrest the bad guys, and then to depart in the trucks and Humvees, to return to base in the equivalent of heavily armed police cars. From the standpoint of mental set, this makes perfect sense; suspects are arrested and trans-

Chapter 9

ported in police cars in every city in America, on an everyday basis, and the Crown Vics and Dodges don't even have machine gun turrets.

However, what was missing in the planning for the Mogadishu operation was the fact that those "police cars" would have to return to base through a combat zone, through ranks of dedicated fighters equipped with military weaponry. Whatever "police mission" gestalts accompanied the convoy to the target area swiftly turned to full-bore military combat on the way out. Not to repeat what has been so well-discussed elsewhere *(Bowden, 2000)*, the convoy was shot up to an incredible degree. Men died, were wounded, were maimed or crippled for life as fire poured in through those damned windows and occasionally through other lightly armored parts of the vehicles.

Many experts think the whole thing would have worked out a lot better, with a lot fewer American casualties, if there'd been a few tanks and APCs along. Fewer Somalis might have died, as well. If the show of force had been more overwhelming, with no prospect of Somali success when armed with APGs and AK-47s against those lethal monster armored Bradleys and tanks, fewer Somalis might have even attempted to attack.

COGNITIVE CONTEXT

The armor question will probably be there as long as the battle is remembered, but ultimately we can see several factors operating here that were clearly also operating at the Battle of the Little Bighorn: mental set, cognitive dissonance, arousal. Mental set is particularly important here. A number of young soldiers reported that the whole experience, people shooting at them and so on, seemed like something *out of a movie (Bowden, 2000)*. It was difficult for them to overcome the passive role of someone watching a movie, and to engage the active role of elite combatants. It will be interesting, and hopefully not catastrophic, to see what happens to modern soldiers, with their general history of video game playing, as they enter the most lethal combat zones. Will they, or will some of them, act as if they are operating in the consequence-free environment of a given computer game? In a computer game, you can usually press the escape button and end the game, or even obtain an extra virtual "life" or two. In reality, when a bad guy is drilling you through the lungs with an AK-47 in the name of God, or trying to drive a knife through your liver before you manage to strangle him, there are few if any computerized options. Time will tell what the relationship of virtual games of murderous violence to the truly terrible, real-world equivalent will be. For the present, we can only say that there is an urgent and immediate need for good research on this issue, and for and the attention of police and military commanders to its potential ramifications.

For the present, with regard to the *"I felt I was in a movie"* thing, we can only say that the role of *mental set* clearly did not die with Custer; it was operating in Mogadishu, too.

Mental set may have been operating even more profoundly on that very hot, very bad day in Somalia. It is extremely unlikely that military commanders would have sent Humvees, trucks, and helicopters into a tank battle; for such a battle, you've got to have tanks. If the commanders were forced into an artillery duel, they would probably provide artillery, and so on.

However, what do you provide if your job is to arrest some people? The answer, generally, is police cars. What is the nearest military equivalent to a police car? Is it, perhaps, the Humvee? The issue of *mission* rears its head again. Were the Delta operators and Rangers supposed to be acting as soldiers, or as police officers in Army uniforms, arresting bad guys? As we have seen, implicit mental set may have been a major driving force in this particular arena; many of these soldiers, and many who did not make it home, drove to battle in the equivalent of heavily armed, relatively tall, bulky four-wheel-drive police cars.

Whether this speculation is accurate or not, Humvees and trucks were sent into an environment in which the survival of their occupants was in extreme jeopardy. Whatever else may be said about this situation, it is fairly clear that *cognitive flexibility* was lacking at some level; possibly at many levels. Failures to notice burning tires; failures to consider the proximity of Bakara Market, the Aidid stronghold; failures to consider what would happen to Humvees faced with what amounted to major infantry forces; failure to consider the near impossibility of detecting, in the teeming streets and crowded buildings of Mogadishu, the guy with the grenade launcher who would destroy the mighty, super-lethal Blackhawk. All might have been defeated, or avoided, through the exercise of feature-intensive command cognitive flexibility.

However, there were powerful psychological forces operating against the deployment of such flexibility. Mental set, cognitive dissonance, arousal; all of these reduce cognitive flexibility, the ability to apply FI processing when needed (and even to recognize when it *is* needed) in the harsh situations encountered by military and law enforcement operators alike. Yet cognitive flexibility can be engendered, and with it the proper interchange needed between feature-intensive, strategic thought and gestalt tactical excellence. We have seen that front-loaded, explicit, feature-intensive training can provide the context, the blueprint if you will, for exactly the type of cognitive

Chapter 9 225

flexibility needed to confront and defeat the treacherous shifts and changes of a tactical environment.

This is not mere optimism; there are historical examples of exactly this type of superior strategic and tactical thinking. Therefore, let us consider one here. Let us take up an example of a situation in which a number of things went right for a change.

Chapter 10
COGNITION IN TACTICAL ENVIRONMENTS III: ARDENNES, 1944, AND THE RELIEF OF BASTOGNE

Actually, things started going right rather late in the situation. Initially, the whole thing looked like a catastrophe. Initially, this was a situation in which nothing looked like it was going to go right at all.

It was late 1944. The Normandy landings had achieved their place in history. American and Allied forces were tearing across Europe with amazing speed in this new era of mechanized warfare, and German resistance was crumbling everywhere. The Germans were finished, at least in the minds of Allied commanders. General Dwight Eisenhower, Supreme Commander, had ruled out the possibility of a major Nazi attack at this late date in the war—the Germans were simply too weak, he believed, to do anything beyond a half-decent defensive front. The politically important Field Marshall Montgomery concurred, believing the Germans incapable of staging major offensive operations. In short, the Thousand Year Reich had had it, after a little more than a decade. Finished. Kaput. They're running away. Completely incapable of organized resistance at this point. In fact, our major military mission at this point, thought the Allied commanders, is to mop up and make certain that fanatic holdouts, such as SS units, do not get away. *Don't let them get away.*

Does the reader hear the ghosts of mental sets past, blending in harmony with the ghost of Custer, and with the spirits of the courageous Rangers and Delta operators who died at Mogadishu, intoning that old, World War II standby expression, never very funny at any time: *"You'll be sorrr-eee ..."*

Even if there were any effective German military left, even if the Germans were to attack, they would certainly not do so through the Ardennes, said the Allied experts. Its wooded terrain makes the passage of tanks and supporting forces difficult. There are few roads, and fewer good ones. The German forces, if there *were* any combat-effective German forces, that is, would certainly not attack though the Ardennes. They would pass north, or south, despite the fact that a previously highly successful German attack had gone right through the Ardennes like a Teutonic knife through tree-infested butter. Even so, they won't come through the Ardennes. So said the experts.

There *had* been some intelligence indications of trouble in the Ardennes. Tanks massing, troop concentrations observed. A military buildup at Cologne. No problem, said the commanders. These are simply spoiler raids. They couldn't be anything else, really, in the minds of the Allied experts. The Allies had built up powerful **mental sets** surrounding German weakness, and they had developed powerful *cognitive dissonance* to support their defense of these mental sets. The Germans are licked; they don't have enough resources left to hit us. We are sure of this, and we are heavily invested in these facts. We are *committed* to these facts.

Not a good sign.

At Mogadishu, the tires burned. At the Little Bighorn, the Rees sang their death songs and gave their warnings—*Otoe Sioux*, plenty Sioux. In the Ardennes, the Germans massed. The Intelligence officers filed their reports, informed their superiors, had quiet military tantrums.

Nobody paid any damn attention. The commanders laughed off the signs of trouble in the Ardennes. Mental sets again: Forests are bad for tanks. Only a few Germans left anyway. They're beaten, defeated, demoralized. We need only a few skeleton security forces across the Ardennes part of the front, just a formality, really. War will probably be over by Christmas.

Custer and the Rangers again, together with the Hindsight Spirits: "You'll be sorrr-eee ..."

If the Germans were defeated, nobody had told them. The German army, luckily smaller, at this point, than the combined might of the Allied armies deployed against it, generally inflicted far more casualties than it took. Their new King Tiger tank, though mechanically not terribly reliable, was even more awe-inspiring than its predecessor, the horrible Tiger. Historians like to point out that the Tiger was also unreliable, which it was; but there are stories of individual Tigers destroying ten, twelve, or more American Sherman tanks before simply running out of ammo. Not, you understand, before being destroyed. The Tigers weren't destroyed—they just went home for more bullets.

The Sherman guys referred to their tanks as Ronsons, after the famous cigarette lighter. The idea was that a Sherman always lit, always caught fire, when it was hit by the first shot from an enemy tank. Underarmored, undergunned. This was the tank that desperately courageous American and British tankers rode against the eighty-eight millimeter dragon-blast, the flaming voice of that ghastly rolling iron brick, the Tiger.

And then there was the powerful Panther tank, less well-known than the Tiger, but more effective, massively more reliable, and unbelievably lethal, supported by the flying artillery battery of the Messerschmitt 109, and occasionally supported by the *jet fighter*—the Germans had *jets*, for God's sake—the terrifying ME-262 jet fighter that could cut and obliterate an Allied bomber formation like an angry Nazi Valkyrie finalizing her divorce.

Chapter 10

In hindsight, always hindsight, do these guys sound anywhere near defeated to you?

No, the Germans were anything but defeated. Their problem was that the Glorious Thousand-Year Reich didn't yet have enough Panthers, or King Tigers, or 262s, not yet, to destroy their many, many enemies. Not yet.

However, a single horrific thrust through the Ardennes, cutting the allies in half and taking the crucial port city of Antwerp, would keep the battles raging. It would give the Third Reich the time it needed to assemble masses of these terrific new weapons. Possibly they could even slap together a few atomic bombs. They were working on it; all they needed was enough time.

The Ardennes battle, the horrible Battle of the Bulge, nearly gave them that time.

Thanks in large part to the mental sets and cognitive dissonance of Allied high commanders, combined with their human tendency to conform to each other's opinions (remember Solomon Asch and his studies of conformity), the German Wehrmacht nearly succeeded in conquering, well, pretty much everybody.

The Battle of the Bulge

The attack on American positions in the Ardennes began in the early morning hours of 16 December. The German forces consisted of four complete armies, two of them Panzer armies. Much of this massive strength was concentrated on the Ardennes, where four American divisions were thinly stretched over an eighty-eight-mile front. Not surprisingly, the Germans began to push through.

When Allied commanders heard the Germans were attacking in great strength in the Ardennes, their response was straightforward. They didn't believe it.

Requests for clarification zipped back and forth across the telephone wires, as fine young American infantrymen, surprised and outgunned, were mowed down by the King Tigers of an all-too undefeated Germany. Eventually, with cities burning and many individual units wiped out, the Allied commanders began to get the idea that something was dreadfully wrong with this whole mental set, this whole Germany-is-defeated thing. However, by that time, the Nazi forces had bulged far into the American lines (hence the term "Battle of the Bulge"); and they had taken Bastogne.

Bastogne was a key strategic town, a road junction. When the attack began, there were some tanks of the 9th Armored already there, but they were nowhere near enough to stem the steel Teutonic tide washing over that particular part of the world. So, the 9th tanks were swiftly reinforced by elements of the 10th Armored Division. These tanks were detached from General George S. Patton's army, fighting to the south in the Saar. Patton was not at all crazy about releasing these units, but his superiors gave him no choice, so off they went; and finally, the famed elite troops of the 101st Airborne roared into town to keep Bastogne safe for democracy.

Still not enough. The American troops were promptly surrounded by massive German forces.

The American troops were stuck there, surrounded by overwhelming enemy armor, for several days. On 22 December, the Germans demanded surrender of the commanding general, Anthony MacAuliffe. The idea was that if he didn't give up immediately, the eighteen thousand men trapped in Bastogne would be put to grisly death.

"Nuts," answered MacAuliffe, ensuring his fame among military historians and English teachers for all eternity.

The Germans had no idea what he meant. It is said that a translation of "Go to Hell" was provided by Nazi linguists. That, the German commanders understood. They fired a few extra artillery shells at the 101st to make themselves feel better.

So, the 101st and the armored troops were trapped. There was no way out. Without the relief of Bastogne, any reversal of the Germans at the Bulge was somewhere between highly unlikely and effectively impossible.

It must be said at this point that no member of the elite 101st ever apparently felt that the division had required rescue at all. However, one might attribute this to the laudable military pride of a unit that would never accept defeat. The fact was that eighteen thousand men were surrounded in Bastogne, and they had to be pulled out.

Now things began to go right.

Enter Patton.

General Patton and the Relief of Bastogne

Like General George A. Custer, General George S. Patton was strange. He practiced his scowling "war face" in front of a mirror. As a boy, to toughen himself, he forced himself to eat an orange while staring at the rotting carcass of a dead frog. As a young officer, with Pershing in Mexico in 1916, he shot two of Pancho Villa's men and then strapped them over the fenders of his car, like trophy deer, to present them to his commander *(Peck, 1970)*. In Sicily, he actually slapped American soldiers he thought guilty of cowardice. He wrote poetry, believed in his own reincarnation as some sort of divinely recycled warrior, and at one point in the North African campaign ordered General Orlando Ward to make certain that more American officers were killed for the benefit of the morale of the American enlisted men *(Atkinson, 2002, pg. 446)*.

He was strange; and at the moment at which the Germans attacked the Ardennes, his men of the 3rd Army were engaged in a life-or-death struggle against German forces in the Saar, far to the south. It was a winter campaign, with all the misery of snow and cold attendant. On 19 December, in the midst of horrible European winter weather, Patton was summoned to a meeting with Eisenhower, together with other commanders, to see if anything could be done about Bastogne.

Patton told Eisenhower he could attack with three divisions in seventy-two hours.

Eisenhower exploded. Other commanders chuckled, looked away, rolled their eyes. Patton was not popular, and this display of exuberant hubris was doing nothing to enhance his social standing. The fact was that nobody could do anything at all. The troops of all of the armies and corps in the vicinity, including Patton's Third Army, were heavily committed. Even if his men had not been embroiled in current battles, Patton's assertion seemed like an idle boast. To disengage a multi-man behemoth like the Third Army from heavy winter combat, to turn it through ninety degrees to face North instead of East, and then to transplant that army in horrible winter weather, all of the ninety miles from the Saar to Bastogne, staggered the imagination. Especially in three days. "Don't be fatuous, George," snapped Eisenhower, as the other commanders sanctimoniously dripped vinegar in Patton's direction.

The thing is, Patton wasn't being fatuous. The operation he proposed looked impossible to everybody else, but he just went ahead and did it. By December 27, the Siege of Bastogne had been lifted, and the Germans had retreated.

It was a tactical miracle. Think of the logistics involved. Patton's maneuvers required the shifting of an army of more than 225,000 men, and all their equipment, to a new front. This front was ninety degrees and ninety miles from their Saar entrenchments. The forces had to disengage from the enemy ahead, and re-engage with the enemy to the side. The staff officers had to coordinate the movement of 133,000 vehicles in the process, and the army had to lay 20,000 miles of new telephone lines and deposit 62,000 tons of supplies in new locations. Furthermore, all of this had to be accomplished in the icy cold and snow of one of the worst winters in European history.

To make matters worse, Patton was known for his indifference to logistical questions *(e.g., Atkinson, 2002, pg. 151)*. He didn't think about supplies a great deal. In view of this disregard, and the fantastic logistical nightmares that had to be overcome, one might expect a total disaster all along his front. George Armstrong Custer was not particularly good at watchful waiting; he charged, and he died. Patton was not particularly good at logistics; one might therefore assume that catastrophe was imminent.

However, here's the thing: Patton himself may not have been good at logistics, but he knew people who were; and they were all working for him.

THE IMPORTANCE OF TEAMS

Law enforcement, like military operations, requires teamwork. Commanders, therefore, assemble teams; and it is a wise commander who considers how the virtues and faults of his or her "players" will contribute to overall mission success, professional effectiveness, and officer survival. It may not be wise to staff a SWAT team with nothing but highly independent patrol officers who work poorly with others. It may not be wise to staff a violent crime suppression unit primarily with older detectives, most of whom have been working white-collar crime for ten or eleven years. Some officers, or soldiers, are good at one thing, while others are good at something else. It is important for any commander to consider the cognitive and behavioral characteristics of the members of any given team; but more than that, it is important to understand how those individuals will think and behave *in context*, when they're under stress and the bullets are flying and the strident demands of *processing under pressure* begin to take over.

This is exactly what Patton was good at.

Patton had picked a group of senior staff men whose strengths complemented his areas of weakness, although it is very doubtful that he would have phrased it that way. Oddly, other senior commanders were singularly unimpressed by Patton's staff. General Omar Bradley, for example, deplored the lack of "outstanding individual performers" among them. However, when officers are working well and closely toward defined goals, each responsible for specific subgoals but contributing ultimately toward the aggregate, the gifted individual may not be visible in sharp relief against the surrounding team activity. It is the team activity itself that becomes visible, and in the case of Patton's staff, this team activity appeared to be a miracle.

The level of activity of Patton's team was not only visible, it was incredible. Each of his highly competent staff officers knew exactly what to do, and each individual had a set of feature–intensive subgoals that were delineated in such a way that redundant or mutually incompatible activities were minimized or eliminated.

The details are illustrative if not essential *(e.g., Farago, 1963)*: Colonel Maddox was responsible for, in effect, unit geometry, changing

Chapter 10

the north-south three-corps front to a four-corps battle line split in two. Half of it ran north to south in the Saar, and the other half ran east to west and rammed violently into Bastogne.

Col. Perry was responsible for the transport of combat and supply units, all hundred and thirty-three thousand of them. Col. Muller established the supply system. Col. Koch prepared the maps and terrain analyses, and Col. Coates moved and set up the field hospitals.

One can imagine the chaotic nightmare that would have ensued if these colonels had decided to display their "outstanding individual performance," instead of working for the common good (*Field hospitals are more important than maps! Are not! Are too! Give me those trucks! No, they're mine! General Patton, Muller took my trucks and won't give them back! Make him stop! Waah!*)

Patton had assembled a team that simply didn't do this. There must have been individual rivalries, of course, together with personal incompatibilities and the other usual problematic social dynamics that occur when high-powered people are forced to work together. However, in this case, these dynamics seem to have been subordinated to the purposes of the overall group mission. Patton's colonels did their own jobs, within the teamwork of the overall organization. The people under them, generally, appear to have done the same thing. As a team, they performed a military miracle; but as a team, they couldn't afford to behave as prima donnas, and for once in human history, they all seem to have known that.

The lesson for the successful law enforcement commander or administrator: *pick teams carefully, with an eye to the individual strengths and weaknesses of each team member, but also with an eye to the context they're going to operate in, and to how those strengths and weaknesses will either collaborate or fall apart under operational stresses.*

Patton needed team players; he wasn't one himself, not by any stretch of the imagination, but he knew one when he saw him. He had put the best team players he could find together, into one big ultra-efficient team. Few authors have ever called Patton "flexible," and in some ways he wasn't. He was inflexible and adamantine in his self-promotion, and in his dissemination of his personal views. However, he clearly had the *cognitive* flexibility to recognize abilities in others that he himself didn't have, although he certainly wouldn't have put it that way. But however you phrase it, this is a quality to strive for.

But what other cognitive miracles let Patton pull this incredible operation off? How did the various colonels know what to do in the first place?

As we have seen, many psychological forces influence thinking and decision making, including and especially decision making in command contexts, and many of these operate for the worst. Yet, Patton succeeded.

> **Let us therefore consider those cognitive influences that we have seen to be most deleterious to the commander in the field, and evaluate the degree to which they were operating in Patton's command in the Ardennes.**
>
> - Mental set—clinging to sets of ideas which do not actually fit the situation.
>
> - Cognitive dissonance—valuing a set of concepts or a series of actions so highly that you cannot deviate from those ideas or those courses of action, usually due to personal investment in the concepts in question.
>
> - Conformity to the opinions of others, rather than response to analysis of real situations as they occur.
>
> - Failure to engage in feature-intensive analysis when needed, in favor of the gestalt responses that must characterize the high-speed, low-drag world of actual tactical operations.
>
> - Failure to front-load the results of feature-intensive analysis in explicit, noninferential terms.

We have seen all of these factors before, at the Little Bighorn and in Mogadishu, and we can now note that they have two major things in common. The first is that all of these factors reduce *cognitive flexibility*, the ability of the commander to alter his or her cognitive behavior in real time to match the demands of current and evolving situations.

The second is that Patton simply does not seem to have been suffering from any of these negative cognitive influences, at least not at the Battle of the Bulge.

Patton's colonels knew exactly what to do because the design for the maneuvers of the Third Army from the Saar to Bastogne, or at least maneuvers very similar to those actually required, had been worked out and front-loaded, in explicit, noninferential, feature-intensive detail, well before they were needed. This feature-intensive analysis had been conducted in the relative calm, or what there was of it, *before the battle began*. Patton and his officers had taken time to operate in the feature-

Chapter 10

intensive strategic mindset before the need for a gestalt tactical mindset had begun.

BUILDING FORESIGHT

Most allied commanders were in the grip of mental set. They believed that the Germans were too weak to attack and that they wouldn't come through the Ardennes.

Patton was apparently not afflicted by this mental set at all. With feature-intensive precision, he realized that the Germans had come through the Ardennes before and that what had been done before could be done again.

Other commanders, in the grip of mental set, ignored intelligence signatures that indicated a major build-up of German forces, in exactly the same way that the commanders at Mogadishu ignored the burning tires.

Patton did not. He made a serious consideration of the G-2 (intelligence) reports that pointed to a German build-up. When G-2 would find a bunch of King Tigers, for example, other officers would interpret the massed armor as preparation for some sort of "spoiling raids." Patton did not. He didn't interpret anything. He saw massed Tigers as nothing more nor less than massed Tigers; and he got ready.

As a result, Patton had told his staff way back on 12 December, *four days before the German breakout at the Bulge*, to anticipate and prepare, just in case, for a German assault into the U.S. First Army zone, into what would become the Bulge. It looks like prophecy; it was actually a feature-intensive analysis free of mental set, cognitive dissonance, or the perceived need to conform to the opinions of other commanders. As a result of this analysis, he actually ordered officers General Gay and Colonel Maddox to prepare a plan for a Third Army counterattack against a possible German thrust in this precise place. In the necessary haste of combat, four days to plan and get ready may be construed as a luxurious eternity; the officers involved were therefore able to make the necessary plans in a way, and at a level of feature-intensive detail, that simply would not have been possible in the free-flowing, gestalt-laden environment that would overflow them all once combat had actually begun.

Patton, unlike Custer, had a team composed of members who were, in general, all pulling together. Again, there must have been individual frictions and rivalries, of course; these are inevitable. However, the positive pursuit of assigned subgoals, on the part of each team member, wound up contributing in aggregate to the collective goals, the strategic and tactical objectives, of the whole. Patton in this instance was free of damaging mental sets; he had engaged the necessary feature-intensive analysis in the calm before the storm, resulting in an explicit, non-inferential set of procedures front-loaded in the minds of his staff and their subordinates; and he was not caught in conformity with the opinions of his fellow commanders (admittedly, never much of a problem with the enormously nonconformist Patton).

Patton did suffer a bit of cognitive dissonance at the beginning, being reluctant to disengage from his considerable military investment in the Saar in order to commit his forces to the Bastogne adventure. However, he was able to overcome this. "What the hell," said Patton to Bradley, "we'll still be killing Krauts" *(Farago, 1963, pg. 674)*.

Callous, inhuman to modern sensibilities, politically incorrect to a pathological degree. Yet Patton used this sentiment to overcome this particular mental set; and he relieved Bastogne.

The carnage of this battle was terrible, far beyond anything ever seen in Montana or Mogadishu. Many historians see the overall Battle of the Bulge largely as a disorganized hell of individual unit combat, a "blood-dimmed tide" *(Astor, 1992)*. Patton's advance, vastly more organized than most of the action of the Bulge, still suffered enormous casualties. This terrible reality is unsurprising; relatively modern forces, of relatively modern great powers, met with all their technology and firepower in a desperate and bitter end-game battle. Thus, there were huge casualties.

But Bastogne was relieved, and the overall Bulge fight concluded, and so there was no German conquest of Antwerp; and so, six months later, there were no atomic bombs being carried aloft by jet aircraft with swastikas on them. Europe, today, is not a neo-feudal Nazi labor camp.

History may turn on instances, such as battles; battles may turn on such apparently trivial factors as the cognitive processes of the commanders, officers, and soldiers in question. This is as true on the streets of urban America as it was in the forest of the Ardennes. It is a wise commander who realizes this, and who arms his or her command with the edge that a knowledge of relevant cognitive processes, of processing under pressure, may provide.

Summing Up—Cognition at the Little Bighorn, at Mogadishu, and at Bastogne

From the standpoint of military history, these three battles provide material for years of contentious study. For the study of *processing under pressure*, however, these battles point to a relatively small set of easily grasped principles, principles that unfortunately have seldom been grasped in the long and bloody history of warfare and of crime.

Still, it's ultimately pretty simple:

There are certain things that you want to do, and certain things that you don't. Here they are:

- **Reduce the factors which lead to stress among commanders and officers, to the degree that this is possible.** Train in realistic contexts to reduce the arousal response that occurs under unavoidable stress. Recognize that even when trained, a physiologically aroused brain will exhibit a systematic set of cognitive reductions, and plan operations accordingly.

- **Examine the teams or individuals who will operate in a given environment.** Determine the degree to which a given environment requires teamwork, or individual initiative, or in some more complex cases, both. Ascertain, in contextual training scenarios that are as realistic as possible, whether or not team members' abilities and personal characteristics are complementary and in synchronization, as was apparently the case on Patton's staff, or whether such factors as personal jealously, history of bad encounters, massive differences in abilities, or the like are likely to cause the team to fail or implode, as was the case with Custer's command. Finally, monitor team cognition to ensure that individual responses are based on analysis of real situations, rather than on conformity to perceived team or command opinion.

- **Plan for contingencies, but add a cognitive perspective to this planning.** Identify the sources of mental set, and of cognitive dissonance, that a commander or subordinates may bring to bear on a given law enforcement or tactical problem. Identify these sources explicitly and non-inferentially, and front-load them prior to careful, feature-intensive consideration of all of the reasonably likely prospects for a given action. Then front-load the necessary training so that smooth gestalt actions and reactions will be available to the right people in the right places in the field.

These courses of action, of course, cannot replace the training and operational characteristics of good work in the military or the law enforcement realm, and they are not intended to do so. However, they provide an extra tool in the box, so to speak, an additional edge to contribute to professional effectiveness and officer survival. This edge, this additional tool for success and survival in environments characterized by processing under pressure, can only be acquired through training. We will discuss issues of training in the final chapter. Before we get there, however, let us examine these principles, in aggregate, in critical areas of law enforcement; specifically, the world of explosives ordinance disposal; the realm of the undercover operative; and specific aspects of the complex world of the patrol officer.

Chapter 11
SPECIAL UNITS - COGNITIVE SCIENCE AT THE EXTREMES

The ideas presented in the previous chapters are generally applicable across the world of law enforcement. The principles of arousal, memory reconfiguration, decision-making; all operate whether the officer, witness, suspect or victim is in the field, at the scene, or in the court.

However, the understanding of exactly how these principles operate, and how they produce their consequences, has to take into account the contexts in which they are operating. Mental set, cognitive dissonance, all the rest- they apply across contexts, but they work in different ways, and have different consequences, for the EOD technician (briefly discussed above in Chapter 8), the undercover operative, the patrol officer, and all the other law enforcement officers who work in their many different professional roles. A complete consideration of all these factors, in all these law enforcement realms, is beyond the scope of this book; but let's consider a few very important examples. Let's start by expanding our discussion of EOD, the Bomb Squad.

Things That Go Boom in the Night: Cognitive Science and EOD

Bomb squads go under different names. They may literally be the Bomb Squad, but usually, they're EOD, Explosives Ordinance Disposal. Overseas, they may be the Explosives Service. But whatever they're called, their primary target is the IED, the *improvised explosive device*. If you think about it, this is a rather sanitized term for a bomb, basically a miniature version of a volcano, the sole purpose of which is to slaughter people in a horrible way.

If Bomb Squad people can get the funding, they go to conferences, keep their skills up, find out what's new in the explosive world. At the conferences, they see photographic slides and grainy digital films. The narrative for these films goes something like this:

> "Now, in City X, this technician had to dismantle the device as it couldn't be elevated safely. You'll see that he removes the cover, and begins to address the timer. Now, (an audible click of the antiquated projection system as the slide advances to a scene of fire, nothing but fire), you see that the device was triggered by a secondary initiation system. The bomb tech died..."

Click.

"Here, in City Y, the tech was beginning to prepare the device for removal and disposal away from the populated area. The weapon detonated (Click- BOOM- fire, nothing but fire), killing the technician and resulting in..."
Click.

"In this scene in City Z, we see the preparation for removal of the device- initiator successfully removed, firing train disabled. However, a secondary device, (click- BOOM- fire, nothing but fire) was initiated under local radio control, resulting in the death of the technician..."
Click. Once again, click.

Bomb techs, of course, wear bomb suits. The suits are impressive, and they can reduce burns, but they can't do much to shield the bomb tech against high-velocity shrapnel, or the concussive force of high explosives. Bomb techs know this. They know it very well.

But back at the conference (click...click...click...), the bomb techs nod. They take notes. They are amazingly calm, reserved, like a bunch of engineers looking at a blueprint, rather than a bunch of cops looking at a possible personal future involving a volcano. And then they go back to their departments (flying economy class, of course), and they fight IED's, those terrible flaming dragon-blast machines, whenever some politically-active lunatic plants one in a dark and evil place.

What can cognitive science offer these people?

Hopefully, quite a lot.

Finding the Bombs in the First Place

In 2013, the Boston bombers struck, during a Marathon race where there would, necessarily, be many spectators. Three people were killed; their names were Krystle Campbell, Liu Lingzi, and Martin Richard. Several other people were horribly, and permanently, maimed by explosive devices. Overall, 264 people had to be treated for bomb-related injuries.

Not bad, if you're a terrorist.

The bombs were disguised as ordinary backpacks. On the ground. Let's face it, you can conceal a decent bomb in practically anything. These were concealed in backpacks.

But *on the ground*?

Backpacks don't belong on the ground, at least not in the street. If they're not in your house, they're—well—on your back. If they're on the ground, something is wrong.

It's like Sesame Street. One of these things is not like the other. One of these things goes boom. One of these things kills three people, and wounds 264.

So, it's kind of important to recognize the bomb before it goes off, and to call in EOD. In time to prevent the carnage.

This means it would be very nice for EOD officers, and for the victims of undetected bombs, to find the damned things before they go off.

Cognitive science can help with this. In two research articles (Sharps et al., 2010, 2014), we introduced the SMOKE system of cognitively based training for IED detection. SMOKE training (based on the acronym for **the five identified types of IED search error, specifically mistakes of Search, Movement, Observation, (failure to) Keep looking, and errors of Evaluation)** literally *doubled* the detection performance of trainees in a single session, and defeated three of the five error types. That was in 2010. In 2014, and as suggested by our earlier work, we incorporated a simple field exercise, also based in cognitive principles, to enhance the SMOKE system. This integrated approach defeated *all five error types*, again at *double the level of untrained performance*.

As will be discussed further in Chapter 12, this research demonstrates the importance of cognitive principles in the development of training. It also provides a highly effective system of training for use in law enforcement applications, and in corporate, commercial, transportation, and educational security environments. This is relatively new research, and the nuances are still in progress; we still need to find out exactly how SMOKE operates in different environments; but to date, *because* it's based in hard cognitive science, it's the most effective system for IED detection training, as far as we know, that's been devised to date.

And we need things like that.

SMOKE: Effective Cognitive and Field Training for IED Detection

The current warfare in the Middle East is well into its third decade at the time of writing, and the detection of improvised explosive devices has become increasingly important, both in the U.S. and overseas (*e.g., Cameron, 2008; Johnson, 2011*). The IED threat is expected to result in large part from the activities of genuine terrorists. However, every law enforcement reader will understand that "copycat" offenders may readily become impressed with the power and notoriety of these weapons, and may use them in a variety of criminal venues, ranging from homicide and gang warfare to the robbery of such hardened targets as banks and armored cars. So, for domestic law enforcement and security applications, as well as for overseas work, there is a strong and growing need for effective, economical training in the detection of IEDs.

At present, IED search-and-detection training may involve practice in the recognition of various types of IED's, and field training in which trainees are exposed to practice environments containing mock explosive devices. As discussed in previous work (*Sharps et al., 2010, 2014*), these types of training are important in the development of hazard detection skills. However, they often lack important cognitive components. The cognitive components in particular are prior frameworks for search methods; explicit connections between the skills employed and their rationales; and the use of specific, feature-intensive training to form smooth, coordinated search methods in the field (*Sharps et al., 2010, 2014*; also see *Bransford and Johnson 1972, 1973; Haviland & Clark, 1974*). As will be seen, these cognitive components, based on sound principles of cognitive science, are critical for the development of the most effective forms of anti-IED training.

Much of what follows derives directly from earlier work (*Sharps et al., 2010, 2014*) and interested readers are directed to those articles for additional information. But in what follows, we're going to go into the SMOKE system in some detail, for readers who may want to consider these principles in relation to relevant contexts in law enforcement.

Initial Considerations

Research discussed in previous chapters has demonstrated the need for the application of cognitively-based principles in visual search training (*e.g., Sharps, Barber, Stahl, & Villegas, 2003; Villegas, Sharps, Satterthwaite, & Chisholm, 2005; Sharps, Hess, Casner, Ranes, & Jones, 2007; Sharps, 2012; Sharps & Hess, 2008; Sharps, Janigian, Hess, & Hayward, 2009*). The need for these principles assumes special significance in the search for IEDs. In our studies, many people looked directly at an *explicit* source of hazard, such as a hand grenade, or at an *implicit* potential source of hazard, such as a military ammunition box situated among street clutter (which might or might not contain explosives), *literally without noticing these hazards* (*Hess & Sharps, 2006, April; Sharps, 2012; Sharps et al., 2007*). You can frequently see the same effects in law enforcement training; even veteran officer trainees, when confronted with the need to move quickly to the scene of a mock violent crime, may completely ignore mock IEDs in plain sight. As mentioned in Chapter 2, in training drills, I have seen veteran officers literally kicking mock IEDs out of the way without noticing them.

SMOKE was designed to use the cognitive factors discussed in this book to defeat these specific problems, and it works; a doubling of IED-detection performance in a single training evolution certainly isn't bad. But exactly what are the cognitive principles involved, and how are they used?

The Cognitive Basis of SMOKE

Training for IED detection involves the enhancement of cognitive skills. The most important principles, as mentioned above, are detailed as follows (see *Sharps et al., 2010, 2014*; also see *Sharps, 2012*). Don't forget these principles; you've seen the bases of them before, and in the rest of this book, with regard to other applications, you'll be seeing them again. A lot.

1. *Training should provide a prior framework for understanding.* The specific purposes and scope for which a given evolution is appropriate should be made clear to all trainees prior to exercises in the given skills (see *Bransford and Johnson, 1972, 1973*). This "front loading" is essential.

2. *Training should be explicit.* Trainees should not have to imply or infer the circumstances under which the training may be useful. The specific skills, and the circumstances under which these skills may be applied, should be explicitly clear to trainees prior to practice exercises (see *Haviland and Clark, 1974*).

3. *Training should initially be feature-intensive in nature.* Trainers should initially provide a step-by-step breakdown of the skills involved in any training evolution. They should provide *explicit* guidance concerning each feature of the skill set in question, together with its use in responding to the reasonable spectrum of eventuality which officers, security personnel, or those who may act in a reserve capacity may encounter in the field. The skills involved should be *explicitly* understood by trainees, *as a prior framework for understanding*, prior to practice exercises (see *Sharps, 2003, 2010, 2012*).

With a prior, explicit, feature-intensive framework in place, practice exercises and subsequent performance will generally be enhanced in effectiveness, ultimately resulting in the smooth, "gestalt" (G) sets of responses necessary for rapid response in the field.

As will be seen in detail in Chapter 12, these are the cognitive bases of success in training for *anything*, and the SMOKE system of training, again specifically for IED detection, is based in these principles. However, training for any specific realm of activity will obviously have to be tailored to that activity, and IED detection is no exception. In other words, you have to identify the most important issues in any given realm, including IED detection, before you can develop training to address them. In the development of SMOKE, we found that a number of specific issues were important to address, discussed in full elsewhere (Sharps et al., 2010, 2014). In summary, these are as follows:

1. Human beings tend to focus their attention on the *core* of a given situation, the center, at the expense of the periphery of the given scene where IED's may be placed (e.g., *Grossman & Christensen, 2004*). This is especially true under conditions of high arousal (see Chapters 1 and 2 above); being in the deeply scary presence of a possible IED is obviously likely to produce such conditions. Therefore, a number of exercises, using a variety of mock IED's, were included to develop strong habits of peripheral as well as central search.

2. These exercises involved violent crime scenes, developed in consultation with law enforcement experts, and incorporating armed and unarmed perpetrators of both sexes. This developed the habit, the *mental set*, of central and peripheral search even in the presence of potentially distracting "core," or central, activity on the part of a given suspect, such as that suspect's holding a gun aimed at a potential victim.

3. Trainees were exposed to a variety of IED types, of different levels of visual salience, in different central and peripheral locations. This established a familiarity with a broad spectrum of weapons, interactive with a broad spectrum of possible locations within the trainee's visual field.

4. IEDs may be disguised, or they may be placed or constructed in such a way that they present an innocuous or ambiguous visual picture to the observer. As mentioned above and in earlier articles, an IED may present itself in such a way that *the major clue to its existence is its inappropriateness to the local environment*. This may be true of a length of pipe which should simply not be where it is, or of a metal container which becomes visually lost among other clutter, but which is definitely *out of place*. Such out-of-place objects would include backpacks lying on the ground in the streets of Boston.

   This problem assumes special significance when a disguised or innocuous object is placed on the *periphery* of a given action. Even when such an object is directly observed, it may be misinterpreted. Therefore, exercises explicitly directed trainees to evaluate the appropriateness of objects for their surroundings, both in central and peripheral locations in a given environment.

5. Trainees were also explicitly shown how to evaluate the prospect that an object might be an IED, based on the relative probability of that type of object's being in the given scene.

This training was front-loaded and explicit, intended to form a prior framework for understanding (*Bransford & Johnson, 1972, 1973*). Finally, the training was based in feature-intensive understanding both of the training protocol and of the types of scenes to which it was to be applied (*Sharps, 2003, 2010; Sharps et al., 2010, 2014*).

As mentioned above, the system was extremely effective. Trainees with no significant level of motivation, and with no prior relevant experience, exhibited a *doubling*, on average, of success in detecting a well-concealed IED, and they took half as much time to detect a given IED, unconcealed but placed among clutter, when compared with a control sample (*Sharps et al., 2010, 2014*).

Errors in IED Search

As noted above, you have to know what issues you're trying to defeat before you can develop training to defeat them. This was certainly true of SMOKE; the acronym is based on the five types of errors which were observed to occur in IED search, specifically, again, errors of Search, Movement, Observation, failure to Keep Searching, and errors of Evaluation. These are described as follows (paraphrased from *Sharps et al., 2010*):

1. Errors of SEARCH. For this error type, respondents focused on only one part of the environment, or only on one plane, failing to look up or down. An interesting finding was that some trainees focused on only one side of a given testing space, failing to notice anything on the other side, perhaps due to some unknown factors with their roots in the lateralization of functions in the brain. Further research should address this possibility. But in short, and for the present, trainees often focused on only part of the environment as their core search area. They failed to notice items on the visual periphery of the given area.

2. Errors of MOVEMENT. Some trainees tended to remain in one place in the environment, frequently at the door. From such a

perspective, many places in the environment, behind things and under tables, were completely invisible to them; there was often no tendency to move about the room in an effort to take different perspectives.

3. Errors of OBSERVATION. Trainees often looked directly at a given IED but did not report it, moving on to look at other things. In some cases, the same error was made repeatedly with a given IED. Just as a person can look at a power screwdriver and see a handgun (*Sharps & Hess, 2008*; see Chapter 5), respondents who made errors of Observation looked, for example, directly at a large, silvery pipe bomb, with a timer and battery pack clearly in view, and saw nothing dangerous at all. This is a little amazing, but it happened, again and again; trainees didn't expect an IED to be there and, although the eyes must have seen it, the brain didn't get the message.

    This, of course, seems counterintuitive; if you're looking at a big silver bomb, with a battery pack and a Casio watch timer attached by colorful wires, of COURSE you're going to see it. And again, your eyes probably do; but if you don't expect it, your brain doesn't see a damn thing. And then it kills you.

4. Failures to KEEP SEARCHING. In these instances, respondents decided they had found everything there was to find. An innocuous object would be identified as an IED, and the individual would report to the experimenter that he or she was finished, even in the presence of additional secondary devices which remained undetected. People are so *proud*—hooray for me, I found the bomb, it is my bomb, it belongs to me, and lo, I see that it is good.

    And then, as they focus on *their* bomb, they miss the other secondary devices in the environment, which, of course, kill them.

5. Errors of EVALUATION. These occurred when respondents identified innocuous objects as IEDs. These objects included a briefcase; a laptop computer; a small pillow; and a wooden box. Some of these objects were plausible disguises for IED's; others were not, ranging from the implausible to the absurd. What is important about these errors, however, is that they *occurred when actual mock IEDs were in plain sight.*

The five letters of this acronym, SMOKE, form a "rehearsal group," a group of perceptions which are processed in the brain at an optimal level for memory organization *(Mandler, 2011)*. Thus, the acronym forms an excellent mnemonic device on which a front-loaded, explicit prior framework for training in IED detection may be based. This may be of special significance when the bomb-searcher is highly aroused (see the first two chapters above), with consequent diminution of cognitive function; when you're looking for bombs, and you're scared out of your mind, it's a REALLY good idea to keep things simple, optimally organized for your brain's fight-or-flight activity.

The original version of SMOKE, consisting solely of Powerpoint-based training (summarized above and described fully elsewhere; *Sharps et al., 2010*), literally *doubled* the performance of trainees, as discussed above. However, only three of the five error types (Search, Observation, and failures to Keep Searching) were defeated by the original training (2010). It was suggested in that work that integration of the Powerpoint training with an appropriate field exercise would increase the effectiveness of the system, potentially defeating all five error types. The multimodal nature of field training, requiring movement through an appropriate environment and the evaluation of a variety of items which might or might not prove to be IEDs, was anticipated to improve performance, and to reduce the two types of errors remaining (errors of Movement and of Evaluation). This field exercise was incorporated into the most current version of SMOKE *(Sharps et al., 2014)*, combining cognitive principles and Powerpoint training with this relevant field exercise to provide optimal training for IED detection.

In the field exercise, three mock IEDs of different types were placed in a moderately cluttered office. Each device was positioned so that it was not visible from the trainee's initial position at the door of the office. Each trainee was explicitly shown the need to move through the room, *to change perspectives*, in order to observe the first of the three IEDs. Then each trainee was instructed to move through the room, guided by the walls, with explicit instructions to look low, middle, and high. Each trainee was directed to a search pattern which would facilitate the detection of the two additional IEDs.

As will not surprise anybody who's read this far, this exercise provided a *prior framework* for *explicitly* understanding the *feature-intensive* characteristics of search which would ultimately lead to success.

These training manipulations were highly successful, producing a top detection rate of 98.72%. Significant success was observed with reduction of all five identified error types, and with success in finding unhidden, partially-hidden, and well-hidden IEDs *(Sharps et al., 2014).*

This boils down to the important fact that those trained in the cognitive skills fostered by Powerpoint training in SMOKE must also have additional, integrated field training, in which they search realistic mock environments. This integrated field training promotes the "movement" and motor skills needed for successful search, and it fine-tunes the skills needed for the evaluation of real-world environments. The incorporation of field training, as discussed in earlier work *(Sharps et al., 2010, 2014)*, and in Chapter 12, provides for optimal memory and retention of the training.

This level of success was directly based in the principles of modern cognitive science.

This emphasizes *the importance of cognitive principles in the development of training for the modern world of tactical exigency.* Again, these principles derive from the "trinity" of modern cognitive training: first, the development of prior cognitive frameworks; second, explicit processing within those frameworks; and third, feature-intensive understanding, both of the *specific* tasks to be performed, and of the environments within which those tasks must be undertaken and applied *(Sharps et al., 2010, 2014; Sharps, 2012).*

The danger of IED attacks, both domestic and foreign, remains high and will probably increase through time. Traditional training approaches to the IED problem have unfortunately been acknowledged to be less than effective *(McClatchy News Syndicate, 2011).* The use of cognitive principles in IED-detection training should be of importance not only to law enforcement, but also to security operations in environments as disparate as educational, commercial, industrial, and transportation facilities.

It is very possible, perhaps probable, that the incidence of terrorism, obviously including IED attacks, will increase in the future *(e.g., Johnson, 2011).* The integrated SMOKE approach shows how effective cognitively-based training to counter this threat can be. Commanders and training officers take note: an awareness of these principles can promote officer effectiveness and survival, and the security of the population you're sworn to protect. *We know how to do this.* We should do it.

EOD and Education

When people, including law enforcement officers, find something they think may be a bomb, they call in EOD. EOD will of course respond, with a variety of generally effective investigative techniques (getting a

Chapter 11

good description of the possible IED, getting a sketch of its location, and so on).

Unfortunately, when EOD is called in, the bomb techs are going to take at least a few minutes to get to the given location. This gives the Bomb Finders the opportunity—God help us—to interact with the bomb. And since bombs are inherently interesting, people frequently start interacting away. EOD friends have told me amazing stories of what Bomb Finders, including other law enforcement officers, have reported to them. Things like this:

"I picked it up and shook it, but it didn't *feel* like a bomb." (Wow.)

"I picked it up and turned it upside down, but I didn't see any wires." (Extra wow.)

"I picked it up and held it up to my ear," (yes, this really happened), "but I didn't hear any *ticking*." (Extra wow with a side of fries).

(A quick technical fact: digital timers don't tick. When I heard this one, I couldn't help visualizing some guy in a black trench coat and a fedora, circa 1917, holding a smoking black cannonball with "BOMB" written on it in white paint, attached to a ticking alarm clock by something vaguely resembling a Slinky. Not your most accurate visual characterization of a modern IED. Which, to reiterate, is vanishingly unlikely to tick.)

The point is that most people, and even many people in law enforcement and security, really don't know much about bombs. But EOD people do. Although they are strongly focused, quite correctly, on the technical aspects of their very intricate operations, it would be good for them (with the blessings and support of sophisticated commanders and Chiefs) to go out and give talks to relevant groups of personnel, both inside and outside of the law enforcement community, on what bombs really are and how you should respond to them. Obviously you shouldn't pick up a bomb, much less turn it over or hold it up to your head; but in the grip of high arousal (see Chapters 1 and 2 above), and given the inherent interest of the situation, many people do. The EOD specialist not only responds to the device, *but also to the people who find the damned thing in the first place and send in the call*; and the bomb tech, and anybody else in the blast radius, would be a lot better off if more people knew how to look for IEDs and identify them.

For example, I wish that there had been people in Boston, back in 2013, who'd been trained in SMOKE. Security officers, firefighters, Boy and Girl Scouts—I don't care. I wish somebody had been trained, with prior-framework, explicit, feature-intensive techniques, in the principle that *one of these things is not like the other*—the knowledge that might have kept 267 people in one piece.

But nobody had this training, and the bombs weren't detected, and there was death and mutilation. Horrible events that could have been prevented with the right kind of education and training.

It would be good to see more proper IED training, widely spread among relevant populations. EOD personnel are the people with this knowledge, and if they have expertise in the relevant cognitive underpinnings, so much the better. It will require the support of law enforcement Chiefs and commanders to foster this type of training; but in the modern world of increased IED threats, such support is certainly warranted.

Mental Sets and IEDs

What follows in this section is basically an expansion of material discussed, very briefly, in Chapter 8 above; but it may be worth your attention, especially if you're a bomb tech, or another law enforcement officer operating in an IED-rich environment.

As we know, once the IEDs are found, the Bomb Squads go into action.

But what kind of action? Most EOD experts with whom I have spoken are aware that EOD duty is fundamentally different, in cognitively important ways, from most other aspects of police work. The EOD context makes a tremendous cognitive difference.

Most cities and towns in the US can't afford a full time bomb squad. So, bomb squad officers have other duties, and they do their EOD work, and their EOD training, on a part-time basis. In my experience, for what it's worth, they do it very well. They meet regularly, and they drill and experiment with explosives on a very expert basis.

But they're still cops.

This means that in their regular duties, motors (motorcycle officers) or traffic or patrol or detectives, they have cop ethics. The number one cop ethic is that *you never stop*. You're sweaty, you're tired, you're injured, but you still keep riding your motorcycle, or your cruiser, until you catch and ultimately book the bad guy. Period.

But EOD officers, in their bomb tech role, *can't* work that way. They're basically in the role of combat engineers. They have to move slowly and patiently, step by step, as they deal with an IED, and a drop of sweat in their eyes can mean that they don't cut the right wire, and, well, BOOM. If a bomb tech's hands start to shake from fatigue, even slightly, or the tech starts missing important structural elements of an IED because of eyestrain or too much sweat in the eyes, he or she needs to stand up, move back, take off the suit, and tell the next tech what he or she did. Then that new tech has to take over. Otherwise, everybody in the blast radius is going to die. Attending closely to your physical state, for the bomb tech, is not optional. If your physical state is impairing your performance, it's very important that you know about it before your glasses fog and you cut the wrong wire.

So, the bomb tech has to be continually aware of the limitations of his or her body, and to respond to them- at least, while in the EOD role. When that role is completed, then that bomb tech, in his or her regular law enforcement role, has to get back on the bike or into the cruiser and into that essential mental set in which you never stop, the limitations of your body notwithstanding.

This means that bomb techs, in those jurisdictions which cannot afford dedicated bomb squads, *must live in two different worlds of mental set*, the mental habits that govern many if not most of our actions. As officers in motors or patrol or detectives, they must ignore hardship, and they must *never stop*. As bomb techs, they must be sensitive to the state of their bodies, and they must stop their work *immediately* if their technical effectiveness is impaired.

Most bomb techs and commanders, in my experience, have a thorough understanding of these facts, expressed in different ways— but such an understanding can take years to develop. Would it perhaps be more effective to provide new bomb techs, in training, with a *prior, explicit, feature-intensive framework* for the understanding of this essential duality, the different mental sets involved in normal law enforcement and in the law enforcement/combat engineer role of the EOD expert?

And, as discussed above, would it not be a good idea to provide EOD experts with the time and resources to provide relevant, cognitively-based education in how to deal with EODs to relevant populations and groups in their jurisdictions?

Finally, would it not be a good idea to provide something like SMOKE training, cognitively-based IED detection training, to those relevant populations and groups?

These are not simple issues, but we do understand them, and we know how to provide the necessary, relevant, cognitively-based training. For a successful future in an increasingly IED-rich world, these ideas are respectfully offered to EOD officers and commanders.

The Undercover Officer- Kurtz's River

Let's discuss another important special-units role, the undercover assignment. Every law enforcement officer knows that the undercover world is *different*, changed from the normal world of everyday law enforcement in many important respects. But there are several cognitive principles that render this deeply weird world more comprehensible, and hence, perhaps safer for the undercover operative.

Please take a few moments to indulge a fictional analogy. You'll see its utility below.

In 1899, Joseph Conrad first published the story which would become his book *Heart of Darkness*. The hero of the story, Marlow, travels gradually up the Congo River to the domains of Mr. Kurtz, a grandiose and sadistic ivory trader who uses his isolation and authority to gratify some deeply bizarre impulses. Kurtz and his followers kill people, quite a lot of people, in very nasty ways. The book was loosely adapted by Francis Ford Coppola in his movie *Apocalypse Now*, with Martin Sheen, as Vietnam-era Captain Willard, in the role of Marlow. Same story, different jungles; in the movie, we see Kurtz (Marlon Brando) engaged in the same inhuman behaviors. Cut off from civilization, human beings tend toward the same inhuman excesses.

Kurtz is effectively cut off from any level of civilization and humanity, and he uses his power to gratify sadistic and power-mad impulses. As Marlow (or Willard) moves up the river, closer and closer to Kurtz's domain, he is increasingly separated from normal human sentiments, until, finally reaching Kurtz's world, there *are* no recognizable human sentiments. Civilization is gone, far away someplace down the river. Practices which would be insanely sadistic by civilized standards become normal in Kurtz's world.

In the book, we follow Marlow's course. As he moves up the river, farther and farther from his normal sources of ethics and reasonable behavior, we are confronted by what would result, in the absence of civilized standards, from the naked excess of power, unconstrained. We are also confronted by what happens to Marlow as he observes the horrors that infest Kurtz's end of the river.

Marlow is fundamentally changed, and not for the better.

Now, here's the point. The book (and the movie) provide a good metaphor for the world of the undercover (UC) officer. He or she (in the place of Marlow or Willard) leaves the normal world of morals and ethics, and enters the realm of organized crime (the world of Kurtz)- a world, to extrapolate to the realm of law enforcement, in which nothing matters except the necessary profit to the *capos* or the gang leaders; a world only of financial result, regardless of the human consequences.

This, for our purposes, is Kurtz's River—the situation in which a typical, competent law enforcement officer leaves normal life behind, and enters a new, clandestine world of terrible consequences and essential concealment.

The concealment part is important, both for the officer's survival, and unfortunately, for the limitations on what we know, scientifically, about the undercover realm. That world is necessarily secret, so research on the relevant psychology is necessarily limited. Unfortunately, some of it is also contradictory.

My colleague, Dr. Devin Kowalczyk, has done an excellent job of synthesizing what is known about this arcane universe, and much of what follows is directly credited to him in our collaborative effort *(Kowalczyk and Sharps, 2015, 2017)*.

To begin with, undercover people often have to move to new, very unfamiliar environments, and to transform themselves in ways that are frequently completely opposite to the ways in which they normally see themselves. These necessary transformations cause problems *(Girodo, 1985)*.

Some of these problems are counterintuitive, and we don't understand them well. For example, successive, short term operations may be more psychologically harmful than single, long term investigations *(Band & Sheehan 1999; Hibler 1994; Vasquez & Kelly 1989)*. At first glance, this doesn't seem right, but it at least makes *psychological* sense; jerking yourself repeatedly from one maladaptive environment to another can't be a good idea, and it may be worse than adopting a single maladaptive identity, even if that identity has to be maintained for a long time.

Also counterintuitively, the *length* of a given undercover operation may not be as important as we might think to the UC officer's psychological well-being *(Girodo 1991a; Love, Vinsom, Tolsma, & Kaufman 2008)*.

This, however, is controversial in the literature (e.g., *Love et al., 2008*). Disparities in results may reflect how the given studies were constructed, but in short, nobody really knows.

However, it does appear that psychological symptoms *may* be more likely to show up after an undercover operation than during the operation itself *(Love et al., 2008)*. This, again, at least makes sense; inconsistencies in character may kill you in the UC role, but they may also surface to your disadvantage once you're back to regular duty and some of the tremendous tension of the undercover role is relieved.

Being isolated from family, colleagues, and normal work environment are major stressors for the UC officer. Farkas *(1986)* found, in a retrospective examination of a broad range of psychological symptoms experienced during undercover assignments, that slightly over half of symptom variance was explained by isolation and changes to relationships.

In other words, changes in how you deal with other people, exacerbated by isolation from your normal human interactions, can cause you to develop a variety of behavioral maladies. Spouses and children may not be particularly sympathetic when you revert, for example, to the personality of a drug-dealing killer on your way to church.

Like Kurtz's river, there is no question that the UC environment has some negative consequences for the officers engaged. Former undercover officers have reported an intention to leave their departments at a rate five times higher than typical of those without undercover experience *(Farkas 1986; French 2003)*. Furthermore, those undercover officers who left their departments reported higher levels of engagement in criminal activity when they were undercover, by comparison with former and active undercover officers who remain with their departments.

In short, when some officers are undercover, they may do things they shouldn't; and the stress and consequences of dealing with those things can blow their careers. It is also tragically true, if unsurprising, that drug use and disciplinary actions positively correlate with undercover experience *(Girodo 1991b)*.

One thing you really don't want in the undercover world is for your officers to sympathize with, or buddy up to, their criminal targets. Everyone connected with the undercover world is entirely aware of that fact.

Yet friendship or loyalty to criminals was reported in almost half of those UC officers interviewed in one early study *(Farkas 1986)*, presumably as a result of the divided loyalties engendered by close contact with criminal elements, and with cognitive dissonance resulting from investment in these loyalties. These connections make sense, but they can cause profound stress for UC officers. Deeper relationships between officers and criminal elements were significantly associated with a greater frequency of psychiatric symptoms.

In short, the more deeply you become involved with your criminal targets, the worse things become for your career and your mental well-being. This is a big problem, because when you're in the deep field in the UC role, you'd better *fake* deep involvement to the point that it can't be detected by the targets; and if you *think about the fact that you're faking it*, you may start to *look* fake, and your targets may notice, and you may wind up dead. So, on the job, it's very important for UC officers to immerse themselves as completely as possible in their roles, as they are frequently and quite correctly trained.

Yet deeper involvement with targets has been shown to be bad for the performance of post-UC duties in a variety of ways, increasing the tendency of officers to engage in criminal activities, and increasing operational complaints and conflict between superiors and sub-ordinates. I'm unaware of any good solution to this problem at present, but commanders, psychologists working with UC operations, and post-operational UC personnel should at least be aware of the relevant facts.

It's hoped that future collaborative research will ultimately provide some solutions to this very difficult question.

But UC operators obviously have to develop effective false personae, and fake sets of behaviors that allow them to look and act like drug dealers, or Mafiosi, or what have you. They have to engage in the relevant behaviors repeatedly, intensely, and with significant emotional investment, and some of those behaviors are fairly nasty. To fake such behaviors consistently and successfully could hardly fail to develop habit systems, *mental sets,* related to the false personae. The problem is that these mental sets frequently pop up later, outside of the UC operational context, when aspects of the given officer's false persona emerge *without the control of the officer* and *outside of an operational context (Girodo, Deck, & Morrison 2002).*

I suspect, but don't know, that this is probably at least part of the source of the depth-of-involvement/post-UC duties problem discussed immediately above. What we do know, however, is that this emergence of the UC persona *frequently happens without the officer's awareness.* It's sometimes noted by the officer, but very frequently it's noticed by the officer's peers or family. The officer may have no idea.

This appears to mean that the longer you adapt to your faked criminal roles, the more likely you are to have cognitive dissonance regarding the relevant behaviors, and the harder it may be to abandon them. Compounding this problem is the fact that *you may not know that you haven't abandoned those behaviors*; some pretty nasty behaviors can pop up just the same.

More research is obviously needed on all of these issues, and it will require active collaboration between commanders, UC operators, and several kinds of psychologists, including research psychologists, in relevant specialties. We certainly can't sort all of these arcane issues out in the present work. But, however these empirical issues eventually shake out in the research, we can say that *former* undercover officers report higher rates of almost all psychological symptoms when compared to many *current* undercover officers, and certainly when compared with mainstream officers who do not have undercover experience.

These facts, in aggregate, appear strongly to apply also to *narcotics* officers, who for obvious reasons regularly use undercover tactics. Narcotics officers have in the past reported increased levels of "burnout" *(Wallace, Roberg, & Allen 1985)*, which is particularly alarming since many departments use new officers, fresh out of the academy, in counter-narcotics UC roles. The very reasonable rationale is that new officers are less likely to have ingrained "cop habits" which may betray them to the bad guys, and bad guys are less likely to recognize new people on the streets anyway, so it makes a lot of sense to put new officers in those roles. The danger here, of course, is that young officers may begin their non-UC careers, typically in Patrol, with some of the mental sets and cognitive dissonance engendered by their early UC experiences.

When you boil down what happens to undercover officers, it's pretty alarming. They tend to feel isolated, they may lose their coping skills, they may feel abandoned, and they may feel sympathy or even friendship for the bad guys.

Cognitive consequences in the UC role can include problems with memory and concentration, and undercover officers may see innocuous situations as threatening. They may also see their UC experiences as unique, things nobody else can understand, which of course can increase the sense of isolation as they return to non-UC duty within their departments *(Kowalczyk & Sharps, 2015, 2017)*. They've been up Kurtz's river, and they have trouble coming back.

There are other factors, of course, that are less quantifiable. A good friend of mine, who is now a senior police commander, did his time undercover. He reports going out, off-duty, with his well-groomed, prosperous, church-going family. Wife and children. It was a nice, but infrequent, break in his daily grind of UC service. The family went for dinner in a suburban restaurant. I believe he wore a suit, but he still had the necessary UC pony-tail and deeply exotic facial hair; let's face it, you can't get a haircut and a shave for one day off.

Anyway, everyone in the restaurant saw his UC coiffure, and they treated him like a contagious leper. Contemptuous looks, sneers, whispers. His wife and children reacted with shame. Any officer with a family can readily imagine his feelings, but there was absolutely nothing he could safely do to relieve them.

And then, next day, he went back into the UC environment; in police service to the same members of the public who'd been sneering at him yesterday.

Another good friend, in a European federal police agency, spent twenty-six years undercover (think about that—*twenty-six years*) before he was betrayed and had to flee his own country. A lot of his work was in the counter-narcotics role against organized crime. He says that he avoided using drugs himself by going into a pretended rage whenever the subject came up— "I sell this s***, I don't use it!" Rage from this guy would be impressive—he's a big man. But, to produce the desired effects, he had full "sleeves" of sex-and-death tattoos permanently engraved on both arms, together with a truly impressive assortment of biker-based facial hair.

You can always shave, of course. But gang tattoos are a much deeper issue. I'm imagining this man as a post-UC officer, in a short-sleeved summer uniform, standing at attention before his immaculately-uniformed Chief, and his colleagues.

And displaying those tattoos.

The Chief looks at those tattoos, snorts derisively, and then goes on to talk to somebody else.

Somebody once said that undercover work takes a part of your life, and will never give it back.

No kidding.

THE SOCIAL BASIS OF UNDERCOVER COGNITION

One of the big problems for undercover personnel is that they are human beings, and human beings should be recognized for their achievements. This is especially true when achievements come at the costs frequently borne by undercover officers. The problem is that when undercover people are recognized for their accomplishments, they frequently wind up dead.

If recognition for undercover accomplishments doesn't actually kill you, it can still have pretty wretched consequences. The case of NYPD Detective Frank Serpico provides an excellent if unfortunate example; having reported on corruption in his agency, in the 1960s, he was forced to flee the country. As far as I know, he's overseas still.

Some of my friends and acquaintances in law enforcement, officers who have actually withstood the stresses of the undercover role, occasionally make fun of the fictional spy James Bond. Readers may recall the old movies, starring Sean Connery. He would stride with perfect posture through casinos in a tailored tuxedo, when everybody else was wearing jeans and a t-shirt. He would draw even more attention by having the most beautiful woman (or women) in the place clinging to his arms.

I once asked a real undercover man, a man of deliberately unexceptional appearance and dress, what he thought of Bond in those movies. "He'd be dead in five minutes," was his reply.

Law enforcement officers, especially those who've been up Kurtz's river, will understand his comment. You don't want to be a world-famous secret agent. There's no future in it, literally, if the bad guys find out who you are, or were. The accomplishments of the undercover operative, however significant, must remain secret, and frequently secret forever. Otherwise the consequences can be lethal.

Yet there are a variety of ways in which former undercover officers can inadvertently give themselves away. For example, gang members often use specific figures of speech or language which are relatively exclusive to their groups. An officer who was formerly under cover against such groups may, from old ingrained habit, inadvertently use the same figures of speech in public, around the wrong people. If those people start wondering about these anomalies of language, the result can be very bad for the officer involved.

Or an officer may have to return to the scenes of former undercover activity, later in the course of other duties. He or she may have changed personal appearance—hairstyle, hair color, facial hair or its absence. Yet all of us walk and move with idiosyncratic mannerisms, and if the given operator happened to be thinking about something else when getting dressed that morning, he or she could wind up appearing to old adversaries in the same clothes worn during his or her time undercover. Maybe with the same idiosyncratic manner of wearing them—jacket habitually half-zipped, shirt bloused or untucked, collar up or down, what have you. Suddenly the operator's movements and clothing click in the mind of a former target who happens to be on the street at the wrong time—and again, the ultimate result can be very bad indeed.

These are among the more common types of field error that have been described to me by law enforcement experts, but it's pretty clear how easy they'd be to make. There are others as well, of course; but these are more operational than cognitive issues per se. The question for the cognitive scientist is more specific—why are such errors made, and how can they be reduced or prevented?

Well, we've already discussed some of the dynamics involved, in the first two chapters on stress, especially chronic stress. Former UC operators need to maintain a level of vigilance that literally lasts *forever*. Not the same vigilance they had in the field, of course; but a kind of watchfulness that will notice changes in environmental and social detail, *and in their own behavior*, that everybody else can safely ignore. Friends and acquaintances of the author, those who have successfully returned from Kurtz's river, have frequently mentioned the necessity of this state of vigilance. Together with the fact that it's fatiguing, that it's stressful, and that every so often, you slip.

Several of these experts have mentioned the fact, however, that some UC training programs (I have no idea how many) do not specifically address these concerns. That, I respectfully submit, is where cognitive science comes in. UC operators, both during and after their operational phases, need to have a *prior, explicit, feature-intensive framework* for understanding which behaviors are safe, and which are not. Relevant training can be provided efficiently, using these principles, and although research will be needed on best practices in such training, it may help to reduce stress, and enhance survivability, in current and former UC officers alike.

BEST PRACTICES FOR PSYCHOLOGISTS AND UC COMMANDERS

Undercover people pose some very difficult problems for psychologists, and for commanders of post-UC officers. What can psychologists do, and what can commanders support, to make life easier for the UC officer?

As a non-clinician myself, I cannot offer clinical recommendations, and I wouldn't presume to do so. Real clinicians, however, have made some serious progress in this regard.

They can use their skills to create family-like structures in UC teams, which appears to help *(Macleod 1995; Miller 2006; Pita 1993)*. They can provide strong and reliable contacts for UC people (e.g., *ABSCAM 1983; Band & Sheehan 1999)*. This can reduce the interference of personal problems, it can reduce UC officers' identification with suspects, and it can help to reduce loss or degradation of personal identity (e.g., Vasquez & Kelly 1989).

Recurrent scheduled interviews can also be very helpful (e.g., *Macleod 1995; Vasquez & Kelly 1989; Wallace, Roberg, & Allen 1985*). Note that symptoms of UC stress are frequently physical, and will include everything from headaches to stomachaches, from nervous tension to blackouts (see *Pita, 1993*). Your brain is part of your body, and your body responds to the stress of the UC world as well.

A competent psychologist can help a lot with that, too. Healthy coping mechanisms, and advocacy for enough time between operations *(Band & Sheehan 1999; Hibler 1994)*, also fall within the province of the competent UC psychologist, although it's important to note that psychologists must operate with regard to necessary operational demands, and *always* with the UC officer's personal survival as the ultimate goal. Psychoeducation in coping techniques may prove paramount, especially in the post UC phase, in which the officer must re-acclimate to normal life and to normal law enforcement operations. It can take a while for UC people to re-integrate into normal life and duty, sometimes as much as three years *(French, 2003)*. It may also take a long time to reintegrate if a UC officer was forced to leave an operation prematurely (*Farkas, 1986*).

It's also very important for UC officers not to imbue the UC experience with too much significance; it's important to see that work as part of a longer career, which is going to continue into the foreseeable future (*French, 2003*).

As a UC officer, you're going to have to readjust. Take the time. Don't use alcohol—it doesn't help. It *seems* to, for about an hour, but when you sober up, you're only going to be more depressed, so it's not worth it. You're going to have the dreams—again—*everybody* has the dreams. They're only dreams. Find a really good police psychologist, somebody who really *gets it*, and go to work. You developed some pretty nasty mental sets in your UC assignments, and you picked up some pretty unhealthy cognitive dissonance, personal investment, as well. But remember, you got through the UC world. If you had the personal qualities to get through that all-enveloping context in one piece, you're sure as hell going to get through this essentially psychological context too.

But no question, context is important. Let's focus on one more very important context, one that has an impact on the lives and survival of a great many officers.

Cognition on Patrol

There are many other special units on which we could focus, of course. SWAT and Hostage Negotiation Teams (HNT), for example. Mental set is hugely important there, as is cognitive dissonance. Time is the enemy of SWAT—you don't want the bad guys to have time to plan their tactics, set up ambushes, revet themselves and their weapons behind barriers. That, if you will, is the SWAT mental set—and you may get pretty damned invested (cognitive dissonance) in that mental set, as well. Time is the *enemy* of SWAT; however, time is the *friend* of HNT. As the bad guy gets tired, gets hungry, questions himself, HNT is more likely to succeed. I know of one HNT case where the bad guy gave up, after a long period of hungry time courtesy of HNT, *for the promise of a pizza.* It takes a lot of time and hunger to produce an outcome like that, even in a *gourmet* bad guy. But it's important to realize that the HNT people become just as invested in their essential mental sets, such as "time is my friend," as the SWAT folks do in the opposite; and conflict becomes inevitable. The wise commander will do his or her best to reduce that conflict.

These are obvious directly-opposed differences, lying psychologically in *investment* (cognitive dissonance) and in the cognitive concept of *mental set* as this regards the variable of time. *Cognitive dissonance* also rears its head as both teams, SWAT and HNT, spend more and more time in the field situation. So, when SWAT and HNT have to get together under a single commander, the cognitive bases of the relevant behavior become increasingly important. We need more research on this, and at the moment, we haven't got it.

But at least we know that these units, HNT and SWAT, are *special* units.

Now, practically nobody thinks of Patrol as a special unit. In at least one agency of my knowledge, Patrol is frequently denigrated. Yet Patrol is the first line of defense, the Thin Blue Line, for every agency. Patrol

Chapter 11 261

officers go out there every day, and God knows what they're going to run into—violent crack addicts with machine guns; savagely angry prostitutes with amazing capacities for vomiting on uniforms; calls to get precious cats out of trees, or to book evil family members who drank the last beer without sharing; lethal domestic calls involving meat cleavers, and homicidal madmen with automatic weapons, crouched behind concrete walls. Patrol sees it all. Patrol *deals* with it all. Every day.

As a civilian, whose personal safety is entirely dependent on Sheriff's Deputies on patrol, I personally see the demands on Patrol officers as very special indeed.

Let's consider only one of the special cognitive factors affecting Patrol officers. It's important.

SCIENCE FICTION IN THE PATROL CONTEXT

This is going to seem a little weird, but please bear with me for a bit. There was an old Star Trek movie (*Star Trek II: The Wrath of Khan*, 1982) in which an evil genetic superman named Khan, played by Ricardo Montalban, got hold of a spaceship and had to be stopped by the Starship commanded by Captain Kirk (played by William Shatner). For a while, Khan was phasering the living hell out of the good guys, but then the late actor Leonard Nimoy's character, Science Officer Spock, realized that Khan *tended to think in two dimensions.* Khan handled his space ship as if it were an infantry column (apparently they don't have air support in the future), concerned only with two-dimensional movements, more or less as if he were on the ground. So Captain Kirk (Shatner) moved his ship in the third dimension (up and down, rather than just back and forth), got into the right position, and phasered the living hell out of Khan's ship right back. Space Justice prevailed.

Readers would be entirely justified in wondering what the hell this has to do with anything.

Well, I remember a case in which two young officers responded to a call. They were at the front door of the residence, focused on everything in front of them. Like Khan, they thought in two dimensions.

They were shot and horribly wounded (thankfully, they were not killed, but they suffered a great deal) by a bad guy who had set up his position on the balcony above them.

These were brave and competent officers; but their *mental set* was two-dimensional. *They didn't focus on the third dimension, height.* And it shot them. The shots came from above, from the third dimension, as they concentrated on the two dimensions of what was immediately in front of them.

In the Kennedy assassination in 1963, Secret Service officers were on the ground, and they were focused on ground attacks. They were prepared for attacks by gunmen or gun teams or vehicles, operating on the ground, *in two dimensions.* On the ground, in front of them.

And then Lee Harvey Oswald, with his mail-order Mannlicher carbine, nailed Kennedy from the sixth floor of the Texas Book Depository.

From the third dimension.

Some officers, in some cities, patrol districts with high-rise buildings. My guess is that those officers think in three dimensions, as a result of long and potentially lethal practice.

Other officers, in other cities or rural areas, patrol a world of one-story ranch houses and one- or, at most, two-story stores. They get used (*mental set*) to looking for threats in two dimensions, in front, in back, and from the side. And then a bad guy climbs onto a roof, or onto a rare upper story.

And he fires down, *in the third dimension.*

As a recent terrorist did in Las Vegas, bump–stocking his way to the death of many of his victims.

We need solid research on this phenomenon which simply hasn't been done yet. Hopefully colleagues in the world of experimental forensic cognitive science, will take up this particular slack. Yet we see it happening, again and again—the focus on a two-dimensional world, at the expense of that all-important, and very lethal, third dimension up and down.

Training officers, please take note. *Up and down* can be as important as *side-to-side.* Please prepare Patrol officers accordingly, depending on your own professionally expert assessment of the relevant patrol environments.

But what form should this training take? Well, the reader will not be surprised at the following opinion: *there should be a prior framework for explicit, feature-intensive understanding.*

A Personal Note to Sergeants, FTOs and Senior Officers

I am an experimental psychologist, not a cop; but as a shrink, I have known many Sergeants, Field Training Officers (FTOs), and Senior Officers. I have the greatest respect for these people, and there is no way in hell I would ever try to tell them how to do their jobs, any more than I would personally attempt to take over an open-heart surgery (Scalpel? This is the SCALPEL? Quick, give me a butter knife! And a SPOON! A really big SPOON!)

Sergeants and FTOs are often between a rock and a hard place, between the troops and the Brass. They have a lot to think about. And all of these command experts, sergeants and FTO's, will recall cases and situations in which *all the pieces of the given puzzle were all over the place,* until they identified the Core Principles, the overarching thematic facts, that pulled all the pieces into place.

With respect, that's the point suggested here. The principles of *cognitive science* can give you *the overarching thematic principles that unite what's going on.* As we will see in subsequent chapters, and to which I've alluded above (quite a few times), there's a kind of Holy Trinity underlying successful training, or success in the field:

1. A solid prior framework for what's actually happening.
2. An explicit understanding of this framework, without the need to imply *anything* in the situation.
3. A feature-intensive understanding, bit-by-bit and piece-by-piece, of the given situation.

The consideration of two-dimensional and three-dimensional factors outlined above is an example. The understanding of this phenomenon, in prior, explicit, feature-intensive terms, can be of great help in unifying what is actually going on in the field, and it may help to keep your people alive.

But all the experimental psychologist can do is to point out these principles, and characterize them for the use of the people who are actually out there in the potentially lethal world of law enforcement. It is the expertise of Sergeants, FTOs, and Senior Officers which will consolidate these perspectives into effective applications in the field, applications which will contribute to officer effectiveness, safety, and survival.

These ideas obviously do not tell you how to do your job; that would be ridiculous. But a consideration of these types of ideas, in any given situation, may help to provide you with an overarching prior, explicit, feature-intensive framework within which to identify and to use the core ideas governing any given field environment or situation.

It is in this spirit that these ideas are respectfully offered.

Summary

Special units have special needs. Some units, such as Patrol, may not typically be seen as "special"; but they still have special requirements which must be analyzed in terms of *context,* in terms of exactly what officers in those units *should be prepared to confront.* I hope that academic researchers, and training officers and commanders at all levels, will collaborate in future to identify exactly what those needs are, to identify exactly what cognitive principles are pertinent in any given situations, and to develop effective ways to defeat the hazards involved.

But for the present, let's see in a bit more detail how these principles can be employed in law enforcement training.

Chapter 12
SYNTHESIS: IMPLICATIONS FOR TRAINING AND ENFORCEMENT IN AN INCREASINGLY RISKY WORLD

In the previous chapters, we have addressed the influence of long- and short-term stress on cognition. We have discussed memory and its failures, the interpretation of what we see around us, and the ways in which all of these factors influence thinking and decision making under conditions of *processing under pressure*, the conditions under which law enforcement officers, commanders, and administrators typically operate. We have discussed the implications and ramifications of these cognitive factors for real-world law enforcement situations, and we have considered how an understanding of these influences can provide an edge, an additional tool or instrument, for law enforcement people to aid in their professional effectiveness and their survivability. In this chapter, we'll summarize these factors. We'll also show how training that takes them into account can be implemented and put into practical use.

At the present time, most training consists of physical demonstrations, followed by practice, of how to do specific things, such as shooting on the move or driving a police car at speed. Modern training has come a long way. As in the past, officers still stand on ranges and fire at targets; but today, they also train with sophisticated force simulators and in field conditions in which they are required to move, take cover, and shoot ambidextrously under simulated combat conditions. Officers still drive real vehicles under the direction of field training officers; but today, many departments also make use of advanced driving simulators that can provide exercise options that are very difficult, if not impossible, to produce under non-simulated conditions.

These innovations are laudable and generally highly effective. Nothing in this book suggests their replacement. However, modern training *can be made even more effective if it is designed and implemented with reference to the cognitive principles discussed here.* If supervisors and field training officers understand the cognitive factors involved in what they do, and if trainees are imbued with an understanding of how their own cognitive processes, and those of the colleagues, witnesses, victims, and suspects with whom they interact, have a direct bearing on the success of their operations and on their own prospects for going home safely at the end of the shift, both their operational effectiveness and their survivability should be considerably enhanced.

Let us, therefore, consider the most important principles for incorporating cognitive elements into training programs.

Training Facilities, Training Scenarios

Virtually all law enforcement agencies face a similar problem with reference to training. This is the fact that it usually takes a relatively low priority. A given agency has a certain number of absolutely defined responsibilities; a certain number of patrol units per district, a certain number of detectives working on cases, etc. In the present climate of diminished resources and increased demand, agency or department finances are usually stretched to rational limits or even beyond, and something has to give. That something is frequently found in the training bureau. In any given city, for example, citizens and local media are often concerned with police response times, and public pressure is brought to bear if these begin to increase. Very few of the same citizens, or reporters, care at all if driving simulators are becoming too old to be reliable, or if new software is essential for the Police Department's force simulator. In fact, very few of these vocal constituencies are even aware that these things exist at all.

However, police commanders are very much aware that these things exist, that active modern training requires resources, and that every successful performance in the field is ultimately dependent upon training. This is true for initial training and also for continued training for more experienced officers, especially with reference to the vast corpus of law enforcement skills that are perishable and that therefore require regular repetition. Training is crucial, and resources are scarce. How, then, are senior commanders and administrators supposed to resolve this situation?

Pooling of resources is of course an option, and it can be effective. A given state or district can create regional training centers so that expensive systems like force and driving simulators, or Hogan's Alley ranges that require a lot of space, can be centrally located for the use of multiple agencies. This, of course, tends to reduce expenses, although secondary expenses such as travel and per diem are necessarily increased for officers from more geographically remote locations to make use of the facilities. Nevertheless, as long as good will prevails among the agencies using such central facilities, and as long as the facilities in question can be easily modified to simulate the mission requirements of the various agencies using them, this is a solid, reasonable option.

However, when you talk to training supervisors and field training officers, the general impression is that training facilities tend to be in use *all the time*, regional or not. The facts are that there are a lot of officers, increasing demands, and only so many resources. Reshuffling those resources is only going to go so far.

INCREASING RESOURCES FOR TRAINING

How can commanders and administrators increase those resources? The answer may be found, to some degree, in the cognitive factors we've discussed above, and in the power of those factors to persuade those who control the resources of the need to contribute more of them to crucial issues of training. There is a whole psychology of persuasion that goes well outside the scope of the present volume. However, certain useful facts in dealing with city councils, state commissions, and federal funding officers emerge from our discussion of processing under pressure. Funding officials have human nervous systems. So do the public and media constituencies that influence their decisions. Therefore, it behooves the commander or administrator who needs funding, and who needs public support for that funding, to recall what he or she knows about cognition. Funding for training, or for anything else for that matter, is unlikely to be forthcoming unless the officials and the public understand the need for it. Therefore, the wise commander or administrator will make an effort to improve that understanding. Together with all of the other machinations of public relations and lobbying techniques, the law enforcement supervisor should meet with funding people, media people, and concerned members of the public with the goal of *front-loading explicit, feature-intensive information* about the relevant needs. If humanly possible, you want this explicit FI information to be in their working memories, immediately available in their minds for consideration, in the immediate context of the decision.

Data can be of enormous help here. Clear, graphic presentations of quantitative performance differentials between officers who have had, for example, simulator training and those who have not, can be front-loaded by means of simple bar graphs or pie charts with simple, explicit prior explanations of what the training is and what it will do. The information should be feature-intensive, rather than gestalt; in other words, "officers with this training exhibited a 17% faster response time" is better than "officers with this training are better police officers, contributing more to the safety of our community." The latter is poetic and satisfying, and you may even want to throw it in for effect. However, it's important to front-load into the mind of the decision maker that there is an explicit relationship between a given specific training expense and a specific law enforcement success (or failure, if the training is not conducted) for which that decision maker will be held accountable by the voters.

Elements of Successful Training

Cognitive principles can therefore be useful in getting the resources you need. However, the next question deals with exactly what those resources should be used for. Obviously, a psychologist such as the author should not presume to suggest specific tactical evolutions for training, but there are psychological factors that can be important across evolutions. The keys to successful training, from a psychological perspective, include the following:

As is typically the case in current training, *repetition of necessary skills* should form a major element. However, there is a trade-off here of which the wise commander or FTO must be aware. As an officer perfects the skills for one type of activity or environment, he or she acquires desirable mental sets. To refer back to the case of Chief McAllister, he acquired the desirable mental set of smoothly taking cover behind a bullet-proof object before engaging the suspect, a mental set painstakingly instilled on the range with appliance boxes in the role of the bullet-proof objects.

However, there is a downside even to desirable mental sets such as this, and that is that they are highly domain-specific. This means that their effectiveness is confined to a relatively narrow range of tactical prospects. For example, a SWAT team trains again and again for entry through a door and into a hostile environment. The way they align themselves as a unit, the positions at which they hold their weapons, the "Groucho walk" as they move from point to point, all are rehearsed to perfection. The team perfects its horizontal entry into the hostile environment of a store or a house. Then comes the real-world call, and they have to make entry vertically through the hatch of a ship, or vertically in the other direction into the belly of a commercial aircraft. Their carefully acquired skills suffer a ninety-degree realignment, and this particular mental set may damage their mission effectiveness and get them killed.

Modern training experts are of course aware of this problem and provide the obvious solution. Training can be provided for aircraft and ship entry, as well. However, not everybody in every agency can afford all sorts of training, and so a terrible trade-off results: Because it's impossible to perfect skills for every possible environment, how does the commander decide which skills to provide?

Chapter 12

REASONABLE TRADE-OFFS

Part of the answer to this question may lie in a reappraisal of the material presented above, on the question of why Patton succeeded while Custer failed. A major part of the answer lies in reasonable cognitive flexibility. Note that word "reasonable."

A reasonable assessment of probable operational environments is key. The experienced officer or commander is in a position to decide *which environments his or her forces may reasonably be expected to confront.*

To take a completely outlandish example, the Carthaginian general Hannibal attacked the Romans with elephants. Therefore, in the modern world, an elephant-borne attack is technically *possible*, albeit very unlikely; and in a perfect world, to provide perfect public safety, a police agency should have a contingency plan for deploying special anti-elephant forces, possibly armed with mice.

In practice, of course, this is absurd, bordering on idiotic. It simply isn't going to happen. Yet law enforcement chiefs must frequently cope with concepts, usually submitted by citizens, that derive from similarly absurd viewpoints. Does a police agency need a policy to deal with a UFO invasion, even after, for example, a mass UFO citing such as that which occurred in Phoenix, Arizona in March, 1997? Semi-hysterical constituents, including some who are extreme devotees of science fiction, would answer with an absolute affirmative (see Chapter 2). Yet even those devotees are in much greater danger from a mugging, especially when their peripheral vision is limited by their space alien masks, than they are from abduction by little green men from the planet Grak. The wise law enforcement commander will therefore consign such concepts, even if supported by a momentary wave of local hysteria, to a file marked "No."

Less crazy examples, however, are legion. Should all forces have units that are trained in entry and operations on container ships? For forces in the coastal areas of Los Angeles who might, in extreme emergency, have to converge cooperatively on the harbor at Long Beach, a reasonable answer might be yes. For the police departments of Salt Lake City, Utah or Denver, Colorado, a "yes" is hard to justify, even in the era of terrorism; the nearest big ships are, quite simply, one hell of a long way away.

How about commercial aircraft entry? For Dallas or Phoenix forces, who operate within screaming distance of major airports, the answer is probably yes, obviously depending in part on collaborative factors regarding local Airport police; for the police force of Laramie, Wyoming, or Trinidad, Colorado, no large aircraft can land at their smaller airports; wouldn't their limited training time be better applied to something more likely?

How about training to deal with terrorists who are operating in high rise buildings? Well, for New York City or Chicago PD, the answer would be a resounding *yes*. For small plains towns in Colorado or Nebraska, where the tallest building is probably a grain elevator, training would be better devoted to the local open-spaces environment (although see Chapter 11 above, with regard to mental sets in single- and multistory patrol environments).

The age of terrorism, of course, has changed public sensibilities on this issue. All sorts of things might be the targets of terrorists. For example, terrorists might attack crops in agricultural areas. However, the wise sheriff will consider the *probability* of terrorists squatting in local fields in the night, gleefully squirting Anthrax onto individual turnips, compared with the certainty that gang members have committed four murders in the county this year. The wise sheriff might also devote some explicit, feature-intensive consideration to the prospect of putative terrorists attacking the local nuclear reactor, say, rather than the local turnips, and act accordingly.

There are only so many resources, and they frequently cannot be allocated with certainty; human beings, in and out of law enforcement, have a poor record of predicting the future. Often resources can only be allocated in terms of probability; and given this fact, prior frameworks for the explicit, feature-intensive consideration of relative probabilities can be a commander's best friend.

History and psychology have shown that wise commanders are cognitively flexible, but not ridiculously so. Patton understood, as his contemporaries did not, the prospect of a German attack in the Ardennes, and he prepared accordingly. However, he did not prepare for German troops to attack on elephants or in UFOs. To reiterate, cognitive flexibility must be tempered with the commander or administrator's best cognitive ally: front-loaded, explicit, feature-intensive information, immediately available in working memory as the decision process unfolds. Such a commander is cognitively flexible, as was Patton, but still makes use of explicit cognitive principles to ascertain the likelihood of given contingencies, and acts accordingly. A flexible commander who makes use of these cognitive principles may still be wrong, of course; but he or she is far less likely to be wrong than the commander who does not.

Once the necessary skills for dealing with reasonably probable tactical environments are identified, a program of training simulations should be created. These simulations should cover those scenarios that are likely, or even diminishingly likely, but not those that are ridiculous. These simulations, however, should not be presented to trainees in isolation. Rather, the trainees should be provided, once again, with front-loaded, explicit, feature-intensive information as to what the given training evolutions are for, how and under what circumstances they will be used in the field, and the range of tactical field situations to which the given tactic is relevant. The major point here is that the physical learning in the situation, the installation of beneficial mental sets, must be accompanied by the right kind of cognitive training as well. The right kind of cognitive training is front-loaded, explicit, feature-intensive, and available in working memory. From a psychological perspective, excellent systems of simulations already exist for specific applications (e.g., the DART system; *Duran, 2008*), as do excellent treatments of tactical issues (e.g., Rayburn's 2003 treatment of advanced patrol tactics) suitable for front-loading in the manner suggested throughout the present volume. The SMOKE system, discussed in Chapter 11 above, provides an example of this type of cognitive construction in the area of training for IED detection. The cognitively aware commander does not have to re-invent the wheel; it already exists.

However, it falls to the cognitively aware commander, training supervisor, or FTO to put the pieces together in a way that optimizes the effects of the training.

> **To summarize, this will take the following form:**
>
> 1. Front-loaded, explicit, feature-intensive training of a "classroom" nature will be interspersed with physical repetition of the necessary skills. This is particularly important in the case of perishable skills.
>
> 2. The skills to be front-loaded and physically practiced will be those relevant to the tactical situations that are *realistically likely* to be encountered by the given agency. Commanders should explicitly consider the spectrum of probability of situations to be encountered by their specific agencies, and should see that the most intense and the most frequent training be directed to the most frequently encountered situations.
>
> 3. The spectrum of training evolutions should include specific examples of the likely situations to be

> encountered, to increase reasonable cognitive flexibility in the field. In other words, don't always put the bad-guy shooter on the first floor; sometimes, place him or her on the second floor balcony. Don't provide only refrigerator cartons as cover; throw in a few old washing machines or dumpsters as well. The officer should be prepared for a *reasonable spectrum of tactical prospects*, rather than for single solutions that may not exist in the field.

Thus far in this chapter, we have been primarily concerned with tactical issues, *but similar considerations obtain for investigative issues as well*. An important example lies in our consideration of eyewitness issues in Chapters 3 and 4 above. In those chapters, we discussed the dynamics of eyewitness memory. However, and once again, the principles governing eyewitness issues are by no means confined to the traditional eyewitness. Every officer reporting on a given tactical situation, every victim, every suspect has a human nervous system; all are subject to the same cognitive laws.

These considerations apply very strongly to police officers as witnesses. For example, officers' eyewitness accounts of a given action frequently change, in terms of verbal details, from statement to statement; the gist of the reported action may be the same, but the words with which it is reported are usually somewhat different in repeated accounts. When internal affairs officers encounter this phenomenon, they may bring charges of a nonexistent integrity violation where, in fact, a given officer simply exhibited the general reconfigurative properties of the human nervous system.

Such verbal reconfiguration, incidentally, is among the most common factors observed in eyewitness memory, including the eyewitness memory of law enforcement officers. Yet knowledge of this fact is not very widespread, and I have seen good officers' careers nearly destroyed by minor verbal inconsistencies on a number of occasions. Everyone concerned in an IA should be aware that human beings very seldom express the same ideas, concepts, or memories in the same words every time; minor verbal inconsistencies are the norm, not the exception, in the recounting of human memory.

Some eyewitness memories are accurate, some are not, and of course some people are simply lying. However, if the reader has come this far, he or she is aware that the dynamics of memory are by no means simple. The wise commander will provide training to patrol officers, detectives, and IA officers in these principles. This training will be front-loaded, explicit, and feature-intensive in nature. Chapters 3 and 4 above, on eyewitness phenomena, can provide a good primer on this information to form the core of such training if desired. The commander or administrator should of course be aware that there are other many other sources on these topics, and vastly more in-depth treatments of this material, in the professional literature. However, a wise commander will also keep time requirements and officer endurance in mind; it may not be possible, or even desirable, to turn every line officer into an expert on eyewitness identification, but it's definitely an excellent idea to provide strong training in the basics and on the most relevant advanced topics. The results will include fewer fruitless investigations, as fewer detectives follow up on fantastic stories with no basis in reality; fewer wrongful IA cases will be based on erroneous witness testimony, together with fewer of the litigations and headaches which invariably result; and fewer errors in court. Solid training on relevant aspects of *processing under pressure* may be viewed as a fabulously cheap but amazingly effective insurance policy, reducing headaches and improving professional efficiency on a number of levels at once.

Training and Experience in the Context of Stress

The basic principles of training outlined above, in this chapter, actually apply to virtually every professional setting, including those unconcerned with law enforcement. However, as we have seen throughout this volume, the law enforcement environment is different from most other professional situations on a number of genuinely important dimensions. Preeminently, of course, this includes the dimension of danger. Law enforcement officers go in harm's way on a daily basis, and this obviously forms a significant source of stress.

As we have seen, this stress can be operationally relieved at least to some degree by repeated and realistic training, again within the realistic sphere of what the given officer is likely to encounter in the field. However, as we have also seen, the effects of stress are cumulative, and many of the stresses of police work are simply unavoidable, regardless of level of training and preparedness. Therefore, in view of these facts, the wise commander or police administrator will take steps to reduce those stressors that *are* in fact avoidable.

Every police psychologist knows that officers, in general, find administrative and bureaucratic requirements far more stressful than the tactical requirements of whatever situations they may encounter in the street. Academics can debate this until the end of time; but the fact is, that's what officers tell us, and their experience clearly has critically important validity as far as they are concerned.

Why is that? Why can't officers just deal with nonoperational stressors? The job is dangerous; everybody knows that. Danger is more—well, *dangerous*—than the need to fill out many reports, or to testify in court or before superiors, or to go to endless community-based training sessions. Physical danger is certainly worse than the stresses attendant on a divorce or family problems.

There is a tacit assumption here—the assumption that peace officers, courageous enough to deal with physical danger, should simply be able to push stress, bureaucratic miasma, and personal problems out of the way. However, they frequently can't, and the reason why may be related to that word "tacit" in "tacit assumptions." The culture of law enforcement has many traditions, and many of them are tacit, implicit, and unspoken. Most of these traditions are highly laudable. These include expectations of physical courage and integrity; a strong sense of duty; a refusal to quit in the face of pain or extreme adversity; and of course the certainty, once a tactical situation has commenced, that defeat is impossible and victory is certain.

The reader will note that these are all *gestalt* concepts, identified in their totality rather than by specific, explicitly definable features. Frequently, especially in the modern world, this is how it must be. To dissect a concept like courage or integrity into its feature-intensive components, in modern language, would prove embarrassing at best and melodramatic at worst to most law enforcement officers (see *Wolfe, 1979*). For most purposes, and for most officers confronting most situations, it may be best to leave the majority of these tacit traditions alone.

Yet sometimes a smart commander should pause to make a feature-intensive analysis of just what the traditions and culture of a particular agency are doing, at least with reference to specific considerations. Consider the tacit idea that an officer never quits (perhaps best exemplified in the venerable Royal Canadian Mounted Police concept of always getting their man, and in the less-official Texas Ranger idea that an officer must always "keep comin'"). In general, these are really good, solid tacit ideas to foster in any given department.

Except in the bomb squad. Recall the Explosive Ordinance Disposal (EOD) officers discussed in Chapters 8 and 11. Unlike officers in most duties, when they get tired, they quit, at least for the moment. They *have* to quit. If they don't, the result will be a resounding "BOOM," accompanied by their own deaths and a lot of what we bloodlessly call "collateral damage." The local bomb squad forms a case in which an active, feature-intensive analysis of tacit law enforcement concepts is not only a good idea, it is absolutely essential. To reiterate earlier discussion, the officers in question are fully aware that their operational tactics and policies are atypical of much of the rest of police culture, and when they are working in their usual, non-EOD assignments, patrol, investigation, traffic, what have you, they deliberately move out of their EOD tactical mindset ("if you get too tired to continue effectively, quit") back into their normal police tactical mindset ("Never quit. Ever. Victory is the only option"). This is an excellent example of what happens when officers and commanders apply feature-intensive reasoning directly to what they have to do in any given range of tactical possibilities, and when they do this well in advance of the point at which those possibilities rear their ugly heads. Fully awake and aware, the successful EOD expert, who has other duties as well, moves smoothly between the needs of the dominant never-quit police culture and the absolute needs of the realm, fraught with insanely high levels of potential disaster, of the unexploded bomb.

Administrative Stress

The work of EOD technicians, and their need for surgical patience in a law enforcement culture more comfortable with high levels of action than with concepts of cognition and fatigue, provides an extreme example of the use of feature-intensive analysis of job and job culture. This type of analysis, used properly, can benefit commanders and administrators, to say nothing of their agencies or departments, to a great degree; and so it is with the reduction of administrative stress. Law enforcement officers operate in a world that has different types of stress than those that occur in most occupations. When these extraordinary sources of stress fuse with the typical bureaucratic and familial stresses encountered by most people, the fusion can be deadly. The police officer does not deal with police stresses, which are considerable, and then with everyday stressors, which are less so, in isolation from each other. As we saw above in Chapter 1 (especially Vignette 1), the officer deals with a fusion of personal and professional stressors that may be significantly worse for professional effectiveness and officer survivability than either would be alone. The combined effects of chronic and acute stress are massively exacerbated for the law enforcement officer. As we have seen, the officer who encounters the acute stress, the shooting or the high-speed chase, may already be on the ropes from cumulative stress and, quite frequently, sleep deprivation.

These are among the reasons why an officer exposed to a long meeting—a truly *long* meeting—after a bad night shift and bad fast food and insufficient sleep and a rocky marriage—may suddenly, and unexpectedly, blurt out something like "THIS MEETING IS A LOAD OF CRAP AND A WASTE OF TIME!" This may be blurted out in front of the City Manager, who called the meeting. Not a great career move, of course, but the reader may remember that the HPA axis in that particular officer doesn't care. The reader may also recall *why* it doesn't care from previous chapters: The HPA axis thinks it's hunting a deer.

This is important. Everyday stress applies to everybody, wherever they work—the phone company, the grocery store, wherever. However, let us now consider the same factors with reference to law enforcement officers. Almost uniquely in modern society, law enforcement officers, like those in the military, have to deal with the "hunting" stressors as well as the everyday ones—the wild two minutes of apprehension of the violent suspect; the terrible moment of the discovery of the mangled body of the murdered child; the exquisitely coordinated actions of the high-speed chase. Then, they have to go back to the station, write and file the reports, go home, and deal with families who frequently have no clue about the reality of police life on the streets.

The great problem is that there is a vast divide between the everyday world of the law enforcement officer and the everyday world of everybody else. Veteran officers, whom the author has had the honor to know or to meet, seem to have a ghastly horror story, a tale of some hideous damned thing that happened, on *virtually every corner of the streets* of their much-patrolled cities. The veteran officer typically has a series of street-by-street blood-soaked nightmares with which he or she must live (*the place where that kid died—I was holding her—the place where that guy looked down and saw the screwdriver coming out of his chest—and he looked surprised, like he hadn't even felt it, but then the blood came up and he—the place where I found that baby—dear God, that baby*).

These are very hard to explain in the context of home redecoration projects and school plays. It's hard for the officer to find people to talk to, people, including family, who will actually *get it*. Veteran officers are not even sure they're *supposed* to talk about this stuff—so the horrible stuff in question festers, in isolation. No matter how brave, how tough, how experienced the officer may be, the stuff festers, and the nightmares begin. Then there is the sudden waking, many times each night, that robs the officer of sleep, and the sudden racing of the heart and the soaking sweat that isn't *really* heart trouble, it's a panic attack—"*but hell, I'm too tough for panic, that doctor must be crazy, but why do I keep getting this damn cold or flu or whatever it is over and over again and have trouble with my guts every time I eat spicy food—never used to, dammit—*"

Chapter 12

These are sources of stress. These stresses can end a career, force long-term stress leaves, reduce organizational efficiency, and produce a significant drain on municipal resources.

They can also destroy the lives and, if you will, the souls, of good, dedicated officers; capable people who should not have to be miserable all the time. These are people who deserve better and who would have gotten it if they knew where to go for competent psychological treatment of these stresses. Such stressors should be reduced or treated if possible. As we have seen, long-term stress is very dangerous for physical health, mental health, and operational performance.

Even so, we are the creatures our ancestors were—we can deal with Selye's alarm state, in general. We can deal with the short-term stress, no matter how nasty it may become. The problem, typically, is not the short-term stress of the bad street situation. The problem is the long-term administrative stress. The present author has yet to meet a single officer who does not find that administrative stresses vastly overwhelm, in terms of personal significance, those inherent in the potentially violent nature of the profession. For many law enforcement professionals, if not for most of them, the need for physical courage in the course of duty is vastly outweighed by the need for whatever skills are required in filling out the forms correctly, filing them properly, and then filling out the new forms that explain why the old ones were filed incorrectly.

So, the officers continue to patrol, and investigate; and they fill out forms, and they deal with computers and with the endless useless updates of the endlessly useless computers. They go to meetings and to public relations things, and they deal with their families and their spouses. Some of them handle it all, depending on circumstances. Others develop ulcers, or acid reflux disease: the consequence of too many years in Selye's state of *resistance*, as discussed in Chapter 1. Others develop heart problems, or circulatory illnesses: same source. People hear about these problems, shrug their shoulders: it's a stressful occupation.

Yet there is something that can be done about these problems, something that can help. It begins with the realization that most officers find administrative stressors to be more personally taxing than those related directly to their duties. This means that law enforcement commanders and administrators are in a direct and crucial position of power with reference to the amelioration of long-term stress. Commanders and administrators have the ability to enhance the operational and economic effectiveness of their agencies (more work completed successfully; fewer sick days required) by means of fairly straightforward actions.

Fixing Problems

This process begins with the realization of how stressful administrative factors can be for officers. It continues with a hard, feature-intensive analysis of how those factors actually interact, in real-world terms, with officer activities and essential operations.

Administrative requirements should be analyzed: is this paperwork required? Who requires it? What does it actually accomplish? Does this computer program actually work? Can people use it successfully, and without spending hours of tax-supported time de-bugging it? If not, did the old program work just fine? Actually, does the given task require a computer at all, or would it be more efficient to do it with a pencil?

Is this mandatory meeting necessary? If not, why is it mandatory? What does it actually accomplish in terms of definable, real-world goals that can be articulated clearly and without verbal sugar-coating, without using words the way squids use ink?

Are my officers isolated? Is there somebody who *gets it*, somebody they can *and will* talk to when they need to? Does our department psychological services specialist provide our officers with information they can use when they've been under combat conditions, or does the shrink mumble about vague theories that our officers find worse than useless? If the latter, should we be looking for a new shrink? Somebody who *gets it*? Somebody who can communicate, successfully and with verbal clarity, about this occupation to the families and loved ones of the officers under my command? Who can help them to create home lives in which my officers can live and live well, without figuratively wanting to chew their own legs off to escape from their respective domestic traps? A shrink who will do useful, real-world things to help to stabilize my officers' lives and to increase those officers' alertness and effectiveness in the field?

The police commander cannot remove the acute stresses from the occupational lives of his or her officers. However, some of the *chronic* stresses are a different matter. An insightful police commander once told the present author about the salutary effect on officer morale, in his agency, of even the *comprehension* of sources of officer stress, let alone their alleviation. In other words, if officers understood that their commanders were aware of the stressors they face, and that the commanders were working to correct them, they felt substantially better. They seemed to perform with greater effectiveness, *even before the problems were corrected*. Morale went up, fewer interpersonal problems were observed, operational demands were met cheerfully, or at least with sardonic optimism and confidence. Feelings are important in this type of context—they translate into enhanced operational effectiveness. The commander who reduces the unnecessary administrative stresses on his or her officers, and who provides reasonable channels for dealing with personal and familial problems, will have a more effective and trouble-free force. There are administrative stresses that result from necessary, non-negotiable factors, and others that can be alleviated by means of relative simple actions on the part of the commander. It is a wise commander who knows the difference, and who is willing to act on that difference.

So, we've discussed some of the chronic effects of long-term stress, together with some considerations for reducing them, to the degree that this is possible in a given agency faced with given demands, resources, and resource limitations. However, the acute stresses remain—the street dangers that are part and parcel of police work. There is no getting rid of these stressors; but there are means of diminishing their power, with the consequence of increased operational effectiveness.

These stressors, of course, are best met by competent, courageous officers, who have had the necessary training; front-loaded, explicit, feature-intensive training, followed by reasonable repetition of necessary skills, under the range of tactical prospects which might reasonably be predicted by commanders who exhibit a high degree of cognitive flexibility.

Cognitive science cannot replace police expertise or experience. Cognitive science, like the rest of psychology, can only provide an additional set of tools for the commander, administrator, or officer to use. Psychological principles, if incorrect or incorrectly applied, can be worse than useless. However, the principles discussed in this book, in all of the previous chapters, are, to the author's knowledge, correct and supported by experimental evidence and by real-world experience. As such, judicious integration of the principles of *processing under pressure* into training and operational practice may provide an additional edge, a solid enhancement of good police work. Not, it must be emphasized, a replacement; but an enhancement, a way of increasing operational effectiveness and officer survivability.

At its best, this additional edge will help more officers to go home at the end of their shift.

Epilogue
A Brave New World?

When I was researching the North Hollywood incident for this book, I went to the Internet to see what was available out there, electronically, on the subject. Initially, I assumed that the general public perception of this horrendous event would be the proverbial no-brainer; the cops were obviously the good guys, the bandits were obviously the bad guys. Nobody in their right mind would see anything admirable about these bandits, blazing away with automatic weapons in the sole service of stealing other people's money, just for reasons of personal greed.

This assumption, on my part, proved that I need to get out more.

There are, at the time of writing, hundreds of thousands of electronic references available through Google on the North Hollywood situation. It's a little difficult to tell what's what, on the Web; many of these references extol the music of a band that, believe it or not, named one of their albums "North Hollywood Shootout."

Let us take a moment to consider the amazing lack of reality contact reflected by this choice—"Hey, let's name an album after a horrible catastrophe involving lots of human death and suffering caused by self-centered greed! On second thought, why not just call it Auschwitz! How totally fun!"

Okay, so after a few moments of marveling at this weird display, I found a few items useful for fact-checking; news reports from that day in 1997, and so on. But then I began to explore a bit further.

Many web sites offered only videos of the incident, without commentary, as if the human tragedy of that day was merely one more action movie. A few mentioned the significance of the incident for modern SWAT training and operation; but the tone of many of the web sites was at least tacitly *positive* about the whole thing.

These sites were not positive about the effective police response, in the face of limited resources, that actually constitutes what positive meat there is to the story. Rather, a number of sites were cautiously, if implicitly, *positive about the robbery itself*. The bandits were glamorized for having made the LAPD "their bitch," for example, in one egregious example. There was even a poem—a poem, for God's sake—*praising the bandits*.

No, I'm not making this up. It's hard to understand how anybody can have so little social awareness that he aligns with the forces that try to destroy his own society, the society on which he depends for his own survival; but people do.

Maybe the authors of these websites imbibed a little too much Robin Hood when they grew up; the fictitious part where he robbed from the rich and gave to the poor, not the real part where he robbed everybody and kept it.

Most people don't know that there was a real Robin Hood, a.k.a. Robin Heud, earl of "Huntingtun." He apparently actually lived in the thirteenth century *(Manchester, 1992)*, and his gravestone (although he's not buried there) still exists in Yorkshire; but he was hardly the green-clad, slightly violent, merry social worker of legend. As William Manchester *(1992)* puts it, "everything we know about that period suggests that Robin was merely another wellborn cutthroat who hid in shrubbery by roadsides, waiting to rob helpless wayfarers" *(pg. 65)*.

No green suit. No social work. No Olivia de Haviland. Just another useless, narcissistic, self-important dirtbag stealing things he hadn't earned.

Why are people so ready to accept the Robin Hood myth, the selfish criminal, the person who is willing to rob and kill *them, personally,* for nothing but cash, as some kind of hero? Isn't that kind of stupid? What's so great about antisocial narcissism and violent theft, whether the bad guy and his men are merry about it or not? The academic literature does not yield a lot of helpful insights here, but the late novelist Michael Crichton *(2006)* offered a rather good one:

> *"(N)obody in this country wants to think of themselves as joiners or civilizers. Just the opposite—we're all rugged individualists. We're all rebels. We're antiestablishment. We stand out, we strike out, we do our own thing, go our own way. The herd of independent minds, somebody called it. Nobody wants to feel that they are not a rebel" (Pg. 154).*

Okay, it's a novel, and it's not scientific, but it's not bad. If everybody's a rebel, exactly what are they rebelling against? If everybody's in the counterculture, what's left of the culture? One frequently encounters, in academic and quasi-academic books, the word "civilization" written just like that, in quotes. An ironic reference; yeah, "civilization," nothing special. Nothing that required five thousand years of development to arrive at a point at which human greed and violence are under enough control that a decent lifestyle is possible. Civilization, phooey—if only we could get rid of that whole "civilization"

Epilogue

thing, or replace it with something else, somehow, then everything would be just dandy.

All I can say is that there are parts of the world in which civilization reigns, and other places where, effectively, it no longer exists, where the forces of legitimate law and legitimate order have broken down. In the latter places, one does not encounter a joyful utopia, where barefoot vegetarians wander about nurturing well-adjusted children, growing organic crops and communing with the happy animals in the serene beauty of their ashrams. One is vastly more likely, in such places, to encounter starvation, chronic illness, hideous parasitic infestations and very high levels of violence.

In such places, there are frequently no legitimate police forces. Instead, every so often, a gang of thugs drives by in an old pickup truck with a machine-gun mounted in the back. They claim to *be* the police, or the army, and they steal whatever is edible or usable in the given village, frequently raping and/or killing anybody who objects to these crimes. Then they burn down whatever passes for housing for the sheer ugly fun of it. Such murderous gangs often replace the police in places where civilization ceases to shed its influence; and as for the "laws," they are frequently proclaimed by some non-elected and possibly crazy Colonel (branch of service, unspecified) who promises to relieve everybody of the insidious influence of Western colonialism, in his wonderful new free country, as soon as his boys steal the last goat.

This may seem melodramatic, but the simple fact is that these events and conditions will be immediately recognized by anyone familiar with history, or by anyone who has traveled in the many places where civilization, with or without quotation marks, has broken down today. Where there are no legitimate cops, there is no valid law or order. Where there is no law or order, the luxuries vanish. These include such luxuries as the time and resources for efficient food production, public health, decent construction, and education. You have to have civilization in order to do these things. You even have to have civilization to put the word "civilization" in quotes at all, or to tell students all about the horrible flaws of your civilization, after you've had a nice lunch in a civilized restaurant.

Of course civilization has flaws; I challenge the reader to find a single human institution that doesn't. However, an ugly fact remains.

> *There seem to be only three real choices facing modern human societies:*
>
> 1. Maintain civilization and recognize that the police are the tip of the spear in that maintenance. Work to sustain the *legitimate* law and order that make a decent life possible.
>
> 2. Let civilization die, and try to survive in the sick, starving, thug-infested violence that remains.
>
> 3. Let civilization deteriorate, just to the point where the toughest strong man becomes your dictator for life. Then the tanks roll out. Into the streets. Readers familiar with history will recognize this as a very popular alternative in the military dictatorships that still infest this planet. Violent anarchy, such as that discussed above, is not the only alternative to civilization; brutal military dictatorships are frequently the result of breakdowns in legitimate police and government powers, and in the subsequent militarization of police and government functions.

If you are a thinking person, I would bet, at this point, that you'd prefer to go with Option 1 above. Civilization is far, far better, than the alternatives, and that's where the cops come in. Cops are the people who keep the civilized from being killed, raped, and robbed by Robin Hood or his North Hollywood colleagues. However, cops, like everybody else, cannot create a perfect world. In general, they just keep the needle of the good-to-evil meter pointed as far from evil as they can. You'd think people would realize this.

You'd think that, of course, if you hadn't read this book. We have discussed gestalt versus feature-intensive (G versus FI) processing. That horrible paragraph I inflicted on you a page or so back, the one with the violent thugs, stands as an example of FI processing, similar to the example of Vignette 5 in Chapter 6. When you read it, you are forced to take a good, long, hard, steamy look at each wretched concept, to create images of it in your mind, to wallow in the features of the given horrible idea until something in your brain, in virtually everybody's brain, begins to prefer a civilized lunch in a nice restaurant to an ugly bad death in a plague-infested war zone. All it takes is a little in-depth FI consideration.

But what is the alternative to such feature-intensive consideration? The answer is gestalt processing, the processing in which we do not

Epilogue

access the details or internal structure of an argument. As we have seen, this seems to be the type of cognition that most people use most of the time. Feature-intensive processing is time-consuming and effortful. It's easier not to do it. It's easier to say, in a gestalt, analysis-free way, something like, "I'm a rebel. I'm different. And" (tossing our hair in imitation of an old TV commercial), "I'm worth it."

Rebelling against what? Different from what? Worth what? Well, in gestalt processing, the question never comes up. You rebel against, you're different from, you're worth—well—"it." "It" remains unspecified.

And there's no question that Robin Heud, and the North Hollywood bandits, and all the other people that police officers have to come up against, are rebels; and oh, boy, are they different, and they absolutely believe that they're worth it. All of which means that the average person who benefits from civilization, the average countercultural rebel who goes his own way, usually in a cubicle, can feel a certain vicarious sympathy with the bad guys. The people who call the police in an emergency can, at all other times at least, share vicariously the rebellious, wind-in-your-hair hatred of Established Order, and of the police, which many real bad guys possess.

So what's the answer? It is, in fact, relatively simple. It lies in education and media that counter the standard depiction of the Evil Cop. This does not require McCarthyism, jingoism, blind obedience or groupthink; rather it requires rational, feature-intensive analysis. People do not need to be indoctrinated; but they do need to be educated. To maintain civilization in a given society, the citizens of that society must be educated, at least to the degree that they will engage in FI processing when they encounter complex social phenomena that require analysis, rather than slogans. People need sufficient education to dissect that word "it" when "it" comes up. They need to learn enough about the world to recognize evil when they see it, and to dissociate themselves from it. Enlightened self-interest can only occur when you know what your interests are. When you understand those interests, a reasonable FI analysis is likely to lead your to the concept that civilization is worth preserving, and that legitimate, law-abiding police forces are a major factor in preserving it.

So, as a civilization, with or without quotation marks, we know what to do. Police officers and commanders need detailed knowledge in order to make sense, FI sense, of the complex situations they encounter. If they have this knowledge, their necessarily gestalt responses in given tactical situations will also make sense.

In the same way, citizens need detailed, FI knowledge. We need to educate people to the point that they'll do the same thing, the rational thing, with their political lives and their social policies.

But how easy will this be to do?

Frankly, not very. Not very easy at all. At this point in our civilized history, we use our technology to create popular video games in which the players are supposed to kill the cops. We broadcast movies upon movies depicting corrupt or insanely violent cops, and damned few movies depicting anything else in the complex world of law enforcement. We've had wildly popular "reality" shows in which you win the prize for lying most convincingly to the police in contrived violent crime situations. These are not marginal media; people watch these shows, and play these games. They watch and play them a lot. People identify with the characters, especially with the ones who are seen as powerful or as rewarded for their actions. Because of this identification, and as suggested by the work of psychologist Albert Bandura (e.g., *1977*), people are very likely to imitate those actions. This is especially true of children, who are of course a huge and much preyed-upon market for violent media.

As a result, we have quite a lot of people today who have grown up wanting to be just like the people who commit violent crimes. It's a very good bet that some of these people want to be just like the North Hollywood bandits.

And a *lot* of these people have web sites.

So, the fact is that universal education in the intricacies of FI processing is going to take a while. People who like civilization, and who really understand who and what Robin Heud and the North Hollywood bandits had in common, have a lot of work in front of them. So do the police officers and commanders who form the tip of the spear, the people who maintain civilization without descent into anarchy, and without descent into military excess. As I hope that this book has demonstrated, a good understanding of the relevant aspects of cognitive science may be very useful to the officer or commander. Knowledge of processing under pressure, of the intricate dynamics of attention, memory, perception, thought: an understanding of how these arcane processes operate in the real world provides an edge. This knowledge can increase professional effectiveness, and enhance officer survivability. It may get you home.

To conclude, and in keeping with the consideration of media in this Epilogue, let us quote from a good book and an old TV series:

It's a brave new world. Be careful out there.

Appendix
THE DEVELOPMENTAL CONTEXT OF FORENSIC COGNITIVE SCIENCE

Teenagers, Tongue-studs, and the Nature of Development

In Chapter 3, we talked briefly about how children and older adults process information as eyewitnesses, and how the age of the given witness can bias eyewitness testimony and the memory processes on which it is based. But the developmental context of thinking and memory goes far beyond the eyewitness role. It can be of critical importance to anyone working in virtually any area of the criminal justice system.

At first glance, you might not think developmental issues to be of much importance in the criminal justice realm, beyond the obvious; children are smaller, weaker, and more helpless on average than adults, and the aging process robs us of some of our physical strength and endurance. But as to our beliefs about the mind: most people today, including legal professionals and potential jurors, seem to think similarly to the way many psychologists thought seventy or eighty years ago.

Specifically, even modern people tend to believe that *everybody thinks in pretty much the same way*, regardless of age. We generally believe that children are only different from adults (albeit shorter and more frequently covered with snot) because they haven't learned as much in the time they've been around, and that older adults are just more easily tired than young people, perhaps because they've been carrying Kleenex around for all those snot-encrusted children for far too long.

Unfortunately, these ideas are incredibly wrong.

Not that people don't keep learning as they age and develop. It's certainly true that learning goes on throughout the human lifespan; you'll hopefully know more about the world at the age of forty or fifty than you did at sixteen, and certainly more than you did when you were six. But is that really all there is to it? Or does *human development* itself rear its head, *changing the processes and products of cognition entirely as we move through the lifespan?*

Consider sixteen year olds. Many law enforcement readers of this book have spent appreciable time and effort, in tactical situations, in *avoiding* having pieces of metal driven into their bodies. Yet those same officers, who fully understand that a piece of metal in a sensitive place is a really bad idea, may come home to find that their sixteen-year old offspring has been to the mall, where he or she *actually paid another adolescent* at the Fun Times Piercing Parlor to drive a good-sized hunk of steel through the offspring's tongue, possibly with a ball-peen or light sledge hammer. The teenaged Offspring in question will display this metal object, which may appear large enough to anchor a small naval vessel, by sticking forth its tongue at you, the Parent, in a proud and defiant manner.

Now, some school health teacher has probably told the Offspring that tongue piercings are not a great idea, in that they apparently open the cardiovascular system to a greater prospect of infection, but damned if the Offspring cares. The Offspring defiantly presents you with a huge fresh silver gleaming-steel tongue stud, together with clots of blood and spit and mucus and other assorted quasi-liquid detritus. The Offspring may even display a certain pride in the oral ooze involved; and when you, the Parent, say something gently parental, like, "ARE YOU INSANE?!? WHAT THE HELL DID YOU DO THAT FOR?," the Offspring will proudly display the steel-perforated organ in question even further as it replies:

"TO INCRLEASHTH MY THEXSHUAL ATTRLACTIVENETHSH!"

Now, we must admit that adults are not exactly paragons of rationality themselves, at least not all the time. Adult cognition can certainly contribute to some amazingly disastrous humdingers as we navigate the course of adult living; but it generally takes an *adolescent* to have a sensitive bit of its mouth drilled in to accommodate a piece of sharpened armor that might have come off the *Graf Spee*.

And so we, as Sensitive Adults, are somewhat stuck with the critical developmental question: *What the hell do adolescents do things like that for?*

The neuroscientists, bless them, have an answer. The brain continues its maturation into young adulthood, especially in the critical area of the prefrontal cortex (see Chapter 1), an area of the brain extremely important for judgment and the weighing of alternatives. So, this crucial part of the brain is not fully developed in the adolescent; therefore, the given adolescent weighs the alternative health of its mouth against the potential sexual attraction of two or three ounces of tungsten carbide or whatever it is stuck through its tongue, and before you know it you have a magnetic teenager. So say the neuroscientists.

This is a nice simple explanation, which takes us neatly from the murky complexity of cognitive science into the relatively clean order of neuroscience. The problem is that it doesn't really work. It's certainly true that the brain develops in exactly the way described; but the real question is how *brain* development in adolescence contributes to *cognitive* and *behavioral* development. This includes the Great Tongue Stud Effect and similar phenomena, and the problem is that the final maturation of the prefrontal cortex may not play as much of a role as we think. No one doubts, of course, that the final elements of brain maturation, in late adolescence or young adulthood, are important; the final unmyelinated prefrontal fibers receive their protective fatty coats of insulation, which also has the effect of increasing their transmission power enormously. But the fact remains that the raw powers of cognition, depending on the context, have not been demonstrated to be all that different between adolescents and adults across all situations. For one thing, if you take adults and adolescents with similar training in science, and give them a physics problem, they generally solve it in the same way and in about the same amount of time. This demonstrates that even with the lag in prefrontal brain development that has been clearly shown by modern neuroscience research, we may need to look elsewhere for much of the cognitive and behavioral difference between adolescent and adult. There doesn't seem to be that much wrong, so to speak, with the adolescent's hardware; it's the software we need to worry about.

There's another problem with the simple, elegant, but unfortunately inadequate pre-frontal development explanation, as well. This is the fact that, in earlier times in history, *those that we now classify as adolescents frequently functioned perfectly well in adult roles.*

Such adolescents still had additional adult learning and experience to attain, of course; but the fact is that teenaged naval midshipmen held small deck commands on European warships as late as the nineteenth century. True, they were usually supervised by older officers or "advised" by older noncommissioned master seamen, but many of them operated effectively, commanding in the field, in the very adult world of naval warfare. The great European sailing battleships of the past centuries actually had *schoolrooms* where these "young gentlemen" completed their education; but the *young gentlemen*, the teenagers, were right there on the gundecks and in the tops with the snipers in every horrible blood-soaked battle, giving commands to adult seamen significantly older than they were, in the terrifying world of naval warfare in the Age of Sail to which no modern adult in his or her right mind would subject a modern teenager. And in their early twenties, with independent commands of sloops and gunboats in the British Royal Navy, many of these "adolescent" captains fought bravely, and with great gusto, against slavery on the 19th century African coasts, as potentates tried desperately to sell other Africans into slavery, and a bunch of young Englishmen, aged 20 or thereabouts, fought like hell to prevent it.

There's more. Cleopatra VII, Queen of Egypt, was a teenager when she began her military and political battles against the fully adult advisors of her adolescent brother, Ptolemy. Alexander the Great was in ultimately victorious command of troops in the field at the age of twenty.

Granted, subjective and cohort-specific historical perspectives may be important here—I, the author, personally come from a place and generation in which if you'd passed your eighteenth birthday, *you were absolutely considered an adult* in every respect except the legal consumption of hard liquor. But, in more modern times, I have heard news commentators refer to the truly adult perpetrators of atrocious crimes, perpetrators only a year or so younger than 20 years of age, as "precious children." Adolescence turns out to be at least as much of a social and cultural phenomenon as a neurobiological artifact, and a hell of a lot of psychology and anthropology supports that opinion, all around the world and deeply into history (e.g., *Mead, 1963*).

The upshot, for law enforcement readers, is that adolescents are perfectly capable of understanding ideas of right and wrong, justice, and crime- but they do have to be taught about these things, at an appropriate level of rigor and abstraction,.

But anyway, it turns out that even with an immature *brain*, there's nothing essentially wrong with the adolescent *mind*—so how do we explain the Incredible Tongue Stud effect, and a variety of other weird age-dependent phenomena as well?

To understand that, we have to take a moment to consider what the process of development actually *is*. We see a baby, a child, or an adolescent, and what we *think* we see is an immature creature *trying to grow up.* But that's only part of the story. A child might *want* to be an adult, because he or she would then have access to credit cards and perhaps military rocket launchers; but at the time, *as* a child, an adolescent, an adult, or an aged adult, each human being has to function *as the kind of creature it is at that time*. Each human, of whatever age, *has to meet the developmental challenges of its particular age*, with the cognitive skills and knowledge of that particular age. In other words, a child has to work as a child, a teenager as an adolescent within the boundaries of local norms, and so on. They're not just trying to grow up, or to move into old age successfully; they're trying to survive and prosper *as what they are at the moment.*

Meeting your needs with your resources, at a particular age, was called *equilibration* by the developmental psychologist Jean Piaget (.e.g, Langer, 1969). Although Piaget's theory has several specific flaws, notably its failure to extend well to all world cultures and to account for extreme variations in developing human behavior, it's generally at least descriptively accurate for most of the cultures most readers of this book will typically encounter. Nobody should be too dogmatic about any given theoretical perspective, including this one; I myself have published scientific papers demonstrating some of the limits of Piaget's theory (e.g., Sharps & Gollin, 1985; Gollin & Sharps, 1987). However, the fact is that we still teach it, and most of it is still generally viewed as generally correct, at least at a descriptive level.

And Piaget teaches us that children, and even adolescents, are not the same as adults at all.

The Young Child as Witness. And as Victim.

Very young children lack mature abstraction powers; they have trouble thinking about things other than as specific, concrete realities. They also think *egocentrically*, which is very weird.

Egocentrism, in this context, does not mean that young children are conceited. It means that the very young child sees the universe in a very specific manner, with reference to his or her own perception and that of everyone else. The very young child *sees itself and the world as one.*

This means that, prior to about the age of 6, generally, *children assume that if they can see something, everybody else can see it too.* The child and the world are the same thing, so his or her awareness is *global.* This is part of what Piaget means by *egocentrism*—if I'm a young child, and I can feel something or see it, I assume you can too, since my world view is literally my whole world.

Not everybody in relevant fields of psychology agrees with this. The Piagetian idea of egocentrism has been repeatedly attacked, and as a student, with Professor E.S. Gollin, I published research many years ago showing exceptions to this concept (e.g., *Gollin & Sharps, 1987*). However, even with some demonstrated exceptions, the overall concept of Piagetian egocentrism appears to be generally right. And that's a huge problem.

One of the most horrible cases of my own experience, as a young psychologist beginning research on forensic issues, involved the molestation, by their father and a gang of his "friends," of very young children. One of the children was two years old at the time of her molestation. The case did not come to light until she was four, but her testimony would have been important. If there had been any testimony.

It's a horrible topic, but consider the molestation of a very young child. Typically, the child has no idea what's going on, but it may be terribly painful, propelling the child to a very high state of arousal and hence more limited cognitive and perceptual processing (see Chapter 1). The molestation may occur in the dark, but even if it does not, the physical orientations of the molestation may prevent the child from having a reasonable physical view of what actually happened. All that the child victim of molestation may know is a dim sense of betrayal, great fear, and great physical pain, further limiting her awareness of the atrocities happening to her. *For which she has no cognitive framework.* All the child understands is that this is some kind of betrayal; and it hurts.

Now, when the molested two year old attained the age of four, she was grilled by police and social workers as to *what had happened to her when she was two.* Not surprisingly, she didn't remember a thing; Piaget referred to the first two years of life as the *sensorimotor period*, and although there is of course cognitive growth during this time, the child's resources *equilibrate* on the basic building of the body and brain; there is very little genuine thought, at least as adults know and understand it, during this period.

But anyway, the cops turned the kid over to a social worker, who used anatomically correct dolls to probe the child's nonexistent memories of the molestation events. All law enforcement and forensic psychologist readers are familiar with this situation, an expanded version of *this doll is you- this other doll is daddy- show me what daddy did to you.*

And of course, the kid had Piagetian egocentrism and the low abstraction powers of early childhood. The child's inner monologue, if there was one, would have been something like this: "So you're showing me a doll. How the hell can that doll be me? I'm sitting right here! The doll's over there, you idiot! The doll isn't me, I'm over here! And what do you mean, that other doll is Daddy? Daddy's not a damn doll, believe me, he's a painful horror in the dark- God knows why you're shoving that doll at me- leave me alone, dammit."

Of course, we're taking some liberties here with the general modalities of speech and thought typically available to preschool children; but the gist is probably accurate, and anyway the end result of this type of forensic evaluation, at this age, is that the poor child typically either bursts into tears or looks away in dissociative madness. Either is a reasonable, if forensically useless, response of the brain to the psychologically unacceptable, incomprehensible events of molestation.

This is why this specific child showed no therapist-discernable response to the anatomically correct dolls. Why would she? In the absence of adult abstraction powers, the idea that this-doll-is-Daddy-and-this-doll-is-me made no sense. Of course it didn't- *the child's developmentally-mediated mental powers were inadequate to the interpretive task imposed on them*; a task imposed by supposedly professional adults who didn't understand that *adults and young children are qualitatively different.* Young children, *as* young children, don't normally need abstractive mental powers, so they don't have them- their behavior and resources are concentrated on other aspects of living and developing.

The social worker in question reported that the child had not been molested, because the child had reported no abstract recreation of the sexual situation. There was a failure to report what happened by a child who had no idea of what had actually happened to her. Therefore, Daddy was innocent. And without additional detective work, which was actually conducted in this instance, that case would have gone South and sideways, as many do. Daddy and his friends would have been free to molest again.

The social worker tacitly assumed adult cognitive capabilities in a four-year old child. And as a result, that case was almost lost. Luckily, other evidence resulted in a conviction.

But this particular social worker may not have been up to speed on the cognitive or developmental characteristics of young children, or may simply have been one of the many people who, after years in medicine or mental health, just can't take one more horrible tragedy. Sometimes, in my experience and for what it's worth, some people may take an essentially unconscious way out, dissociating from the horrors they see in their professional capacities—nothing to see here, Daddy didn't really do these horrible things, because *nobody* would do that, they *couldn't,* I don't have to think about this anymore, let's think about something else. Something pleasant.

But serious professionals in the worlds of forensic psychology, mental health, and criminal justice simply can't afford that lovely dissociated treacherous way out. *You have to see reality for what it is,* even when it's incredibly unpleasant. And this is why it's so vitally important for everybody in the relevant fields to have a basic understanding of psychological development. It's very, very important.

And the very important fact is that very young children simply don't have the cognitive resources to create coherent eyewitness accounts. Without other evidence, their limited abstraction and egocentrism may sometimes render them worse than useless as witnesses. Of course, *that doesn't mean you shouldn't pay attention to what they say.* Frequently they may get something right, even if it's presented in childish terms. But don't treat them like adult witnesses. They aren't.

This, of course, can be a huge problem. Some of the most horrifying and emotionally devastating crimes are those perpetrated on children, and, as we've already seen (Sharps et al., 2013), when crimes are especially horrible, people tend to find the suspects guilty faster and they also tend not to notice holes in the evidence. Therefore, a jury may be strongly convinced by a child witness to something awful, especially an appealing child witness, when that witness is actually incapable of remembering the incident or of providing a coherent account. This is an important point, to say the least. Obviously no one wants the guilty child molester to go free; but we should also make sure that the innocent, who are accused of terrible crimes, actually do receive fair trials. Fair trials may require at least a basic understanding, on the part of the court, of the developmental principles which influence children's testimony.

Cognition in Early Childhood; Or, Why Young Children Are Basically Alien Beings

Cognitive Organization. Between the age of two and six, Piaget says that kids are in the *preoperational period*. They're still egocentric, as we've seen, and there are some other odd bits. If I ask you how a knife, fork, and spoon are alike, you'll probably tell me it's because they're all silverware. A child under six will tell me it's because they're *used* together. This is the difference between *syntagmatic* (under age 6) and *paradigmatic* reasoning (past age 6.) We as adults generally label things as what they *are*, in terms of what category they come from (silverware, furniture, vehicles, etc.). Kids under 6 generally label things with regard to their common *use* in the Western world (e.g., Sharps & Gollin, 1985). Now, this doesn't work in all world cultures; there are some societies in which the way people live their life does not contribute to this *syntagmatic/paradigmatic shift*. But in most of the cultures most of the readers of this book work in, this is how the mind works. There's a major shift, around age six, of the way children see things. Before that age, children tend to see things as how they're *used*. After that age, people tend to see things as what they *are*. Law enforcement readers may see how this could be important in the use of relatively atypical objects as weapons. Suppose a young child is cognitively fixed on the fact that knives are used with spoons and forks, as "kitchen things" (things used together at mealtimes), but does not fully understand the inclusion of knives, including kitchen knives, in the overall categories of "weapons" or "potential weapons." Children may organize their thinking in terms of how things might be *used*, rather than what those things actually *are*, with obvious negative consequences for the coherence of their eyewitness accounts. Again, readers in law enforcement or law can readily see how the relative categorical incoherence of a young child's accounts of a crime in these respects, especially when formalized and entered officially into the proceedings of a courtroom proceeding or criminal investigation, could derail the understanding of the relevant evidence very effectively.

Perspective Taking. Another rather weird factor we see in the preoperational period is a typical failure of *spatial perspective taking*. There's the usual academic disagreement about exactly how it works, and there are often experimental ways around it (e.g., Gollin & Sharps, 1987), but in general, children under the age of six are very hazy on whether or not you see things from a different angle or position than they do, or *whether you see things exactly as they do*, from whatever your position is in the given scene. Many authorities (but of course not all) would suggest that this is another aspect of *egocentrism*—the child egocentrically assumes that if he or she can see whatever it is, *so can you*; and if the child can't see it, *you can't either*. Anyone with investigative experience can see how this could play howling hell with eyewitness testimony. For example, a child witness might assert that there was no body in a given room, when there actually was one, simply because the child was not in a position to see it; therefore, in this hypothetical example, the child might state positively that the adult witness who *was* in line of sight with the victim's body couldn't possibly know that the body was there, either. The reader can easily construct mental pictures of how this could be important in terms of witness accounts of weapons, vehicles, important aspects of cover or concealment, or any of the other myriad objects and object positions for which accounts must be generated in any investigation (see previous chapters).

Granted, as mentioned above, spatial perspective taking does not always fail in preoperational children (see Gollin & Sharps, 1987)- that depends in part of the conditions of the observation, and in part on individual differences and the age of the child. However, it's another good reason for the responsible investigator to do everything possible to test and verify the young child's accounts of persons, relevant objects, and relative positions in any given crime scene.

Life and Death for the Preschool Child.
There's yet another very weird factor in children between aged 2 and 6, of great criminal justice importance: *animism*. This one can be a very big deal.

Suppose you break a glass in your kitchen, and I ask you if you broke it. Your answer: Yes. But suppose I ask you if you *hurt* it. Did it feel *pain*?

Either you will assume that I have a different linguistic background, and that I'm confusing the words for *pain* and *damage*, or you'll wonder what the hell is wrong with me.

As an adult, you can *break* a glass; but you can't *hurt* it in the English language sense of that word. You can't cause a glass to feel pain. It's an inanimate object.

But children under six don't really know this. For them, says Piaget, *everything is at least somewhat alive;* and everything can feel pain.

This concept, *animism*, is one that doesn't always work cross-culturally. In many places around the world, some inanimate objects are considered animate, even by adults; anthropologists and devleopmentalists have documented this in many world cultures. But in most of the cultures with which most readers of this book will interact, pretty much all the adults believe that a glass or a salt-shaker can't feel pain, but a person or a puppy can.

But this is not true for kids under about age six.

They may not think the glass hurts more than you would if *you* were broken, but they're pretty sure that it's in pain, and that the glass-breaking culprit is guilty of inflicting that pain. Detectives, prosecutors, and investigative psychologists take note: if your witness is a preschooler, you may be investigating the murder of a coffee cup.

I remember a clinical case in which a preschooler was repeatedly dragged by authoritarian parents to religious services that lasted an objective hour, but subjectively, to the preschooler, seemed to go on for years. He used to sneak a little plastic car into the service, in his pocket, presumably to fantasize about escaping in it from the service. Anyway, Mom found out about the car, and stomped on it, smashing it with her shoe in the service of the Lord.

The kid went into mourning.

I'm not kidding. He was wailing in agony. He was an only child, and only children often develop stronger than normal attachments to toys; but this kid had won the Preakness of mourning. He was sobbing and incoherent.

The parents came to the shrinks in the facility in which I was working at the time. Their compassionate parental questions and remarks: What the hell is wrong with our rotten kid? Why is he crying over a damn plastic toy? He's damn lucky to have any toys, since when we were kids, there were no toys and we had to play with dead rats and old rusty barbed wire, and we even had to catch the rats ourselves, which is what we used the barbed wire for, the rotten little bas- kid is damn lucky to have parents like us, and is there a military school we can send him to?

My account of the parental compassion here may have involved a little poetic license, but these parents were basically as advertised above; their child-rearing strategies were unhealthily authoritarian, to say the least.

But anyway, the explanation of the child's behavior is pretty straightforward, in terms of the *animism* of Piaget's *preoperational period*. That car, before Mom stomped on it, was *alive*. For the kid, Mom had not just broken a replaceable toy. Mom had *killed* his car. Its little Matchbox soul had gone off to Hot Wheels Heaven. For young children, the breaking of an inanimate object may be viewed as a death to be mourned.

Law enforcement readers: do you see how *alien* young children are, by our adult standards? They're equilibrating on completely different issues than those that even *matter* to adults- and we haven't even gotten back to adolescents and their tongue-studs yet.

And what does this concept of Piagetian animism mean to the young child witness to a dead body? This is not the sort of question that typically finds its way into the mainstream literature on child development; but for those involved in the criminal investigations which may surround the horrendous crimes that can happen to children, such issues are very central. The fact is that we desperately need a lot more research on what we might call *forensic cognitive developmental science* than has been conducted to date. Such research is desperately needed. It would help a lot.

Parenting; Or, God Help Us

Parents, by the way, come in a variety of different versions and flavors (see *Baumrind, 1971*). The ones who remember limping uphill to school, both ways, every day including weekends, in terrible heat through four feet of snow and heaps of frozen dead rats, like the Matchbox Car-Stomping Assassin Mommy of the case recounted above, are usually termed *authoritarian* parents. They're often characterized as "cold" but "demanding" in character. No kidding. And not surprisingly, their parenting outcomes, in terms of their offsprings' eventual conduct, are not usually of the best.

The other end of the parenting spectrum, however, comprises the *permissive* parents, who are characterized as "warm" but "undemanding." They're nice, so you might expect better outcomes, but frankly, no. The permissive parents don't seem to give rise to more successful outcomes than the authoritarian ones, and a moment's reflection will probably tell you why. If parents repeatedly bail their kids out of every academic and disciplinary conflict, if they give the kid whatever it wants depending on the volume of its tantrums, and they merely express Sadness and Remorse when the kid tries to barbecue its baby-sitter on a spit, you can see how they'd produce—well—Caligula. And apparently, they frequently do.

In view of the many types of lifestyles modern parents have adopted, several new parenting classifications have been added to Baumrind's original (1971) work, and, as always, not everybody agrees. The present volume has neither the space nor the scope to deal with these issues in depth; but the research literature still seems to coalesce on the *authoritative* (not *authoritarian*; sorry, they sound a lot alike) parenting style as the best. The successful *authoritative* parenting style is generally characterized as "warm" but "demanding." You don't murder your church-going child's little Hot Wheels buddy, but you do insist the kid continue with assigned chores until they're done. You do take the kid camping, but insist that he or she help collect the firewood and wash the frying pan, even the big heavy one. You do take the kid to Disneyland, but the kid's souvenirs have to come out of the kid's allowance, and if you let that stretch it should come out of a definite advance on said allowance, to be repaid in additional chores, or something similar. And so on. The kid learns responsibility and pleasure, simultaneously, and everybody's happy.

That's the official story, of course, and in general it seems to be pretty accurate; but there are parents who believe, quite sincerely, that they did everything right. In fact, as far as anybody can tell, they can prove they were the model authoritatives, warm but demanding; but they still gave rise to a terrifying offspring who might have been confused with the young Nero, and who, as a young adult, is now the Fuhrer of the "Destroy America and Beat the Kittens With Hammers Club" at the local university. For those parents, for what it's worth, I'm sorry. There are such things as individual differences, and the study of human development is not an exact science. Having served through a long career as a professional shrink, I can testify to many instances in which, as far as I can tell, the parents did everything right; but they still wound up with Lee Harvey Oswald crossed with a Gila monster as the result of their apparently ideal parenting strategies. Human

Appendix 299

development is so complex that we can't even begin to model it mathematically. If, as a parent, you did everything you could, *and you still wound up with a disaster*; well, the fact is that at least part of it *could* be your fault, *but it may not be your fault at all*. The sad fact is that, without a time machine, you'll never know. Get professional help if you need it, but pick up the pieces and get on with your life. Things are as they are, and the past cannot be changed. Move forward, in your own best interest, and look back as little as possible. It doesn't help.

The Elementary School Years; Or, Why it Is Not Possible to Assemble a Working Model of a Volcanic Magma Chamber at the Last Minute from Items You Picked up at 11:58pm at the Quik-e-mart Because Your Kid Forgot the School Assignment for the Last Eight Weeks and It's Due Tomorrow. Let's move on, from the preschoolers and first graders of the preoperational period to the "school-aged" children between age 6 and adolescence. These children, for Piaget, are in the *concrete operational* stage of development; moving toward adulthood, but still *equilibrating* for their age group.

An important point for law enforcement readers: at this age, child witnesses may give you more false positives on a lineup than adults would. Nobody seems to know why; it's an important topic for future research.

As any parent can testify, children of this age generally have great difficulty with scheduling, as this involves abstract concepts moving into the future; concrete operational children still have a lot to learn in terms of the processing of abstractions. Hence, at least in part, your child's failure to remember school assignments, models of magma chambers or whatever, until midnight before the due date. Children of this age still do not deal well with abstract concepts of time or space.

But children in this age group also have a powerful imagination, in ways they partially share with pre-operational children, but at a somewhat more sophisticated level. The relevant processes have not really been worked out very well. Except by Bill Watterson, the cartoonist author of the old comic strip *Calvin and Hobbes*.

I wish Watterson had kept drawing Calvin and Hobbes, partly because it was one of my favorites, and partly because it beautifully illuminated and illustrated the cognitive world of the young child, vacillating between preoperational and concrete operational cognition. In the comic strip, Calvin was supposed to be six years of age, but his behavior was often more typical of a very advanced and somewhat older child, somewhere in elementary school. Granted, Watterson used a mildly anachronistic view of childhood cognition for very effective comic effect. In Watterson's hands, again for comic effect, Calvin's cognitive world was frequently too advanced for his age at a conceptual level, and Calvin used a vocabulary far beyond that of typical childhood; but for those readers who remember the comic strip, or who can get hold of it in book form today, you'll recall the *constantly shifting viewpoints of Calvin's childhood.*

These are the crucial points here. Hobbes, Calvin's toy tiger, was at one moment a stuffed toy animal, at the next a wise advisor or tactical ally, and at the next a potential predator if Calvin got sick. Calvin's classmate Susie was at one moment an academic ally, at the next a hated adversary, at the next a love object, and at the next a space alien. There was no cognitive consistency in Calvin's childhood world, and none was needed; in fact, he was somewhat irritated when adults attempted to impose cognitive consistency on his equilibrative childhood imagination. Watterson beautifully captured the constantly shifting frameworks of childhood; he created a kaleidoscopic vision of childhood which was frequently accurate in terms of the always-malleable frames of reference, Calvin's advanced vocabulary and conceptual life aside.

But, for those law enforcement readers who remember the comic strip, can you imagine Calvin as an eyewitness? Think about the constantly changing frames of reference of the preschool child, or even the young school-aged child- and if you're a criminal investigator, you'd better.

I recall a case reported by another investigative psychologist. It dealt with a murder by decapitation, in a trailer. Two school-aged boys reported a suspect dropping the bloody head of the deceased into a bucket, and the suspect's taking the head, in its bucket, to a local creek for dumping. The boys' account was sufficiently compelling that divers from the swift-water recovery divisions of local law enforcement agencies were apparently deployed to scour and "drag" the creek bottom to find the head of the victim.

The problem was that the physical circumstances of the murder would have prevented the boys from even *seeing* the crime; the arrangement of the windows of the trailer, with reference to the internal walls, demonstrated that they could not possibly have observed the murder or the body. As to the dumping of the head into a bucket, and subsequently into the creek: these elements of the "crime" devolved from an entirely different source. The trailer-court superintendent had been painting a shed, and a can of red paint had fallen off his stepladder, soaking his painter's coveralls. He had stripped off the paint-soaked clothes where he stood, dropped them into a

Appendix

bucket and carried them down to the creak for preliminary cleaning. He was not the killer; he was just a working man dealing with a paint accident. But the child witnesses in question saw his reddened overalls as a bloody head in a bucket.

Kids get things wrong. A lot. Their brains are focused on their development, which involves imaginatively taking on many different identities, and their reports of reality are frequently incorrect. This does not mean that they're always wrong. It does mean that we need to be especially careful in evaluating their evidence, including and especially eyewitness evidence. Their imagination is still a part of their perception of the external world, even the external world of the eyewitness.

These are major cognitive factors important in the forensic realm in childhood. There are of course many other aspects of childhood cognition of direct importance here, especially in the interaction with the cognitive characteristics of childhood, as these develop, with children's affective and social lives, including their interactions with adults. Any reader who works with children is encouraged to obtain as thorough a grounding as possible in developmental psychology, at least those aspects of development which intersect with the forensic realm. As children metamorphose into adolescents, they seem increasingly adult; *but they are not.*

Okay. That's childhood, at least in summary, and for our purposes. What about adolescents? And their tongue-studs?

Adolescents as Witnesses; and as Gang Members. Oh, and as "Child" Soldiers

In our brief consideration of adolescents and their tongue-studs above, we saw that it is certainly true that the prefrontal cortex of the teenager is in flux, continuing to grow and to myelinate into young adulthood. However, both historical and experimental evidence indicate that there's nothing really wrong with young people's intelligence. So, as many an aggrieved parent of an adolescent will agree, we are faced with a fundamental question concerning the cognition of adolescents:

WHAT THE HELL IS WRONG WITH THEM?

Granted you're more likely to hear this from wailing parents than from academic authorities, but anyone might ponder why it is that adolescents comprise the age group most likely to play "chicken" with combine harvesters on the bank of an irrigation canal; or to see how many times they can spin a car on a lake covered with thin ice ("less than once" tends to be the answer to that one); or to see how many cherry bombs can fit into the toilet and then light the fuse. These activities tend to be the unique province of the adolescent, and some of the less amusing manifestations of teenage hijinks can bring the relevant adolescents fairly firmly to the attention of law enforcement. Why?

Piaget proposed a fairly reasonable explanation of adolescent behavior, rooted in his concept of *adolescent egocentrism;* like all things Piagetian this concept has come under considerable academic attack, literally for decades, but the concept at least makes sense. It's not the same thing as the egocentrism of early childhood, not at all, in mechanism or consequences. The basic idea of *adolescent* egocentrism is that the adolescent may have fully developed cognitive powers ("formal operations" is the term for the basic operations of both adolescent and adult cognition in most formulations), but the problem is that *the adolescent lacks adult experience.* In the absence of that experience, the adolescent tends to see his or her characteristics and reactions to life as *central and unique;* everyday events are imbued with special meaning for adolescents, and questions that are relatively simple for the adult become terrifyingly significant as the child enters the teens.

For example, *kissing*—where do the noses go? Adults don't worry about this—things just seem to work out somehow—but this can be a hugely significant question for seventh-graders, along with the problem of braces. That story about the two kids whose braces locked together while they were kissing, and the custodian had to separate them with the Jaws of Life or something—it's part of the mythology of every middle school in America, and it obviously never happened, but it gives some idea of the hyperdramatic approach to life that adolescent egocentrism tends to foster. So does the typical adolescent attitude toward pimples. When an adult notices a Facial Zit, he or she usually just squeezes it, wipes the detritus off the mirror, and gets on with life; but do you remember the terror of a Facial Pimple on the day before the Big Dance, or the Big Game, or the Big Whatever, trying to cover it with a bandaid, and then a different-colored bandaid, and then some gel pen or Liquid Paper (all of which must have been tried at some point by some desperate zit-besmirched adolescent)? Adolescents *will write poetry to their acne* (Oh, such a great Zit have I, Alas...) without having a clue that none of the other adolescents will even notice. They're all too worried about their own zits.

This, for Piaget, is the power of *adolescent egocentrism,* power to alter the adolescent view of the world in very fundamental ways; but, also for Piaget, this adolescent egocentrism has an additional and very dangerous downside—the phenomenon of *adolescent invulnerability*.

If, as an adolescent, I am central and unique, then in a way I am the hero of my own story, with thoughts and feelings and ideas that (as far as I know) no one else has ever had, at least not with this level of intensity. Yes, in a way I am a hero- and, in general, heroes don't get written out of the script. In other words, my *adolescent egocentrism* seems to confer a kind of quasi-invulnerability upon me. Maybe bad things just won't happen to me—and if they do, my lack of adult experience may shield me from understanding just how bad an accident with a combine harvester, or explosives in the toilet, or guns or knives or the other arcana of violence can actually be. *Adolescent invulnerability* inclines me to a relatively Gestalt view of personal immortality, of immunity from harm; and this, all by itself, may predispose me to danger.

Again, many modern developmental psychologists regard this viewpoint as at best oversimplified, but the fact is that you can see this phenomenon operating in the field on a daily basis. If you approach a middle-aged man and tell him that you have an amazing drug that only tough guys can handle, or that you want him to join your street gang, he'll typically tell you to scram or he'll report you to your probation officer; and when you tell him you don't have a probation officer, he'll ask you if you want one.

But the same approach to an *adolescent* male can turn him into a crack-smoking member of the Horribly Dangerous Evil Hamster Gang or whatever, just by appealing to his teenaged machismo and his sense of invulnerability. Teenaged girls have also often been known to make very bad decisions, some life-threatening or at least life-altering, under social pressure that wouldn't phase them at all as adult women; and "girl gangs" are a relatively new phenomenon that merits serious study.

The theoretical nuances of these concepts may be justifiably criticized. Some of them can be refined, or even replaced conceptually, under the remorseless academic glare of the more precise members of the developmental fraternity; but, in the field, you'll see these phenomena operating on a daily basis in the worlds of drugs and gangs. This is why the criminals involved in illicit drug sales and gang recruitment target young adolescents, and even children in the upper elementary grades- the relevant approaches work on these age groups when they wouldn't work on anybody else.

My own field experience indicates that Piaget was on the right track with these concepts, at least descriptively if not at the most refined processual levels. Years ago in Southeast Asia, I interviewed a number of teenaged veterans of infantry combat, in the constant brush wars and border conflicts that have often plagued that part of the world, but which are virtually never covered by Western media.

These adolescents weren't supposed to be in the army at that age, let alone two or three years younger when they'd signed up, but their families received a food bonus if they joined the military, so they lied about their ages.

These children had become adolescents in vicious combat, and *not one of them showed the slightest sign of adolescent invulnerability.* They'd seen other kids, their own age, blown down by rifle fire, or cut in half by Claymore mines. They knew damn well they could be killed in a heartbeat and they were very keen on avoiding it; and as for adolescent *egocentrism,* they also knew their best chance of survival *was as part of a team,* of a cohesive rifle squad in which the individual had to suborn his teen angst to the problems of combat survival. Their prefrontal cortices were presumably the same, in terms of developmental myelination, as those of any ninth- or tenth-graders who actually had the privilege of going to school rather than to the front lines; but there wasn't a shred of the adolescent egocentrism or invulnerability we see rather consistently in more conventional Western settings. Piaget's ideas may have been oversimplified in parts; but based both on experimental developmental psychology and field experience, I would not dismiss his ideas out of hand. You see Piagetian dynamics operating too frequently, and too powerfully, in the admittedly grim real-world realm of forensic cognitive science and actual law enforcement.

Adolescents and the Technology of Death. And speaking of grim real-world things, modern law enforcement professionals and forensic mental health people have yet another problem in dealing with adolescents that previous generations could only rejoice in being without- and it has to do with the interaction of human development with technology.

Some of my readers have had the dubious pleasure of hefting a Garand M-1 rifle, or a .45 Thompson submachine gun, or, God help us, a BAR, the Browning Automatic Rifle, which feels like a ton of steel and the heaviest wood found in nature, and having it slam back against your shoulder with a force that would dent an elephant.

Ok, these weapons aren't really that bad. In fact, a fair-sized adult can heft, fire, and otherwise handle any of these weapons with a minimum of practice and training. This is also true of the old Model of

Appendix

1911 .45 ACP pistol, the standard sidearm of the American military for most of the last century.

But to a child or adolescent, handling any of these mighty weapons would be like strangling an elephant. So, the "child soldier" of the past tended to be a *servant* of the actual combat personnel, as many girls and young women in the "service" of various movements around the world still are.

But technology has intervened. The modern 9mm sidearm that replaced the old .45, and the 5.56 mm infantry rifles that have replaced the Garand and the Thompson, are made out of very light, space-age materials, and to anyone used to an older generation of weaponry, they have practically no kick at all.

They can, therefore, be used by children and adolescents, who are apparently using them, in actual combat roles in many places around the world.

Nobody knows what active armed combat experience will do to the development of a child, or a teenager. Sociologists may suggest parallels with growing up in a gang. (And children do grow up in gangs. I worked on a homicide case in urban California in which the suspects were members of a *five-generation* gang family. Nobody in the extended family had apparently ever had a job outside of criminal gang activity, and children were literally born into the gang.)

But the gang parallel, here, is almost certainly useless unless the linguistics involved are taken into consideration. Gangs do not behave like armies. The journalist and military historian Gwyn Dyer said it best *(1985, pg. 116)*: "If they (gangs) behaved the way armies do, you'd need trucks to clean the bodies off the streets every morning." Although gang members frequently view themselves as "warriors," their criminal operations are typically very different from the world of actual battle; in the examination of many crime scenes, both direct and vicarious, I have yet to encounter one where you had to figure out which pieces of which bodies went together, the grim duty of Graves Registration people and their modern equivalents in the aftermath of every genuine battle.

So there are differences in perspective; the gang member views the word "warrior" in very different ways than does the combat veteran, and the words "child," or "teenager," may be seen very differently by a suburban American teacher or school counselor who must now deal with a refugee "child" who has killed people in battle, and who just brained the kid who cut in front of him at Milk Time. The modern world, thanks in part to the light, modern weapons which have made the true "child soldier" possible, has caught up with our developmental theorizing, requiring research advances at a rate and of a magnitude which were previously unheard of. New research on what are relatively grim developmental realities is desperately needed, by law enforcement and by those in the mental health communities who must deal with completely unprecedented developmental, clinical, and educational problems.

It would be a very good idea to conduct this research in time. Now, in fact.

Right now.

Aging and the Criminal Justice System

Human development progresses through childhood and adolescence, and into adulthood—but it doesn't stop there. As we saw earlier, dealing with older adults as witnesses, the aged population also presents special challenges to law enforcement, to forensic psychology and the criminal justice system.

Who are "the aged?" Nobody really has a good definition, and older terms like "the elderly" are now under attack in various quarters as being potentially discriminatory. The classic age of retirement is 65, and that might give us a starting point; but current economic realities have rendered retirement at 65 increasingly unlikely for many people, and anyway, it's completely arbitrary—apparently, when Otto von Bismarck "unified" Germany, many of his political enemies were over that age, so he introduced 65 as the age of retirement and got rid of the lot at one stroke.

Nevertheless, there is certainly some "agism," unwarranted negative stereotyping of the aged, out there. When I've asked freshman college students the proportion of those over 65 who become "senile," the usual answer is 50-70%. Then they tell me stories about Grandpa losing his car keys.

The actual figure is around 8%.

Eight percent or so is not great news, and it gets worse the older you get. If everybody in the world lived for several centuries or so, everybody would probably die of Alzheimer's disease.

But they don't and in a normal lifespan you've got about a nine out of ten chance of aging in the absence of the truly terrible consequences of the senile dementias.

The aged, however you want to define them, may come into contact with the criminal justice system. Sometimes as perpetrators, and when they do, essentially, nobody knows what to do with them. Old people are more prone to disease, especially under crowded conditions such as those typical of jails and prisons. They're more physically fragile, so

God help them in the relatively violent world of genpop (the general population) in any given prison. Additionally, when injured, older adults heal more slowly if at all; I personally will never forget the continued agonized screams of an elderly patient, with a simple fracture which became gangrenous, as the surgeons cut off more and more of her leg over time and the painkillers gradually lost their effectiveness.

We need far more *forensic developmental research* on the older population, and it is hoped that the current cohort of professional researchers and students will direct more focus to these issues.

But what do we know *now* that can help us with the aged, if not as potential perpetrators, as witnesses and victims? We've already seen that older adults face disadvantages as eyewitnesses or as witness/victims. Is there anything we can do at least to reduce these problems, if not to eliminate them?

To make sense of the forensic psychology of the aged, we must first ask *why older adults exist in the first place.* This is not a facetious question; in most large mammals, death occurs within a year or so after loss of reproductive competence. Humans live about twice as long as they are reproductively competent. Why are humans so different?

Characteristics of the Aging Process. Older adults have some difficulty in *retrieving* information from long term memory, but they are especially bad at *encoding* new information (e.g., Sharps & Martin, 1988). This is why, for example, a Viet Nam veteran can remember practically every detail of everything that happened in Quang Tri province in 1968, but damned if he knows what happened last Tuesday. Quang Tri was encoded back *when he had an eighteen-year-old brain,* encoding away with the exuberance of youth; Tuesday was encoded with a brain over seventy years old.

Now, the fact that the elderly have more trouble with encoding than retrieval is a problem, because when they are witnesses, or victim/witnesses, there's not much you can do to enhance their encoding processes, at the scene of the crime; that bird, so to speak, has flown.

However, what can you do to assist their recall of the given crime situation? How can you aid their retrieval?

As we age, we lose some brain cells, and that's a problem. With a few exceptions in specific parts of the brain (the jury is still out), adult brain cells can't reproduce themselves. So, when the cells of specific circuits die, at least theoretically, the messages they might have carried may have to travel around inside the brain in more circuitous routes. This results in the single most important factor in cognitive aging, a general *reduction in cognitive speed* (see Sharps, 2003 for summary and references). The speed loss is not huge, but it's there, and it means that older adults have more trouble not just with encoding and retrieving, especially under stressful circumstances, but also more trouble dealing with highly effortful mental tasks requiring sustained concentration, and more trouble dividing their attention in complex situations. These factors are all true of the normal aging process, not just aging in the presence of something like Alzheimer's disease.

What about older adult *intelligence*? Well, it changes too. Performance intelligence, often involving mechanical and spatial tasks which must be done quickly (there's the speed loss again) tends to diminish. Verbal intelligence, however, tends to increase with age. "Fluid" intelligence, which we use in dealing with new and unfamiliar situations, also tends to diminish; but "crystallized" intelligence, dealing with familiar problems and issues, tends at least to remain stable or even to increase in some areas with age.

Note that, not surprisingly, there is some disagreement in the field about these conclusions, and even with the ways intelligence is theoretically divided up; but, if you look at the entire picture of cognitive aging from this perspective, a reasonable pattern emerges, and it tells us a little bit about why older adults typically survive far beyond their reproductive years, unlike other large mammals, and what you can do to help them as witnesses.

Most large mammals are specialists, but humans are not; we live in practically every habitat on Earth, exploiting every food resource from deep-sea fish to edible alpine plants and everything in between. We therefore have to rely on *knowledge* more than does any other known creature.

So what's the problem? We have books, magazines, we used to have newspapers, and we still have an incredible source of dubious information in the Internet. *But we didn't always.* Before humans had developed ways of recording information outside our own bodies, *we had to rely on our own brains for our information.* Whose brain was likely to have the most useful data in any given emergency? The person *who had lived through that particular emergency before*, perhaps more than once; in other words, the tribal elder.

Suddenly the pattern of cognitive aging makes sense; we don't need Grandma or Grandpa to build a jet engine (performance intelligence), we need them to be verbally coherent in recounting their *knowledge of past emergencies*. We don't need them to invent new technology (fluid intelligence); we need them to tell us how to deal with the many things that happened in the *past* (crystallized intelligence) and which may be happening again now, dammit. We don't need them to learn all the new stuff; we'll handle that. We don't even want the aged dividing their attention in complex mentally-effortful situations, like war or dangerous hunting; back in the day, the elderly were relatively rare, and their knowledge correspondingly valuable, and the last thing we wanted was the tribal repository of wisdom out there getting run over by a mammoth. We wanted them where they were most useful; *dispensing a usable understanding of the past*. Granted this is no longer, in general, the cultural function of the aged; but we are creatures of our past as well as our present, and the relevant cognitive factors are still very much in evidence.

Is this an accurate view of the history of cognitive aging? Again, many in the field disagree, but the overall picture certainly makes sense in terms of the actual history of the human race. This is especially true in view of the fact that in the old American West, one of the most recent repositories of traditional cultures, most of the war chiefs were young men, with all that fluid and performance intelligence, and most of the peace chiefs, the speech-makers with their verbal and crystallized understanding, tended to be relatively old by local standards.

But shouldn't older adults be better at retrieval, then? Well, yes; but note that their *retrieval* deficits aren't as bad as their *encoding* systems can become, and that gives the investigator an edge. You can help the older witness or victim to remember more effectively, but only if you understand these characteristics of the aging process.

When interviewing older adults, don't interrupt them. You'll interfere with the flow of their attention. Don't ask questions quickly; accommodate the cognitive slowing of the aging process, allowing the narrative to flow from the older adult at his or her own rate (this, by the way, is how traditional peoples generally elicited knowledge from older adults; slowly, conversationally, with all the time in the world). In the modern world, we don't think that way; we want our information *immediately*, and if we don't get it, we tend to interrupt with what we believe are clarifying questions, and hurry the witness along; but if you want to confuse an older witness or victim, reducing the accuracy and the level of detail that aging memory can provide, that's exactly how you would do it.

When dealing with older adults, *go slowly*.

You can assist older adults' retrieval with *accurate visual aids*, pictures and models of important aspects of the given criminal situation (obviously only to the degree that this will not bias witness accounts); ancient peoples used pictures, varying from the "winter counts" of the old American West to complex pictorial allegories in the European Middle

Ages (Carruthers & Ziolkowski, 2002). You must be careful not to bias memory incorrectly with such visual aids, of course; but used correctly, they can help to augment aging retrieval processes enormously.

In my laboratory, we've been able to augment older adults' memory of experimental situations to the point they were indistinguishable from teenagers, through the use of speed manipulations (go slow) and appropriate visual aids (see Sharps, 2003 for summary). Research on how to apply these principles to different and specific investigative situations is desperately needed; but at least we now have the principles on which those research applications can be based, to the benefit of the criminal justice system at large and to rapidly-expanding elderly population which must interact with that system.

IN SUMMARY

Young children, older children, adolescents, and adults of all ages are all human beings, with all the rights and privileges pertaining thereto; but we don't let preschool children drive roadgraders. Legally, there are some distinctions among age groups, as every investigator knows; but we tend to ignore the psychological distinctions, which may be at least of equal importance for the success of a criminal investigation. Once again, more research in these specific areas, as they pertain not just to criminal justice but to specific investigative situations, is desperately needed; but, simply stated, the investigator who is aware of the developmental factors discussed here will be more successful than the one who is not. It is to be hoped that an increased awareness of these critical aspects of forensic psychology will be of direct benefit to the criminal justice system and to the diverse populations it serves.

And once again, it's a Brave New World.

Be careful out there.

Bibliography/References

ABSCAM (1983). *ABSCAM Ethics: Moral Issues and Deception in Law Enforcement.* Cambridge, Mass.: Ballinger.

Ahlberg, S.W., & Sharps, M.J. (2002). Bartlett revisited: Reconfiguration of long-term memory in young and older adults. *Journal of Genetic Psychology, 163,* 211-218.

Anderson, J., with Cassidy, M. (1999). *The Newhall Incident: America's Worst Uniformed Cop Disaster.* Fresno, CA: Quill River Books.

Asch, S.E. (1956). Studies of independence and conformity I: A minority of one against a unanimous majority. *Psychological Monographs, 70* (9, Whole No. 416).

Associated Press (2007, February 13). Police: Man pointed cordless drill at officer. Retrieved February 15, 2007, from http://www.kirotv.com/news/11004849/detail.html.

Astor, G. (1992). *A blood-dimmed tide.* New York: Dell.

Atkinson, R. (2002). *An army at dawn.* New York: Holt.

Baddeley, A. (1990). *Human memory.* Boston, MA: Allyn & Bacon.

Bailey, K. (1987). *Human paleopsychology: Applications to aggression and pathological processes.* Hillsdale, NJ: Erlbaum.

Band, S. & Sheehan, D. (1999). Managing Undercover Stress: The Supervisor's Role. *FBI Law Enforcement Bulletin, 68*(2), 1-6. http://leb.fbi.gov/1999-pdfs/leb-february-1999.

Bandura, A. (1977). *Social learning theory.* Upper Saddle River, NJ: Prentice-Hall.

Banich, M.T., & Compton, R.J. (2018). *Cognitive neuroscience* (4th ed.). Cengage.

Bartlett, F.C. (1932). *Remembering: A study in experimental and social psychology.* Cambridge, UK: Cambridge University Press.

Bartlett, J.C., & Memon, A. (2007). Eyewitness memory in young and older adults. In Lindsay, R.C.L., Ross, D.F., Read, J.D., & Toglia, M.P. (Eds., 2007). *The handbook of eyewitness psychology* (Vol 2., pp. 309-338). Mahwah, NJ: Erlbaum.

Baumrind, D. (1971). Current patterns of parental authority. *Developmental Psychology,* 4(1, Pt.2), 1–103.

Bazerman, M.H. (1998). *Judgment in managerial decision making* (4th ed.). New York: Wiley.

Bergman, E.T., & Roediger, H.L. (1999). Can Bartlett's repeated reproduction experiments be replicated? *Memory and Cognition, 27,* 937-947.

Bergreen, L. (2007). *Marco Polo: From Venice to Xanadu.* New York: Alfred A. Knopf.

Bisby, J.A., Burgess, N. & Brewin, C.R. (2020). Reduced memory coherence for negative events and its relationship to posttraumatic stress disorder. *Current Directions in Psychological Science, 29,* 267-272.

Blades, H.B. (2005). The Washington, D.C., sniper case: A case study in how eyewitness identification of vehicles can go wrong. *Forensic Examiner, 14,* 26.

Blanchard-Fields, F. (1986). Reasoning in adolescence and adults on social dilemmas varying in emotional saliency: An adult developmental perspective. *Psychology and Aging, 1,* 325-333.

Bowden, M. (2000). *Blackhawk down.* New York: Penguin.

Bransford, J.D., & Johnson, M.K. (1972). Contextual prerequisites for understanding: Some investigations of comprehension and recall. *Journal of Verbal Learning and Verbal Behavior, 11*, 717-726.

Bransford, J.D., & Johnson, M.K. (1973). Considerations of some problems of comprehension. In W.G. Chase (Ed.), *Visual information processing*. Orlando, FL: Academic Press.

Brewin, C.R., Andrews, B., & Mickes, L. (2020). Regaining consensus on the reliability of memory. *Current Directions in Psychological Science, 29*, 121-125.

Brown, Dee. (1962). *The Fetterman massacre*. Lincoln: University of Nebraska Press.

Brues, A. (1977). *People and races*. New York: Mamillan.

Bugliosi, V. (2007). *Reclaiming history: The assassination of President John F. Kennedy*. New York: Norton.

Burke, A., Heuer, F., & Reisberg, D. (1992). Remembering emotional events. *Memory & Cognition, 20*, 277-290.

Camerer, C.F. (1995). Individual decision making. In J.H. Kagel & A.E. Roth (Eds.), *The handbook of experimental economics* (pp. 587-703). Princeton: Princeton University Press.

Carbon, C., & Albrecht, S. (2012). Bartlett's schema theory: The unreplicated "portrait d'homme" series from 1932. *Quarterly Journal of Experimental Psychology, 65*, 2258-2270.

Carruthers, M., & Ziolkowski, J.M. (2002). *The medieval craft of memory*. Philadelphia: University of Pennsylvania Press.

Cesario, J., Johnson, D.J., & Eisthen, H.L. (2020). Your brain is not an onion with a tiny reptile inside. *Current Directions in Psychological Science, 29*, 255-260.

Cialdini, R.B. (1988). *Influence: Science and practice* (2nd ed.). Glenview, IL: Scott, Foresman

Clifford, B.R., & Richards, V.J. (1977). Comparison of recall by policemen and civilians under conditions of long and short durations of exposure. *Perceptual and Motor Skills, 45*, 503-512.

Connell, E.S. (1985). *Son of the morning star*. New York: Promontory.

Conrad, J. (1899, reprinted 2003). *Heart of darkness*. New York: Barnes & Noble.

Correll, J.T. Daylight precision bombing. (2008). *Air Force Magazine: Journal of the Air Force Association, 91*, 60-65.

Cowen, R. (1999). Math error equals loss of Mars orbiter. *Science News, 156*, 229.

Craik, F.I.M., & Lockhart, R.S. (1972). Levels of processing: A framework for memory research. *Journal of Verbal Learning and Verbal Behavior, 11*, 671-684.

Crichton, M. (2006). *Next*. New York: Harper-Collins.

Custer, C.G. (1995, reprinted). *My life on the plains*. New York: Promontory Press,

Cutler, B.L., Penrod, S.D., & Martens, T.K. (1987). The reliability of eyewitness identifications: The role of system and estimator variables. *Law and Human Behavior, 11*, 23-258.

Department of Justice (1999). *Eyewitness evidence: A guide for law enforcement*. Washington, D.C.: National Institute of Justice.

Donovan, J. (2008). *A terrible glory: Custer and the little bighorn*. New York: Little, Brown & Co.

Dorner, D. (1996). *The logic of failure: Why things go wrong and what we can do to make them right*. New York: Metropolitan Books

Bibliography/References

Duran, P.L. (2008). *Duran advanced role-play training system.* New York: Looseleaf Law Publications.

Dyer, G. (1985). *War.* New York: Crown.

Elliot, M.A. (2007). *Custerology: The enduring legacy of the Indian wars and George Armstrong Custer.* Chicago: Chicago University Press.

Farago, L. (1963). *Patton: Ordeal and triumph.* New York: Dell.

Farkas, G. M., & US Dept of, J. (1986). Stress in Undercover Policing (From Psychological Services for Law Enforcement, P 433-440, 1986, J Reese & H A Goldstein, eds. - See NCJ-104098). *Stress In Undercover Policing (From Psychological Services For Law Enforcement, P 433-440, 1986, J Reese & H A Goldstein, Eds. - See NCJ-104098).*

Fenici, R., & Brisinda, D. (2004, October). Cardiac and psycho-physiological reaction during police action and combat shooting. Society for Police and Criminal Psychology, Rome, Italy.

Fenici, R., Ruggieri, M.P., Brisinda, D., & Fenici, P. (1999). Cardiovascular adaptation during action pistol shooting. *Journal of Sports Medicine and Physical Fitness, 39*, 259-256.

Festinger, L. (1957). *A theory of cognitive dissonance.* Evanston, Il: Row, Peterson.

Fisher, R. P., & Schreiber, N. (2007). Interview protocols for improving eyewitness memory. In Toglia, M. P., Read, J. D., Ross, D. R., & Lindsay, R. C. L. (Eds.), *The Handbook of Eyewitness Psychology* (Vol 1., pp. 53-80) Mahwah, NJ: Erlbaum.

Force Science News (2009, February 13). I. New study: When civilians would shoot … and when they think you should. *Force Science Research Center, Transmission #117,* www.ForceScienceNews.com

Ford, D. (2007). *Flying tigers.* New York: Smithsonian/Collins.

Fort Phil Kearny/Bozeman Trail Association (1993). *Portraits of Fort Phil Kearny.* Banner, Wyoming: Fort Phil Kearny/Bozeman Trail Association.

Freedman, J.L., & Fraser, S.C. (1966). Compliance without pressure: The foot-in-the-door technique. *Journal of Personality and Social Psychology, 4,* 195-202.

French, N. (2003). *Identity stressors associated with the reintegration experiences of Australasian undercover police officers* (Doctoral Dissertation). Retrieved from eprints.quit.edu.

Fresno Bee Staff (2009, May 31). Boston mayor opposes military rifles for police. *Fresno Bee,* A-8.

Garnham, A., & Oakhill, J. (1994). *Thinking and Reasoning.* Oxford, UK: Blackwell.

Gauvain, M. (1993). The development of spatial thinking in everyday activity. *Developmental Review, 13,* 92-121.

Gelles, M. (2006, October). Behavioral threat assessment: Law enforcement considerations. Society for Police and Criminal Psychology, Washington, D.C.

Gilovich, T. (1992). *How we know what isn't so.* New York: Free Press.

Ginet, M., Chakroun, N., Colomb, C., & Verkampt, F. (2019). Can the cognitive interview reduce memory conformity in an interview context? *Journal of Police and Criminal Psychology, 34,* 381-391.

Girodo, M. (1985). Health and legal issues in undercover narcotics investigations: Misrepresented evidence. *Behavioral Sciences & the Law, 3*(3), 299-308.

Girodo, M. (1991a). Symptomatic reactions to undercover work. *The Journal of Nervous and Mental Disease, 179*(10), 626-630.

Girodo, M. (1991b). Drug corruption in undercover agents: Measuring the risk. *Behavioral Sciences and the Law, 9,* 361-370.

Girodo, M., Deck, T., & Morrison, M. (2002). Dissociative-type identity disturbances in undercover agents: Socio-cognitive factors behind false-identity appearances and reenactments. *Social Behavior and Personality, 30*(7), 631-644.

Gladwell, M. (2005). *Blink.* New York: Little, Brown, & Co.

Gollin, E.S., & Sharps, M.J. (1987). Visual perspective-taking in young children: Reduction of egocentric errors by induction of strategy. *Bulletin of the Psychonomic Society, 25,* 435-437.

Gollin, E.S., & Sharps, M.J. (1988). Facilitation of categorical blocking depends on stimulus type. *Memory and Cognition, 16,* 539-544.

Grossman, D. (1996). *On killing.* Boston: Little, Brown.

Grossman, D., & Christensen, L.W. (2004). *On combat.* PPCT Research Publications.

Hackworth, D. (1997). *Hazardous duty.* New York: William Morrow.

Haffner, C. (Director), & Gillam, M. (Writer). (2003). Wake Island: Alamo of the Pacific (Documentary motion picture). United States: Greystone Communications, History Channel.

Haviland, S.E., & Clark, H.H. (1974). What's new? Acquiring new information as a process of comprehension. *Journal of Verbal Learning and Verbal Behavior, 13,* 512-521.

Herrera, M.R., Sharps, M.J., Swinney, H.R., & Lam, J. (2015). Deadly force or not? Visual and cognitive interpretation of rifles and BB guns in crime-scene context. *Journal of Police and Criminal Psychology, 30,* 254-260. (DOI 10.1007/s11896-014-9158-x).

Hess, A.B., & Sharps, M.J. (2006, April). Identification and interpretation of peripheral sources of hazard in complex crime situations. Western Psychological Association, Palm Springs, CA.

Hibler, N.S. (1994). The effects of undercover duty on the family. In J. T. Reese, E. M. Scrivner (Eds.), *Law enforcement families: issues and answers* (pp. 93-100). Hillsdale, NJ, England: Lawrence Erlbaum Associates, Inc.

Hope, L., Lewinski, W., Dixon, J., Blocksidge, D., & Gabbert, F. (2012). Witnesses in action: The effect of physical exertion on recall and recognition. *Psychological Science, 23,* 386-390.

Horwitz, S., & Ruane, M.E. (2003). *Sniper: Inside the hunt for the killers who terrorized the nation.* New York: Random House.

Kahneman, D., & Tversky, A. (1972). Subjective probability: A judgment of representativeness. *Cognitive Psychology, 3,* pp. 430-454.

Kahneman, D., & Tversky, A. (1979). Prospect theory: An analysis of decision making under risk. *Econometrica, 47,* pp. 263-91.

Kassin, S.M., Tubb, V.A., Hosch, H.M., & Memon, A. (2001). On the "general acceptance" of eyewitness testimony research: A new survey of the experts. *American Psychologist, 56,* 405-416.

Kieras, D.E. (1978). Good and bad structure in simple paragraphs: Effects on apparent theme, reading time, and recall. *Journal of Verbal Learning and Verbal Behavior, 17,* 13-28.

Kintsch, W. (1979). On modeling comprehension. *Educational Psychologist, 14,* 3-14.

Kintsch, W. (1994). Text comprehension, memory, and learning. *American Psychologist, 49,* 294-303.

Bibliography/References

Klinger, D. (2004). *Into the kill zone: A cop's eye view of deadly force.* San Francisco: Josey-Bass.

Kowalczyk, D., & Sharps, M.J. Best practices for reduction of physical and psychological health consequences of undercover work in law enforcement officers. Society for Police and Criminal Psychology, Atlanta, Georgia, October 1, 2015.

Kowalczyk, D., & Sharps, M.J. (2017). Consequences of undercover operations in law enforcement: A review of challenges and best practices. *Journal of Police and Criminal Psychology, 32,* 197-202.

Krause, K.W. (2016). Biological race and the problem of human diversity. *Skeptical Inquirer, 40,* 33-39.

Lamb, H. (1940). *The march of the barbarians.* New York: Literary Guild.

Laney, C., Campbell, H.V., Heuer, F., & Reisberg, D. (2004). Memory for thematically arousing events. *Memory & Cognition, 32,* 1149-1159.

Langer, J. (1969). Theories of development. New York: Holt, Rinehart, & Winston, Inc.

Lee, C. (2005, March 15). A list with bullets: NYPD shooting deaths of civilians, starting with Diallo and not ending. *Village Voice.* Retrieved January 19, 2007, from http://www.villagevoice.com/news/0511,lee,62083,5.html.

Lee, R. B., & DeVore, I. (Eds.). (1968). *Man the hunter.* Chicago: Aldine.

LeMay, C.E., & Kantor, M. (1965). *Mission with LeMay.* Garden City, New York: Doubleday.

Lesgold, A.M., Roth, S.F., & Curtis, M.E. (1979). Foregrounding effects in discourse comprehension. *Journal of Verbal Learning and Verbal Behavior, 18,* 291-308.

Lindsay, R.C.L., Ross, D.F., Read, J.D., & Toglia, M.P. (Eds., 2007). *The handbook of eyewitness psychology* (Vol 2, pp. 257-282). Mahwah, NJ: Erlbaum.

Loftus, E.F. (1975). Leading questions and the eyewitness report. *Cognitive Psychology, 7,* 560-572.

Loftus, E.F. (1979). *Eyewitness testimony.* Cambridge, MA: Harvard.

Loftus, G.R., & Bell, S.M. (1975). Two types of information in picture memory. *Journal of Experimental Psychology: Human Learning and Memory, 1,* 103-113.

Loftus, E.F., & palmer, J.C. (1974). Reconstruction of automobile destruction: an example of the interaction between language and memory. *Journal of Verbal Learning and Verbal Behavior, 13,* 585-589.

Love, K. G., Vinson, J., Tolsma, J., & Kaufmann, G. (2008). Symptoms of undercover police officers: A comparison of officers currently, formerly, and without undercover experience. *International Journal Of Stress Management, 15*(2), 136-152. doi:10.1037/1072-5245.15.2.136

MacLin, O. H., Zimmerman, L. A. & Malpass, R. S. (2005). PC_Eyewitness and the Sequential Superiority Effect: Computer Based Lineup Administration. *Law and Human Behavior, 29(3),* 303-321.

Macleod, A. D. (1995). Undercover policing: A psychiatrist's perspective. *International Journal Of Law And Psychiatry, 18*(2), 239-247. doi:10.1016/0160-2527(95)00009-7

Manchester, W. (1967). *Death of a president.* New York: Harper & Row.

Manchester, W. (1992). *A world lit only by fire.* Boston: Little, Brown, & Co.

Mandler, G. (1967). Organization and memory. In K.W. Spence & J.T. Spence (Eds.), *The psychology of learning and motivation* (Vol. 1). Orlando, FL: Academic Press.

Mandler, G. (2011). From association to organization. *Current Directions in Psychological Science, 20*, 232-235.

Marsden, W. (1948, trans. & ed.) *The travels of Marco Polo the Venetian.* Garden City, New York: International Collectors Library.

McGaugh, J.L. (2003). *Memory and emotion: The making of lasting memories. Maps of the mind.* New York: Columbia.

McKinnon, M.C., Palombo, D.J., Nazarov, A., Kumar, N., Khuu, W., & Levine, B. (2015). Threat of death and autobiographical memory: A study of passengers from Flight AT 236. *Clinical Psychological Science, 3*, 487-502.

McClatchy News Syndicate (2011). Pentagon has little success fighting IED's despite billions spent. *McClatchy Newspapers* http://www.timesfreepress.com/news/2011/mar/27. Retrieved December 7, 2011.

McRae, K., Sharps, M.J., & Kimura, N. (2015). Error and accuracy in memory for firearms. *Forensic Examiner, 24*, 1-6.

McRae, K. Sharps, M.J., Power, J., & Newton, A. (2013). Eyewitness memory for typical and atypical weapons in cognitive context. *Journal of Investigative Psychology and Offender Profiling, 10*, DOI: 10.1002/jip. 1410

Mead, M.'(1963). *Sex and temperament in three primitive societies.* New York: Dell.

Mecklenburg, S.H., Larson, M.R., & Bailey, P.J. (2008). Eyewitness identification: What chiefs need to know now. *The Police Chief, 75*, 68-81.

Mecklenburg, S.H., Bailey, P.J., & Larson, M.R. (2013). Eyewitness identification: An update on what chiefs need to know. *The Police Chief, 80*, 60-63.

Medin, D.L., & Bazerman, M.H. (1999). Broadening behavioral decision research: Multiple levels of cognitive processing. *Psychonomic Bulletin & Review, 6*, 533-546.

Meissner, C.A., & Brigham, J.C. (2001). Thirty years of investigating the other-race effect in memory for faces: A meta-analytic review. *Psychology, Public Policy, and Law, 7*, 3-35.

Meissner, C.A., Sporer, S.L., & Schooler, J.W. (2007). Person descriptions as eyewitness evidence. In Toglia, M.P., Read, J.D., Ross, D.R., & Lindsay, R.C.L. (Eds.), *The handbook of eyewitness psychology* (Vol 2, pp. 1-34). Mahwah, NJ: Erlbaum.

Memon, A., & Bull, R. (1991). The cognitive interview: its origins, empirical support, evaluation and practical applications. *Journal of Community and Applied Social Psychology, 1*, 291-307.

Memon, A., Zaragoza, M.S., Clifford, B., & Kidd, L. (2010). Inoculation or antidote? The effects of cognitive interview timing on false memory for forcibly fabricated events. *Law and Human Behavior, 34*, 105-117.

Miller, G.A. (1956). The magical number seven, plus or minus two: Some limits on our capacity for processing information. *Psychological Review, 63*, 81-97.

Miller, L. (2006). Undercover policing: A psychological and operational guide. *Journal of Police and Criminal Psychology, 21*(2), 1-24.

Miller, L. (2015). *PTSD and forensic psychology: Applications to civil and criminal law.* Springer International Publishing.

Moore, L. (2006, November). *Conference on the use of force in law enforcement.* Office of the United States Marshal, Fresno, California.

Monnett, J.H. (2008). *Where a hundred soldiers were killed.* Albuquerque: University of New Mexico Press.

Montejano, D. (2004, November). *Fresno Police Department Conference on stress in police work.* Fresno, California.

Morgan, C.A., Hazlett, G., Doran, A., Gattest, S., Hoyt, G., Thomas, P., Baranoski, M, & Southwick, S.M. (2004). Accuracy of eyewitness memory for persons encountered during exposure to highly intense stress. *International Journal of Law and Psychiatry, 27,* 265-279.

Munsterberg, H, (1908). *On the witness stand.* New York: Doubleday, Page, & Co.

Narby, D.J., Cutler, B.L., & Penrod, S.D. (1996). The effects of witness, target, and situational factors on eyewitness identifications. In S.L. Sporer, R.S. Malpass, & G. Koehnken (Eds.), *Psychological issues in eyewitness identification* (pp. 23-52). Mahwah, NJ: Erlbaum.

National Institute of Mental Health. Post-traumatic stress disorder: What is post-traumatic stress disorder? http://www.nimh.nih.gov/health/topics/post-traumatic-stress-disorder-ptsd/index.shtml. Retrieved January 6, 2015.

Nelson, T.O. Metzler, J., & Reed, D.A. (1974). Role of details in the long-term recognition of pictures and verbal descriptions. *Journal of Experimental Psychology, 102,* 184-186.

Park, D.C., (1992). Applied cognitive aging research. In F.I.M. Craik & T.A. Salthouse (Eds.), *Handbook of cognition and aging* (pp. 449-493). Hillsdale, NJ: Erlbaum.

Paulo, R.M., Albuquerque, P.B., & Bull, R. (2019). Witnesses' verbal evaluation of certainty and uncertainty during investigative interviews. *Journal of Police and Criminal Psychology, 34,* 341-350.

Payne, J.W. (1973). Alternative approaches to decision making under risk: Moments versus risk dimensions. *Psychological Bulletin, 80,* 439-453.

Payne, J.W. (1982). Contingent decision behavior. *Psychological Bulletin, 92,* 382-402.

Peck, I. (1970). *Patton.* New York: Scholastic.

Pica, E., Sheahan, C., Pozzula,o, J., Vallano, J., & Pettalia, J. (2019). The influence of familiar and confident eyewitnesses on mock jurors' judgments. *Journal of Police and Criminal Psychology, 34,* 362-361.

Pita, M. (1993). *Stress and burnout in police officers.* (Doctoral Dissertation). Retrieved from Proquest (9316122).

Pozzulo, J. (2007). Person description and identification by child witnesses. In Lindsay, R.C.L., Ross, D.F., Read, J.D., & Toglia, M.P. (Eds.), *The handbook of eyewitness psychology* (Vol 2, pp. 283-308). Mahwah, NJ: Erlbaum.

Rasmussen, A., Verkulien, J., Jayawickreme, N., Wu, Z., & McCluskey, S.T. (2019). When did posttraumatic stress disorder get so many factors? Confirmatory factor models since DSM-5. *Clinical Psychological Science, 7,* 234-238.

Rayburn, M.T. (2003). *Advanced patrol tactics: Skills for today's street cop.* New York: Looseleaf Law Publications.

Reed, S.K. (1992). *Cognition* (3rd ed.) Pacific Grove, CA: Brooks/Cole.

Schraer, M. (2012, May 9.) Setting the record straight on the Newhall Incident. *Police 1.* Police1.com, Lexipol, Copyright 2020, retrieved December 17, 2020.

Selye, H. (1976). *The stress of life.* New York: McGraw-Hill.

Sharman, S.J., & Powell, M.B. (2013). Do cognitive interview instructions contribute to false memories and beliefs? *Journal of Investigative Psychology and Offender Profiling, 10*, 114-124.

Sharps, M.J. (1990). A developmental approach to visual cognition in the elderly. In T. Hess (Ed.), *Aging and cognition: Knowledge organization and utilization* (pp. 297-341). Amsterdam: Elsevier.

Sharps, M.J. (1991). Spatial memory in young and elderly adults: Category structure of stimulus sets. *Psychology and Aging, 6*, 309-312.

Sharps, M.J. (1997). Category superiority effects in young and elderly adults. *Journal of Genetic Psychology, 158*, 165-171.

Sharps, M.J. (1998). Age-related change in visual information processing: Toward a unified theory of aging and visual memory. *Current Psychology 16*, 284-307.

Sharps, M.J. (2003). *Aging, representation, and thought: Gestalt and feature-intensive processing*. Piscataway, NJ: Transaction.

Sharps, M.J. (2012). The mental edge: Effective cognitive processing in law enforcement. *The Police Chief, 79*, 100-105.

Sharps, M.J., & Antonelli, J.R. (1997). Visual and semantic support for paired-associates recall in young and older adults. *Journal of Genetic Psychology, 158*, 347-355.

Sharps, M.J., Barber, T.L., Stahl, H., & Villegas, A.B. (2003). Eyewitness memory for weapons. *Forensic Examiner, 12*, 34-37.

Sharps, M.J. Foster, B.T., Martin, S.S., & Nunes, M.A. (1999). Spatial and relational frameworks for free recall in young and older adults. *Current Psychology 18*, 241-253.

Sharps, M.J., & Gollin, E.S. (1985). Memory and the syntagmatic-paradigmatic shift: A developmental study of priming effects. Bulletin of the Psychonomic Society, 23, 95-97.

Sharps, M.J., & Gollin, E.S. (1987a). Speed and accuracy of mental image rotation in young and elderly adults. *Journal of Gerontology, 42*, 342-344.

Sharps, M.J., & Gollin, E.S. (1987b). Memory for object locations in young and elderly adults. *Journal of Gerontology, 42*, 336-341.

Sharps, M.J., & Gollin, E.S. (1988). Aging and free recall for objects located in space. *Journal of Gerontology: Psychological Sciences, 43*, P8-P11.

Sharps, M.J., Herrera, M.R, Dunn, L. & Alcala, E. (2012). Repetition and Reconfiguration: Demand-Based Confabulation in Initial Eyewitness Memory. *Journal of Investigative Psychology and Offender Profiling, 9*, 149-160.

Sharps, M.J., Herrera, M.R., & Price-Sharps, J.L. (2013). Situationally equivocal eyewitness evidence and the violence of crimes. *Journal of Investigative Psychology and Offender Profiling, 10*, DOI: 10.1002/jip.1398

Sharps, M.J., Herrera, M.G., & Lodeesen, A.L. (2014). SMOKE: Effective cognitive and field training for IED detection. *Inside Homeland Security, 2*, 9 pgs., http://www.abchs.com.ihs/SUMMER 2014/ihs_articles_5.php. (Simultaneously published online in *Forensic Examiner, 23*, 7 pgs.).

Sharps, M.J., & Hess, A.B. (2008). To shoot or not to shoot: Response and interpretation of response to armed assailants. *Forensic Examiner, 17*, 53-64.

Sharps, M.J., Hess, A.B., Casner, H., Ranes, B., & Jones, J. (2007a). Eyewitness memory in context: Toward a systematic understanding of eyewitness evidence. *Forensic Examiner, 16*, 20-27.

Sharps, M.J., Hess, A.B., & Ranes, B. (2007b). "Mindless" decision-making and environmental issues: Gestalt/feature-intensive processing and contextual reasoning in environmental decisions. *Journal of Psychology, 141,* 525-538.

Sharps, M.J., Hess, A., Price-Sharps, J.L., & Teh, J. (2008). Heuristic and algorithmic processing in English, math, and science education. *Journal of Psychology, 142,* 71-88.

Sharps, M.J., Hess, A.B., & Ranes, B. (2007). "Mindless" decision-making and environmental issues: Gestalt/feature-intensive processing and contextual reasoning in environmental decisions. *Journal of Psychology, 141,* 525-538.

Sharps, M.J., Janigian, J., Hess, A.B., & Hayward, B. (2009). Eyewitness Memory in Context: Toward a Taxonomy of Eyewitness Error. *Journal of Police and Criminal Psychology, 24,* 36-44.

Sharps, M.J., & Martin, S.S. (1998). Spatial memory in young and older adults. Environmental support and contextual influences at encoding and retrieval. *Journal of Genetic Psychology, 159,* 5-12.

Sharps. M.J., & Martin, S.S. (2002). "Mindless" decision making as a failure of contextual reasoning. *Journal of Psychology 136,* 272-282.

Sharps, M.J., Martin, S.S., Nunes, M.A., & Merrill, M. (1999). Relational frameworks for recall in young and older adults. *Current Psychology 18,* 254-271.

Sharps, M.J., Martin, S.S., Nunes, M.A., Neff, A., & Woo, E. (2004). Relational and imageric recall in young and older adults under conditions of high task demand. *Current Psychology, 22,* 379-393.

Sharps, M.J., Matthews, J., & Asten, J. (2006). Cognition, Affect, and Beliefs in Paranormal Phenomena: Gestalt/Feature Intensive Processing Theory and Tendencies toward ADHD, Depression, and Dissociation. *Journal of Psychology, 140,* 579-590.

Sharps, M.J., McRae, K., Partovi, M, Power, J., & Newton, A. (2015). Eyewitness memory for firearms: Narrative accounts and specific questioning in the elucidation of accurate information. *Journal of Police and Criminal Psychology, 30,* DOI 10.1007/s11896-015-9184-3.

Sharps, M.J., Nagra, S., Hurd, S., & Humphrey, A. (2020). Magic in the house of rain: Cognitive bases of UFO 'observations" in the Southwest desert. *Skeptical Inquirer, 44,* 46-49.

Sharps, M.J., Newborg, E., Glasere, M., Hayward, B.A., & Scholl, M. (2010). Finding IED's before they find you: The SMOKE system of training for hazardous device detection. *Forensic Examiner, 19,* 48-59.

Sharps, M.J., Newborg, S., & Van Arsdall, S. (2010). Paranormal encounters as eyewitness phenomena: Psychological determinants of atypical perceptual interpretations. *Current Psychology, 29,* 320-327.

Sharps, M.J., & Nunes, M.A. (2002). Gestalt and feature-intensive processing: Toward a unified model of human information processing. *Current Psychology, 21,* 68-84.

Sharps, M.J., & Pollitt, B.K. (1998). Auditory imagery and the category superiority effect. *Journal of General Psychology, 125,* 109-116.

Sharps, M.J., & Price, J.L. (1992). Auditory imagery and free recall. *Journal of General Psychology, 119,* 81-87.

Sharps, M.J., Price, J.L., & Bence, V.M. (1996). Visual and auditory information as determinants of primacy effects. *Journal of General Psychology, 123,* 123-136.

Sharps, M.J., & Price-Sharps, J.L. (1996). Visual memory support: An effective mnemonic device for older adults. *The Gerontologist, 36,* 706-708,.

Sharps, M.J., & Price-Sharps, J.L. PTSD past and present. Society for Police and Criminal Psychology, Scottsdale, AZ, September 25, 2019.

Sharps, M.J., Price-Sharps, J.L., Day, S.S., Nunes, M.A., Villegas, A.B., & Mitchell, S. (2005). Cognition at risk: Gestalt/feature-intensive processing, attention deficit, and substance abuse. *Current Psychology, 23,* 91-101.

Sharps, M.J., Price-Sharps, J.L., Day, S.S., Villegas, A.B., & Nunes, M.A. (2005). Cognitive predisposition to substance abuse in adult attention deficit hyperactivity disorder. *Addictive Behaviors, 30,* 355-359.

Sharps, M.J., & Tindall, M.H. (1992). Relational and item-specific information in the determination of "blocking effects." *Memory and Cognition, 20,* 183-191.

Sharps, M.J., Villegas, A.B., & Matthews, J. (2005). Cognition at risk: Gestalt/feature-intensive processing and cigarette smoking in college students. *Current Psychology, 23.* 102-112.

Sharps, M.J., Villegas, A.B., Nunes, M.A., & Barber, T.L. (2002). Memory for animal tracks: A possible cognitive artifact of human evolution. *Journal of Psychology, 136,* 469-492.

Sharps, M.J., & Wertheimer, M. (2000). Gestalt perspectives on cognitive science and experimental psychology. *Review of General Psychology, 4,* 315-336.

Sharps, M.J., Wilson-Leff, C.A., & Price, J.L. (1995). Relational and item-specific information as determinants of category superiority effects. *Journal of General Psychology, 122,* 271-285.

Smith, A.M., & Leach, A. (2019). Confidence can be used to discriminate between accurate and inaccurate lie decisions. Perspectives on Cognitive Science, 14, 1062-1071.

Spoehr, K.T., & Lehmkule, S.W. (1982). *Visual information processing.* San Francisco: Freeman.

Sporer, S.L., Malpass, R.S., & Koehnken, G. (1996). *Psychological issues in eyewitness identification.* Mahwah, NJ: Erlbaum.

Star Trek II: The Wrath of Khan (1982). Paramount Pictures.

Steblay, N.M. (1992). A meta-analytic review of the weapon focus effect. *Law and Human Behavior, 16,* 413-424.

Suefeld, P. (2008). *Uses of history: Space analogues revisited.* Paper presented at the Annual Meeting of the American Psychological Association, Boston, MA, August 14, 2008.

Tietjen, T. (2005). *The impact of job related stress on individuals in law enforcement.* Fresno, CA: Presentation, Fresno Police Department, Sierra Education and Research Institute, and Alliant International University.

Toglia, M.P., Read, J.D., Ross, D.R., & Lindsay, R.C.L. (Eds., 2007). *The handbook of eyewitness psychology* (Vol 2, pp. 257-282). Mahwah, NJ: Erlbaum.

Tregaskis, R. (1943). *Guadalcanal diary.* New York: Random House.

Turner, T. (2001). *Wild Bill Hickok: Deadwood City- End of Trail.* Old West Alive.

Tversky, A., & Kahneman, D. (1972). Subjective probability: A judgement of representativeness. *Cognitive Psychology, 3,* 430-454.

Tversky, A., & Kahneman, D. (1973). Availability: A heuristic for judging frequency and probability. *Cognitive Psychology, 5,* 207-32.

Tversky, A., & Kahneman, D. (1974). Judgement under uncertainty: Heuristics and biases. *Science, 125,* 1124-31.

Bibliography/References

Utley, R.M. (1973). *Frontier regulars: The United States Army and the Indian, 1866-1890.* New York: MacMillan.

Vasquez, J. & Kelly, S. (1989). Management's commitment to the undercover operative. *FBI Law Enforcement Bulletin, 58*(2), 3-12.

Villegas, A.B., Sharps, M.J., Satterthwaite, B., & Chisholm, S. (2005). Eyewitness memory for vehicles. *Forensic Examiner, 14,* 24-28.

Wallace, P., Roberg, R. & Allen, H. (1985). Job burnout among narcotics investigators: an exploratory study. *Journal of Criminal Justice* 13, 549-559.

Warren Commission (1964). *Report of the president's commission on the assassination of President Kennedy.* New York: St. Martin's Press.

Wells, G.L., Memon, A., & Penrod, S.D. (2006). Eyewitness evidence: Improving its probative value. *Psychological Science in the Public Interest, 7,* 45-75.

Wells, G.L. (1993). What do we know about eyewitness identification? *American Psychologist, 48,* 553-571.

Wertheimer, M. (1982, reprinted from 1945). *Productive thinking.* Chicago: University of Chicago Press.

Wilstach, F.J. (1926). Wild Bill Hickok. New York: Garden City.

Wogalter, M.S., Malpass, R.S., & Burger, M.A. (1993). How police officers construct lineups: A national survey. In *Proceedings of the Human Factors and Ergonomics Society* (pp. 640-644). Santa Monica, CA: Human Factors and Ergonomics Society.

Wogalter, M.S., Malpass, R.S., & McQuiston, D.E. (2004). A national survey of police on preparation and conduct of identification lineups. *Psychology, Crime and Law, 10(1),* 69-82.

Wolfe, T. (1979). *The right stuff.* New York: Bantam.

Yarmey, A.D. (2001). The older eyewitness. In Rothman, M.B., Dunlop, B.D., & Entzel, P. (Eds.), *Elders, crime, and the criminal justice system* (pp. 127-147). New York: Springer.

Index

.45 automatic colt pistol (ACP) ... 113
10th Mountain Division ... 218
Acute stress ... 29
Administrative stress ... 275-279
Adolescent cognition ... 288-290, 301-306
Adrenal cortex ... 15
Adrenal glands ... 15
Adrenal medulla ... 16
Adrenaline ... 16
Aging and cognition ... 306-310
Aging process, characteristics of ... 307
Aidid, Mohamed ... 218
Aircraft and air tactics ... 160, 161, 163, 164
AK-47s ... 223
Alarm state ... 19
Alcmaeon ... 5
Alcohol, PTSD and stress ... 52, 124
Aldosterone ... 15
Amadou Diallo ... 135
Amygdala ... 14
Animal tracks, memory for ... 70, 72
Animism ... 296, 297
Apocalypse Now ... 252
Arapaho ... 199
Ardennes ... 227-235
Army Rangers ... 217
Arnold, Gen. H.H. ... 160
Arousal and emotion ... 94-96
Asch, Solomon ... 100
Assault weapons ... 113
Automatic brain structures ... 7
Automatic Colt pistol (ACP) ... 113
Automatic pilot ... 33
Baddeley, A. ... 183
Bandura, Albert ... 286
Bartlett ... 66-68, 81, 89, 110, 111, 125, 145
Bastogne ... 229-236
Battle of the Black Sea ... 217
Battle of the Bulge ... 229
Battle of the Little Bighorn ... 197

Behavior decision research	175
Beretta	71, 81, 111
Bigfoot and cryptids	37
Black Hawk Down	217
Black Hawk helicopters	217
Blood pressure	17
Bomb Squad	239-241, 250, 251
Bomb technicians	240, 241, 249-251
Boston marathon	240
Bowden, Mark	217
Bradley, General Omar	232, 236
Brain size	8
Bransford and Johnson	179
Bransford, J. D.	179
Breathing rate	17
British Royal Air Force	161
Bugliosi, Vincent	124
California Highway Patrol	33
Cavalry	189
Cerebellum	13
Chemically-impaired witnesses	91
Cheyenne	199
Children as witnesses	88
Children's cognition	291-301
Christensen, L.W.	30
Clark, H. H.	181
Clifford & Richards, 1977	65, 92
Cognitive asynchrony	90
Cognitive consequences	256
Cognitive dissonance	191, 209, 220, 223, 224, 228, 229, 234-237, 260
Cognitive flexibility	212, 224, 233, 234, 269, 270, 272, 279
Cognitive interview	82, 83
Cognitive mediation	137
Cognitive organization	294
Cognitive science	239
Collateral damage	195, 274
Combat fatigue	47
Combat reload	69
Compensatory reasoning	175
Compound errors	138
Concrete operations	299-301

Index

Cone cells	76
Conformity	99, 101, 229, 234, 236, 237
Conformity to the opinions of others	234-236
Connery, Sean	257
Conrad, Joseph	252
Contextual information	184
Correll, John	161
Cortex	7, 8, 12, 22
occipital lobe	13
parietal lobe	13
prefrontal	12
temporal lobe	13
Cortisol	16, 18
Cross-racial identification	86, 90, 114
Cross-racial identification, disguise, and weapon focus	85
Cross-racial IDs	85
Custer, George Armstrong	197
Daisy BB gun	113
Dark adaptation	77
Decision making	157, 159, 174, 175, 178
Delta Force operators	217
Depth of processing	114
Diallo, Amadou	135
Digestion	17
Disguise	86
Dissociation	37
Donovan, J.	199
Dorner, Dietrich	175
Dreams and sleep	50
Driving simulators	265
Ecological validity	8, 70, 125
Egocentrism, Piagetian	291
Eisenhower, General Dwight	227
Emotion and eyewitness memory	94
Equilibration	291
Errors of interpretation	137
Estimator variables	73
Exhaustion	19
Expertise	112
Explicit information vs implicit	10, 171, 181, 190, 192, 210, 234, 267, 271, 279
Explosive devices	131

Explosive Ordinance Disposal 213, 239
Explosive Ordinance Disposal (EOD; "bomb-squad")................213, 239-
    241, 248, 250, 251, 274
Exposure time..88
Eyewitness..109, 139
    confidence...74, 75
    imaginative errors...145
Eyewitness arousal...91
Eyewitness errors at Little Big Horn..206
Eyewitness memory...............66-68, 88, 89, 96, 107, 109, 111, 113, 116,
    118, 120, 121, 124, 129, 141, 166, 206, 272
Factors in good decisions (summary)..185, 192
Failure to engage...234
Farago, L..232
Feature-Intensive (FI) Processing and analysis..............11, 45, 88, 110-
    115, 119, 121, 125, 144, 148, 163, 164, 167-174, 176, 182,
    186, 190, 192, 193, 205, 206, 208, 210, 212, 213, 215, 224,
    234, 235, 267, 271, 272, 274, 278, 279, 284, 285
Feature-intensive analysis..45
Fenici, Prof. Riccardo..41
Festinger, L..191
Fetterman Massacre..56, 203
Field identification procedure (showup)..102
Field Training Officers (FTOs)..262
Fight-or-flight...17
Fight-or-flight complex...7, 15, 17, 18, 25
Fight-or-flight response...17
Fighter aircraft...160, 163
Firearms identification...112
Forensic cognitive science..287
    aging...306
    elementary school years...299
    gangs..305
    preschool child..296
    teenagers..287
Foresight..235
Front-loading frameworks for understanding............11, 171, 179, 190,
    192, 210, 224, 234, 236, 267, 270, 272, 279
Frontal lobes..12
Functional fixedness..187
G/FI tradeoffs...171
Game theory..175

Index

Gangs 305
Garrison, Gen. William 217
General George S. Patton 230
General Omar Bradley 232
German armor & aircraft, WWII 228, 229
Gestalt processing 110, 111, 114, 115, 119, 120, 125, 133, 144,
            148, 153, 163, 164, 166-169, 171-174, 186, 190, 192, 205,
            207, 208, 210-212, 214, 215, 220, 223, 224, 234, 235, 237,
                                                    267, 274, 284, 285
Gestalt/Feature-Intensive (G/FI) Processing Theory 110, 111
Gladwell 135
Glock 109, 112, 158
Grassy knoll 122
Grossman, Lt. Col. Dave 30
Grummond, G.W. 57
Gustavus Adolphus 189
Hackworth, Col. David 221
Handbook of Eyewitness Psychology 72
Haviland, S. E. 181
Heart of Darkness 252
Heart rate 39
Height and weight numerical estimates 129
Hemispheres of the brain 12
Henry repeating rifles 204
Hickok, Wild Bill; death of 58
Hindsight Spirits 158, 159, 164, 228
Hippocampus 18
Historical analysis 196
Hitler, Adolf 165
Homeostasis 14
Hostage Negotiation Teams (HNT) 260
HPA Axis 15, 19, 22
Humvees 219, 222
Hunters and gatherers 9
Hunting 9, 18, 31, 43, 70, 171, 201, 276
Hyperfocus 10
Hypothalamus 14
Hypothalamus-Pituitary-Adrenal (HPA) 15
Ice pick 109, 112, 115
Illinois State Police 105
Imagination & eyewitness errors 145
Improvised explosive device (IED) 239

Improvised explosive devices (IED's) 28
Interpretation 127, 129, 131, 137-145, 148, 149, 151, 153, 155,
                                                166, 200, 206, 211, 265
Interview 168
Intrusive thoughts 36
Johnson, M. K. 179
K-9 133
Kennedy, John F.; assassination of 122
Klinger, Dr. David 30
Kowalczyk, Dr. Devin 253
Kublai Khan 176
Lakota 18-24, 56, 198, 218
Lemay, Curtis 47
Lighting 76-81
Lineups 96, 102, 130
Lobes of the brain 12
Loftus, Elizabeth 68, 110
Long-term (chronic) stress 17
Los Angeles Police Department (LAPD) 157-159, 161, 165, 222,
                                                                                             281

MacAuliffe, Gen. Anthony 230
Machine gun 190
Malta 47
Manchester, William 124
Mannlicher-Carcano carbine 122
Marco Polo 176
Marital and career dissatisfaction 177
Mars orbiter 175
McAllister, Chief Darryl 42, 268
Memory 8, 67
    ancient 70
    effective use of 182
    long-term 182
    working 182
Memory distortions 36
Memory loss 36
Memory, importance of 63
Mental set 188, 204, 208, 212, 215, 219, 220, 222, 224, 227-229,
                                                234, 235, 237, 268
Military eyewitnesses 92
Mindlessness 175

Index

Mindset
    strategic 172
    tactical 172
Mnemonic devices 71
Mogadishu 217
Montgomery, B. L. 227
Moonlight 77
Motor cortex 12
Munsterberg, Hugo 66
Muskets 188
Mutual collaboration in research 126
NASA 196
National Institute of Justice 102
Naturalistic approach 125
Nebulous orders 211
Neisser, Ulric 2
Newhall incident 33
Night shift 20
Non-compensatory reasoning 176
North Hollywood Shootout 157, 161, 164, 165, 168, 174, 180, 188, 222, 281
Occipital lobe 13
Occultation 78
    interaction of darkness 79
Officer Involved Shooting 150-155
Older adults as witnesses 89
Oswald, Lee Harvey 122
Paranormal sightings and beliefs 37
Parietal lobe 13
Patrol and tactical rifles 158
Patrol officers and operations 261, 262
Patrol resources 116
Patton, General George S. 230-236
Perceptual and attentional anomalies 30
Peripheral Processing 11, 31
Perseverative behaviors 28
Perspective taking 295
Pesticides 175
Phoenix Lights 37
Physiological arousal 91, 207
Pituitary gland 15
Police car 222

Police cars	169
Police department budgets	116
Police response times	266
Positive feedback	29
Post-event information	68, 71, 81, 96, 101, 109, 115
Post-traumatic stress disorder (PTSD)	45
Pre-frontal cortex	25
Precision bombing	160
Prefrontal cortex	12, 288, 301
Premotor cortex	12
Preoperational period	294
Preschool child	296
Prior frameworks for understanding	179, 186, 211
Psychology of persuasion	267
PTSD	
arguments against	54
past and present	55
Push of pike	188
Quick Reaction Force	218, 229
Quick Reaction Force (QRF)	222
Reconfiguration of memory	67-69
Ree scouts	200
Reno, Janet; Attorney General	102
Reno's Hill	206
Repetition of necessary skills	268
Reptile brains	5
Research collaboration	126
Resistance	19
Response to short-term stressors	19
Revolver	109
Richards, V.J.	65, 92
Rifling	189
Robin Hood	282
Rocket-propelled grenades	220
Rod cells	76
Satisficing search	103, 104, 176
Selye, Hans	19
Sequential double-blind procedures	105
Serpico, Frank	257
Seventh Cavalry	198
Sherman tanks	228
Showups	96, 102, 107

Index

Simulators, driving and force 265, 266
Single-light sources 77, 98, 101
Situational variables 73-82
Six pack photo arrays 105
Six-pack line-up identification 128
Sleep and eyewitness memory 81
Smith & Wesson 112
SMOKE 241-245, 247-249, 271
Social pressure 101
Socrates 167
Somalia and Somalis 218, 219
Sound anomalies 30
Springfields 204
State-dependent learning 91
Steblay, N. M. 88
Strategic mindset 212
Streetlight 77
Streetlights 77
Stress 17, 24, 273-279
Subcortical realities 13
Subcortical structures 7, 14
Submissive behavior 40
Supplementary motor cortex 12
Surveys 169
SWAT 126, 133, 157, 182, 214, 232, 260, 268, 281
Syntagmatic/paradigmatic shift 294
Tactical mindset 212
Tactical speed 140
Tanks and armored vehicles 219-222, 228
Target variables 73, 85
Taxonomy 139
Teamwork 232, 233, 237
Teenagers 287
Temporal lobe 13
Temporary paralysis 37
Terrorist operations 127, 146, 270
Training 11, 266
Tunnel vision 10, 31
Tunnel-vision 209
Tyrannosaurus 5, 7
UFOs 269
Undercover officers and operations 251-259

United States Army Air Corps 160
Uzis 113
Variables
    passage of time 81
    single-light sources 77
Variables under law enforcement control 95
Varnum, Lt. Charles 199
Vasodilation 17
Vehicle identification 115, 117
Verbal reconfiguration 272
Video game 223, 286
Violation of expectations 132
Wagon Box Fight 203
Warren Commission 122
Washington Sniper case 115
Weapon focus 87, 88, 114
Weapon identification 112, 127
Wertheimer, Max 2
White boards 186
Winchester repeating rifles 204
Witness credibility and confidence 74
Witness retelling of accounts 81
Witness variables 73, 88
    chemically impaired 91
    children 88
    older adults 89
Working memory 182-186, 190, 192, 193, 270
World War II air campaign 160

NOTES

OTHER TITLES OF INTEREST FROM LOOSELEAF LAW PUBLICATIONS, INC.

METTLE: Mental Toughness Training for Law Enforcement
by Lawrence Miller, Ph.D.

Police Suicide
Prevention, Assessment and Intervention
by Thomas E. Baker, Lt. Col. MP USAR (Ret.)

Reasonable, Justified and Necessary
Exploring the Professional, Physical and Psychological Complexities of Deadly Force
by Dan Bernouli, Ed.D.

Lethal Force and the Objectively Reasonable Officer
Law, Liability, Policy, Tactics and Survival
by John Michael Callahan

The Verbal Judo Way of Leadership
Empowering the Thin Blue Line from the Inside Up
by Dr. George Thompson and Gregory A. Walker

Conflict Resolution for Law Enforcement
Street-Smart Negotiating
by Kyle E. Blanchfield, Thomas A. Blanchfield and Peter D. Ladd

Path of the Warrior - 2nd Edition
An Ethical Guide to Personal & Professional Development in the Field of Criminal Justice
by Larry F. Jetmore

No One Trips Over a Mountain
Enhancing Officer Safety by Doing the Little Things Right
by Det. Joseph Petrocelli and Prof. Matthew Petrocelli, Ph.D.

Law Enforcement Management
What Works and What Doesn't
by Michael Carpenter & Roger Fulton

A Practical Career Guide for Criminal Justice Professionals
by Michael Carpenter and Roger Fulton

Developing the Survival Attitude
A Guide for the New Officer
by Phil L. Duran

(800) 647-5547   www.LooseleafLaw.com